TABEGIRL

Jun

TABEGIRL - THE ART OF JUN

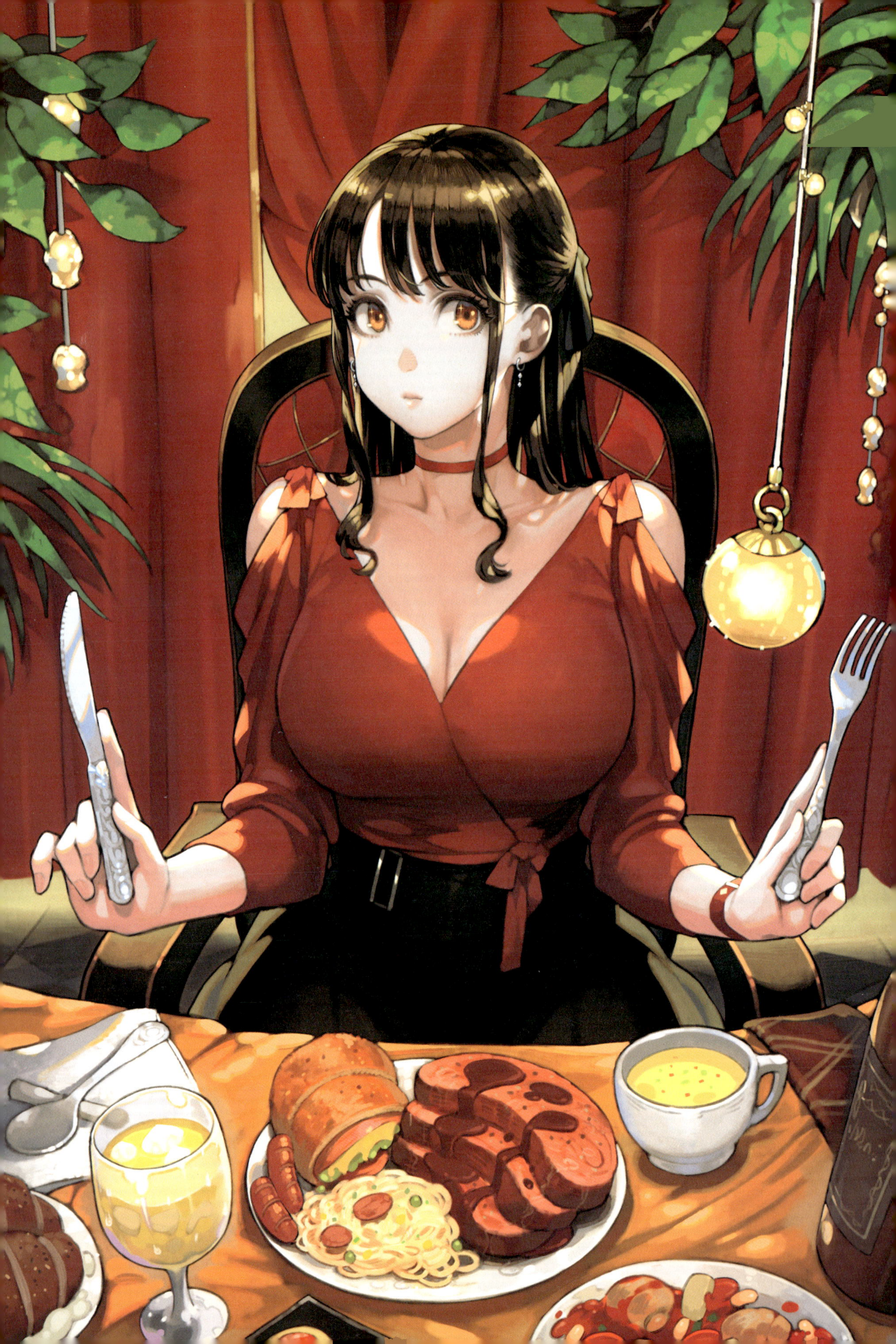

Let's Eat!

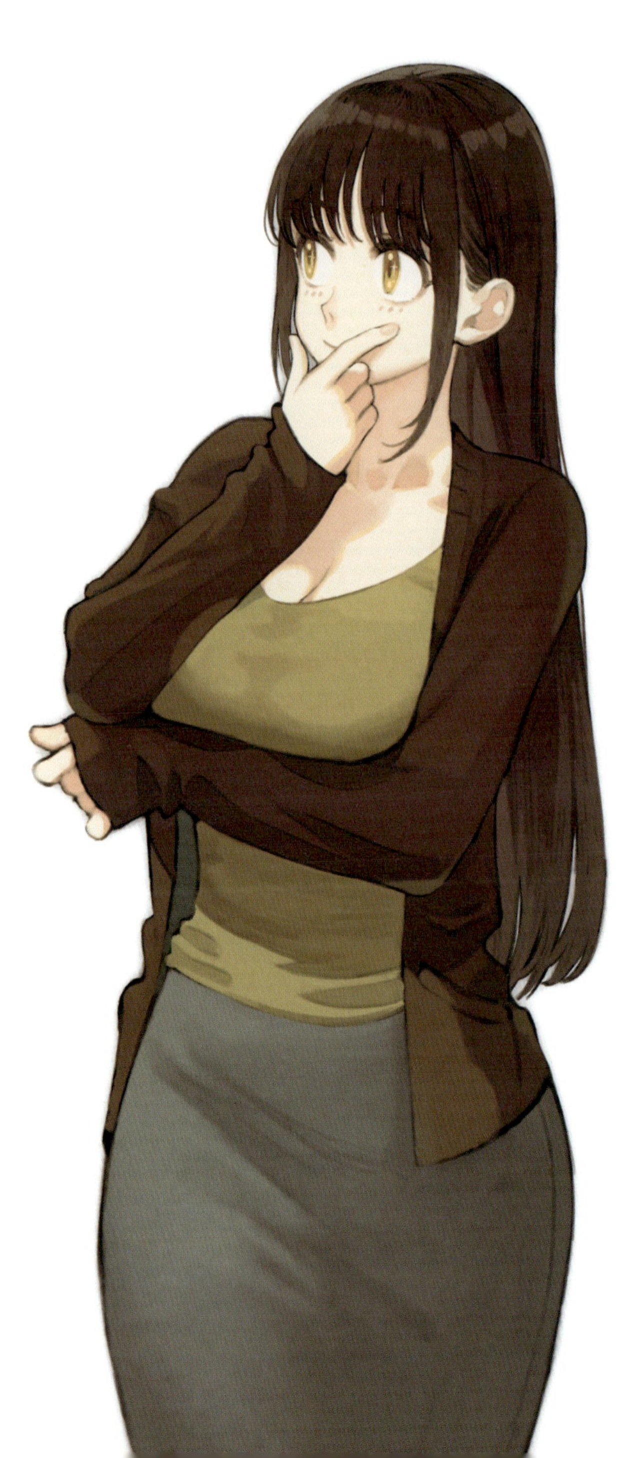

CHAPTER 1

"TABEGIRL"

In 2019, Jun started the hashtag "#tabegirl" (#タベガール) on *Twitter*.

They started by single-mindedly posting illustrations of girls eating ("tabe-girls") with this hashtag. Then numerous other illustrators started using the tag and it is now a thriving movement of active illustrators on *Twitter*.

Introduction

CONCEPT

"TABEGIRL"

"What is Tabegirl?"
Text by Jun

"Tabegirl" is a gluttonous fantasy that I started drawing around the simple theme of "Girls who want to eat more and more." It's a series of illustrations focused on main characters who are sisters that steal and are stolen from in "the war of the dinner table." Something those of you who have siblings will have experienced at least once!

I truly hope you enjoy the sisters' cuteness and full-blown appetites, and their battles over food!

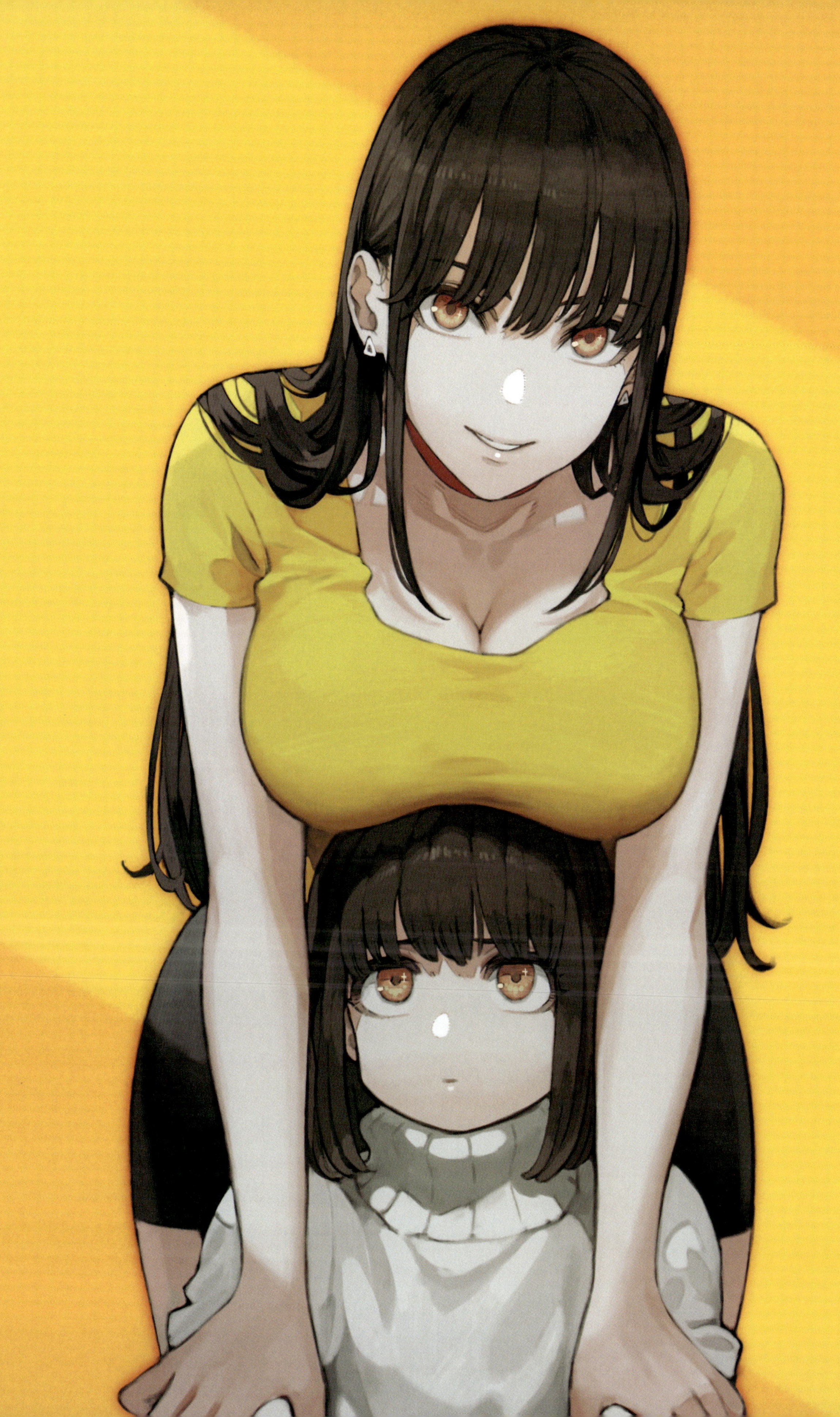

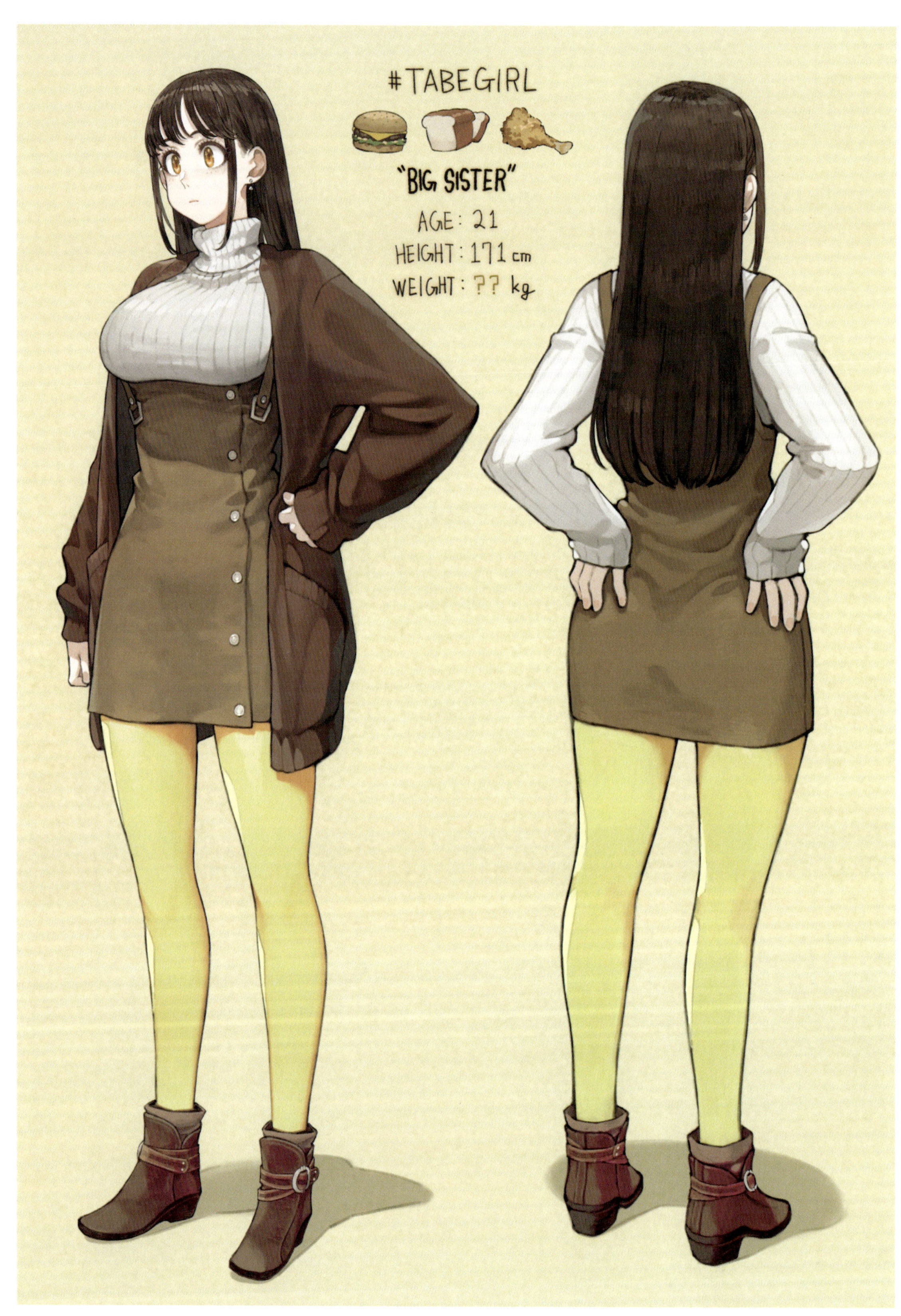

TITLE

"Sisters: Big Sister"

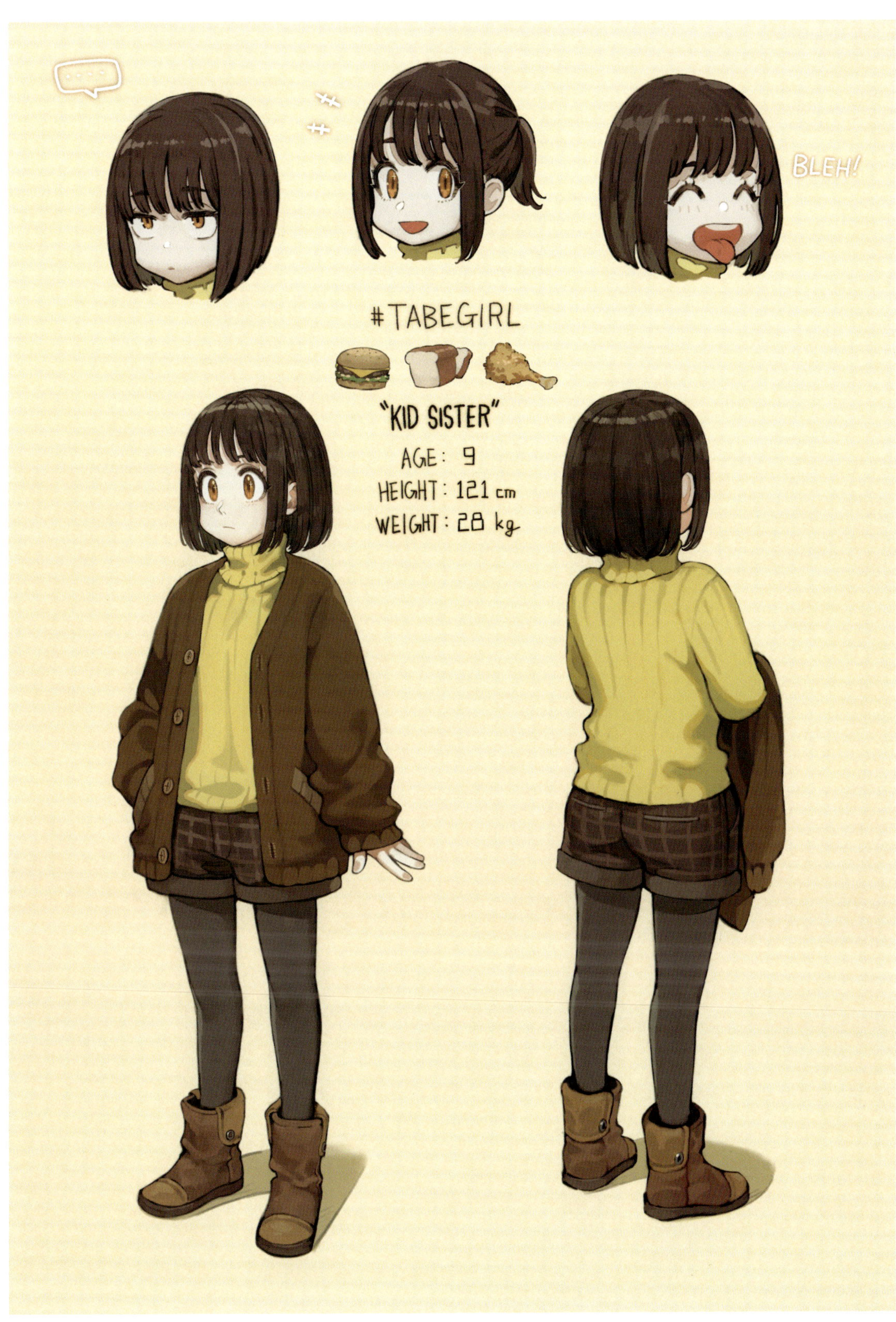

TITLE

"Sisters: Kid Sister"

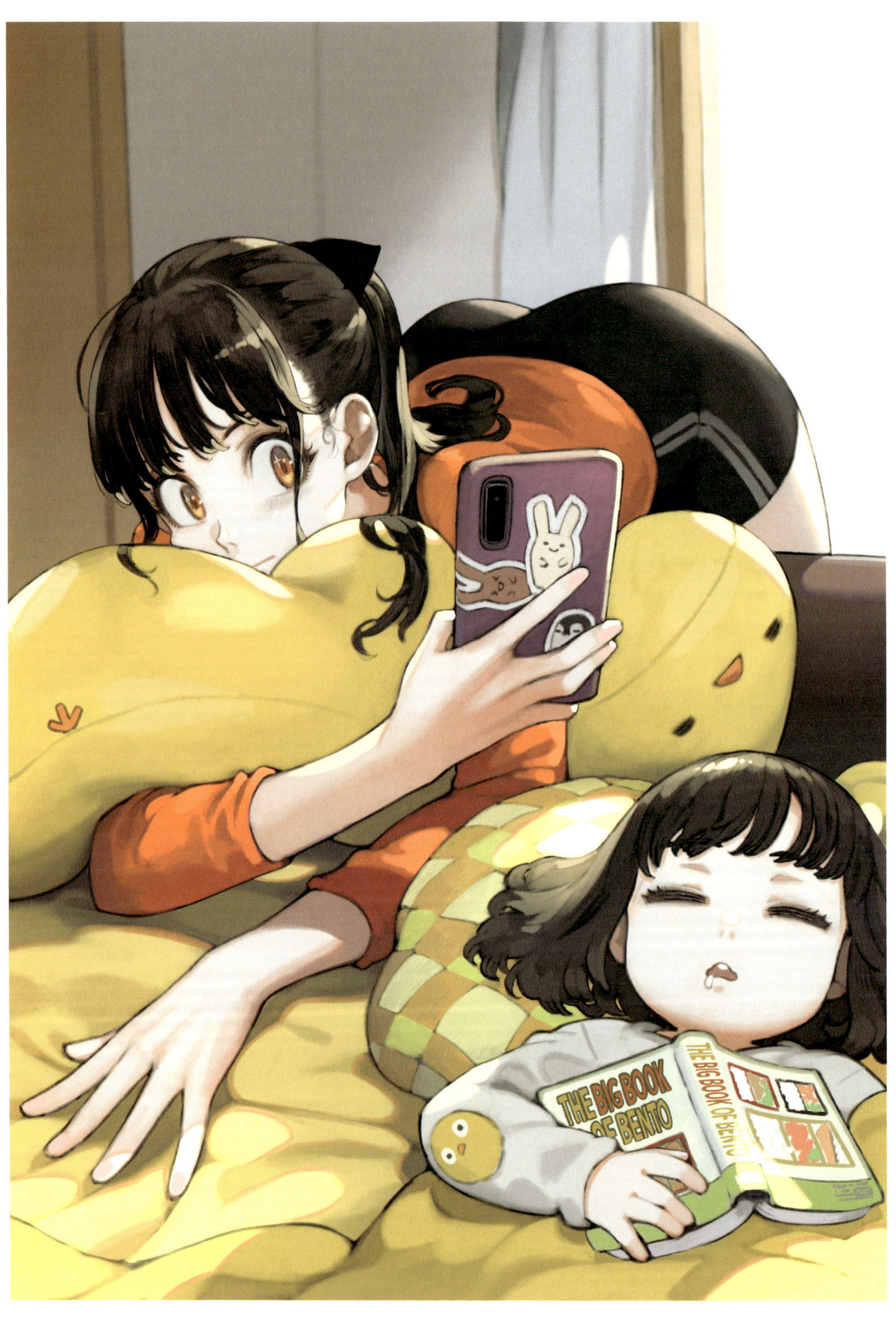
THE BIG BOOK OF BENTO
THE BIG BOOK OF BENTO

TITLE

"Alarm" (new illustration)

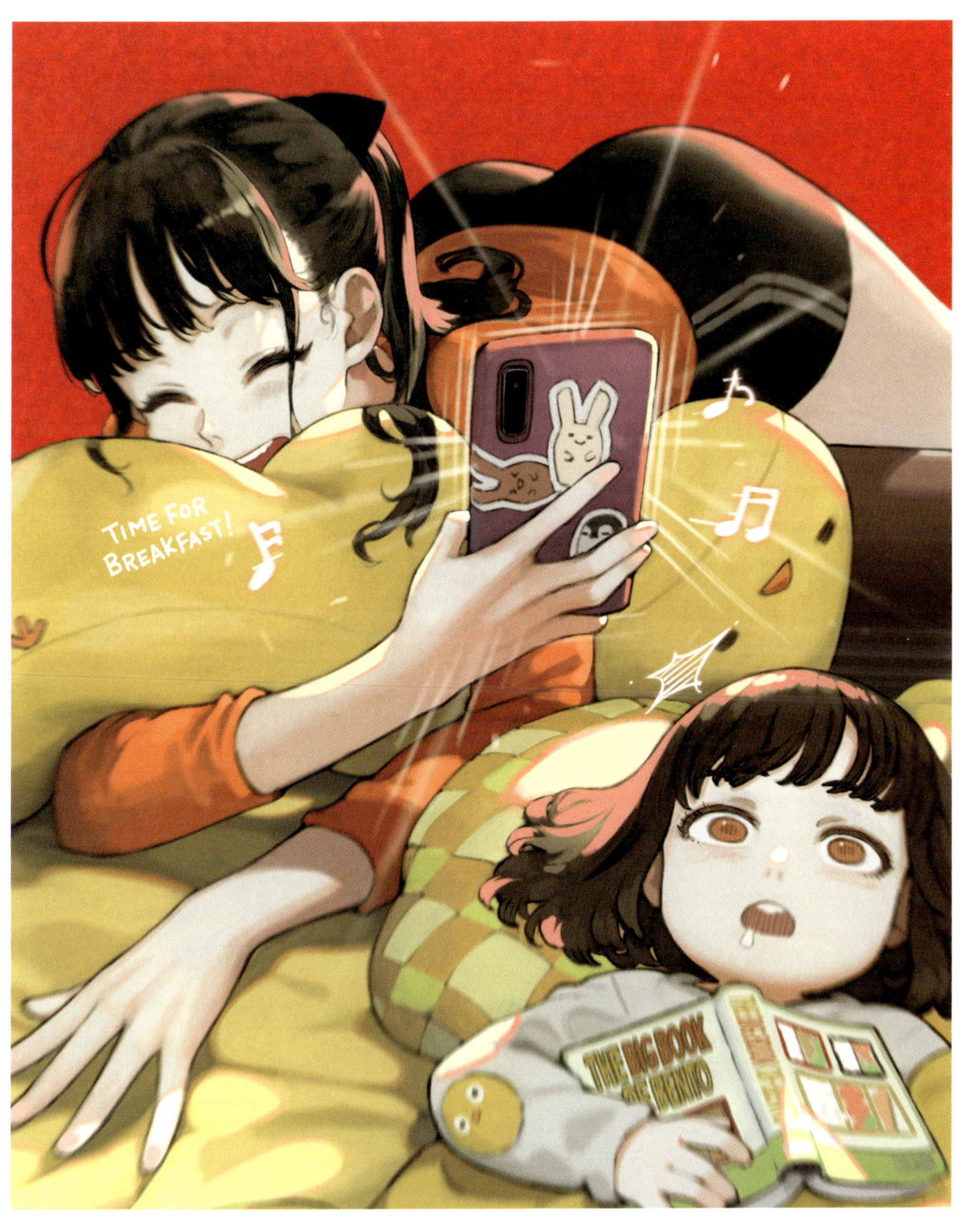

TITLE
"Tonkatsu Breaded Pork
Cutlet" (new illustration)

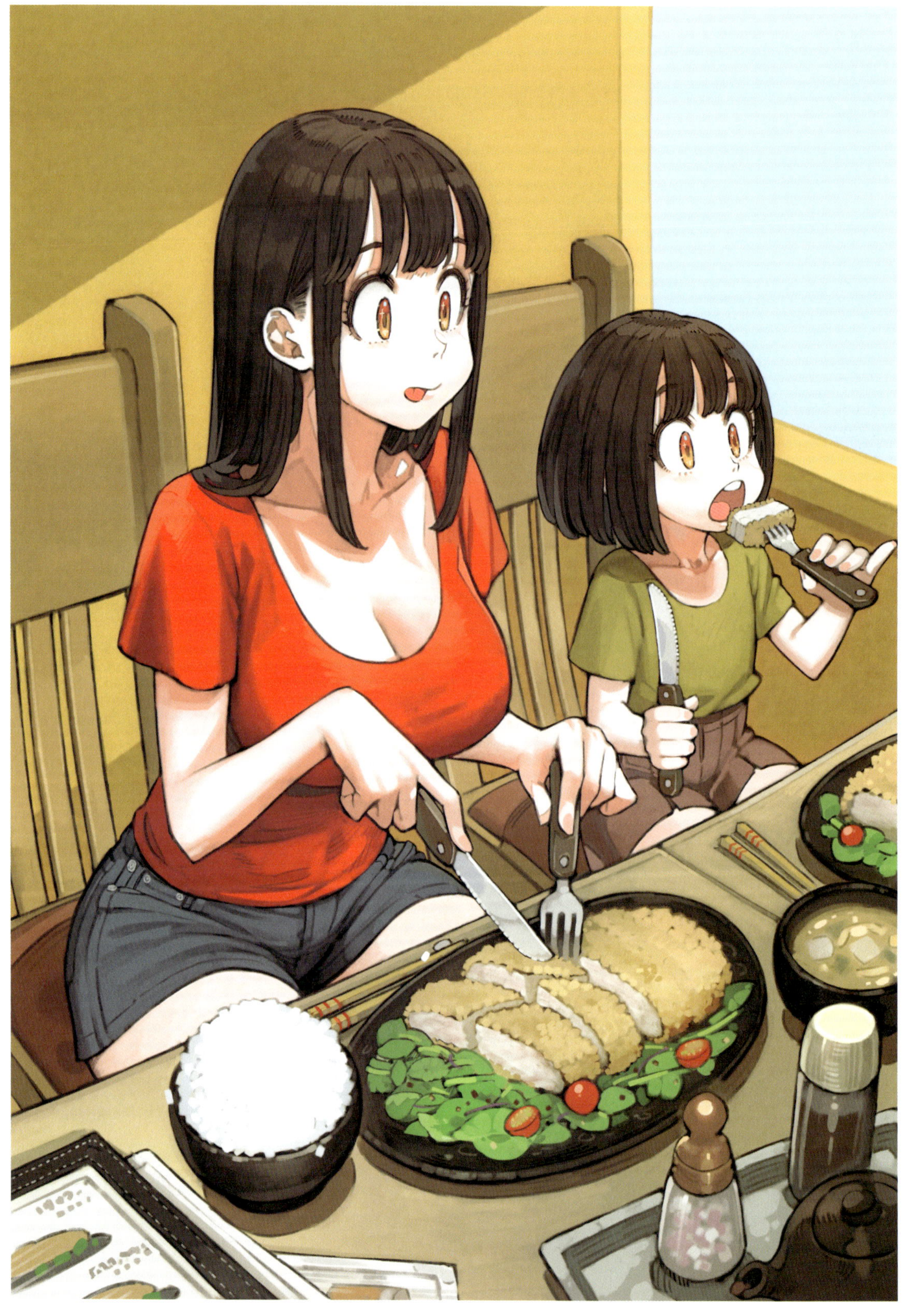

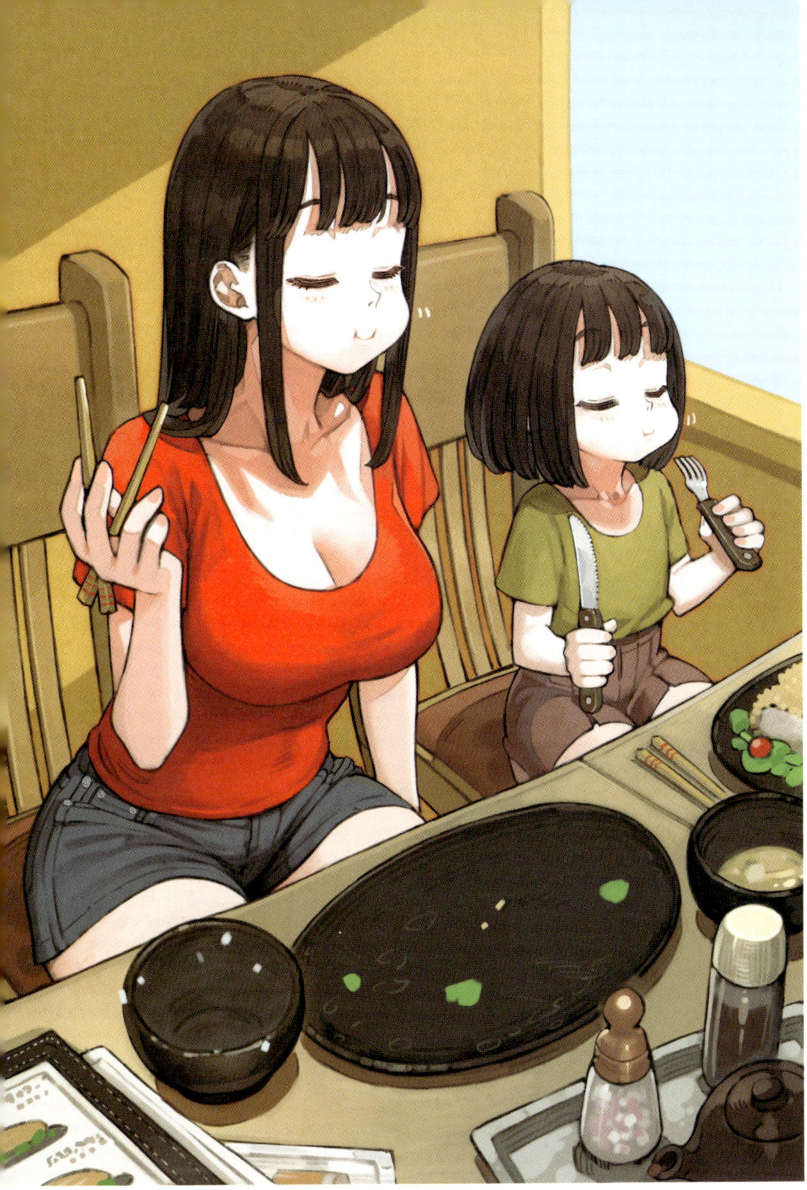

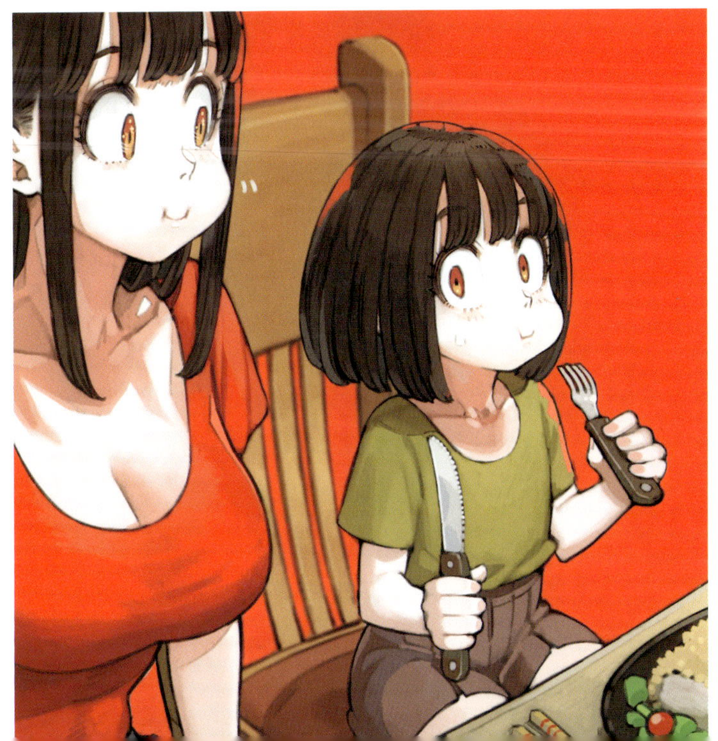

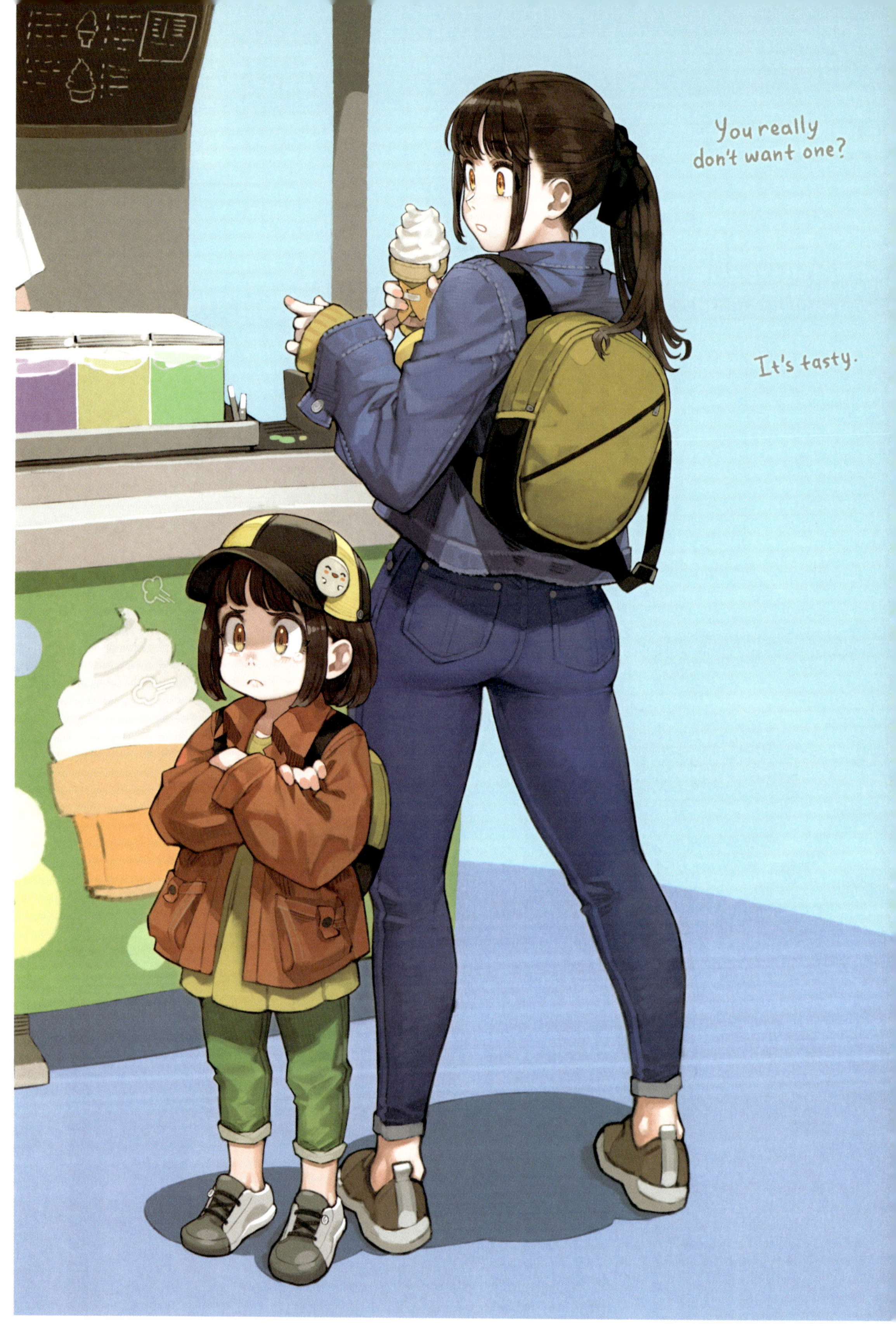

TITLE

"Pouting" (new illustration)

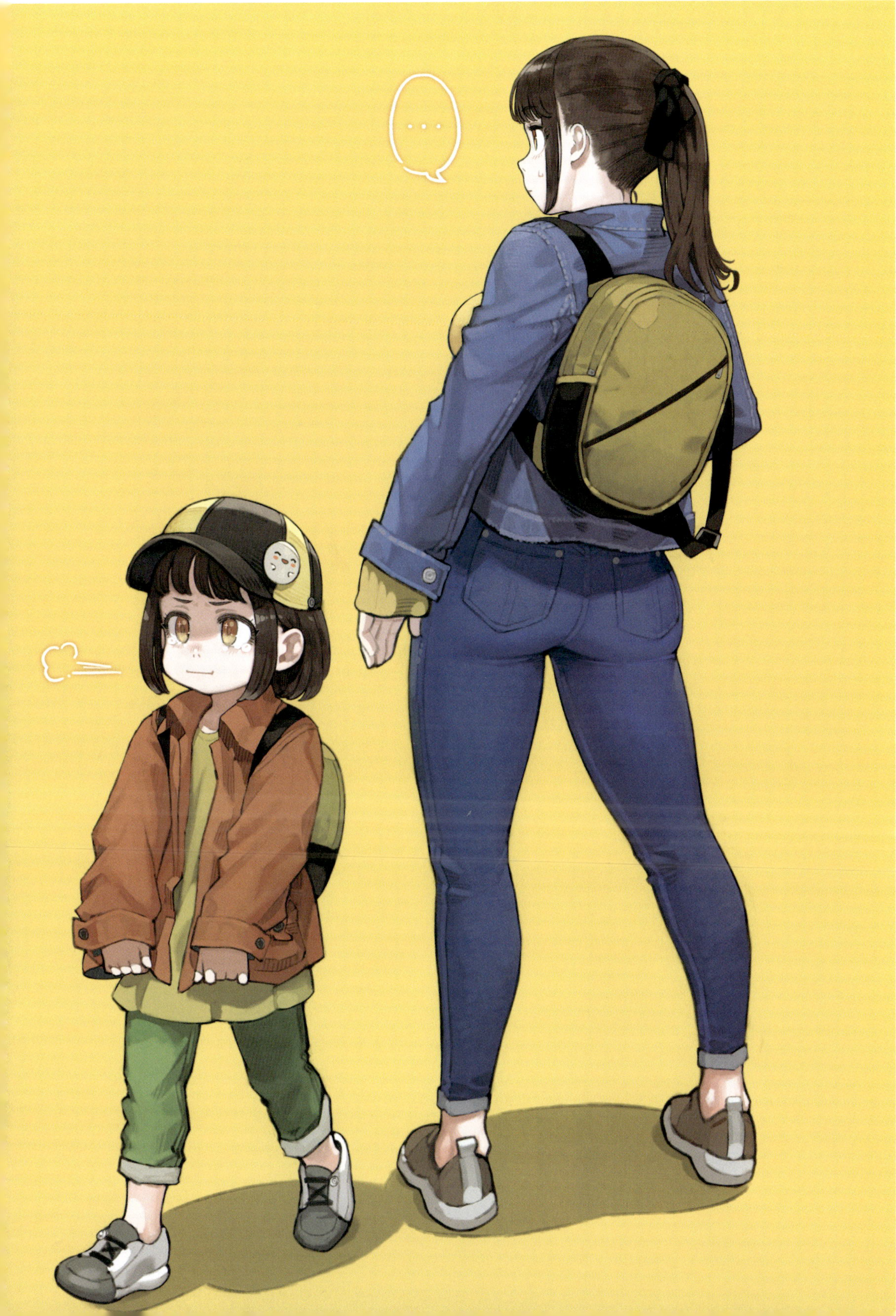

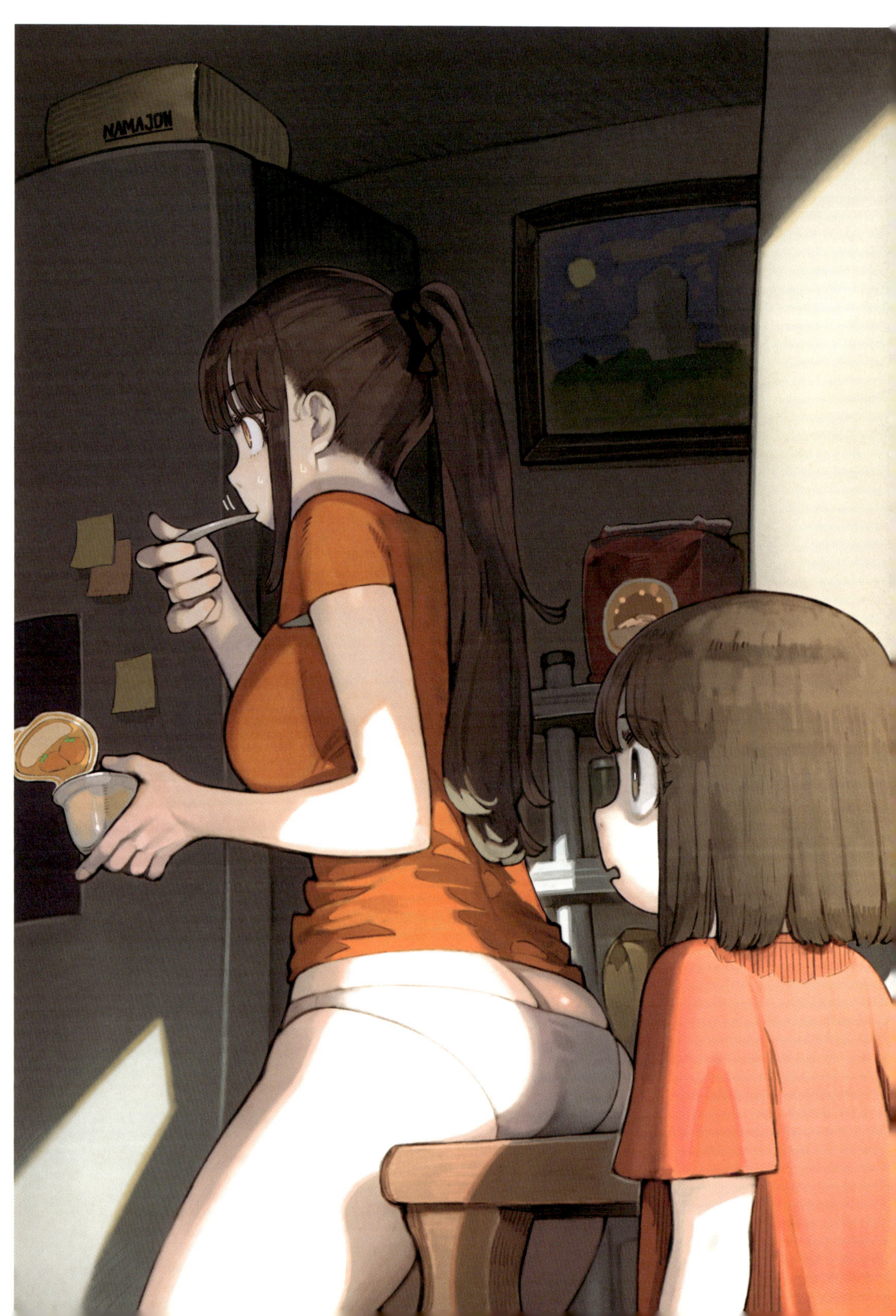
NAMAJON

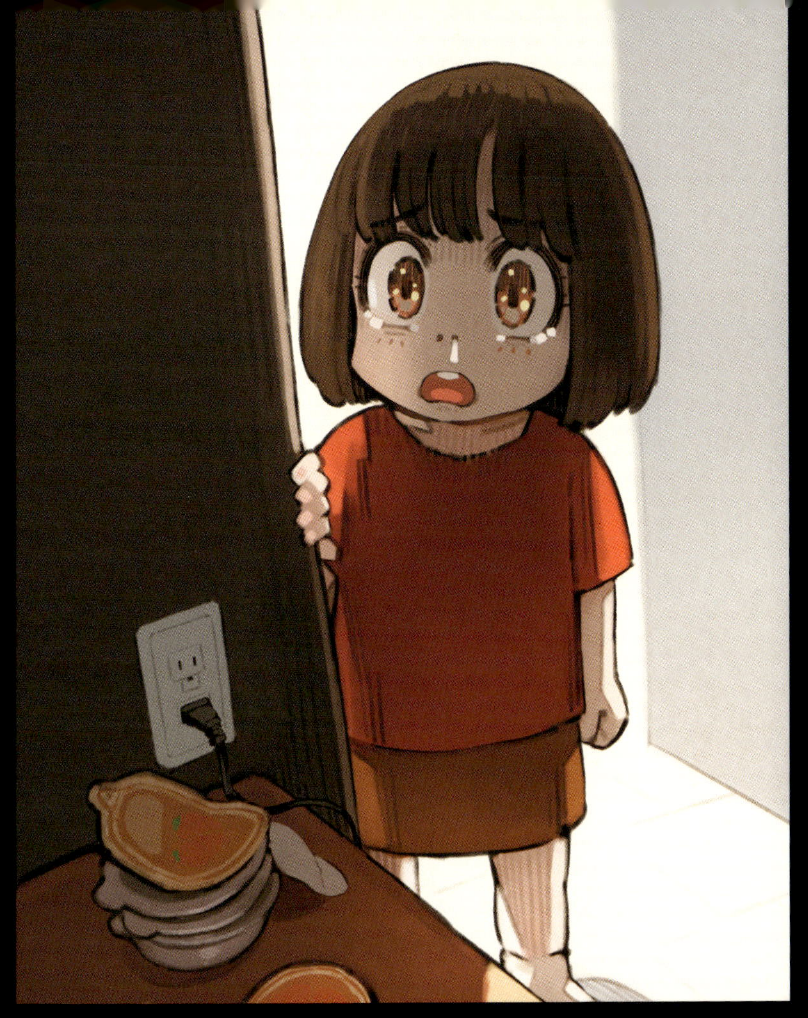

TITLE

"That's My Mandarin Jelly..." (new illustration)

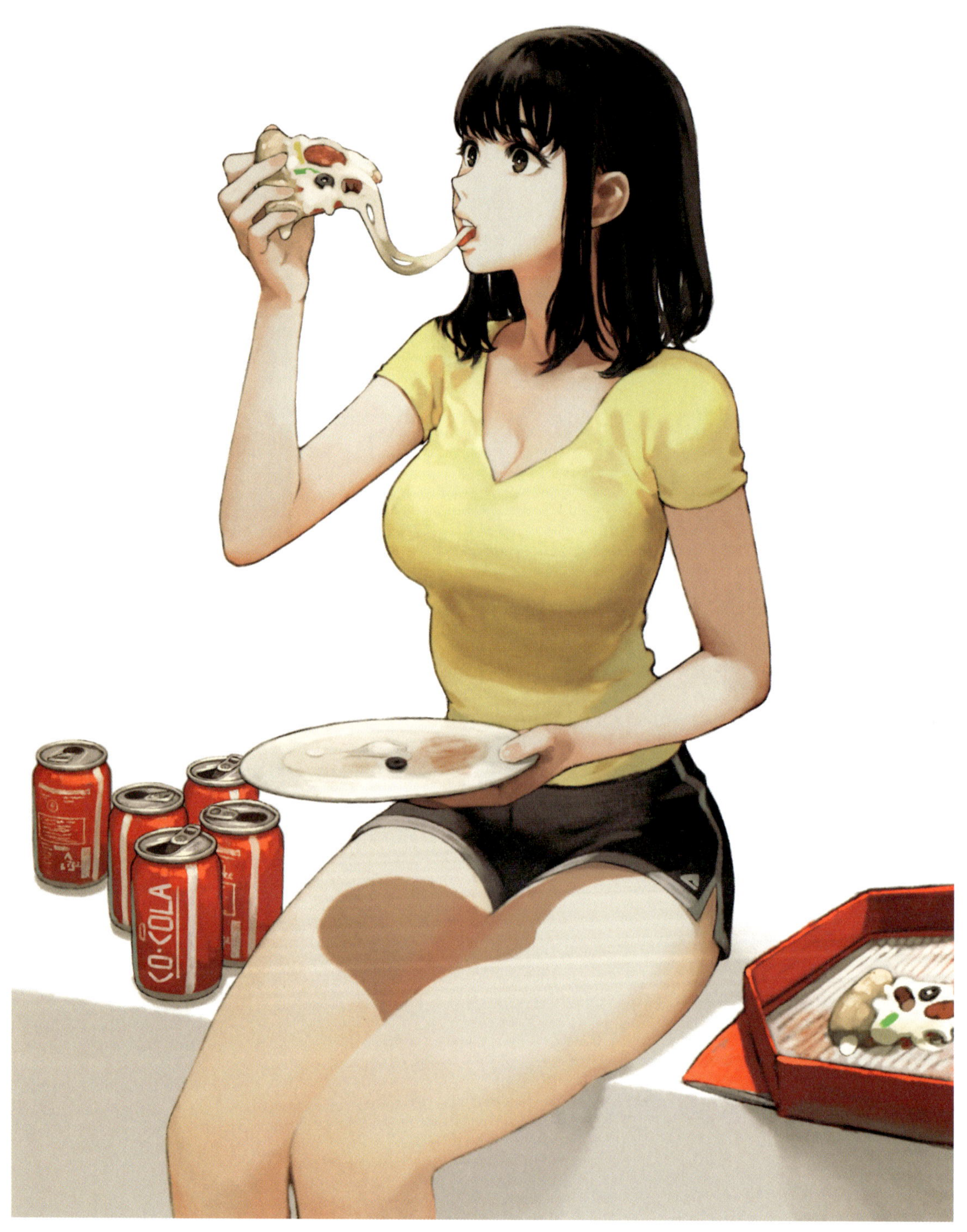

TITLE

"Pizza"

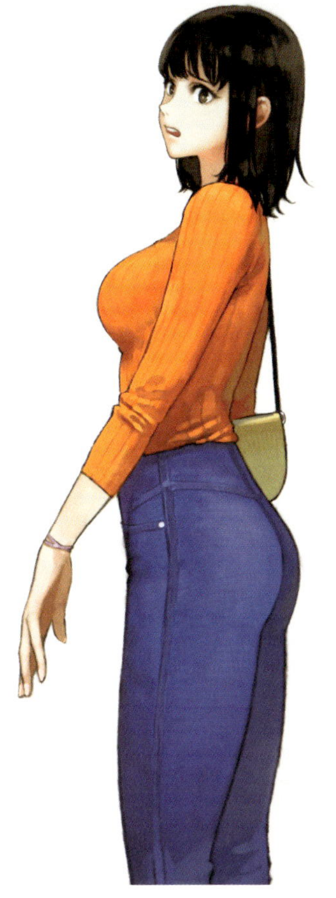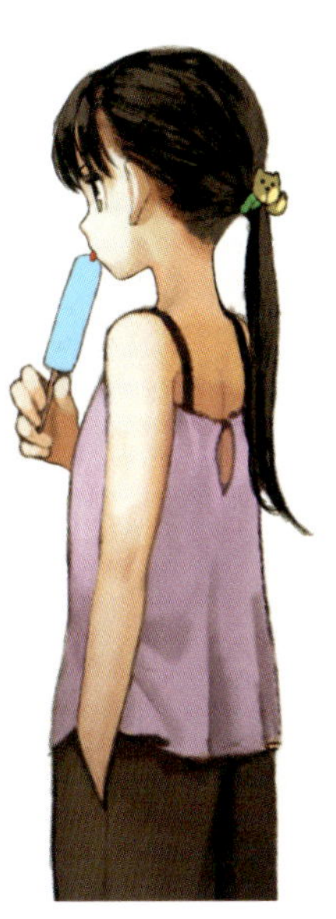

TITLE

"Have I Been Gaining Weight?"

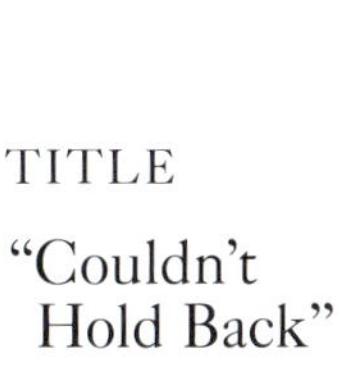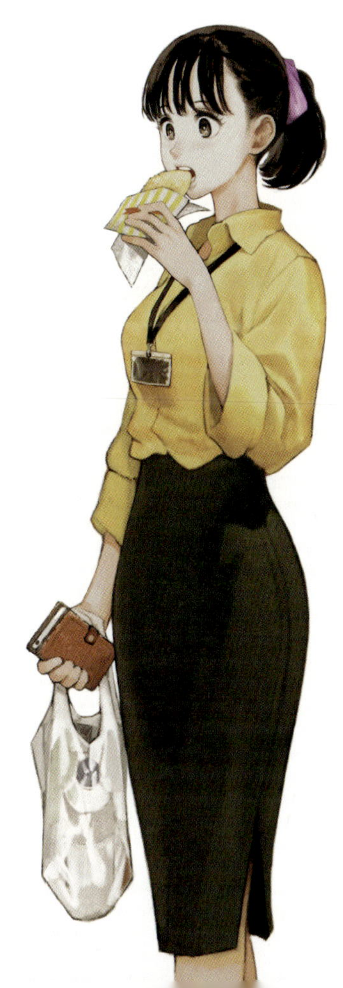

TITLE

"Couldn't
 Hold Back"

TITLE
"Junkie"

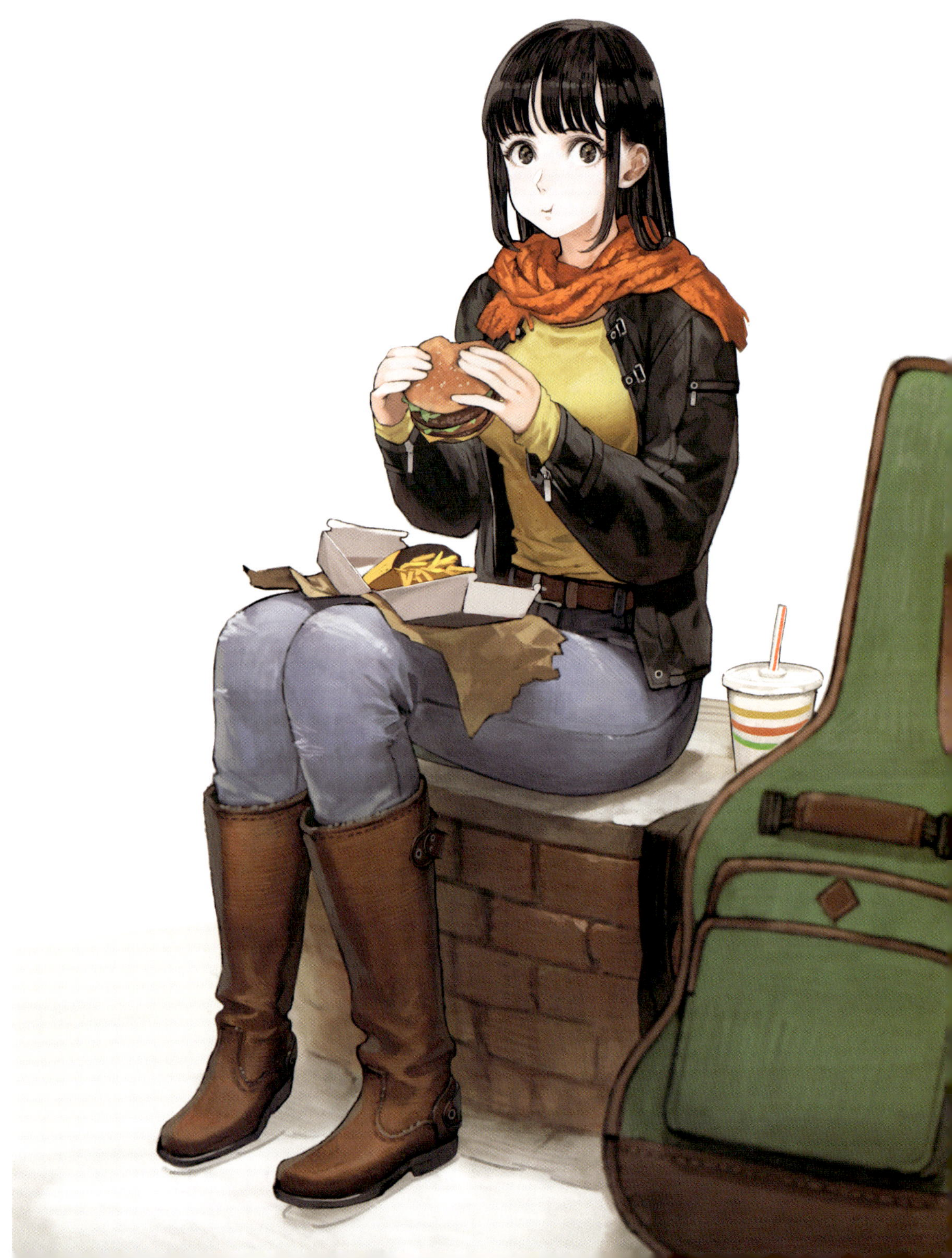

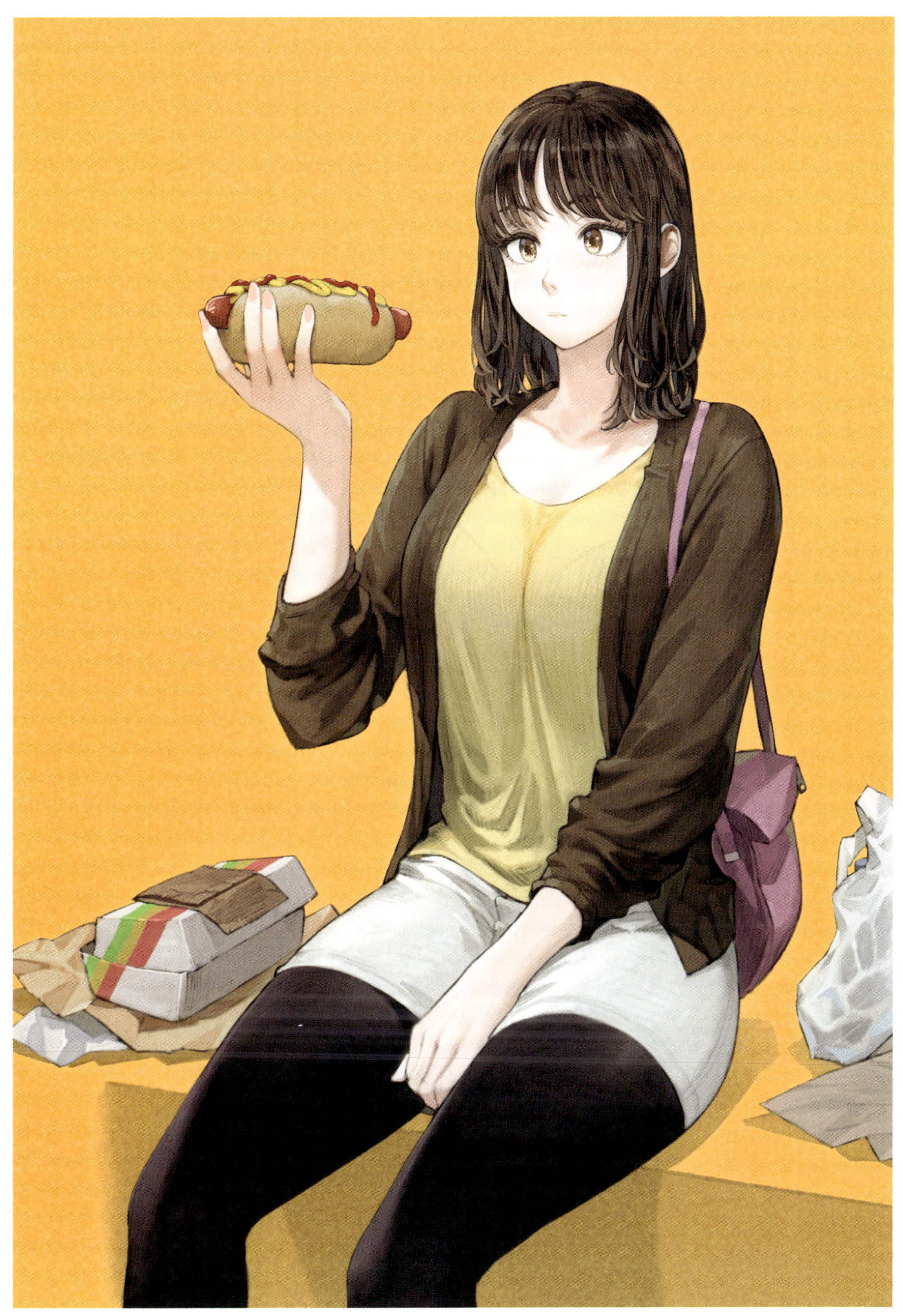

TITLE

"Hot Dog"

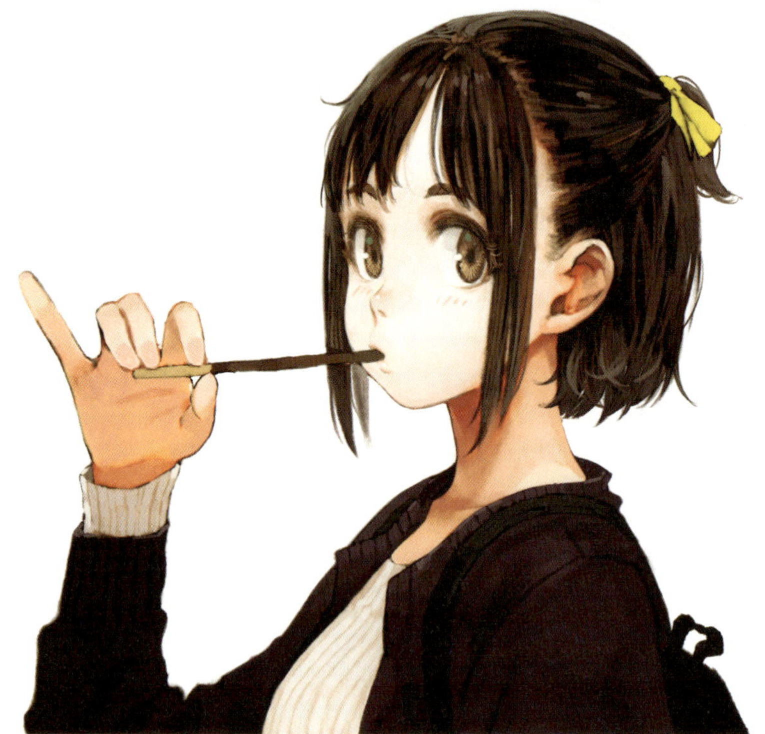

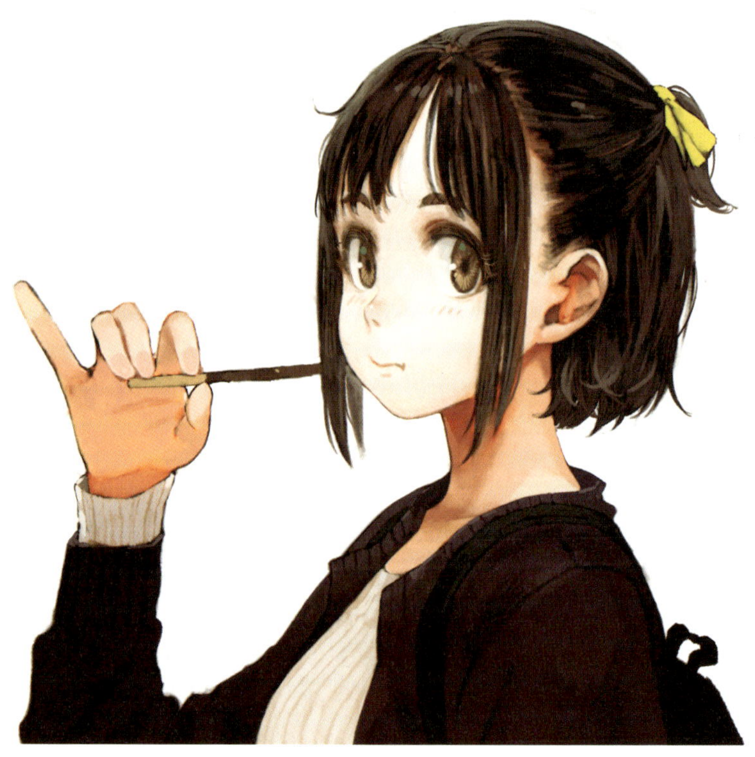

TITLE
"What?"

TITLE
"Ramen"

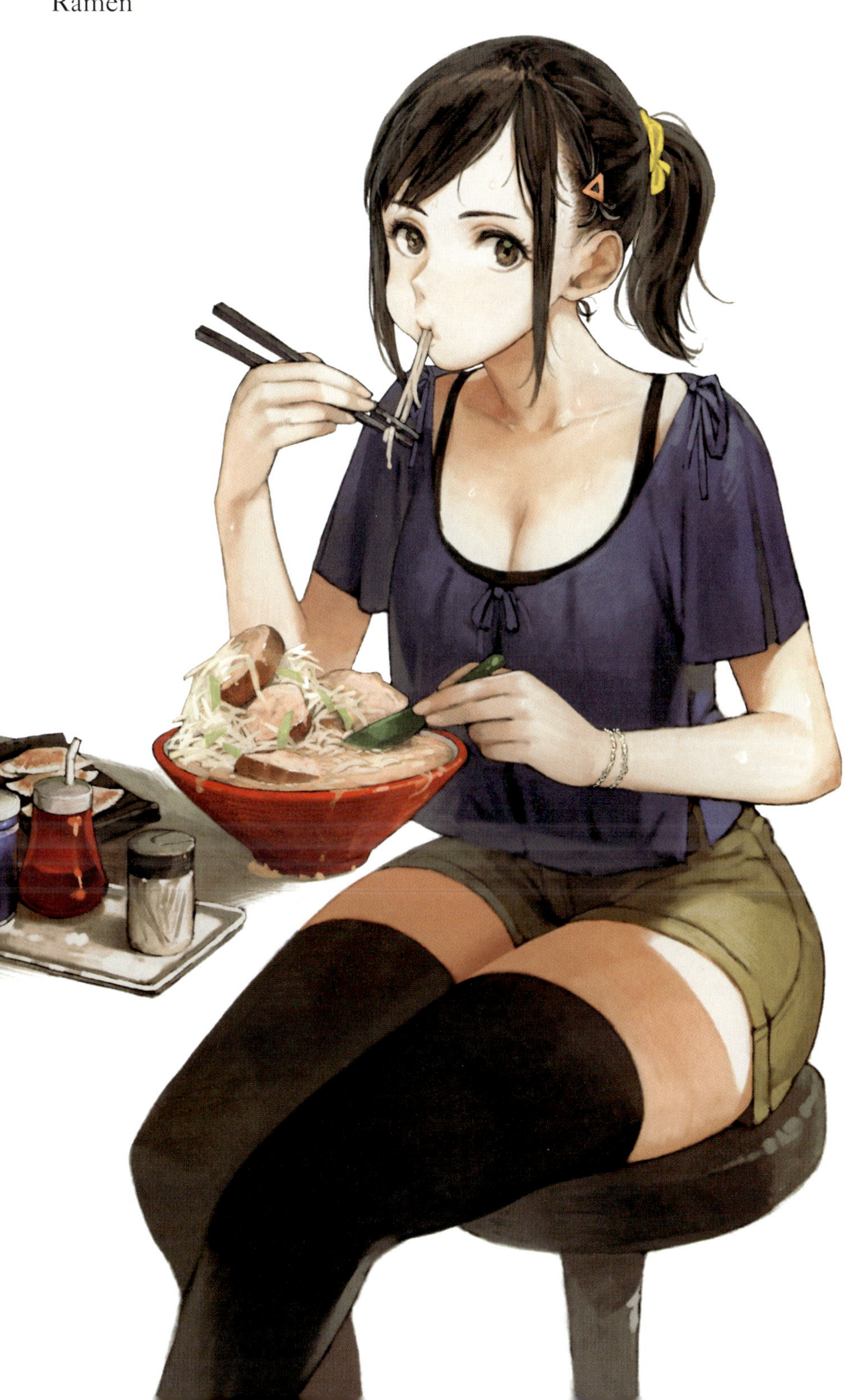

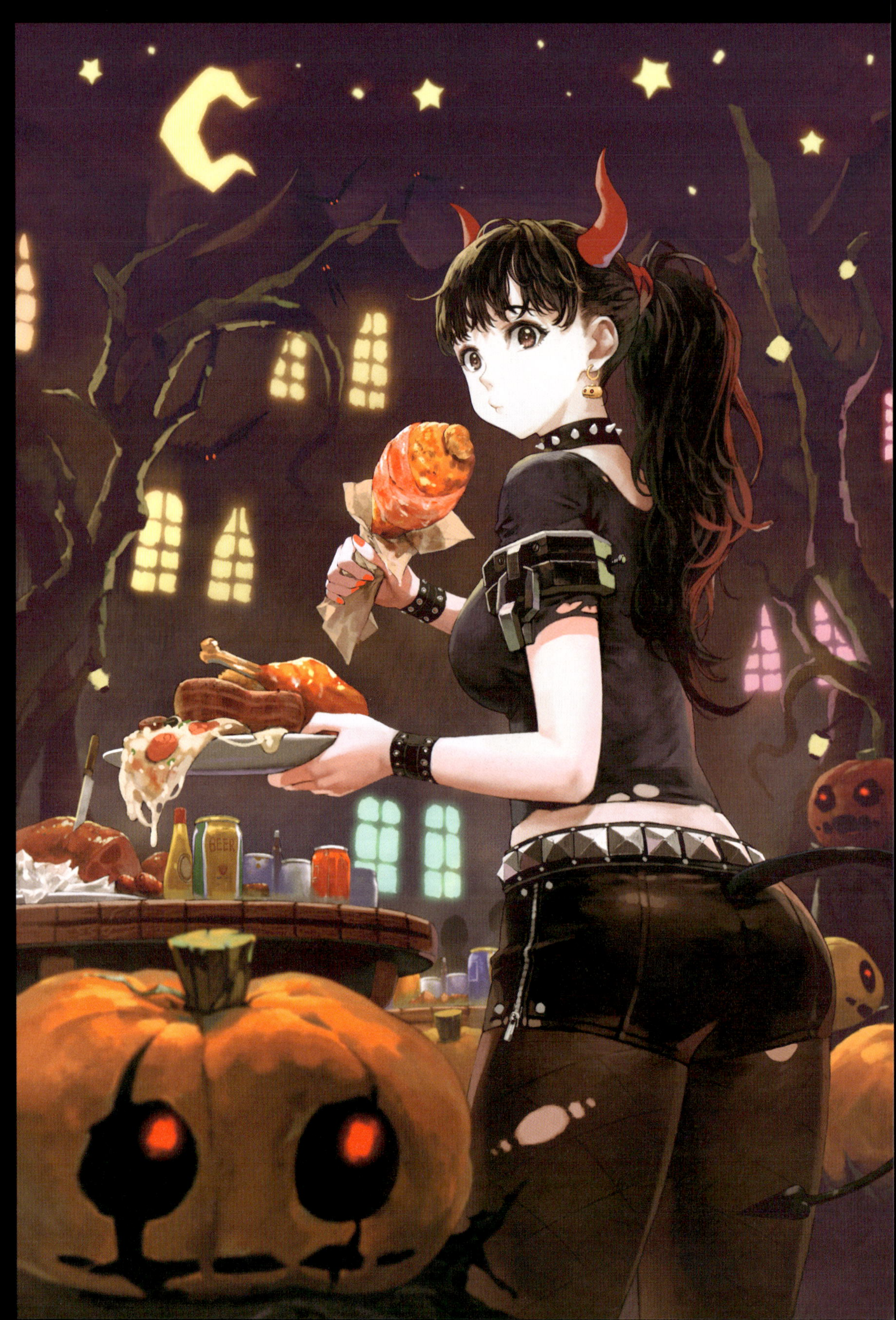

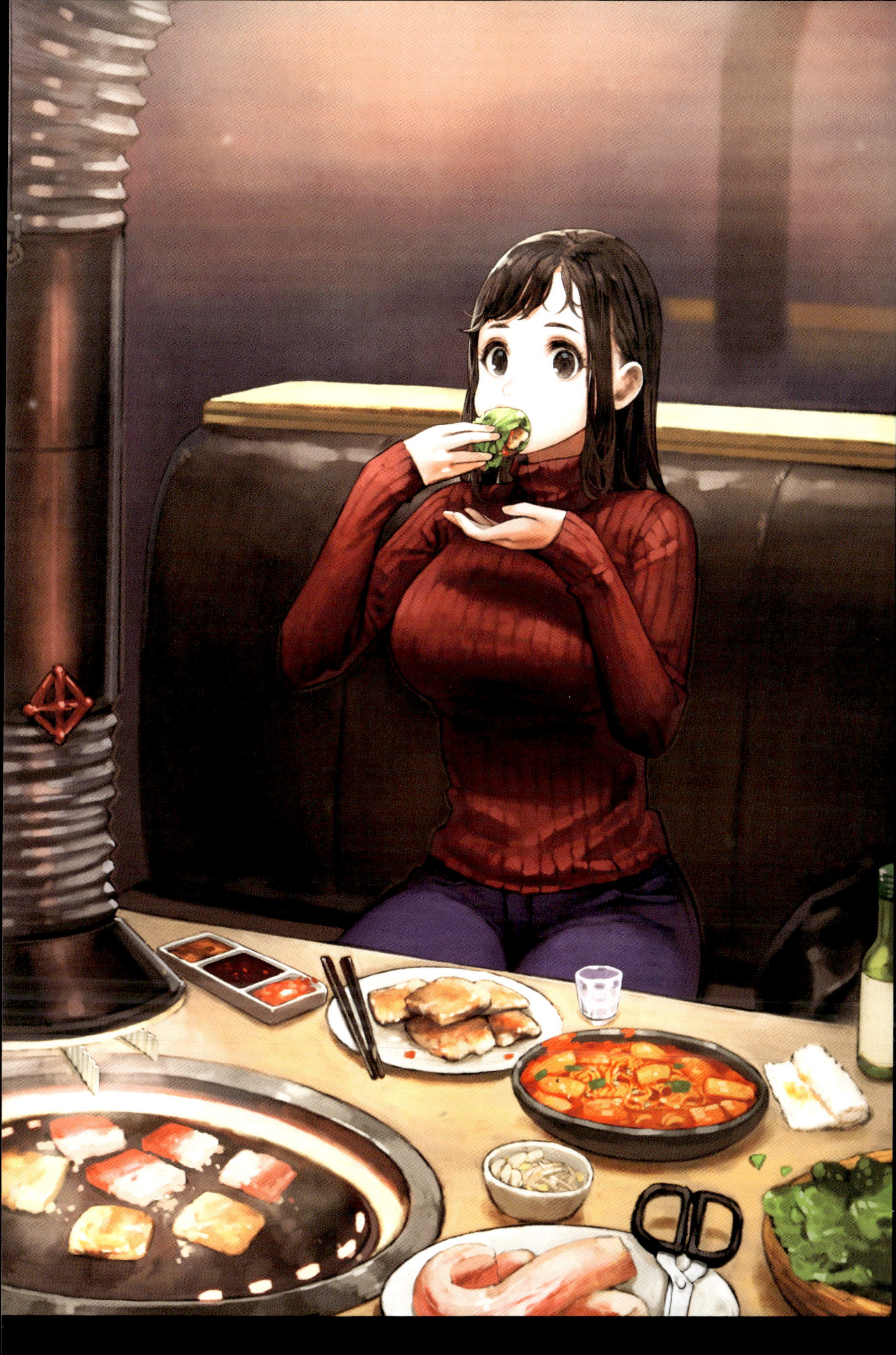

TITLE

"Do I Eat It Like This?"

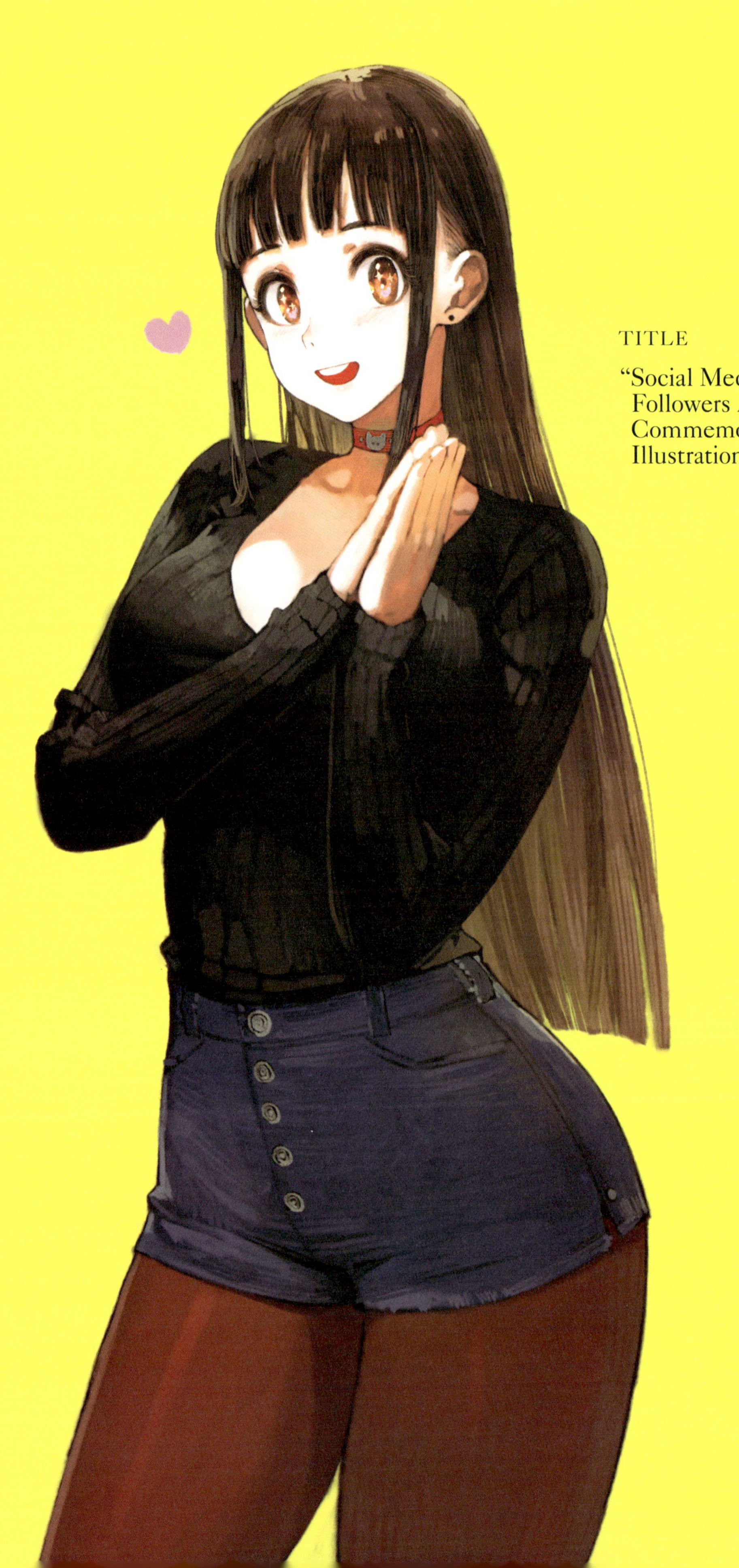
TITLE

"Social Media
Followers Achievement
Commemoration
Illustration 1"

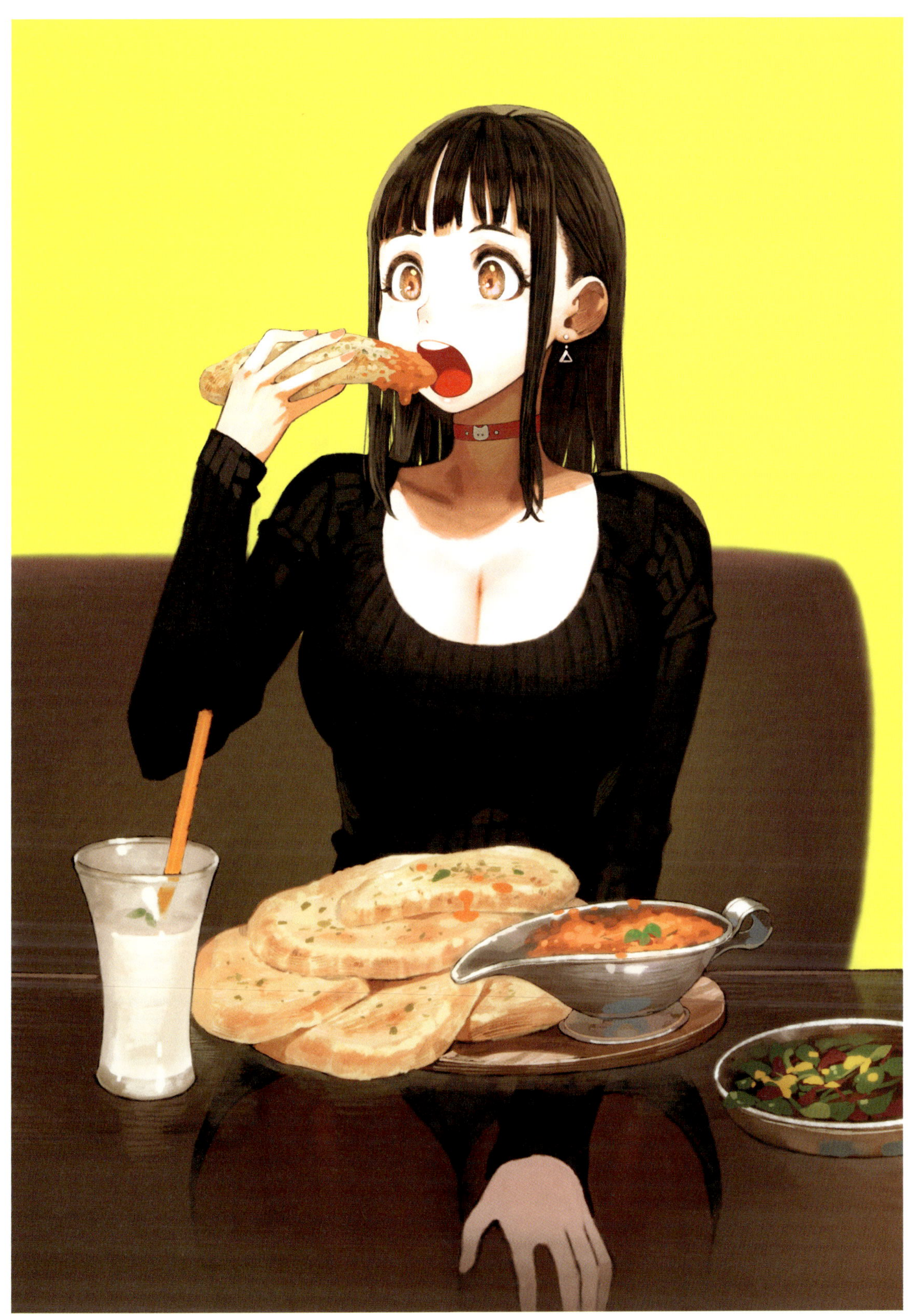

TITLE

"What Naan?"

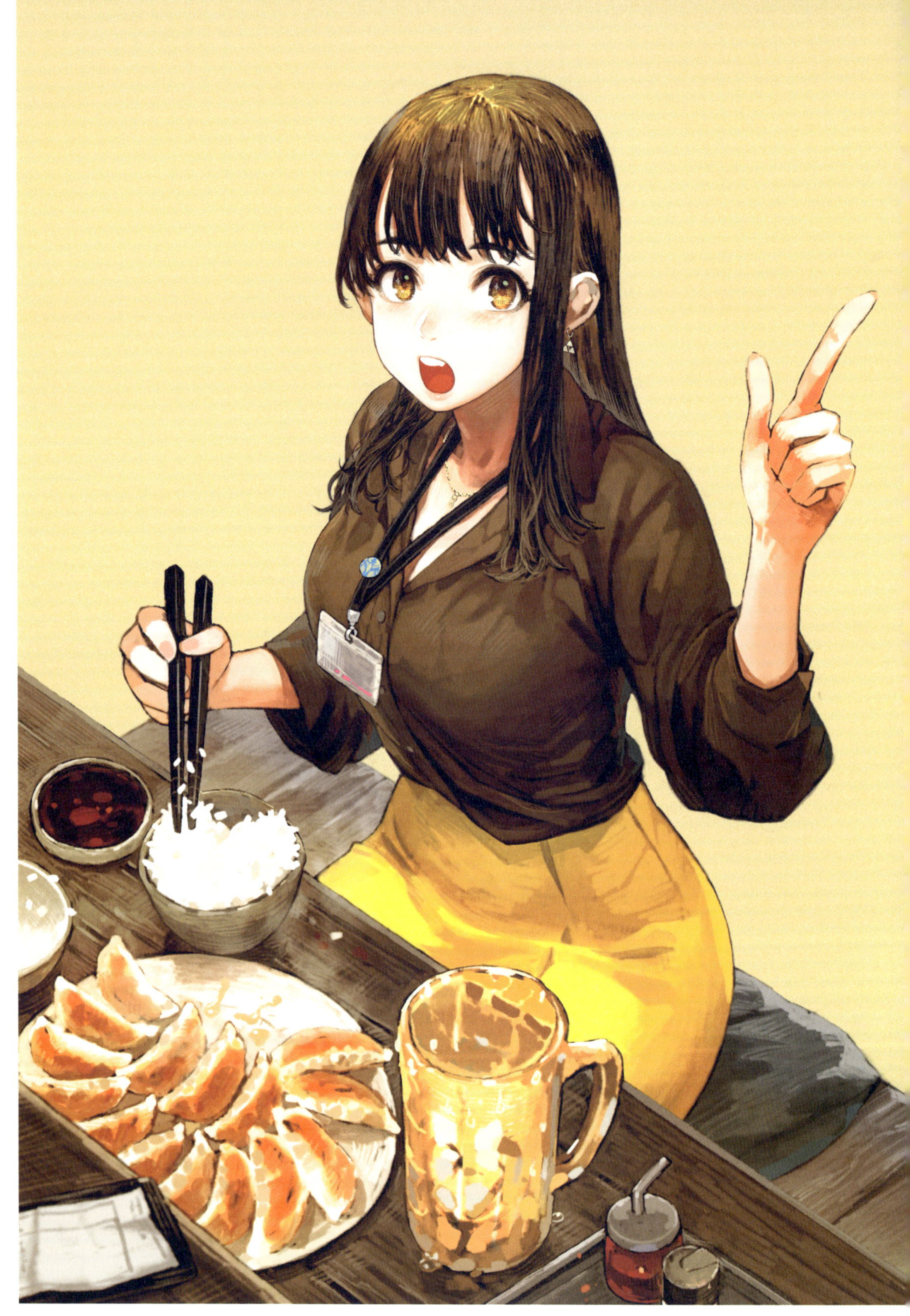

TITLE

"One Draught Beer, Please!"

TITLE

"Aren't You Hungry?"

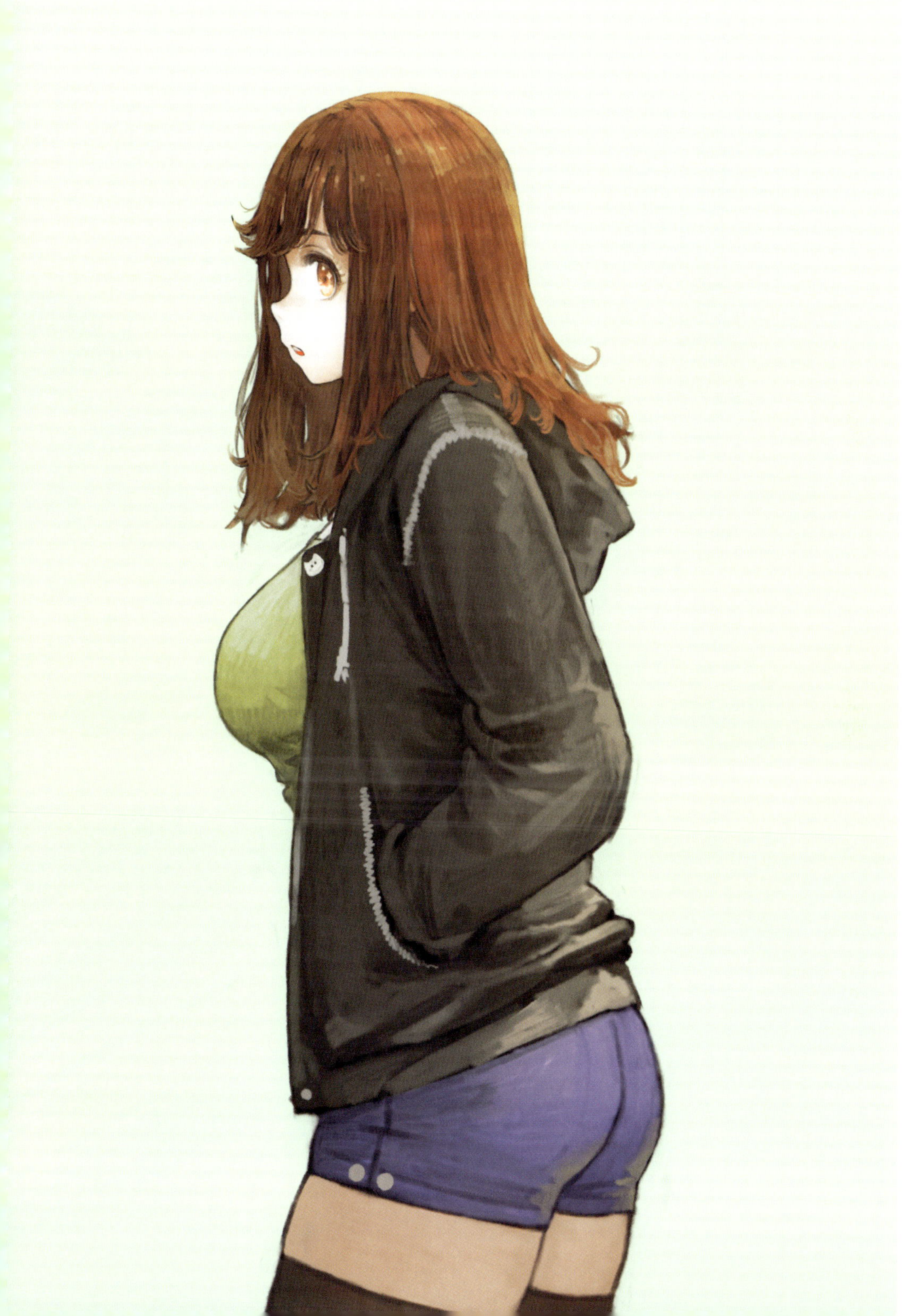

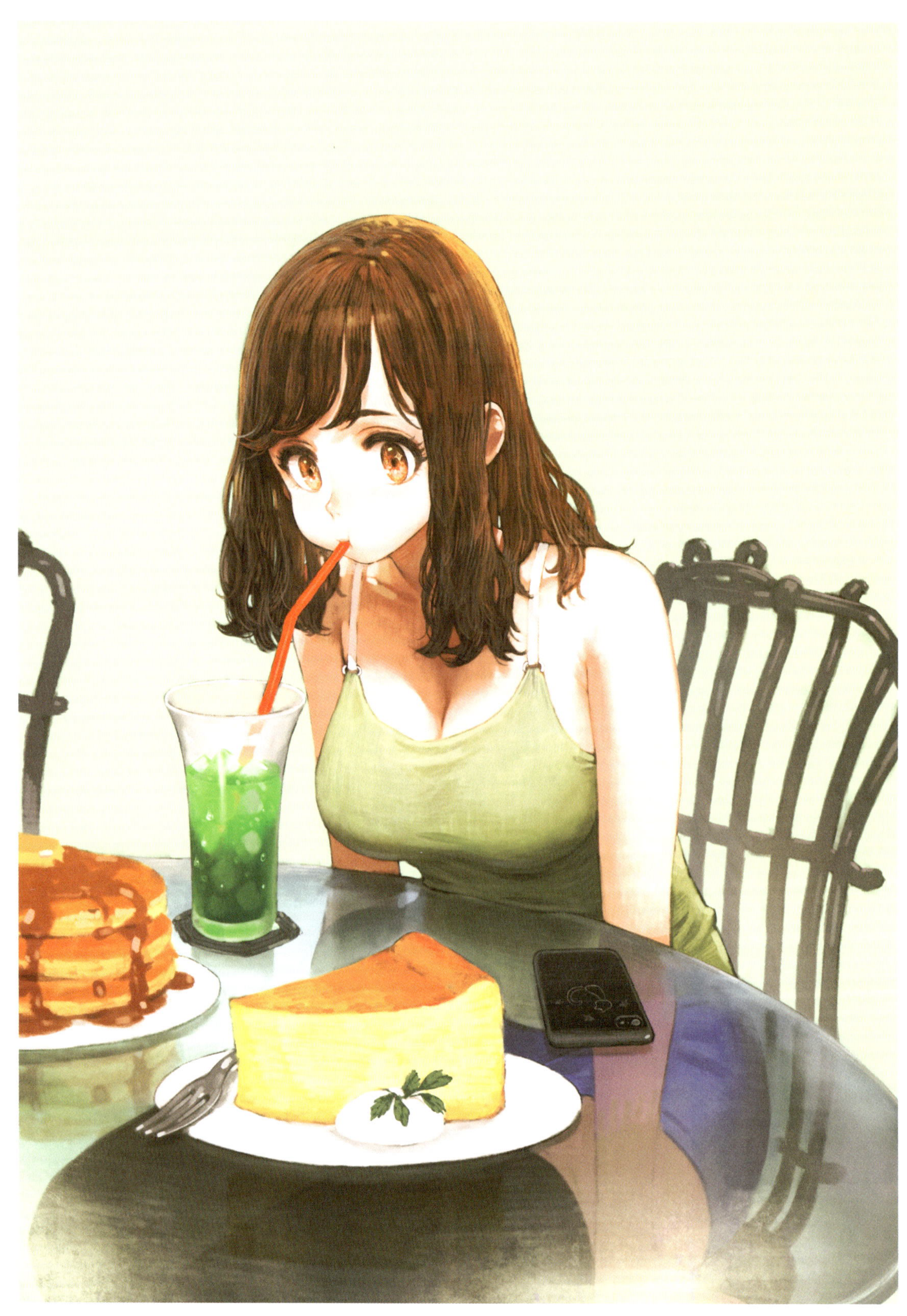

TITLE
"Sweets"

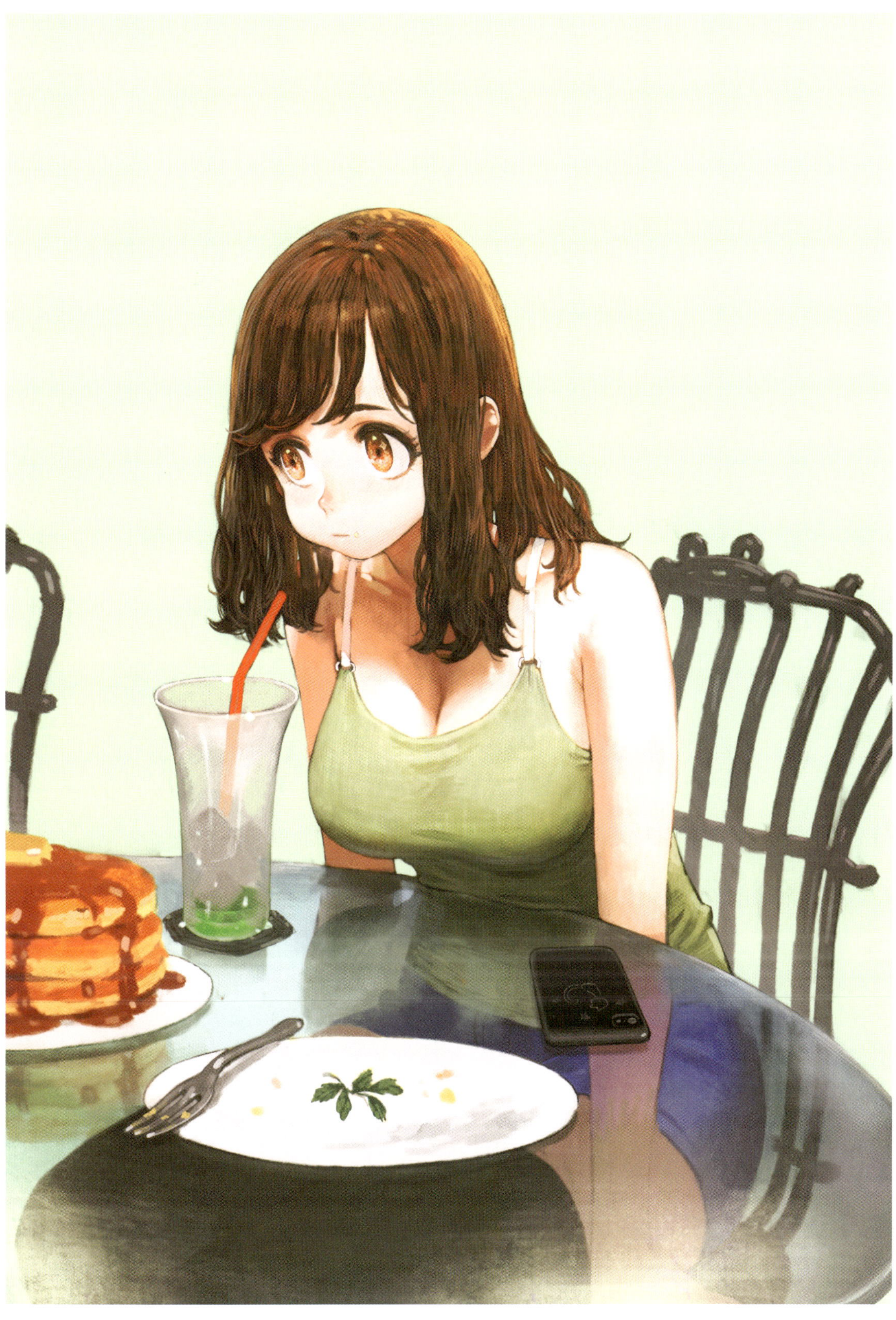

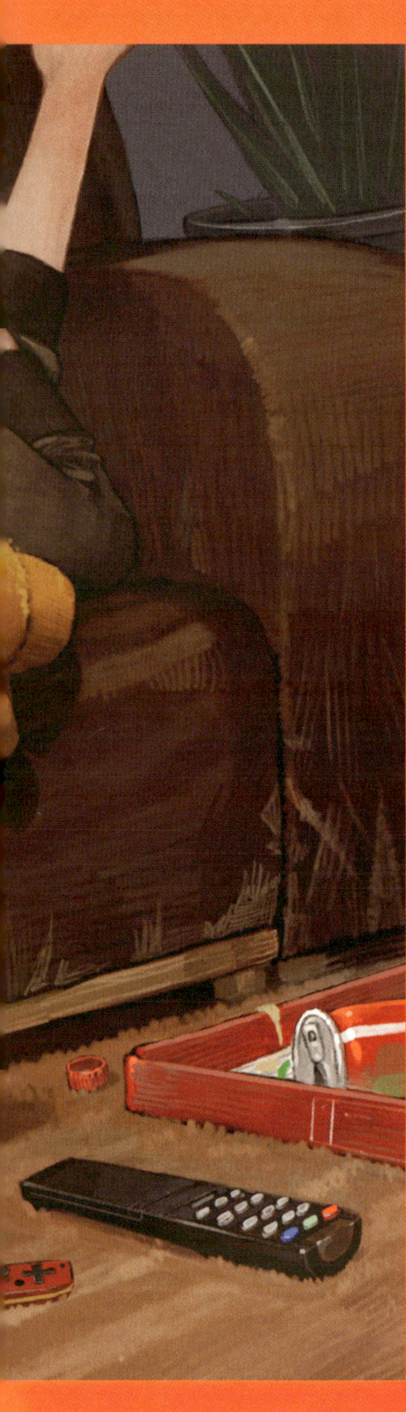

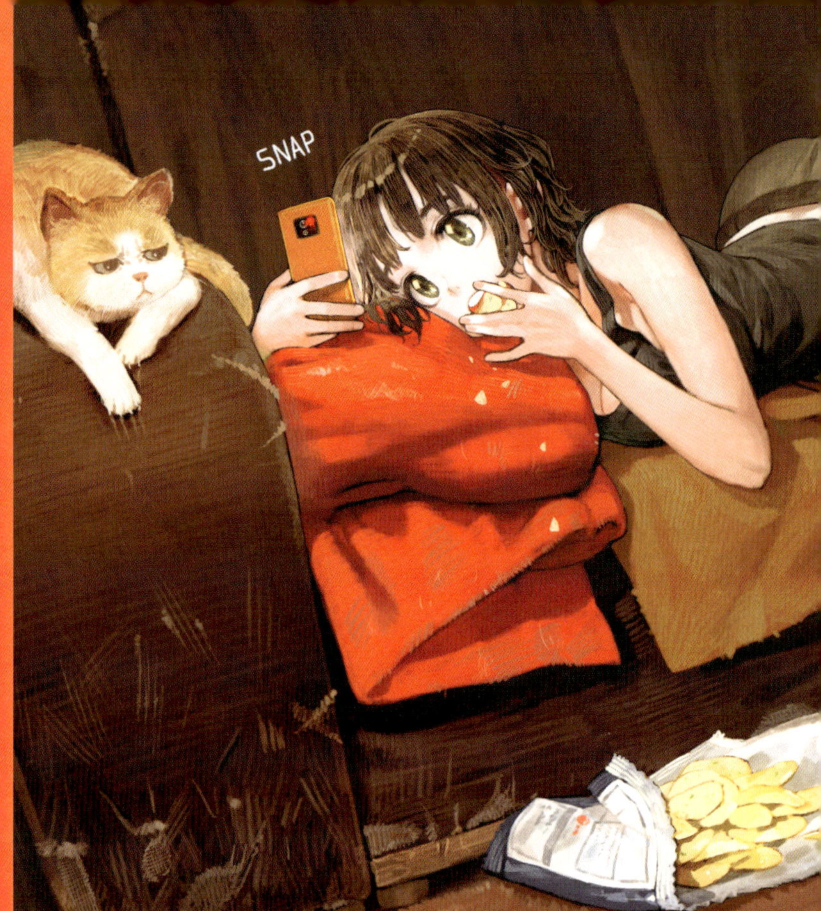
SNAP

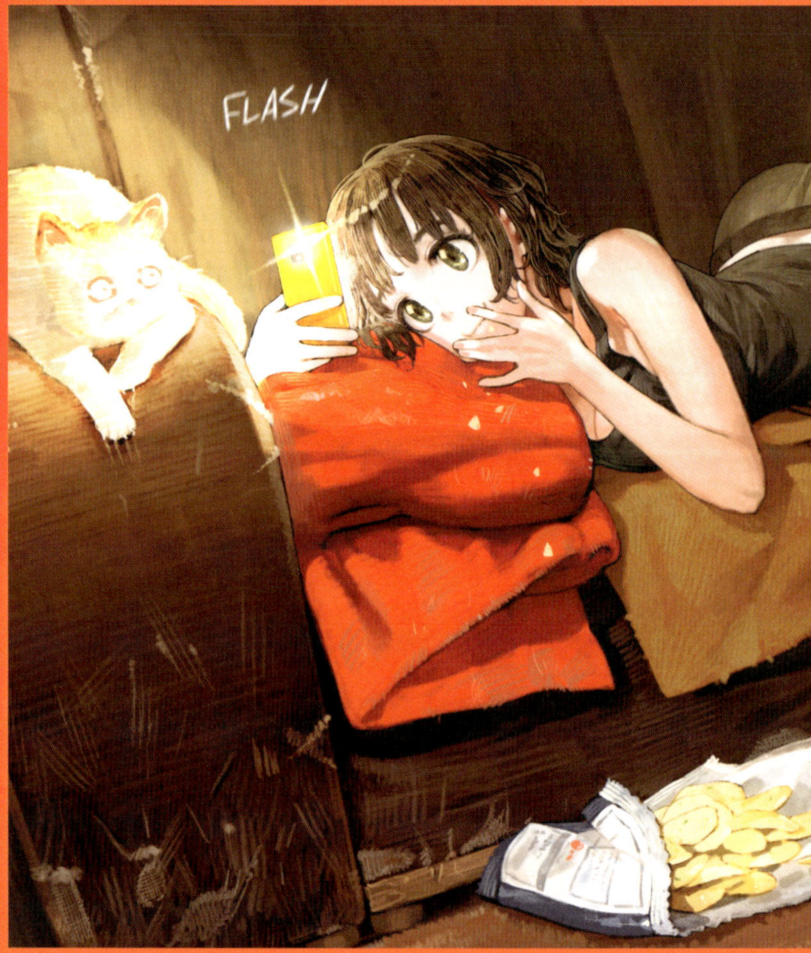
FLASH

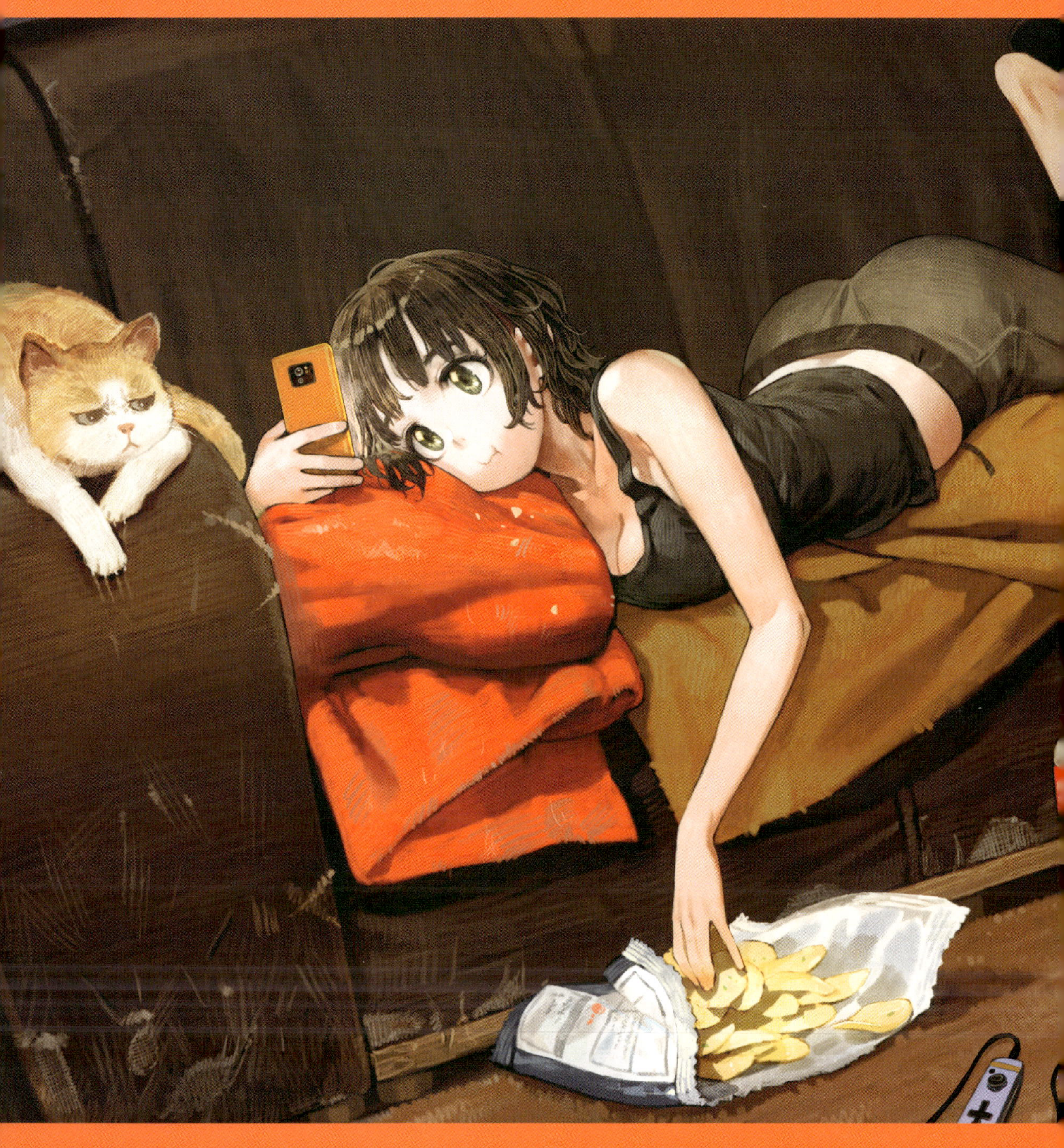

TITLE
"Potato Chips"

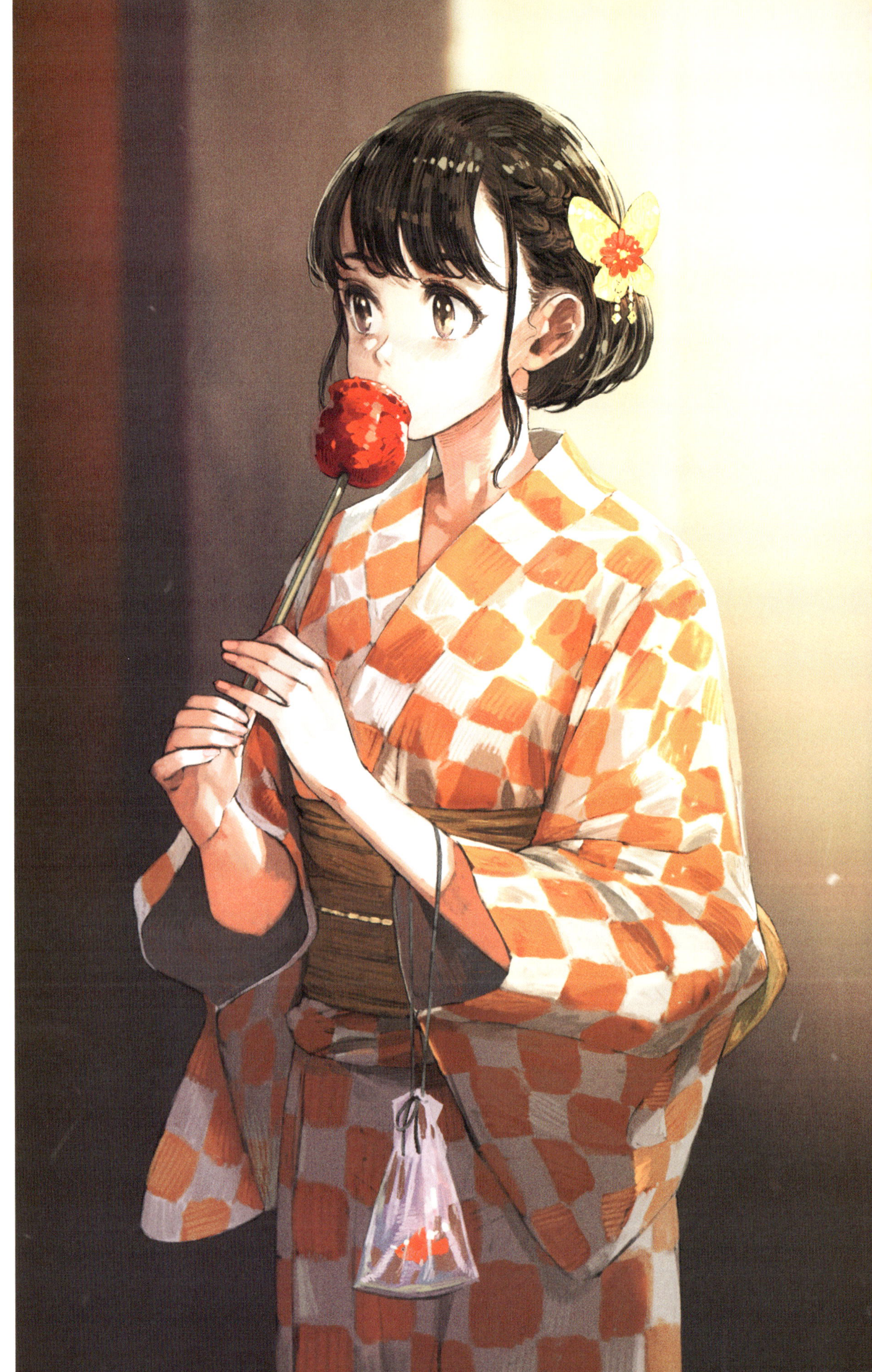

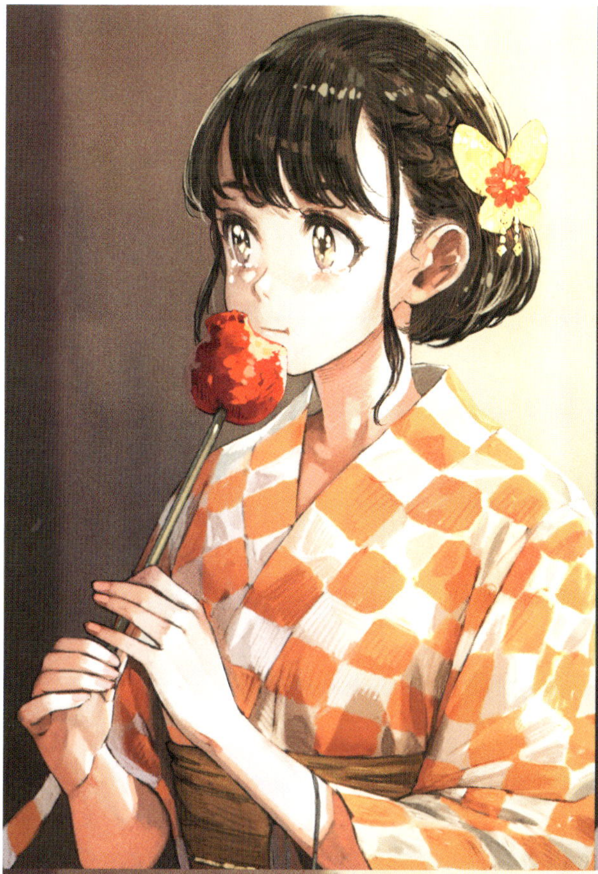

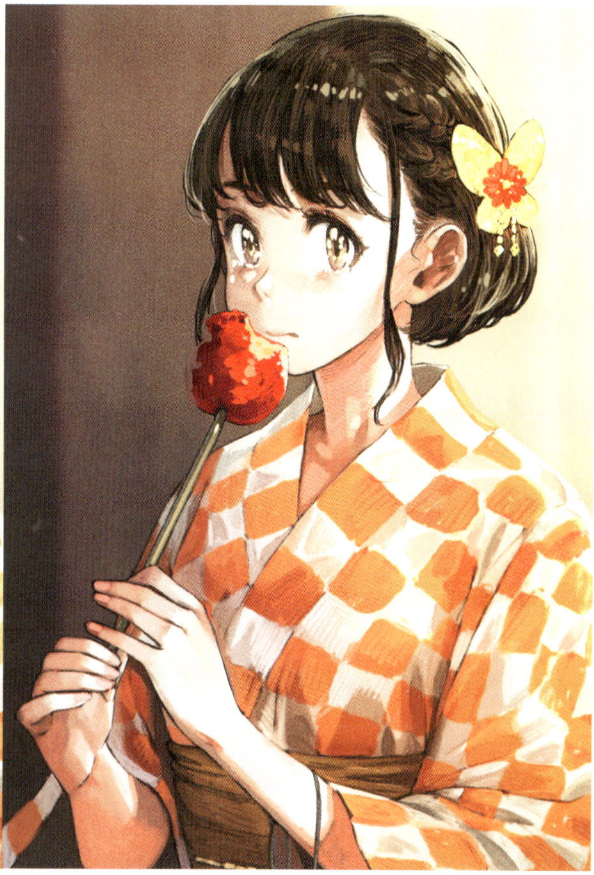

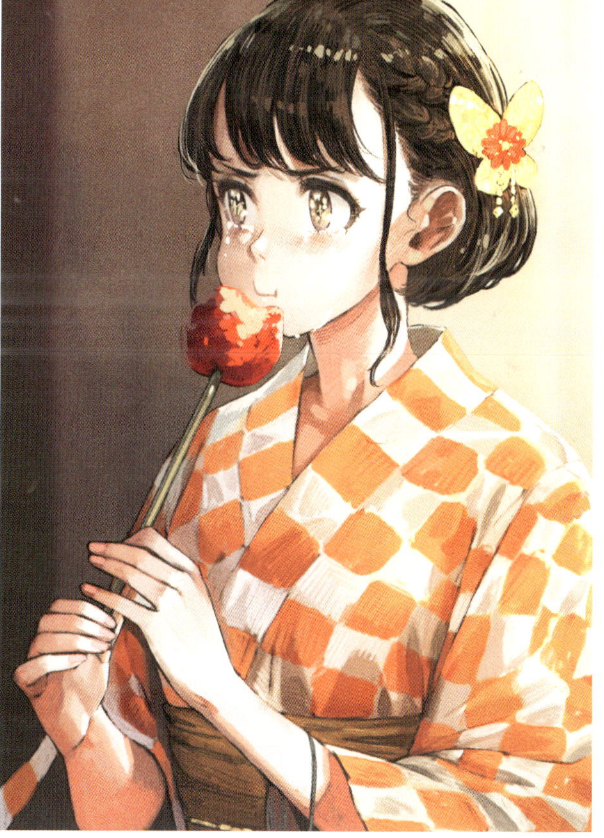

TITLE

"Festival"

TITLE
"Ice"

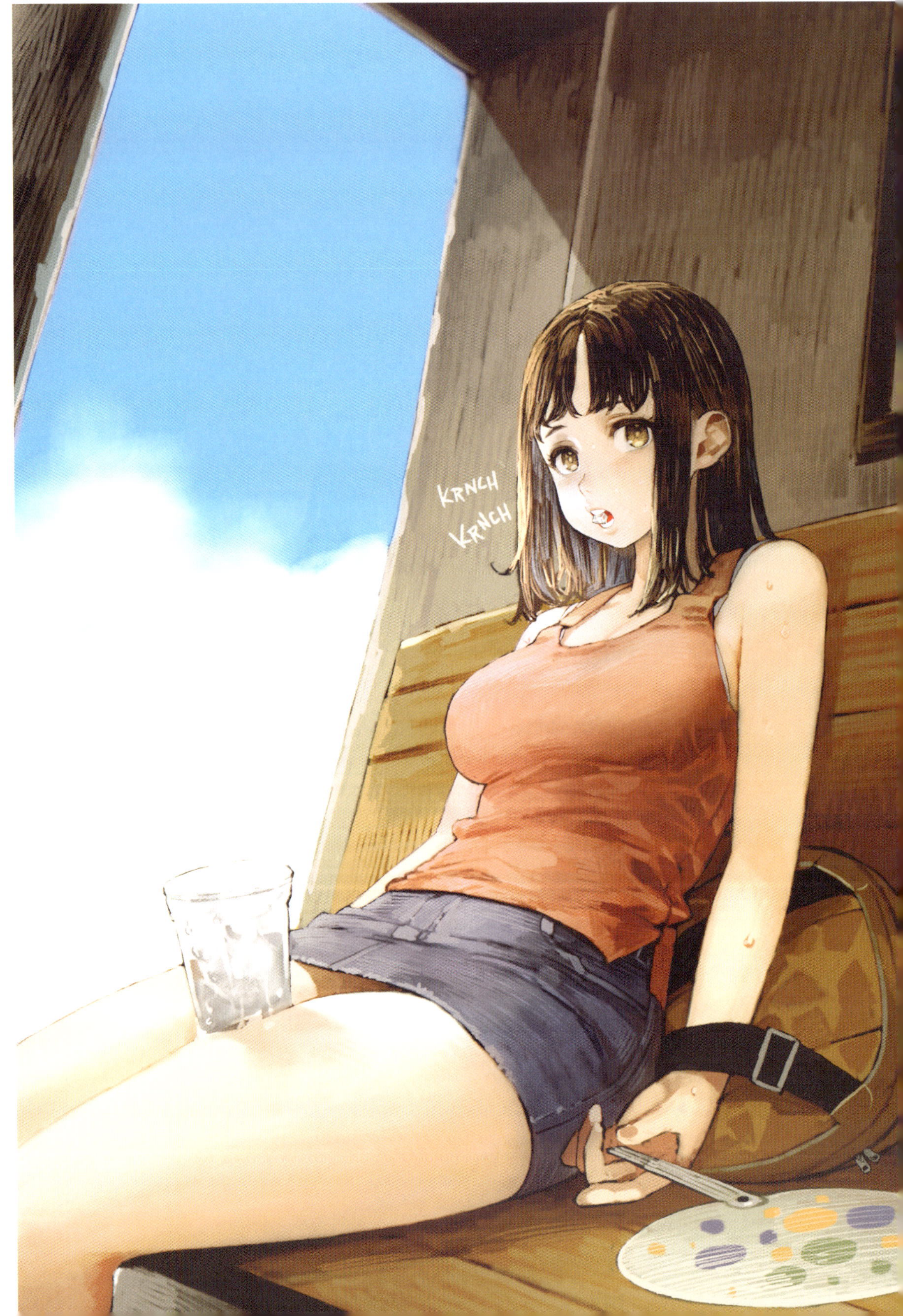
KRNCH
KRNCH

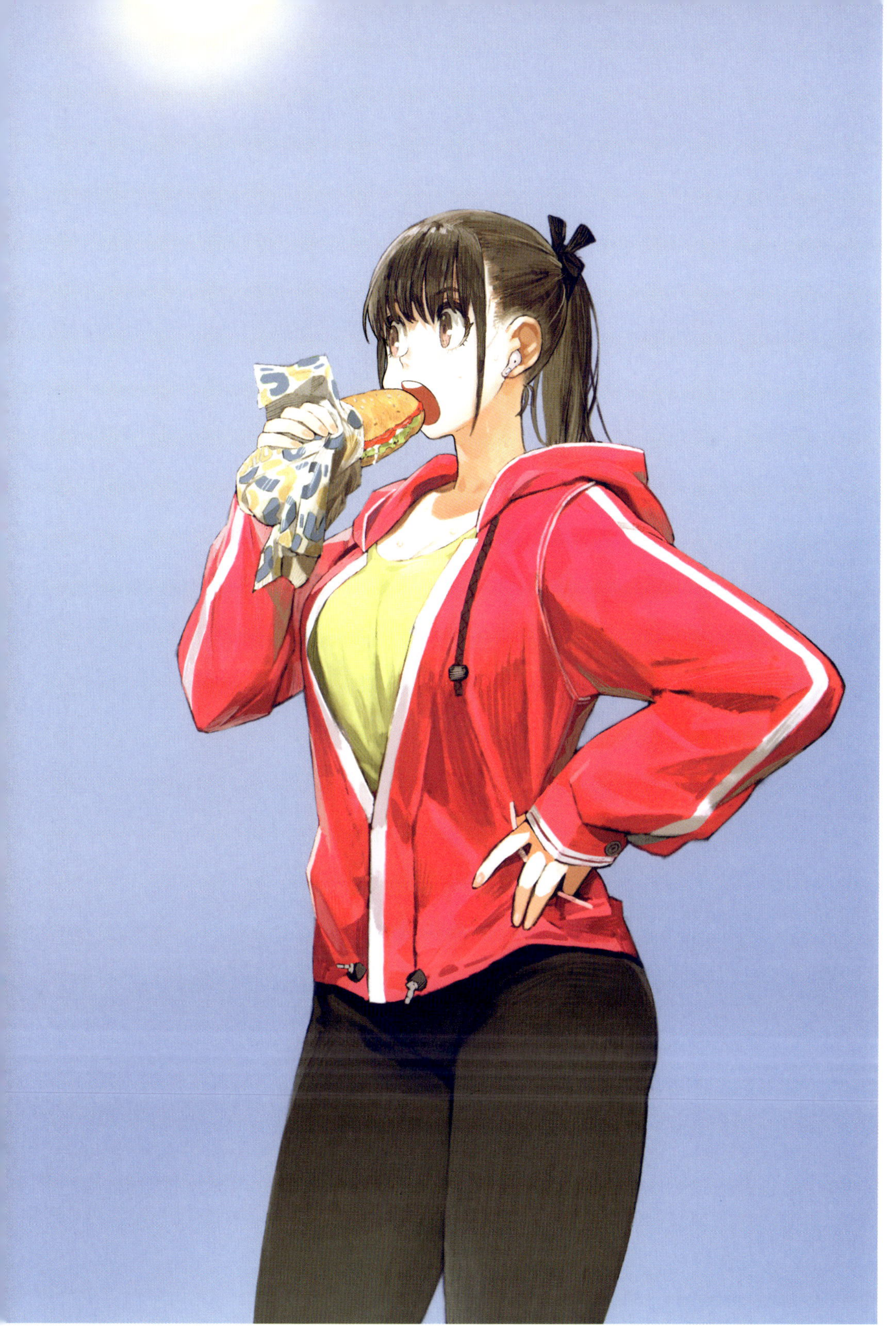

"Recharging"

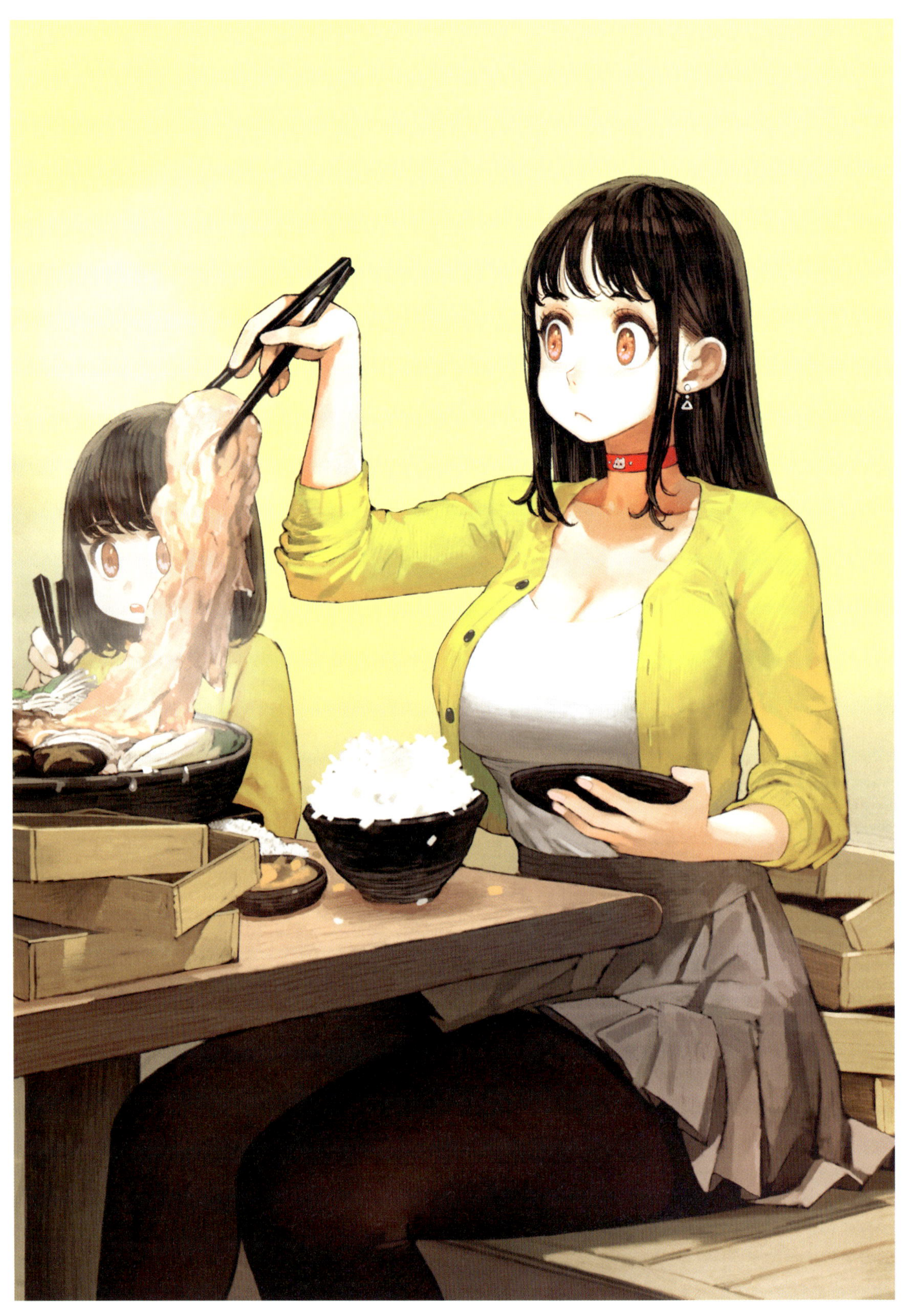

TITLE
"Shabu Shabu Hot Pot"

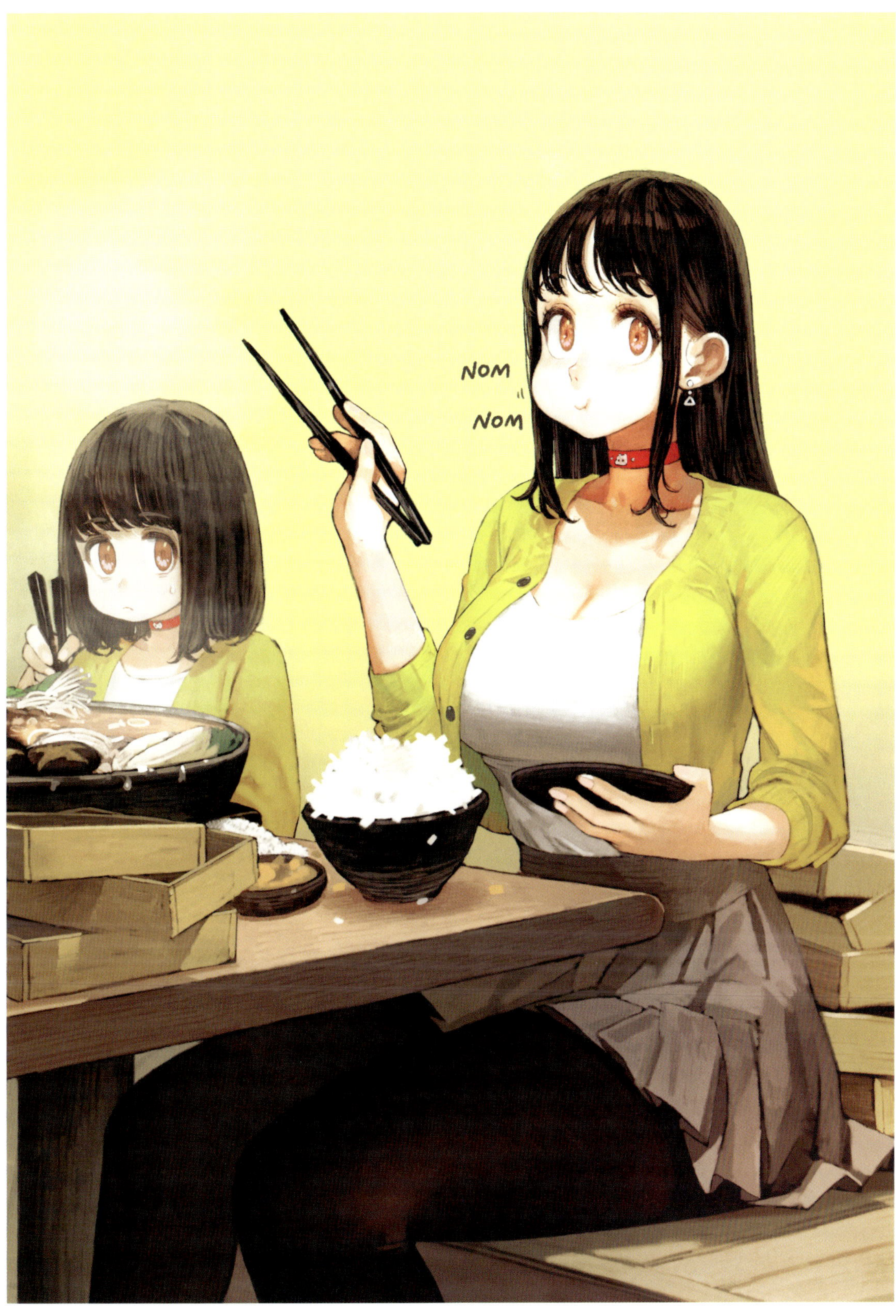
NOM
NOM

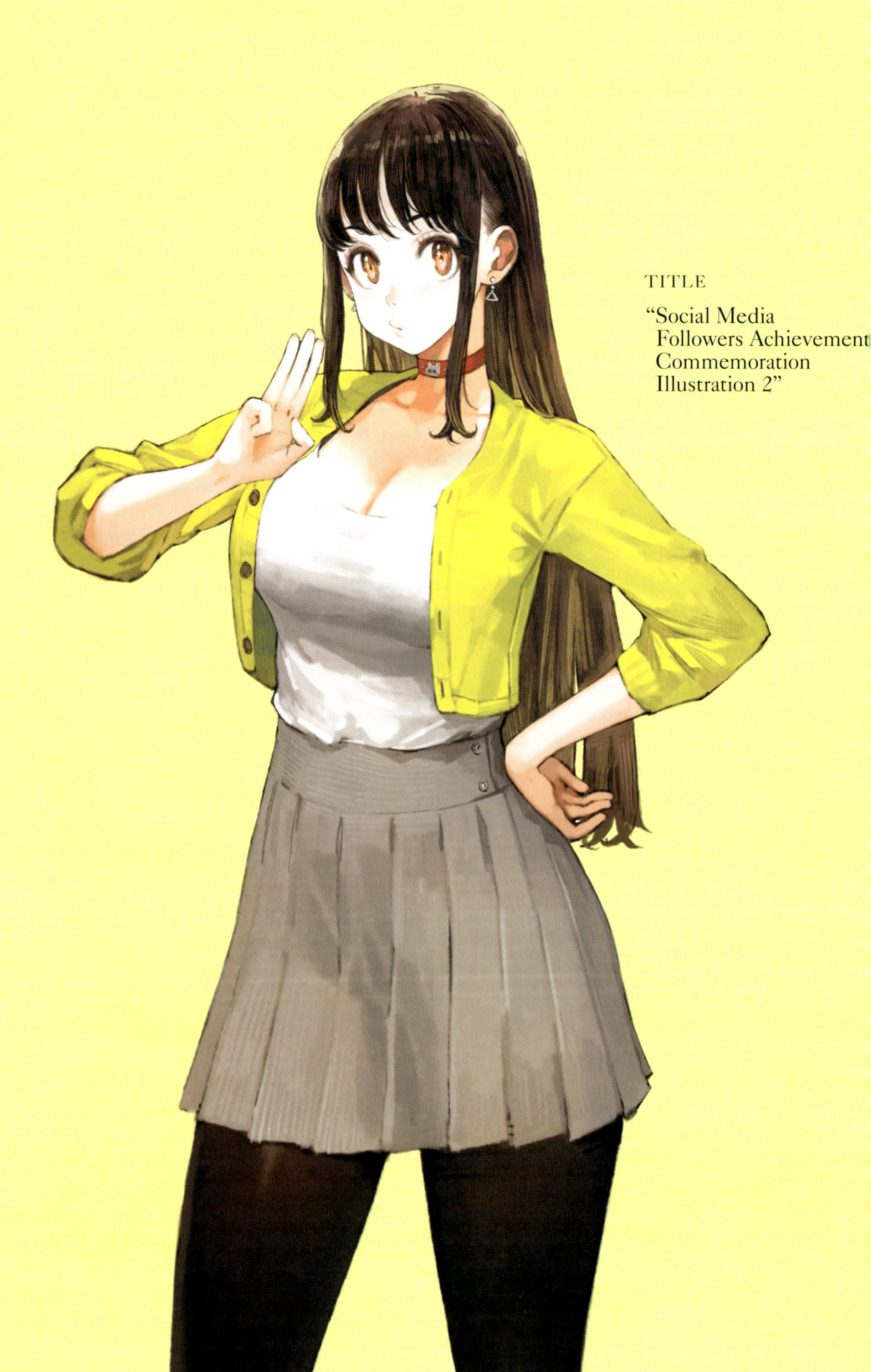

TITLE
"Social Media
Followers Achievement
Commemoration
Illustration 2"

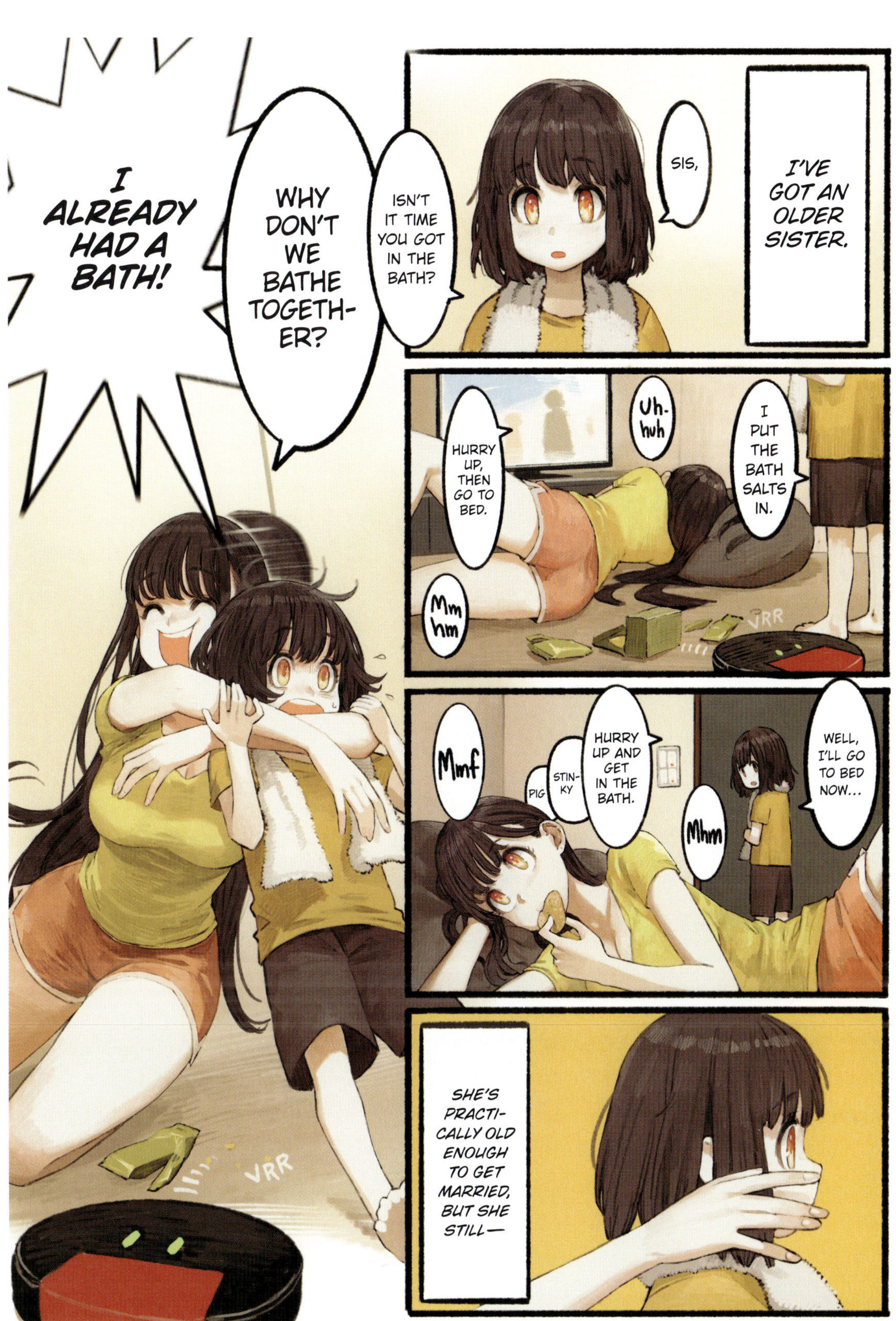

TITLE

"Sisters"

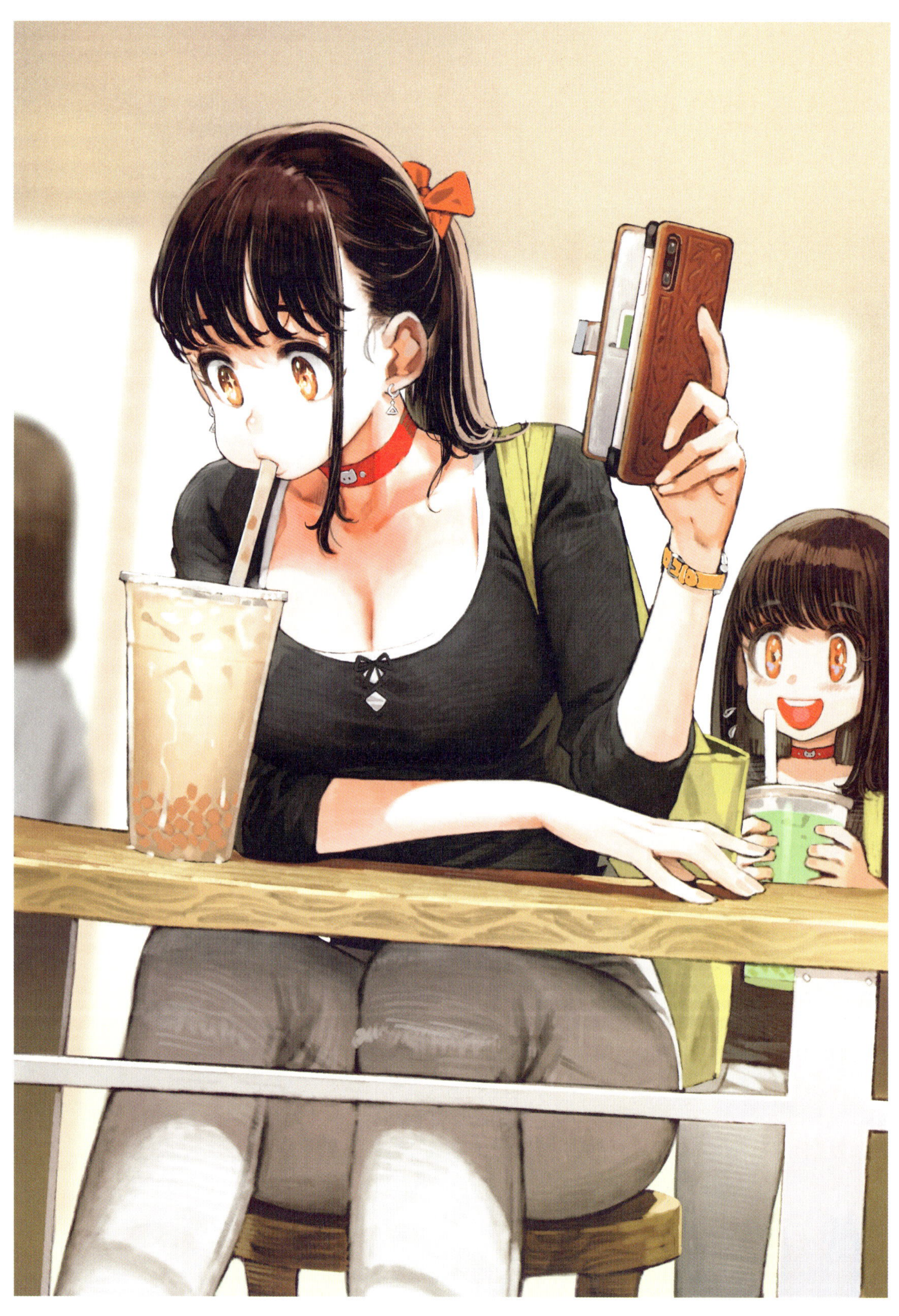

TITLE

"Big Sis, Trade Sips…?"

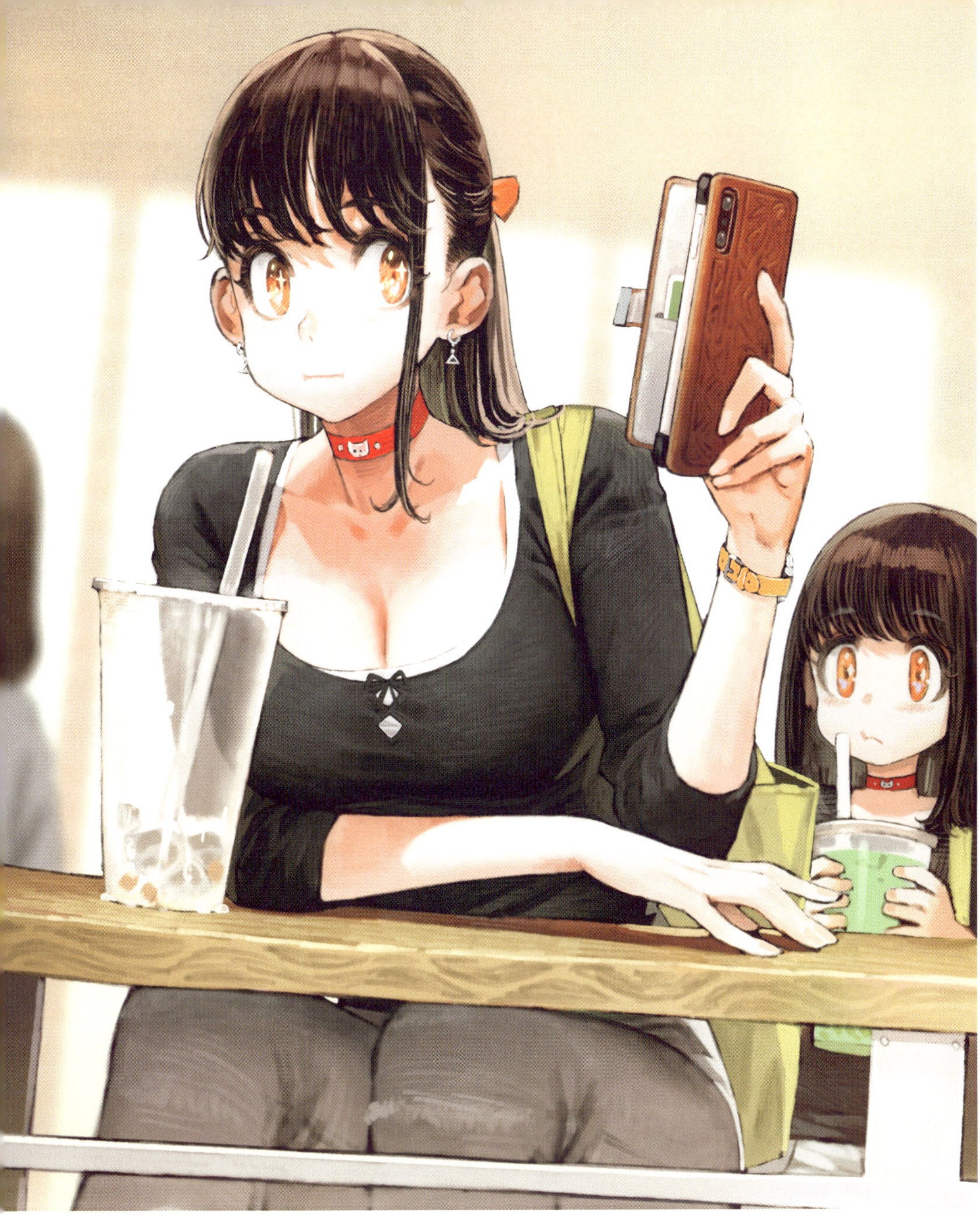

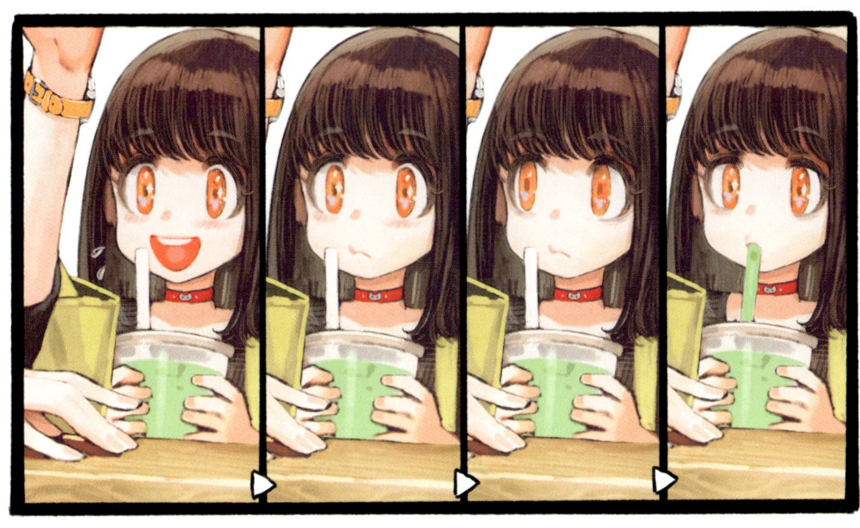

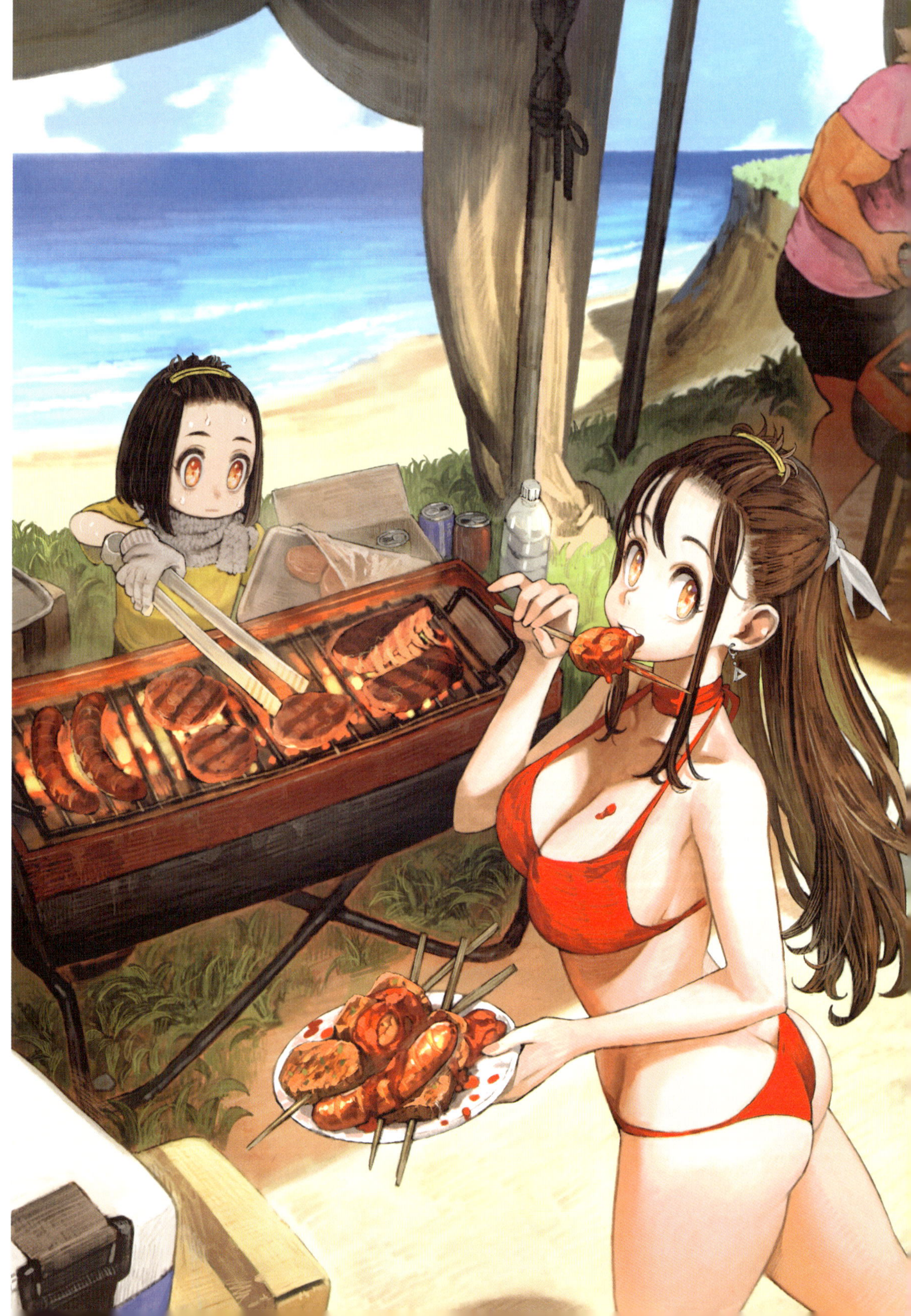

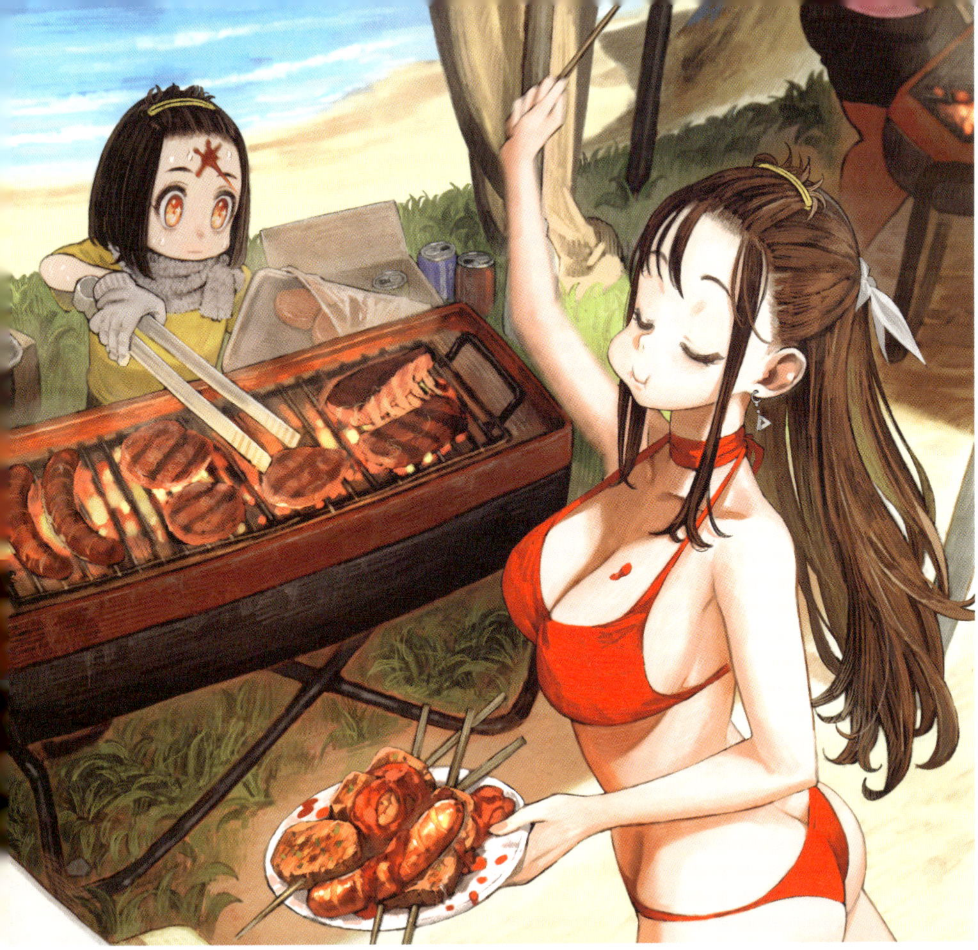

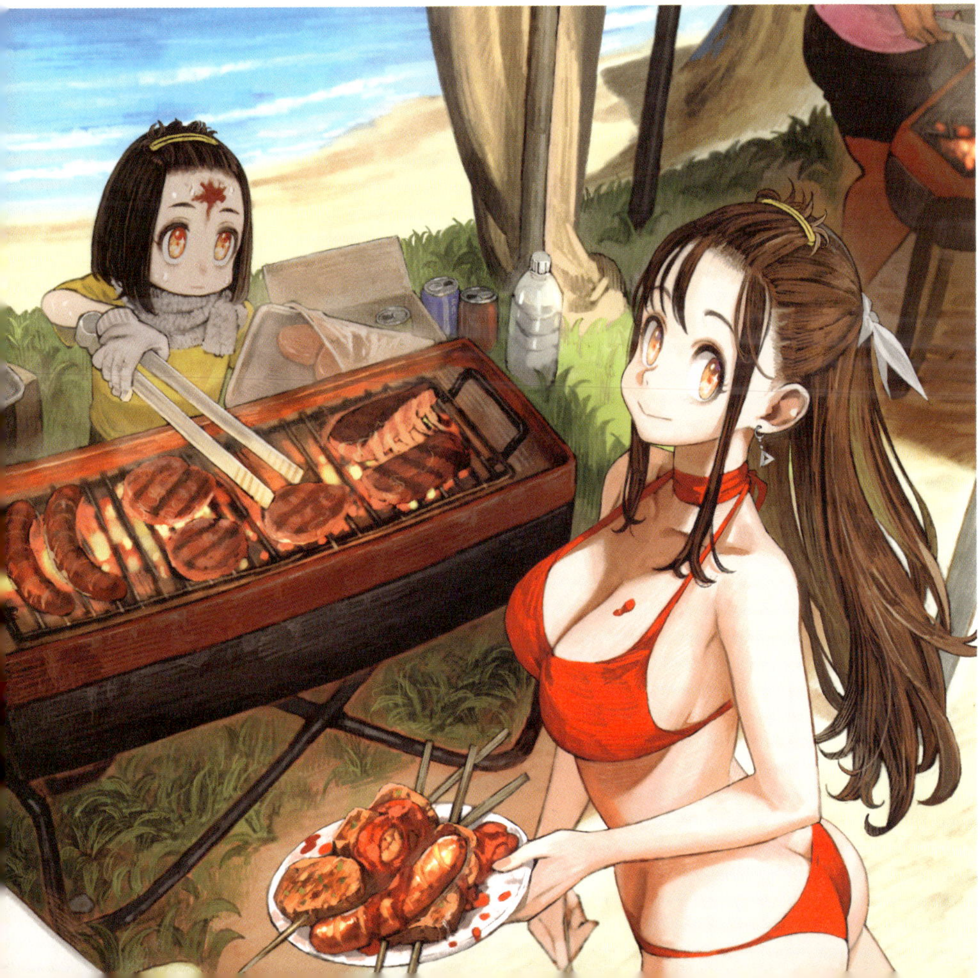

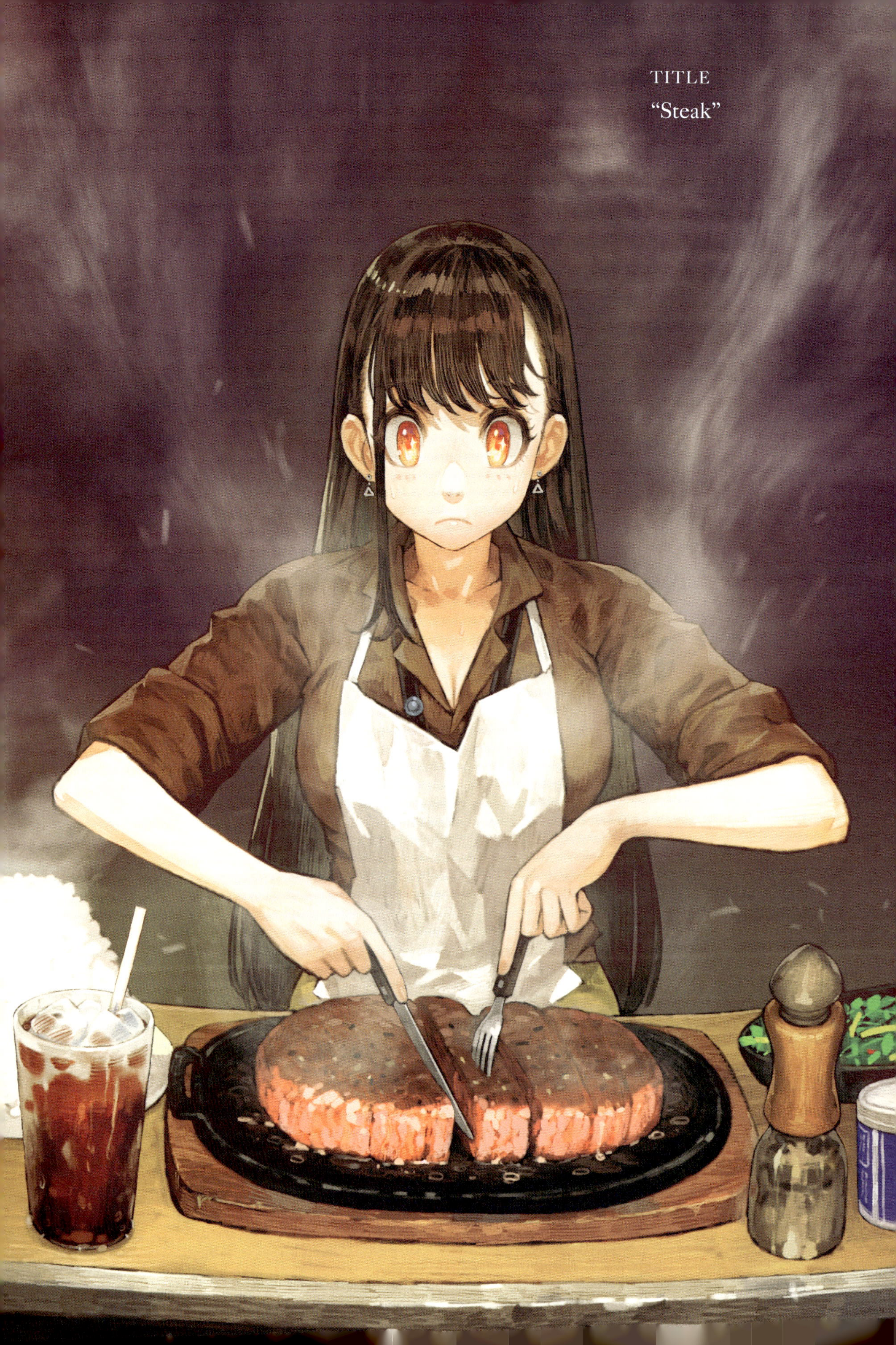
TITLE
"Steak"

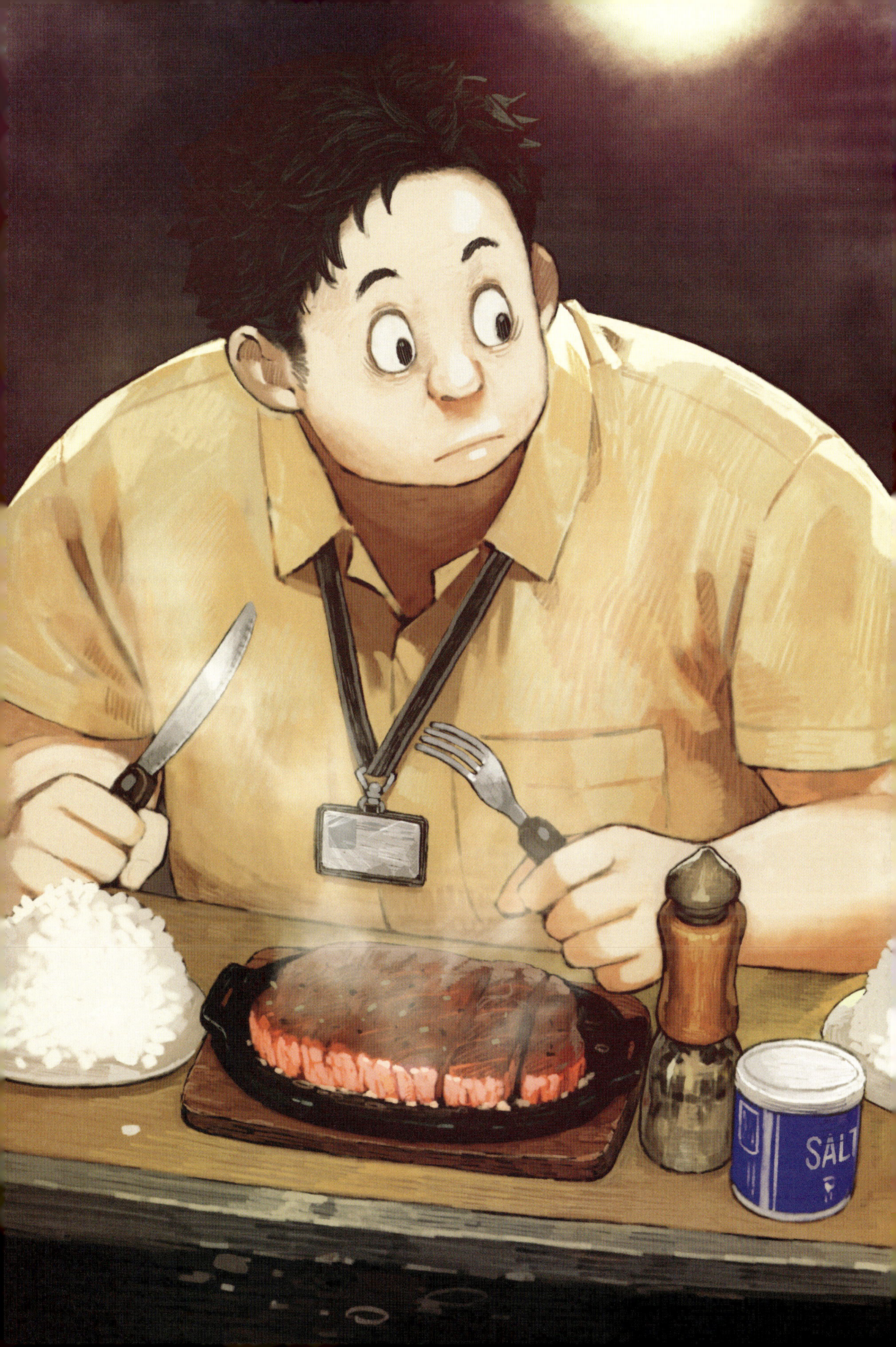

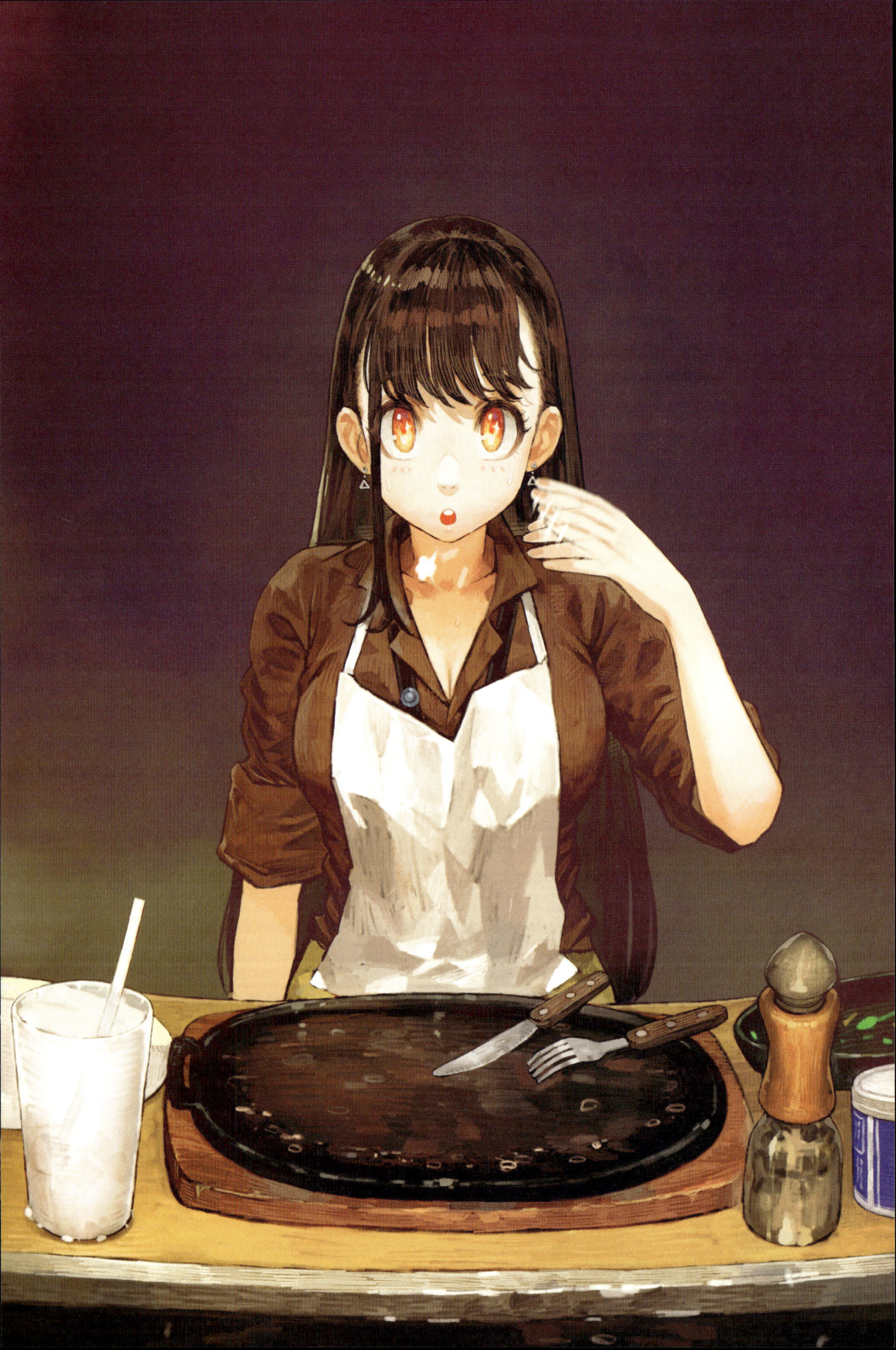

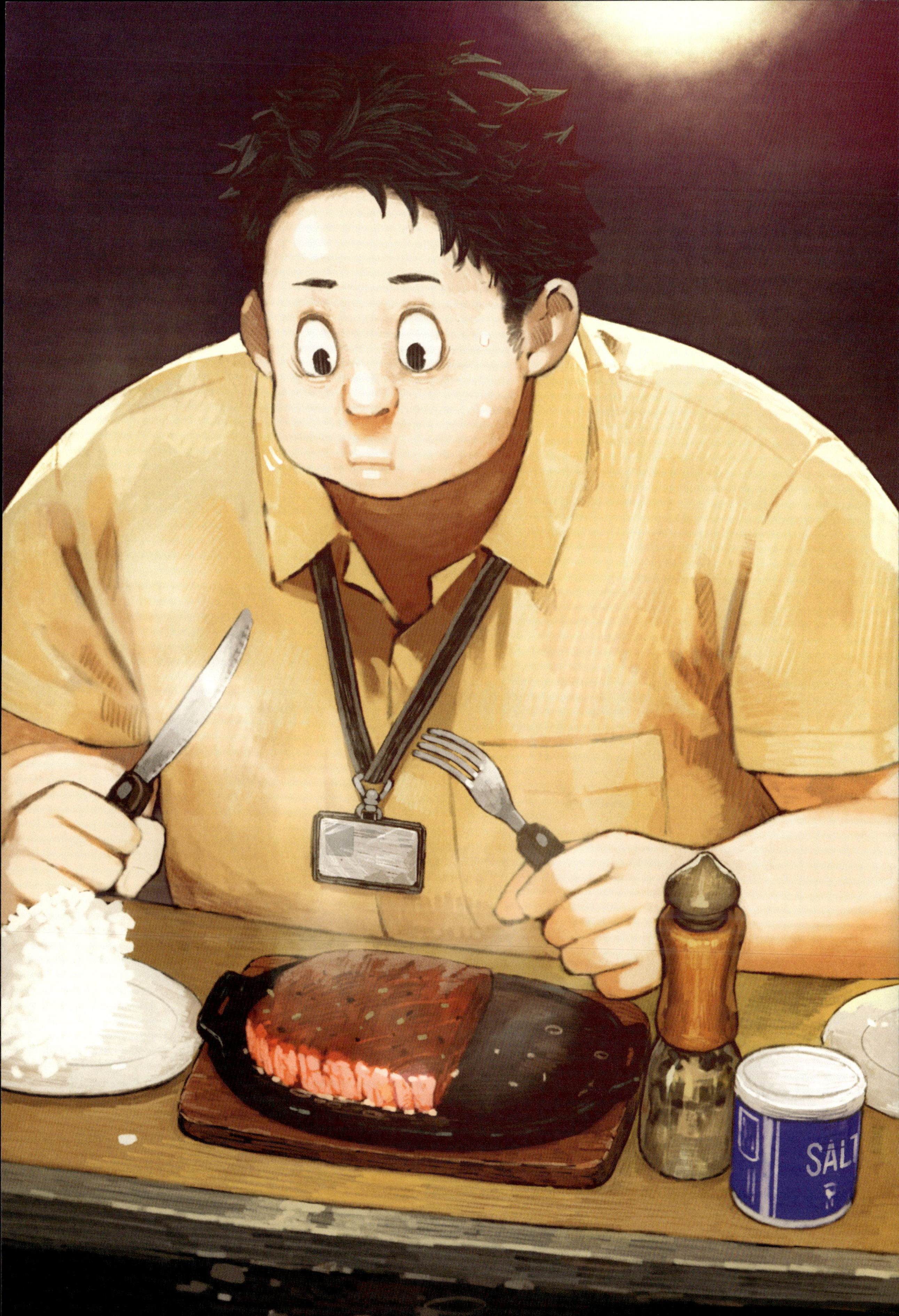

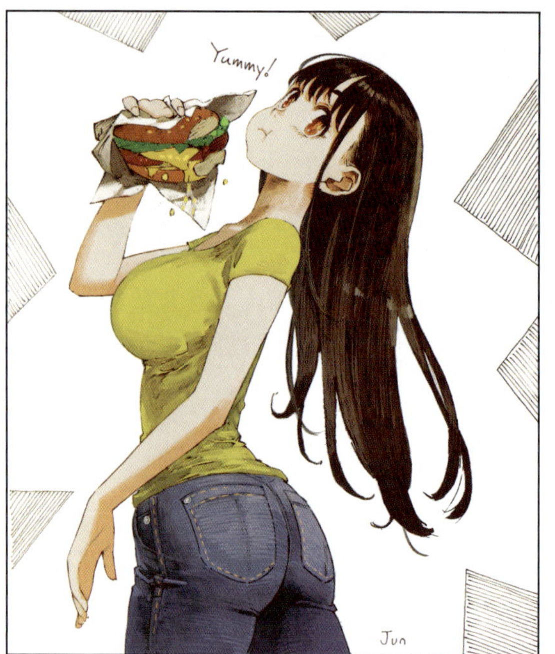

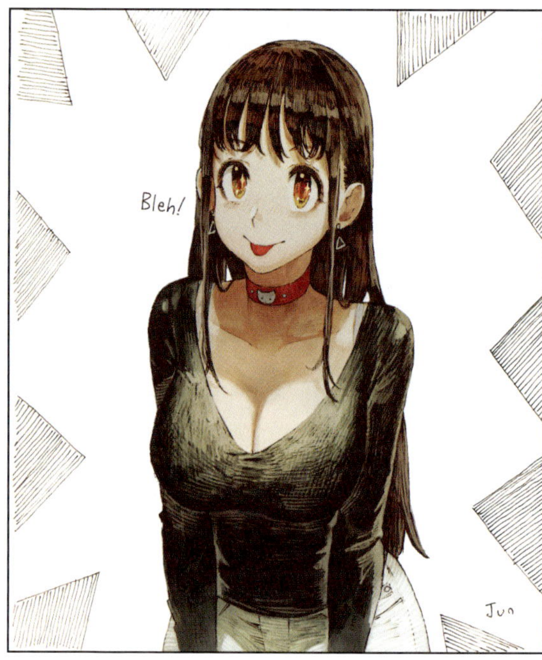

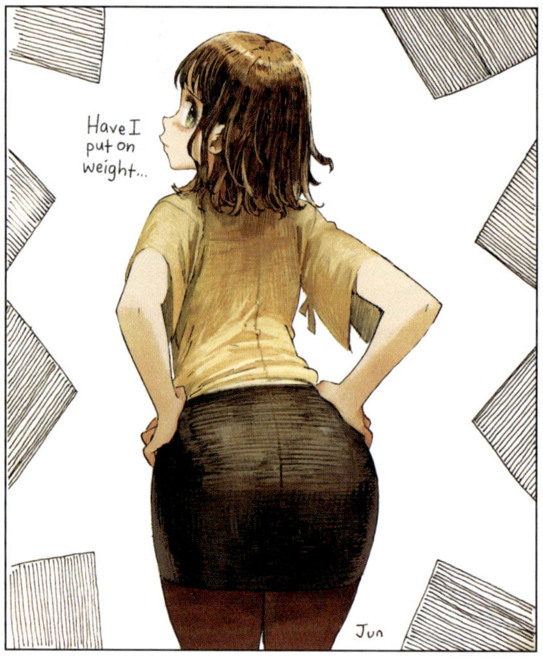

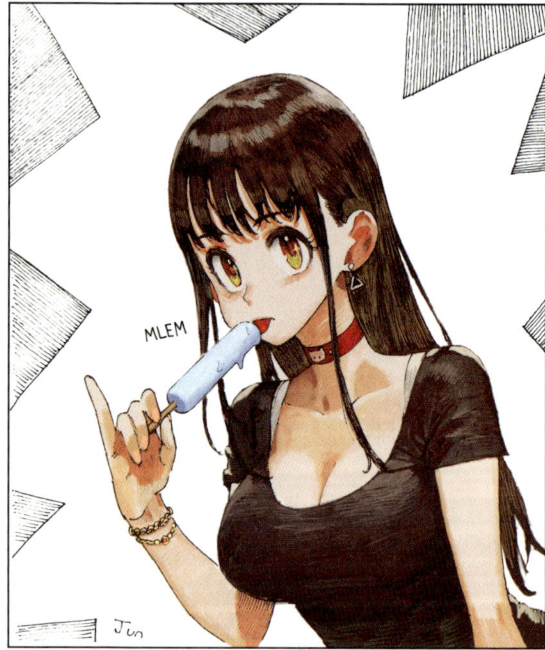

TITLE

"Autograph Boards for Comitia"

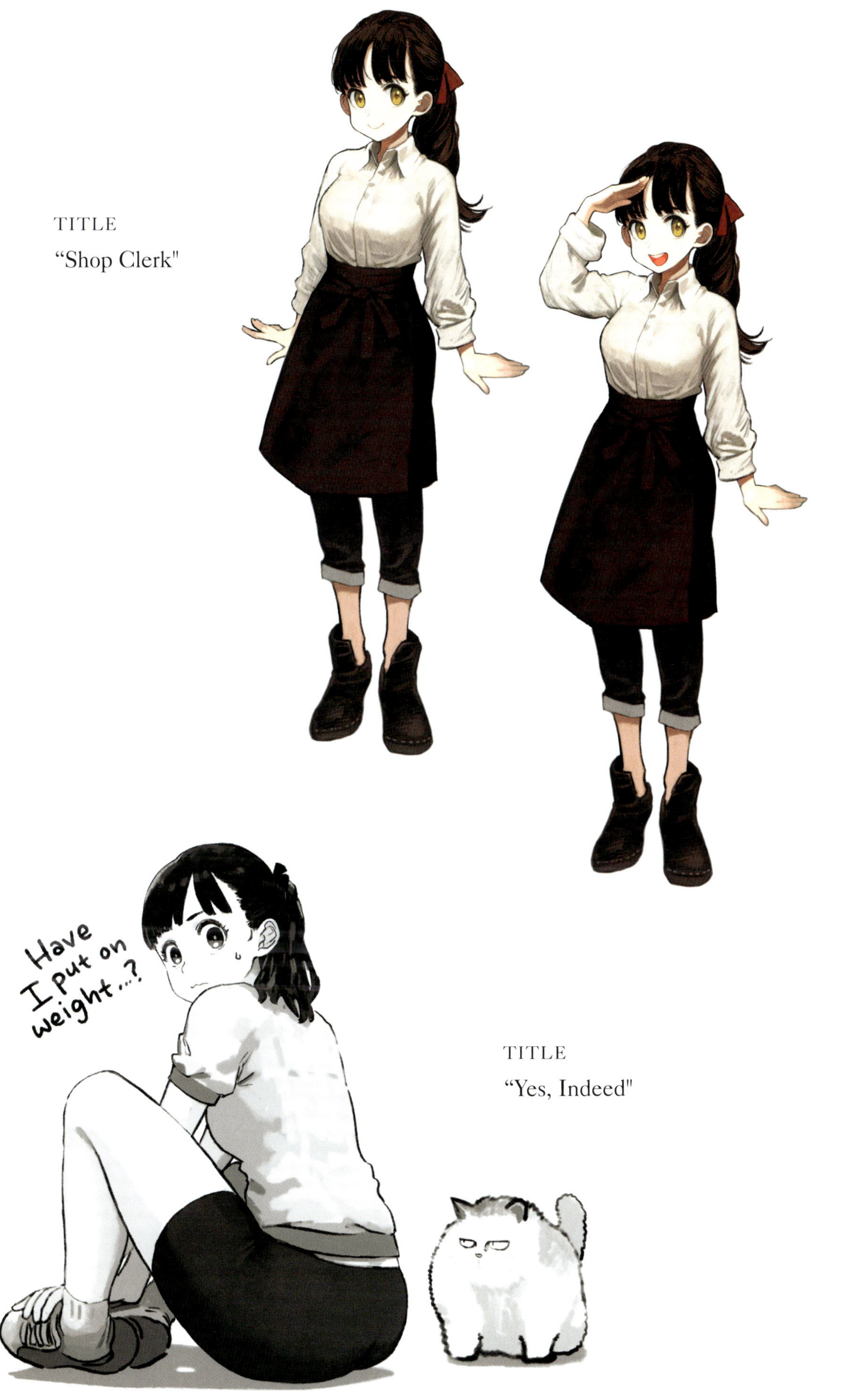
TITLE
"Shop Clerk"
Have I put on weight...?
TITLE
"Yes, Indeed"

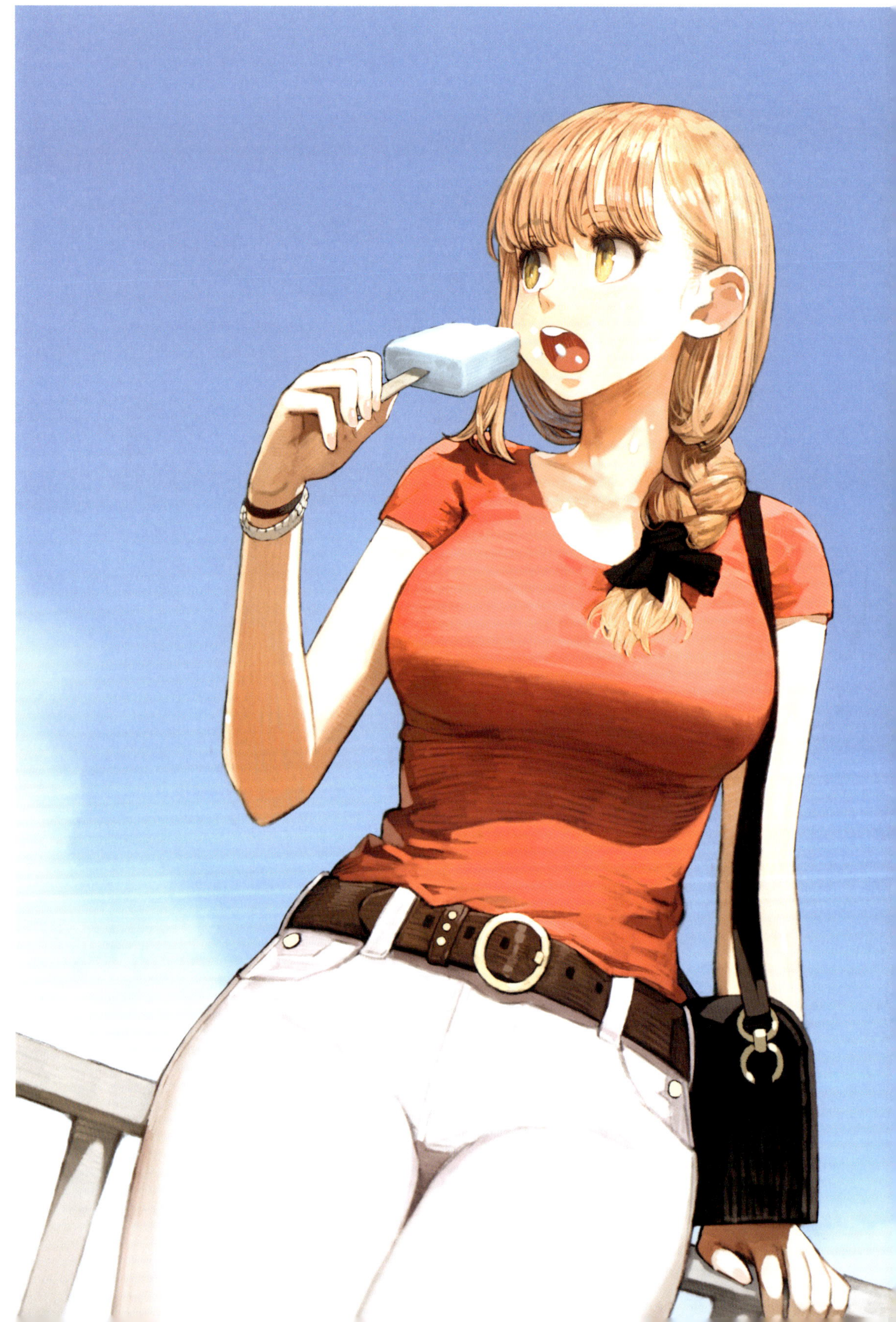

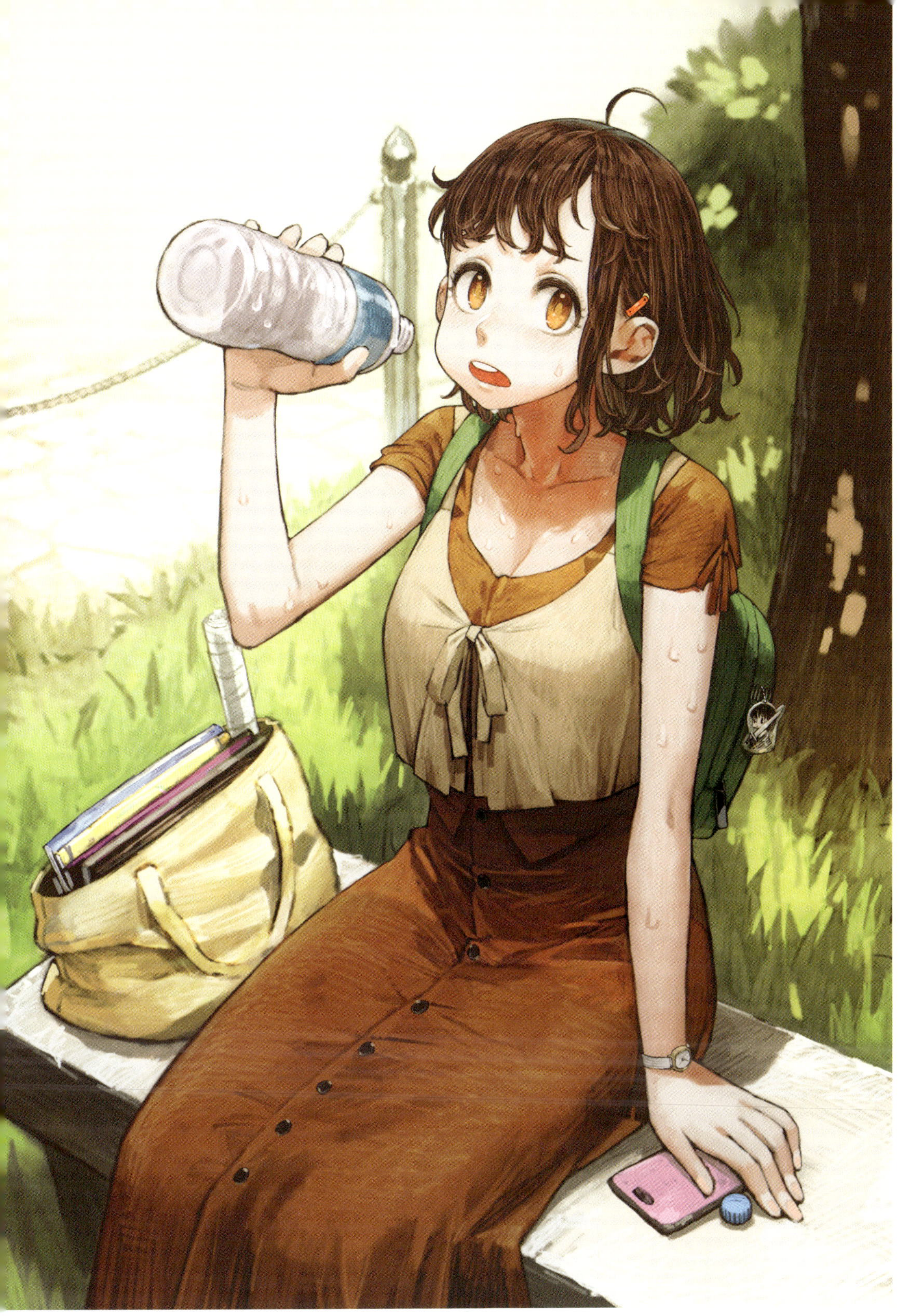

TITLE

"Replenishment"

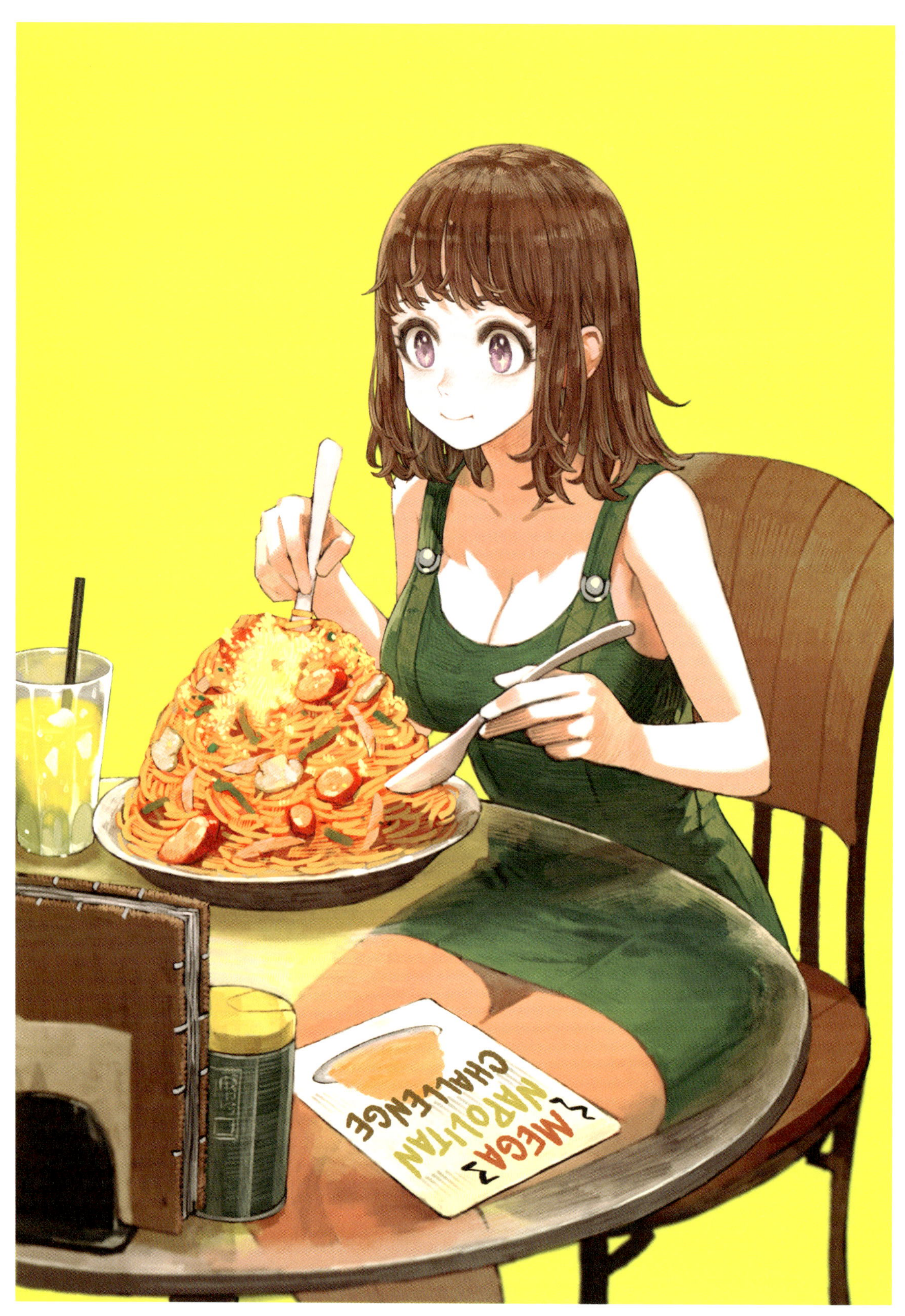

TITLE

"Japanese Ketchup Pasta"

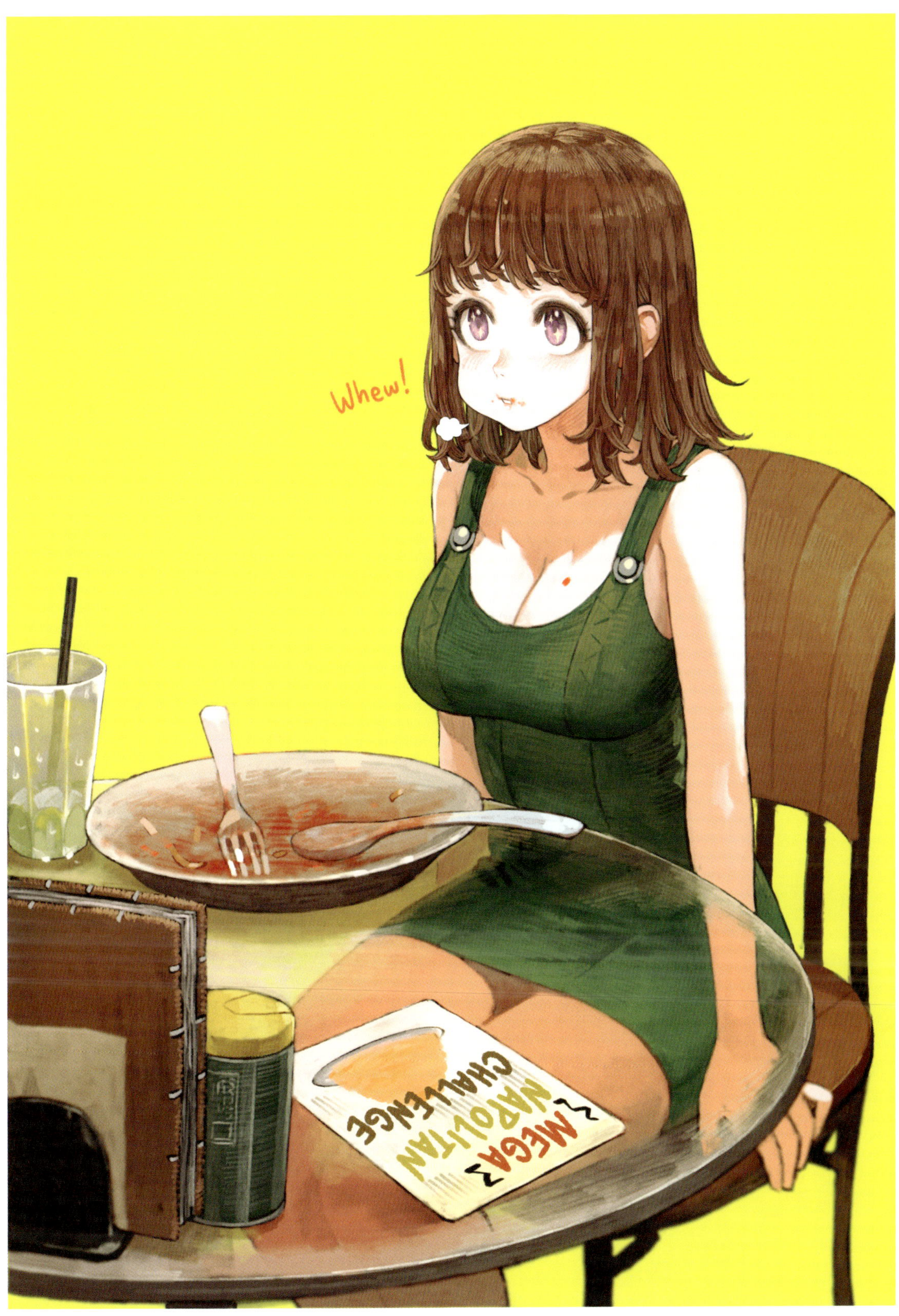
Whew!
MEGA NAPOLITAN CHALLENGE

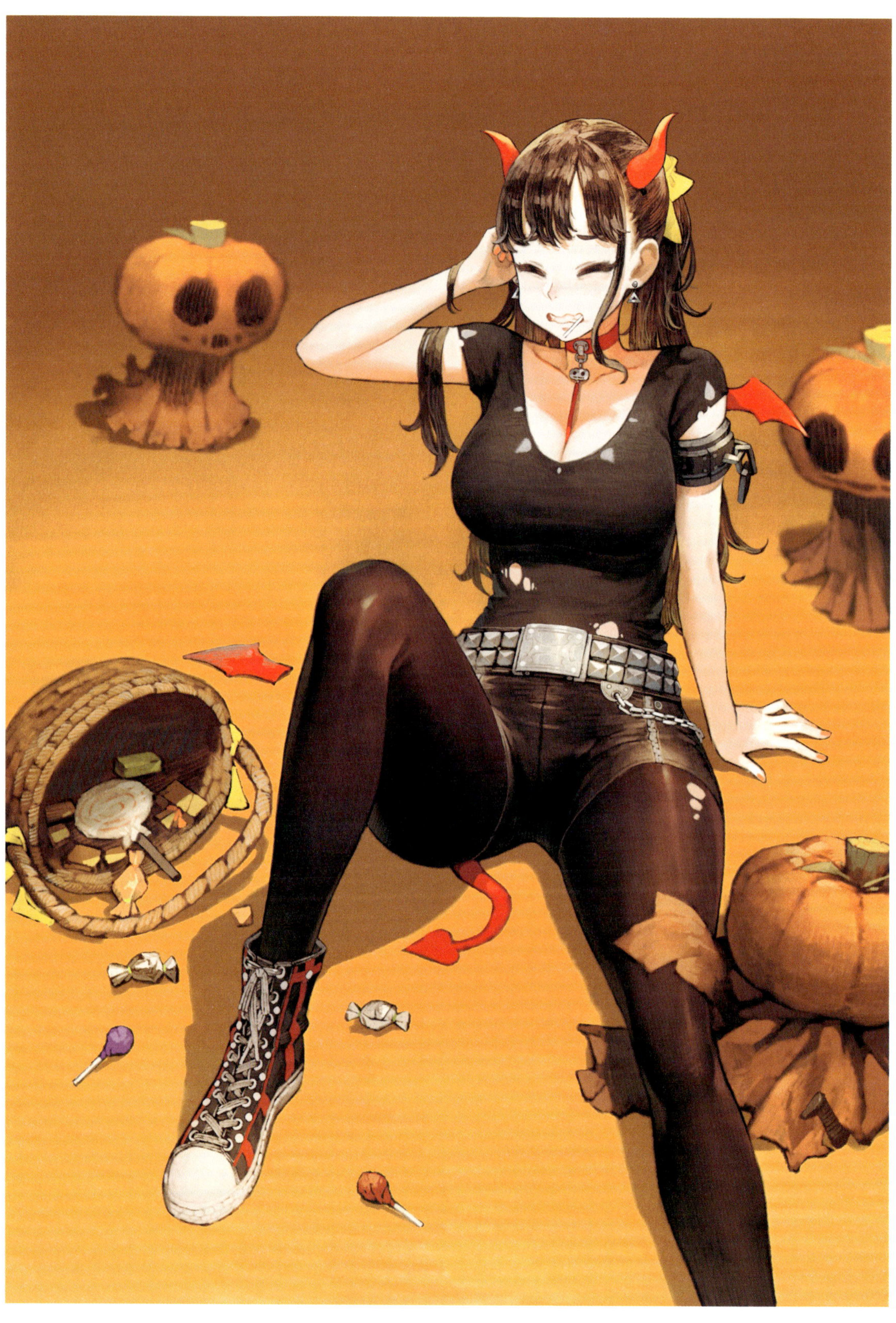

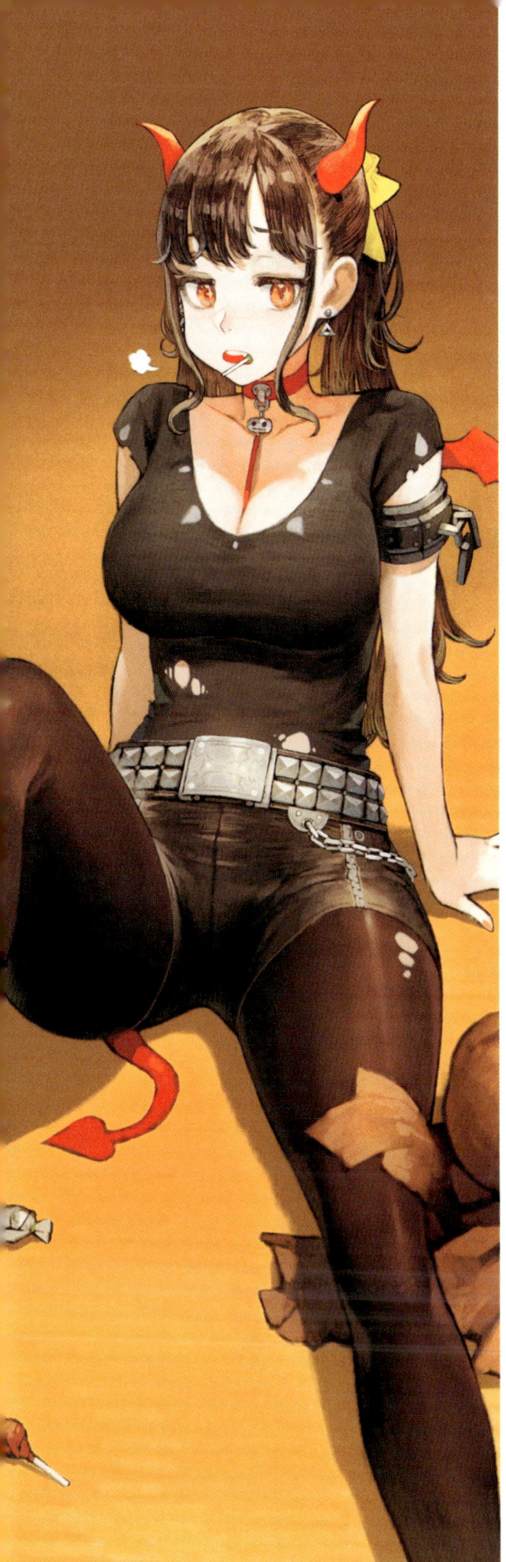 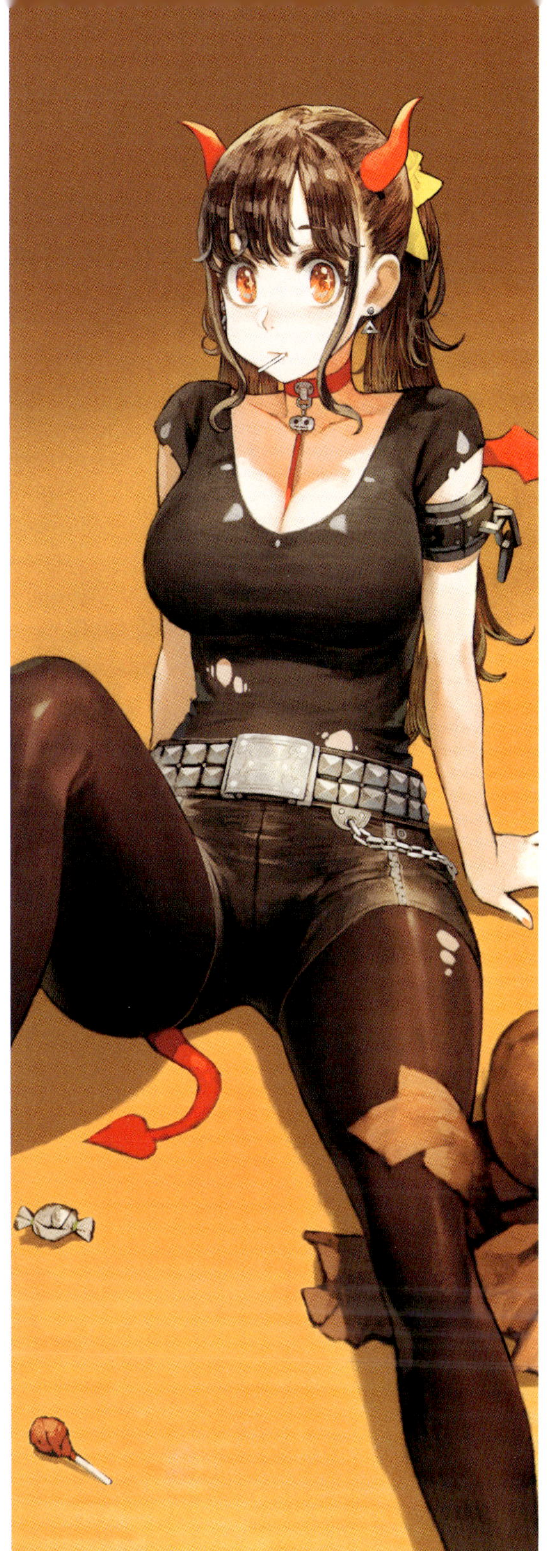

TITLE
"Collision"

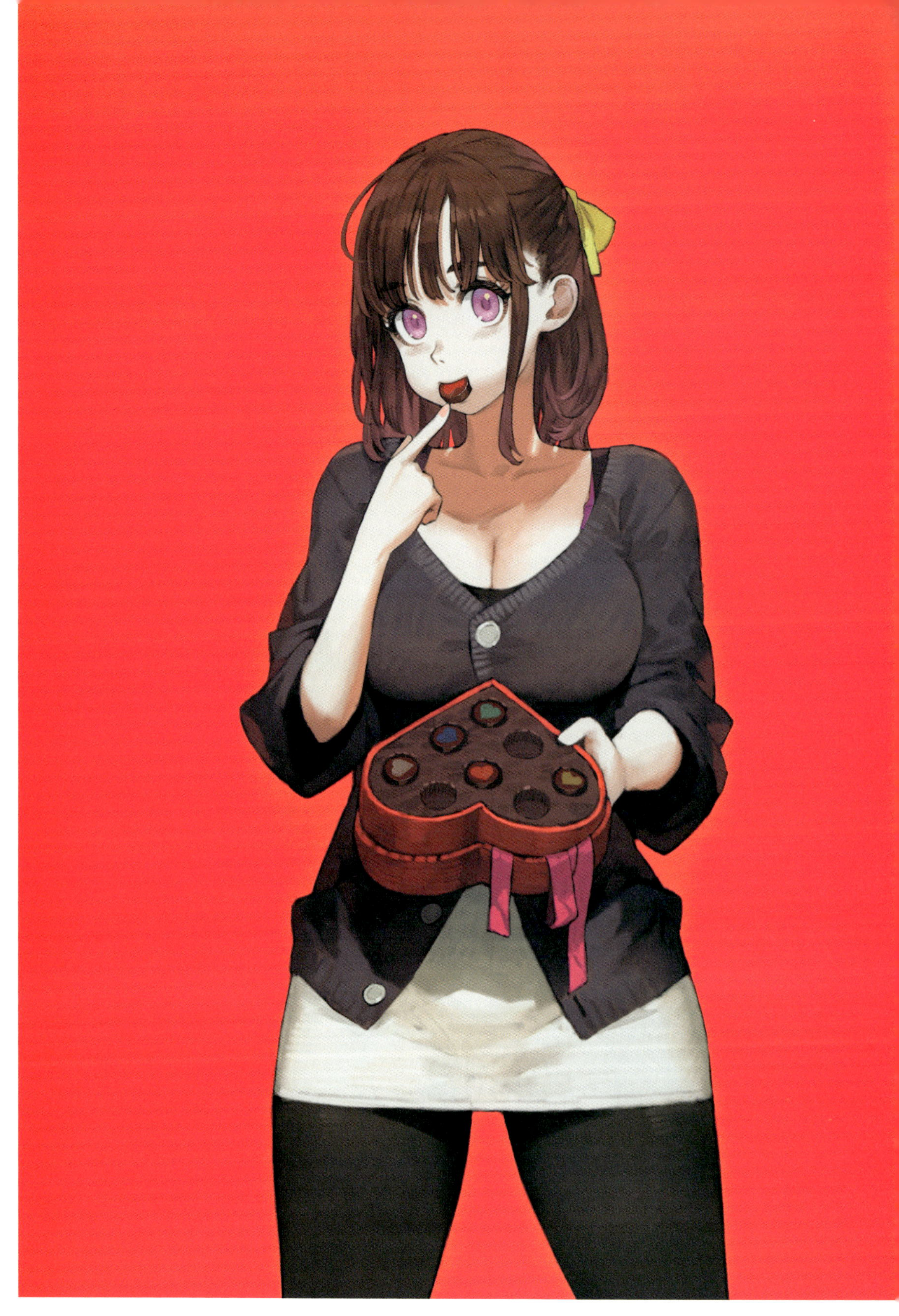

TITLE

"Want One?"

TITLE
"Street"

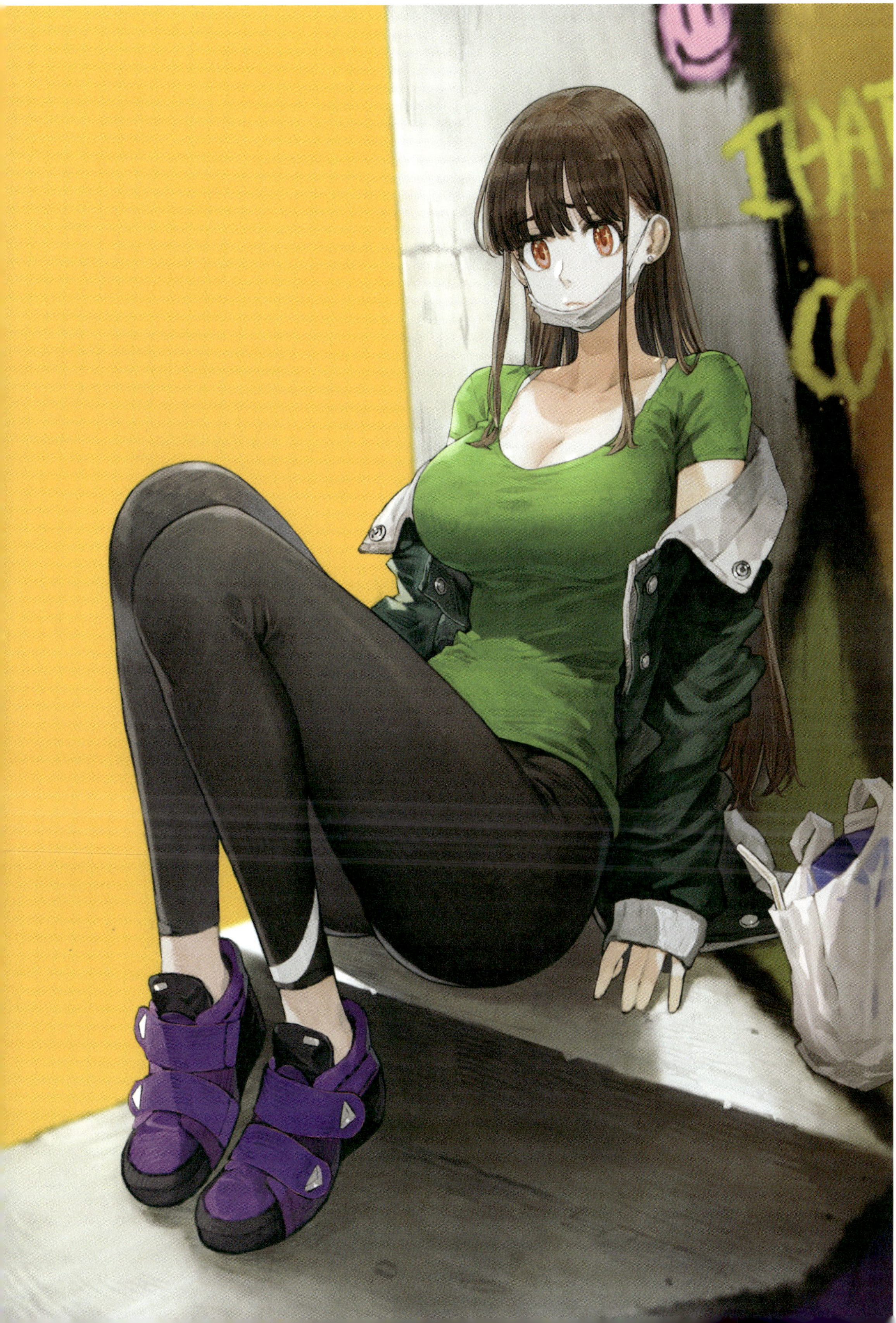

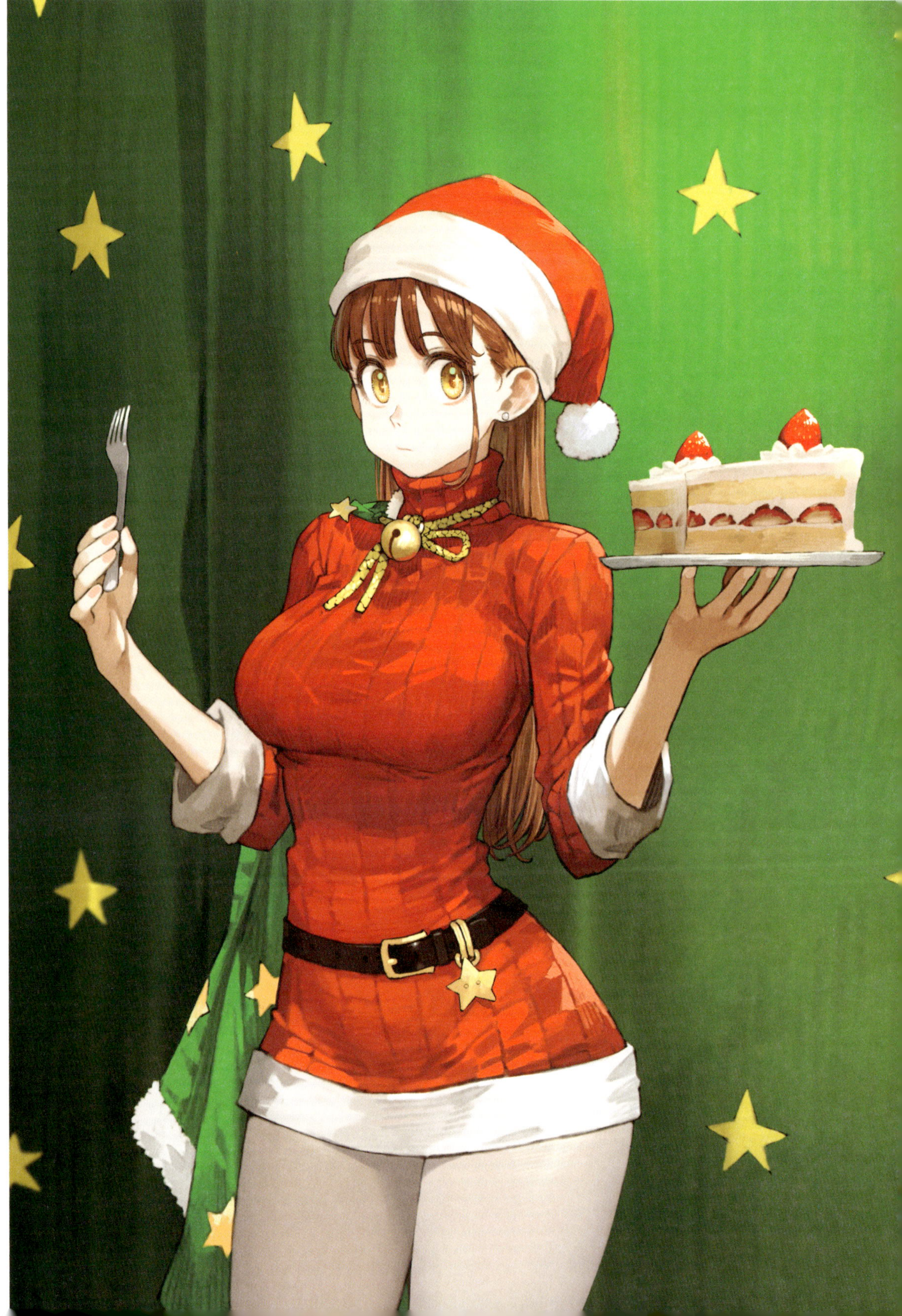

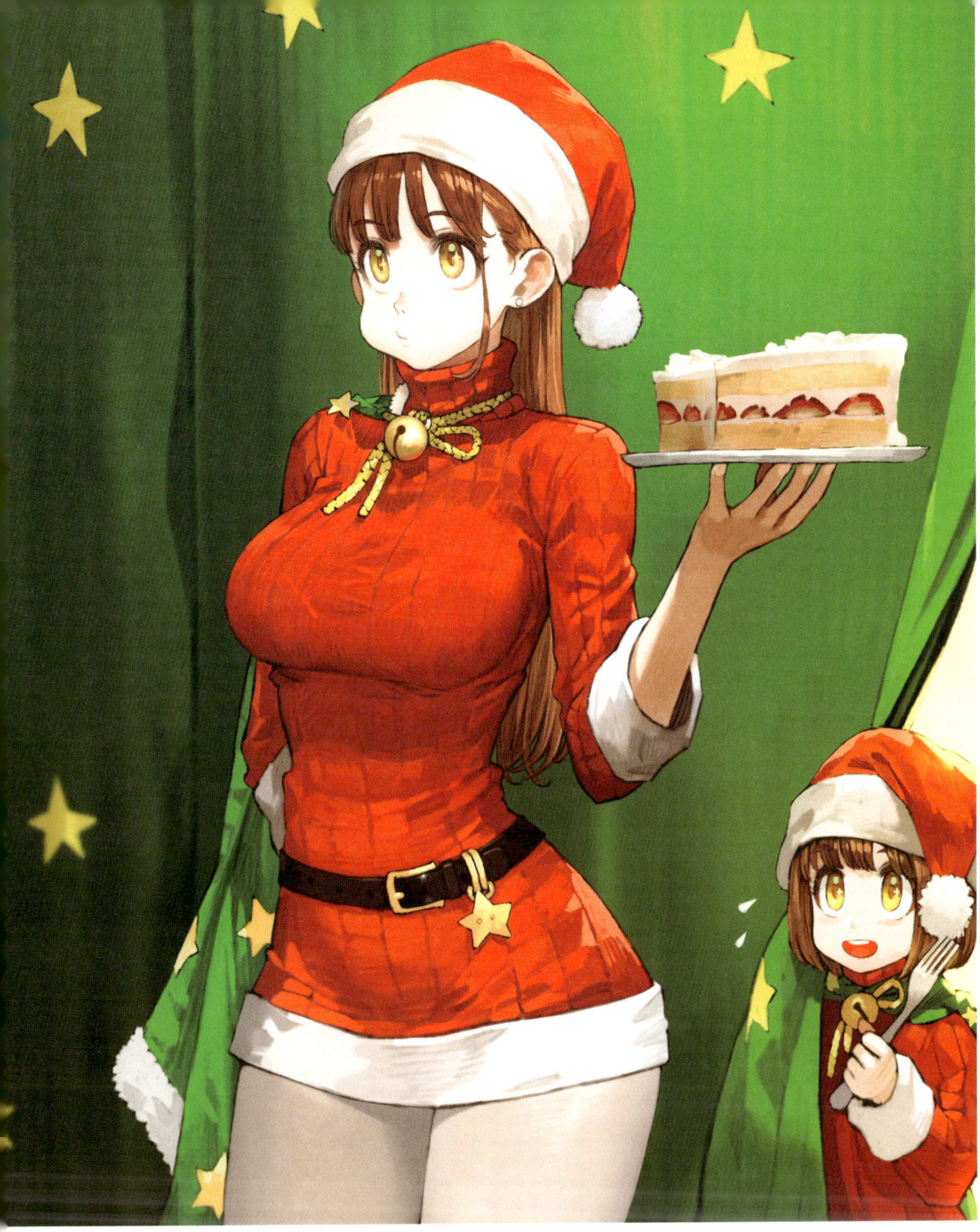

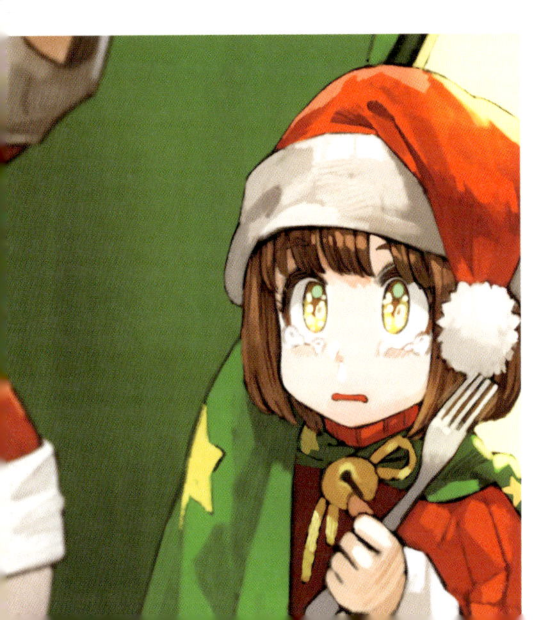

TITLE

"What Happened to the Strawberries…?"

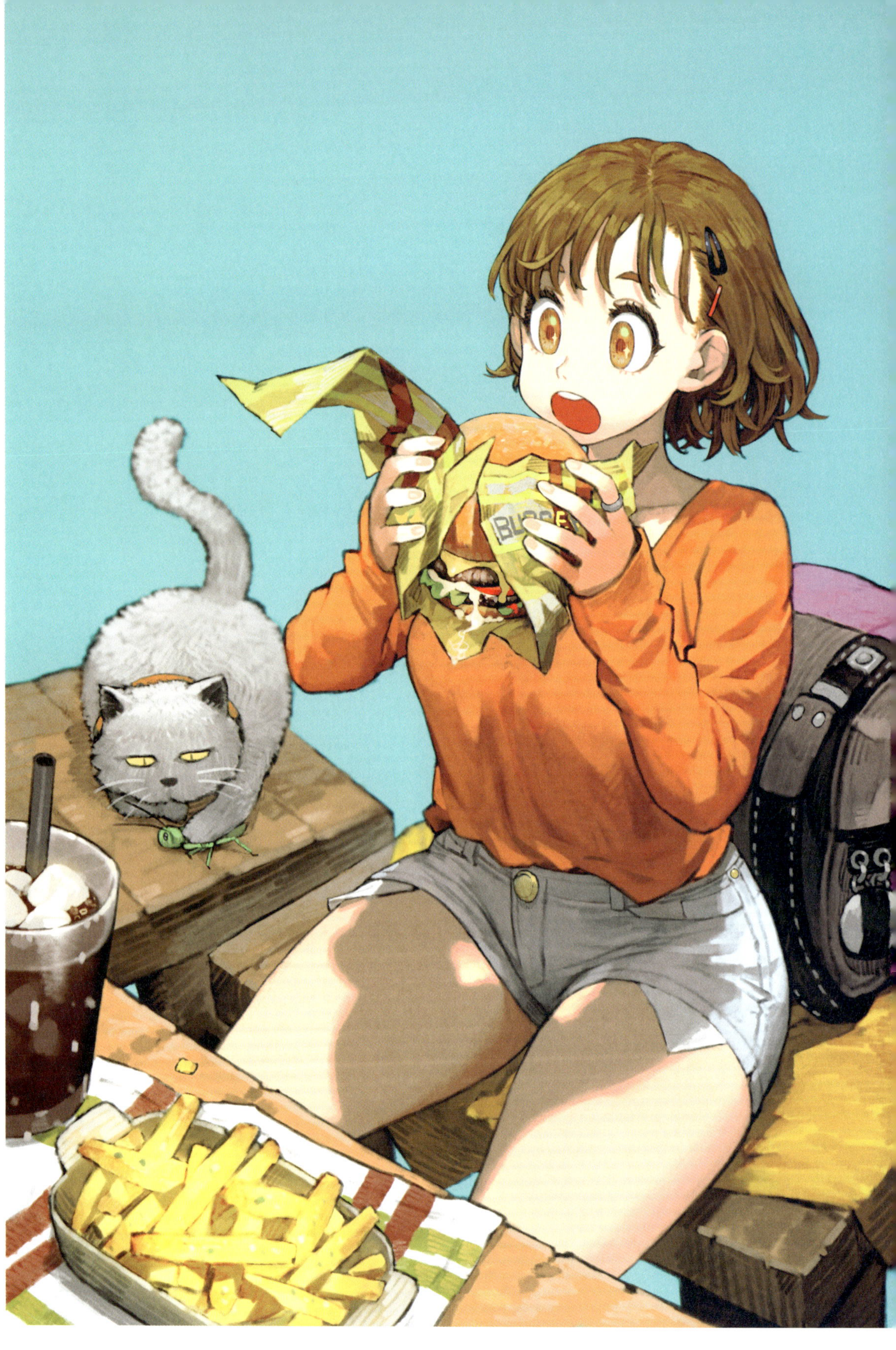
BURGER

TITLE
"Burger"

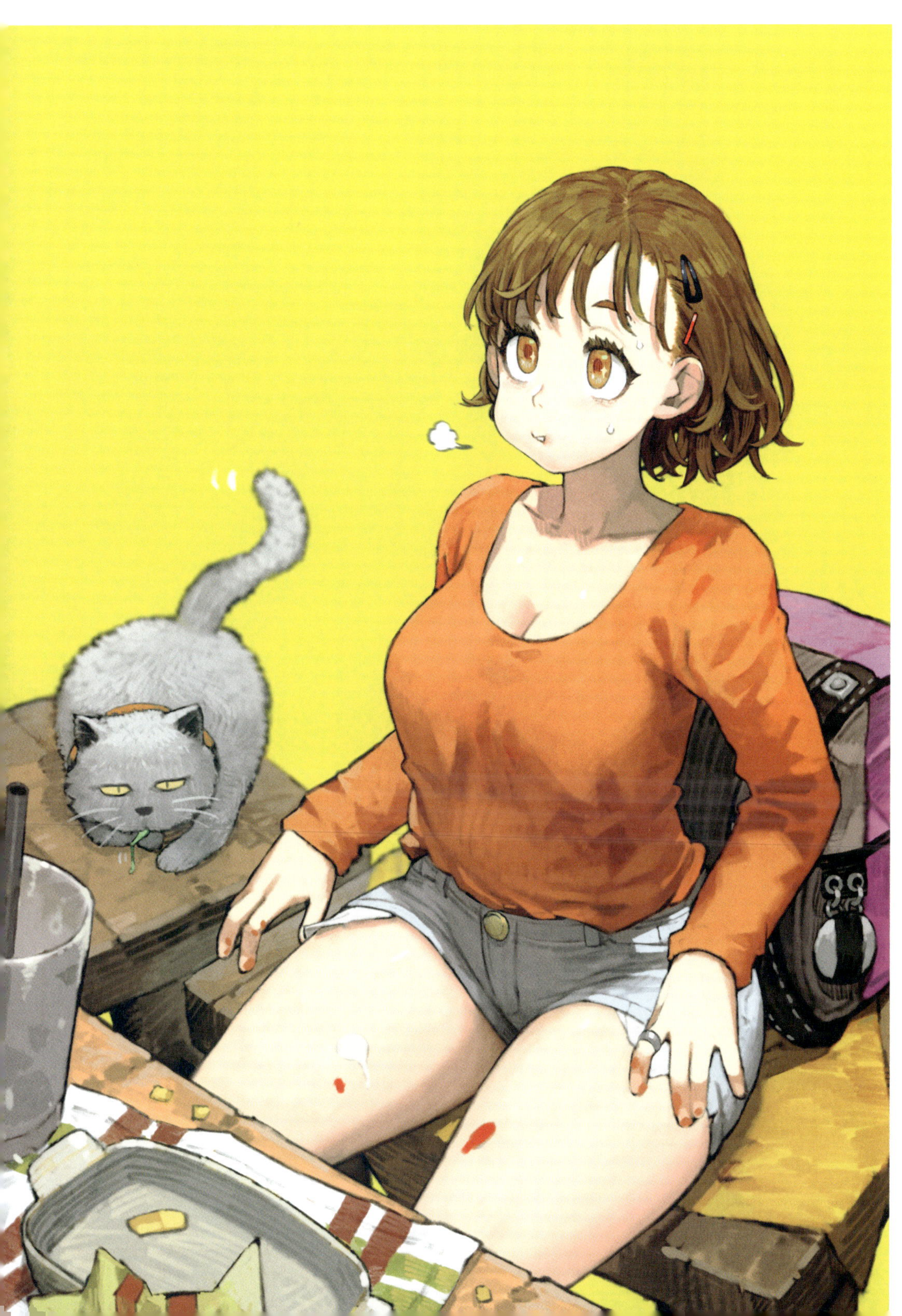

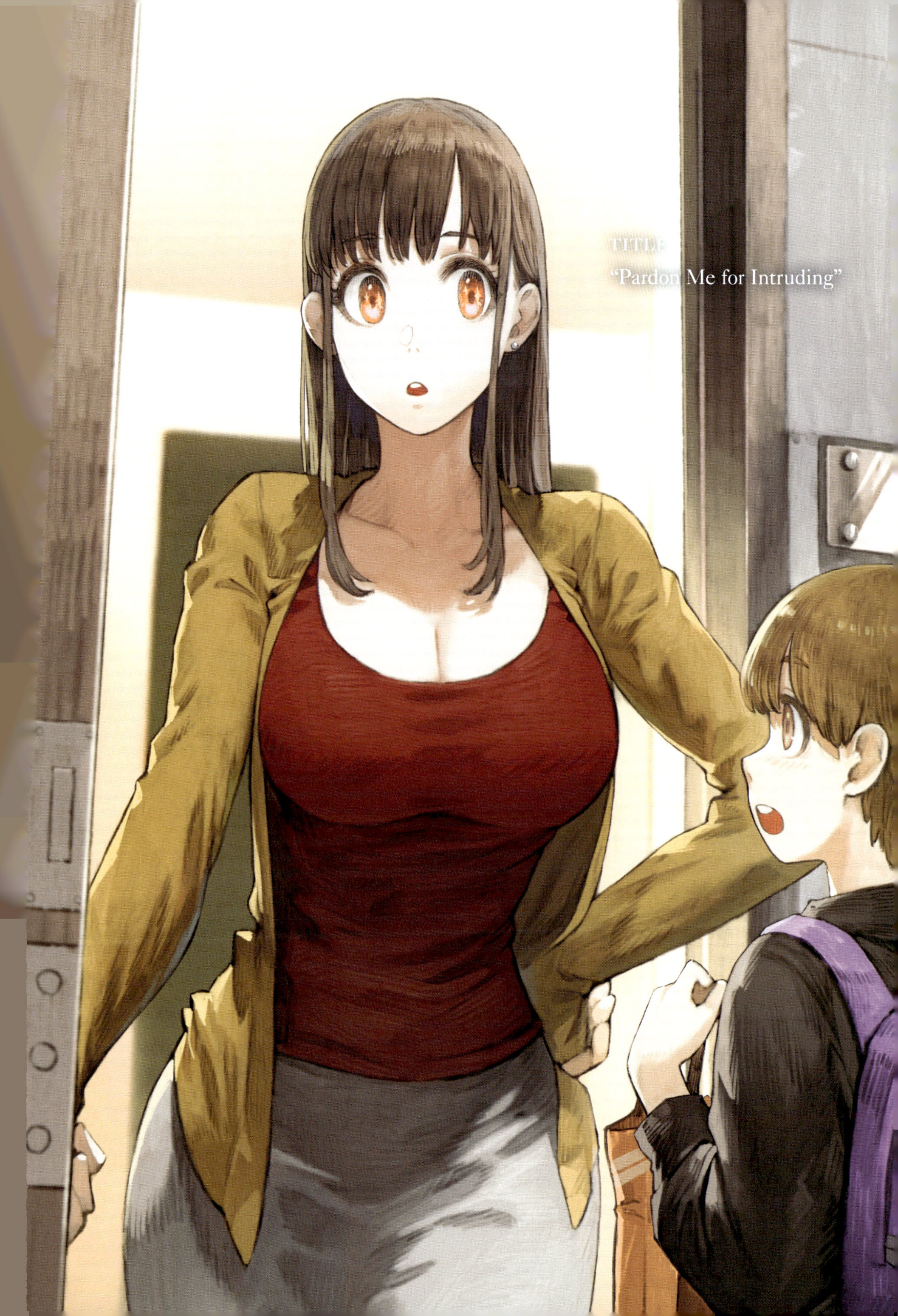
TITLE:
"Pardon Me for Intruding"

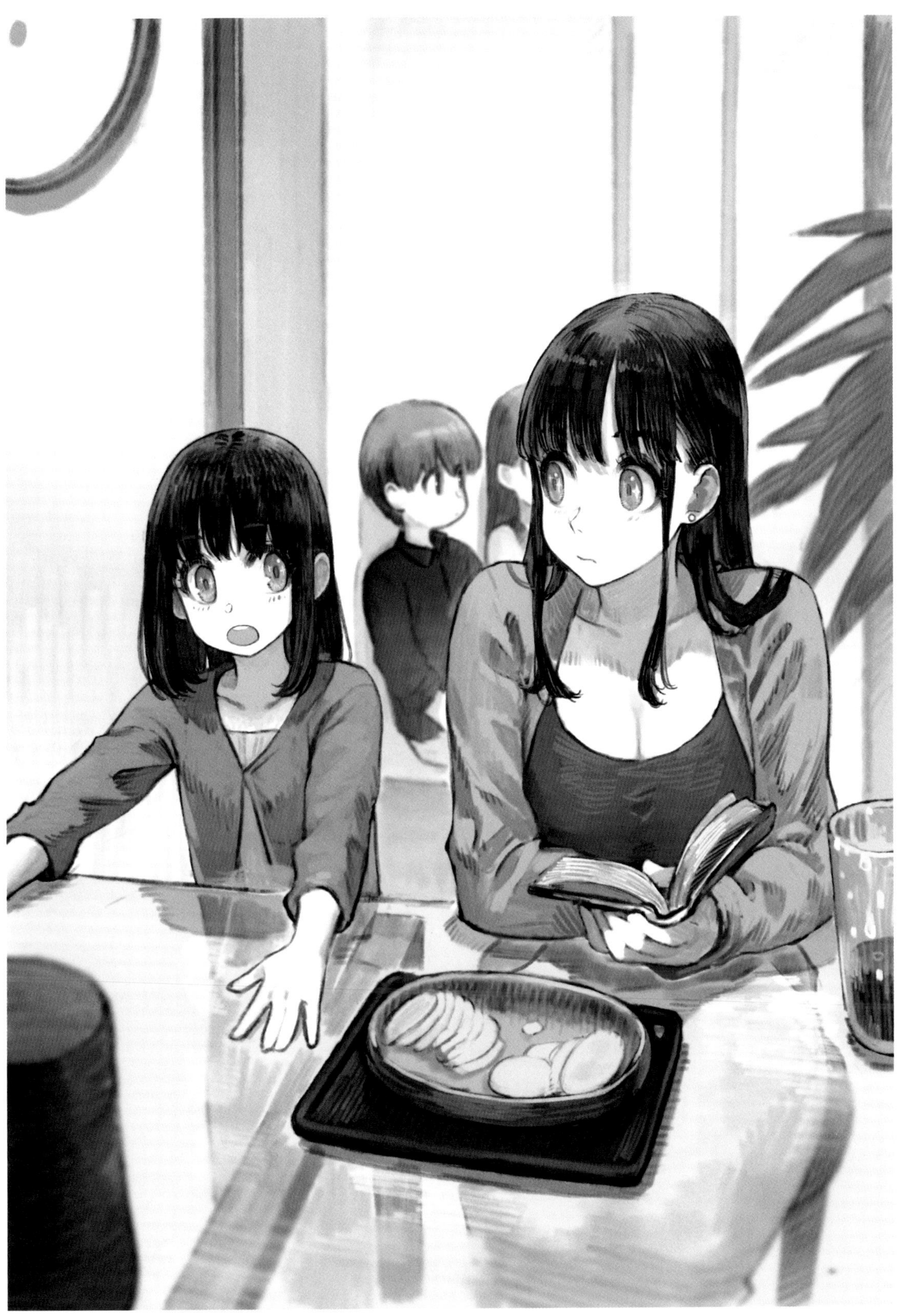

TITLE

"Big Sis, I'm Hungry!"

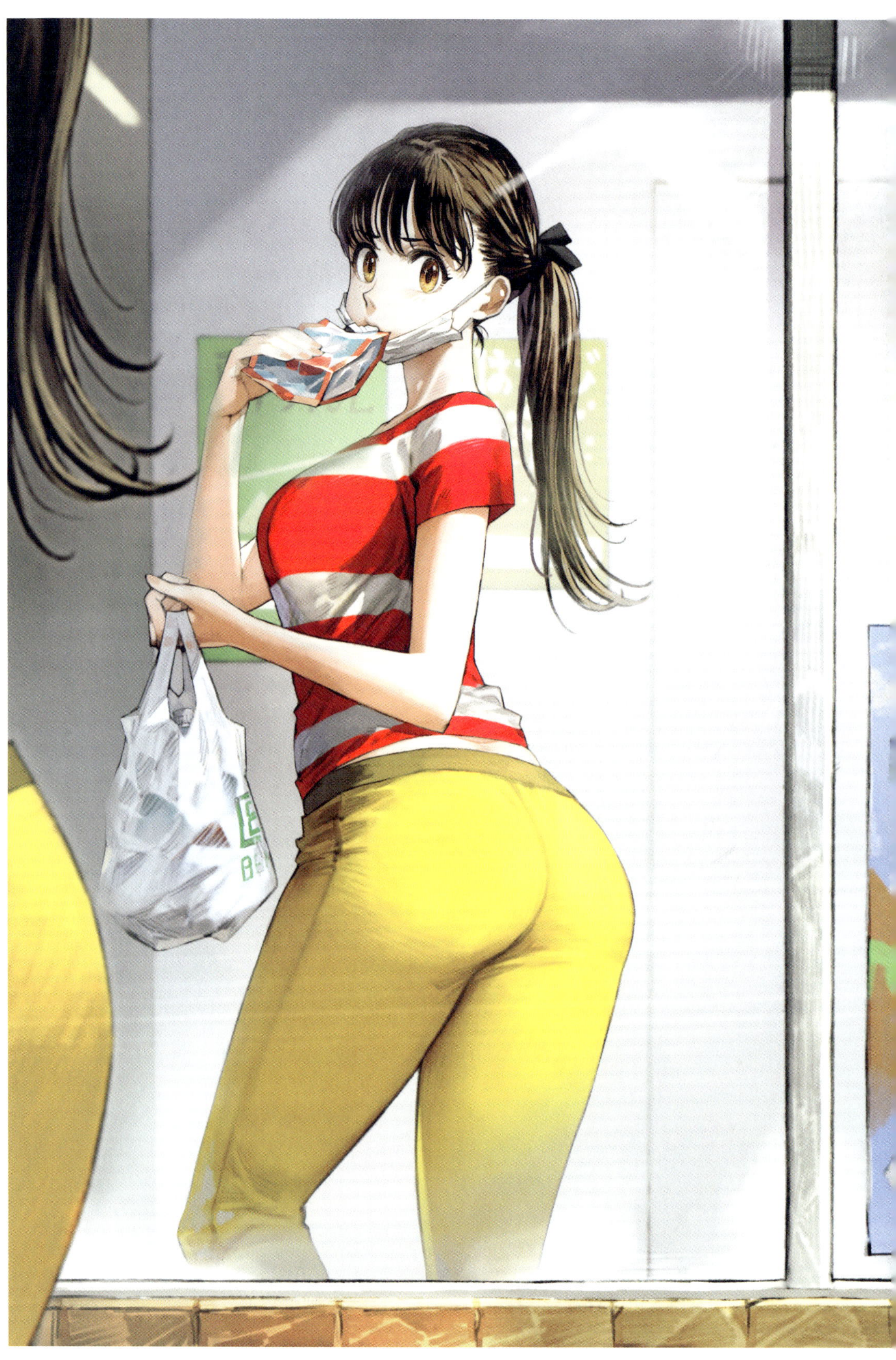

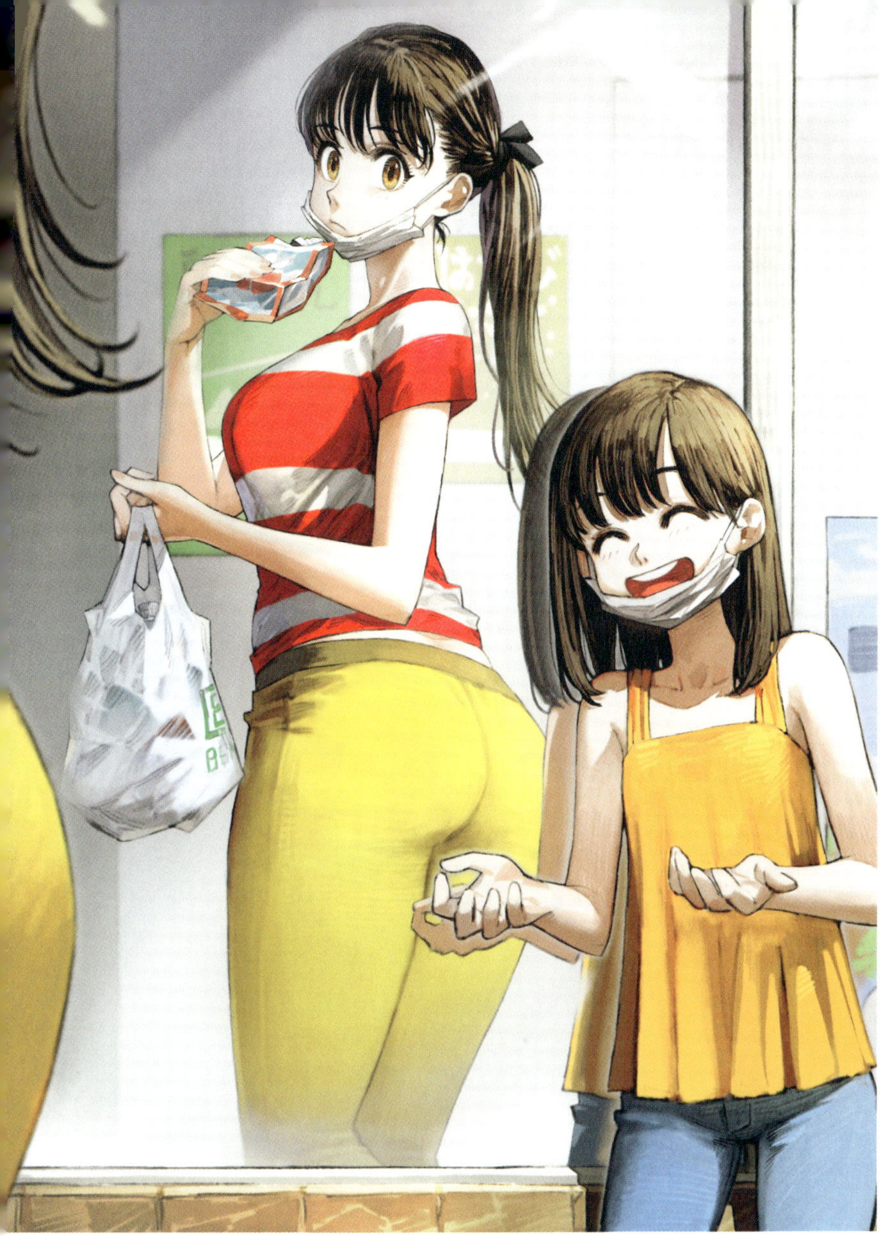

TITLE

"You're Getting Big!"

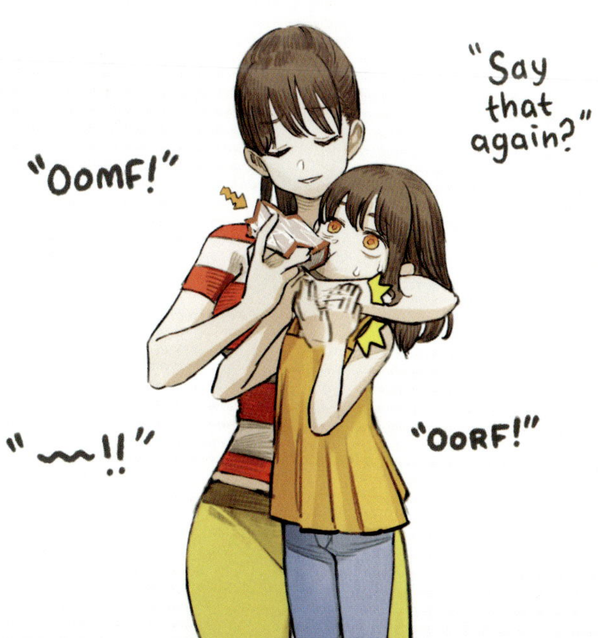

TITLE
"Chewy Mochi
Rice Cakes"

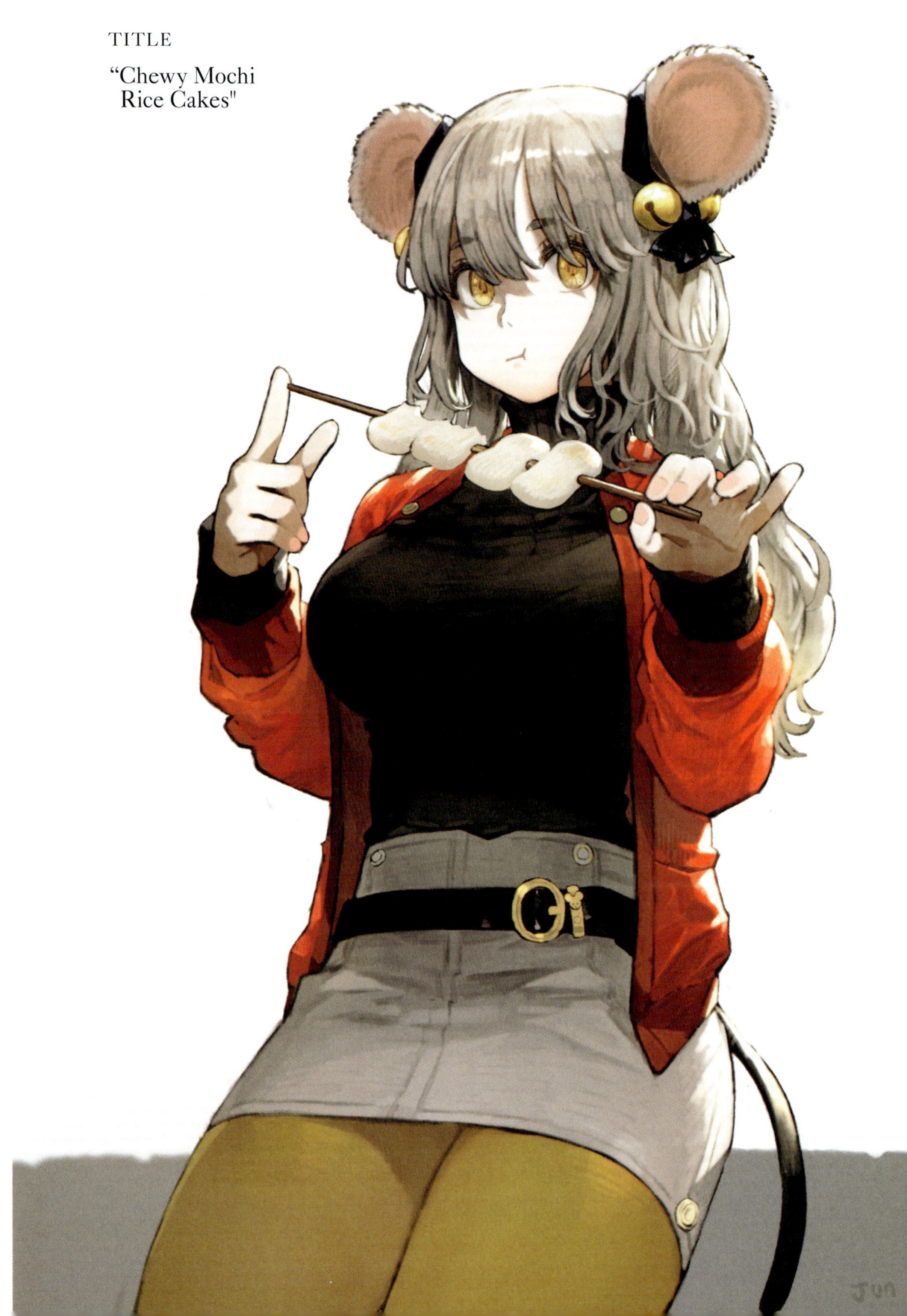

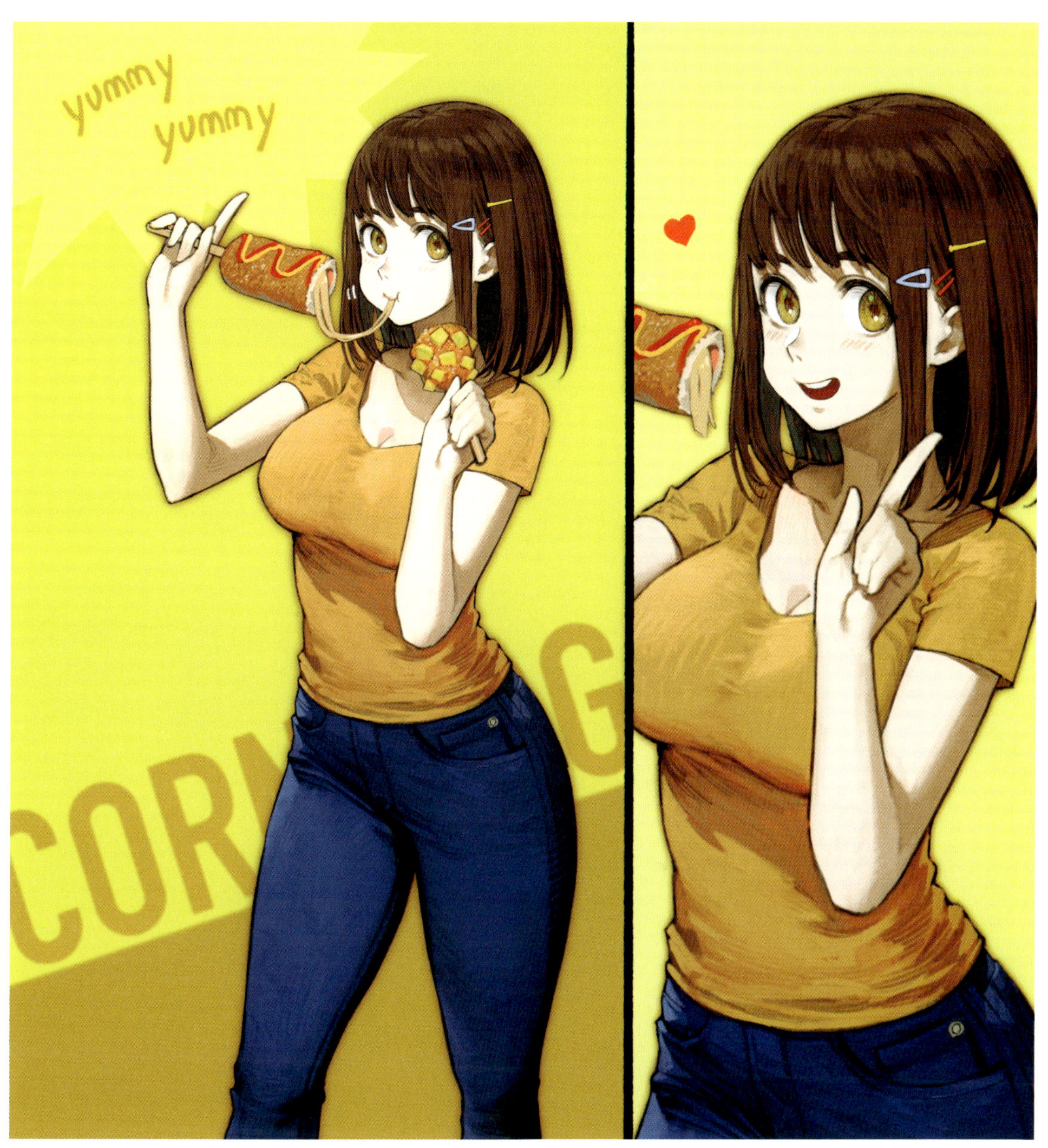

TITLE

"1+1"

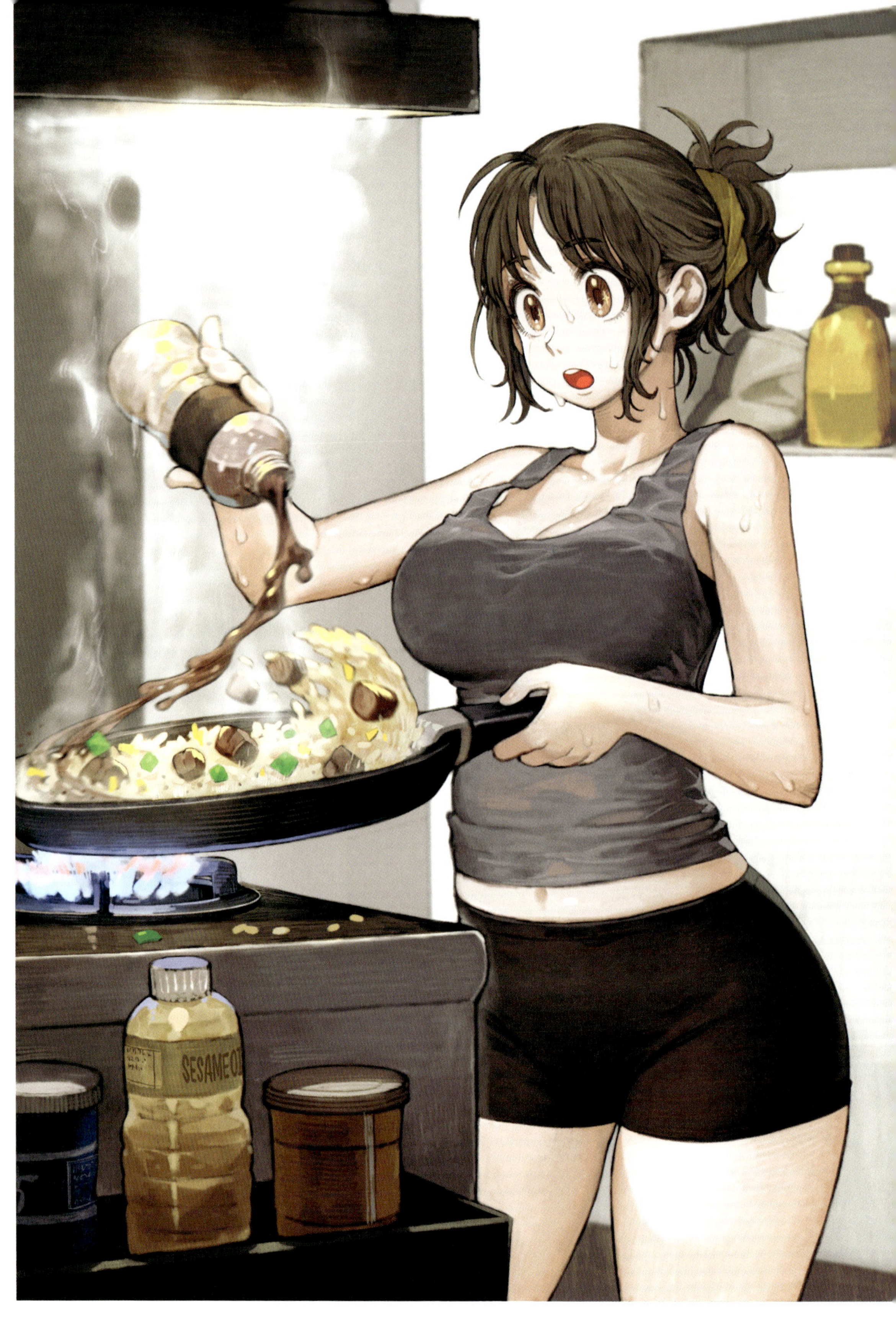

TITLE

"Fried Rice"

TITLE
"Corn"

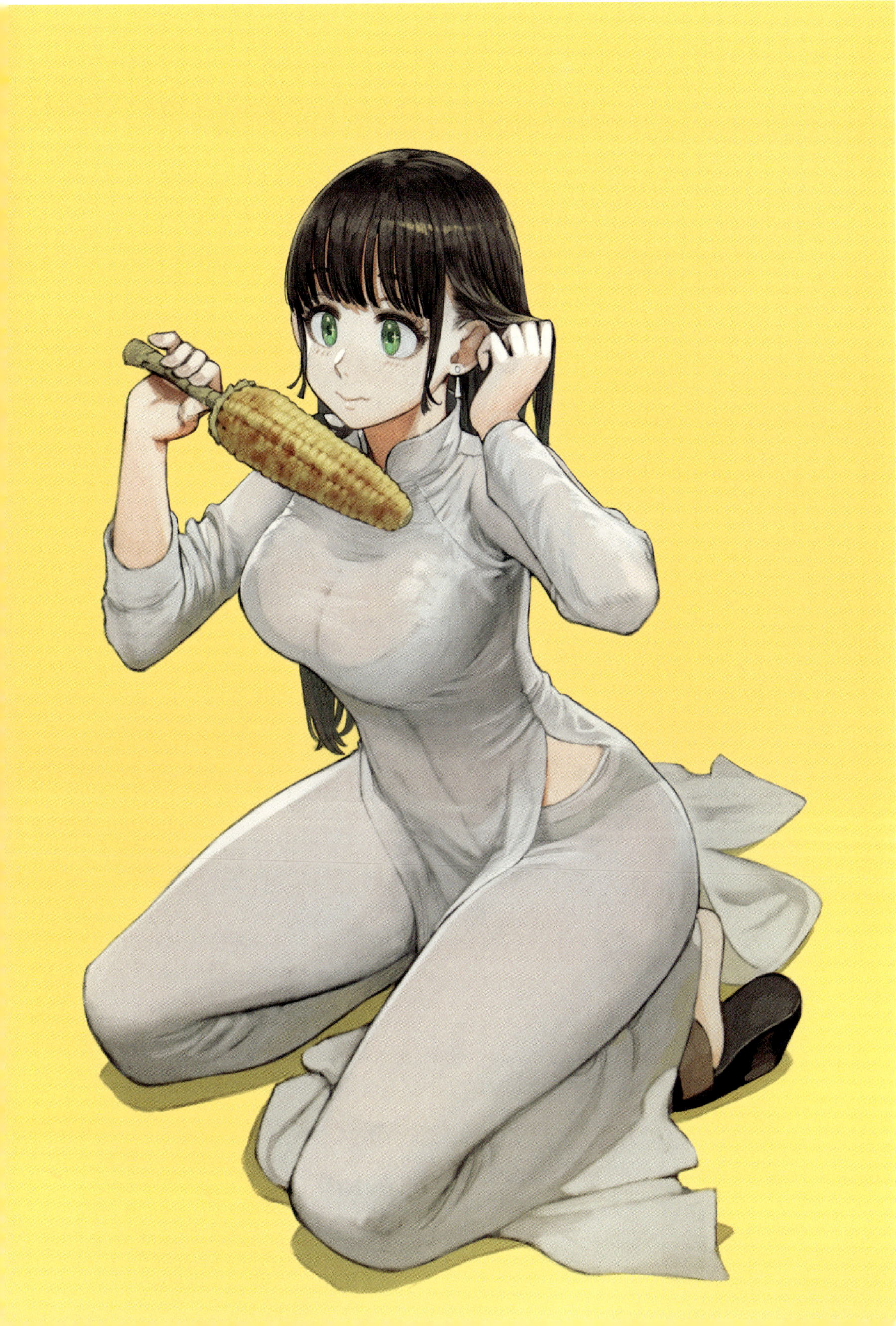

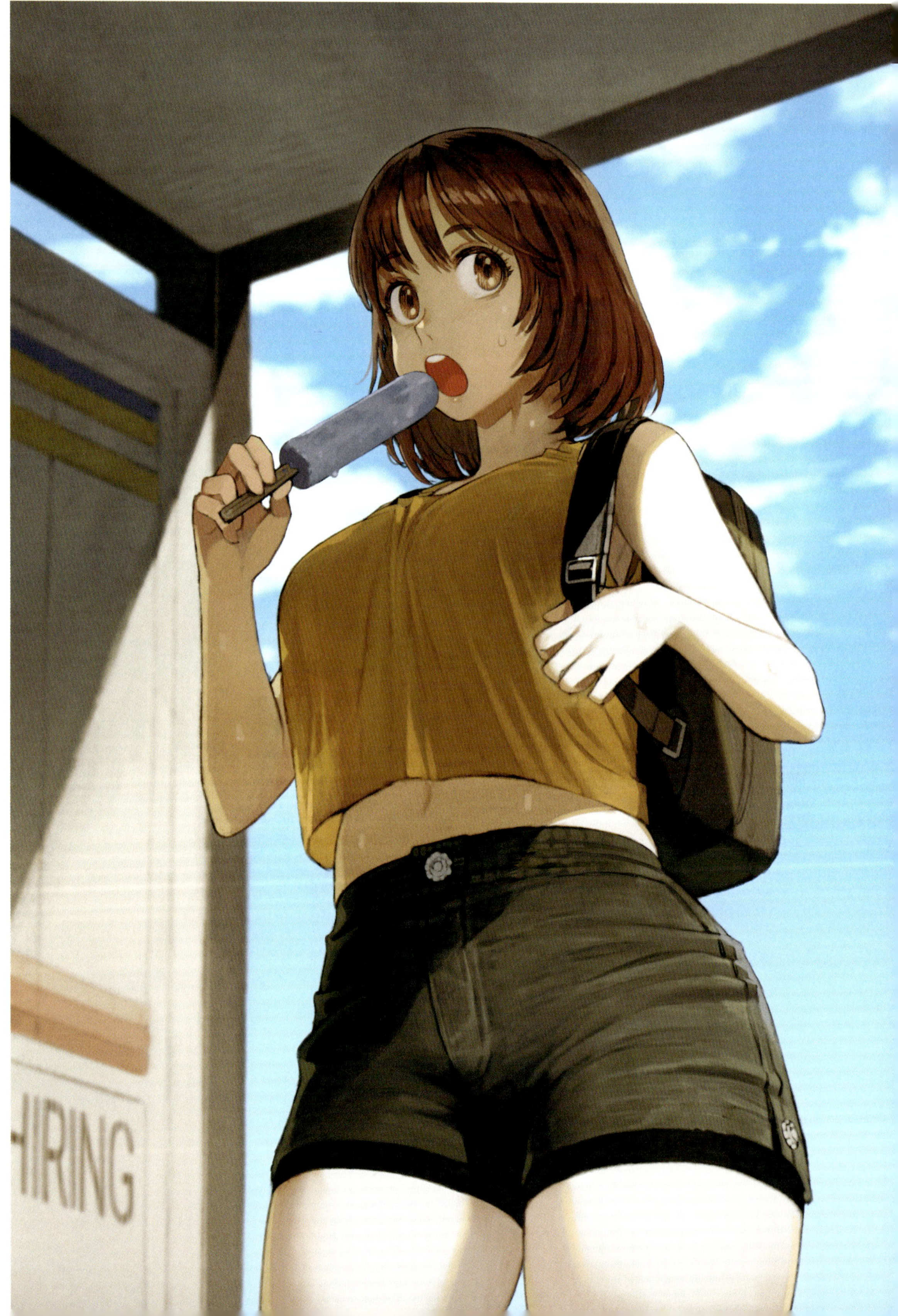
HIRING

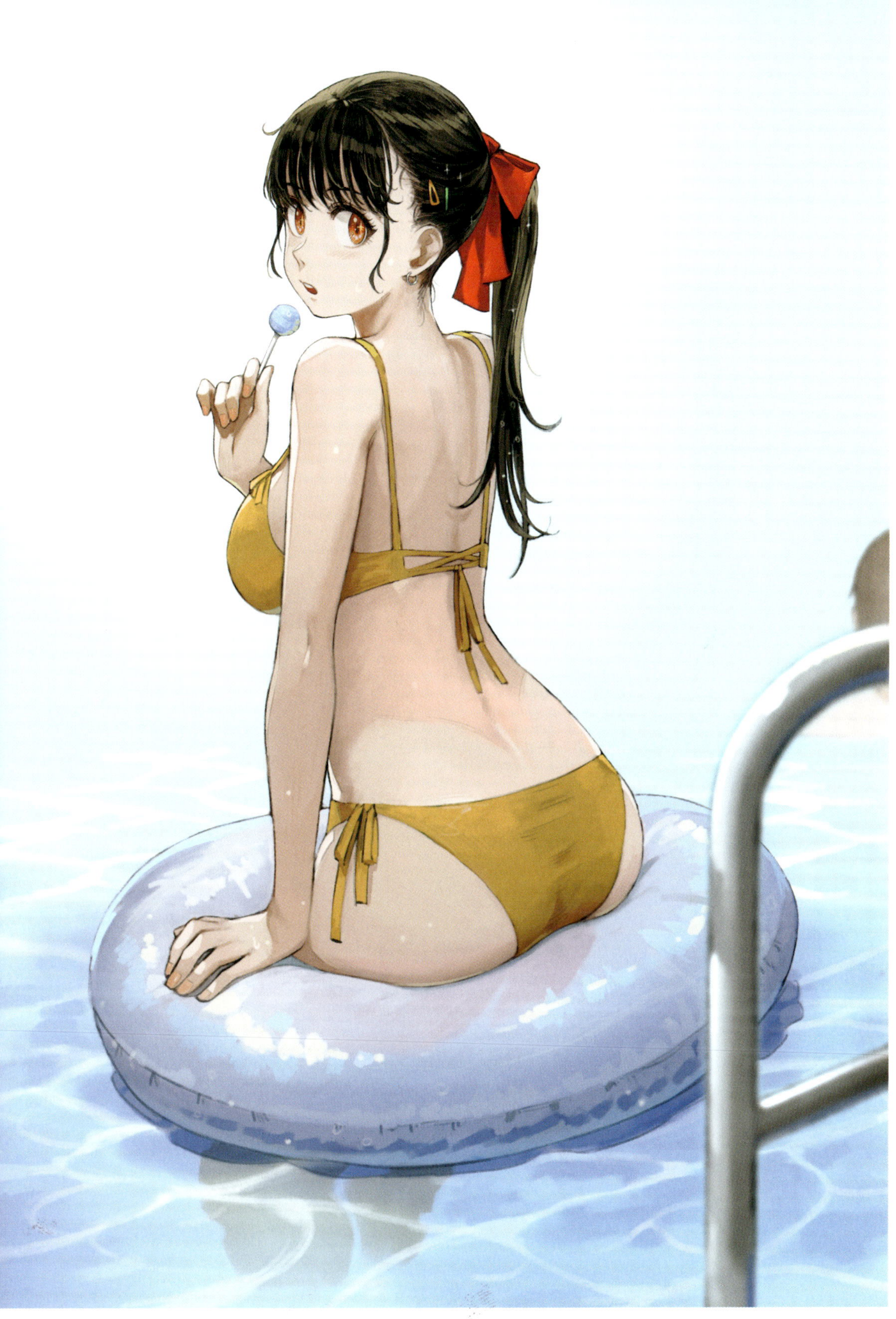

TITLE
"Pool"

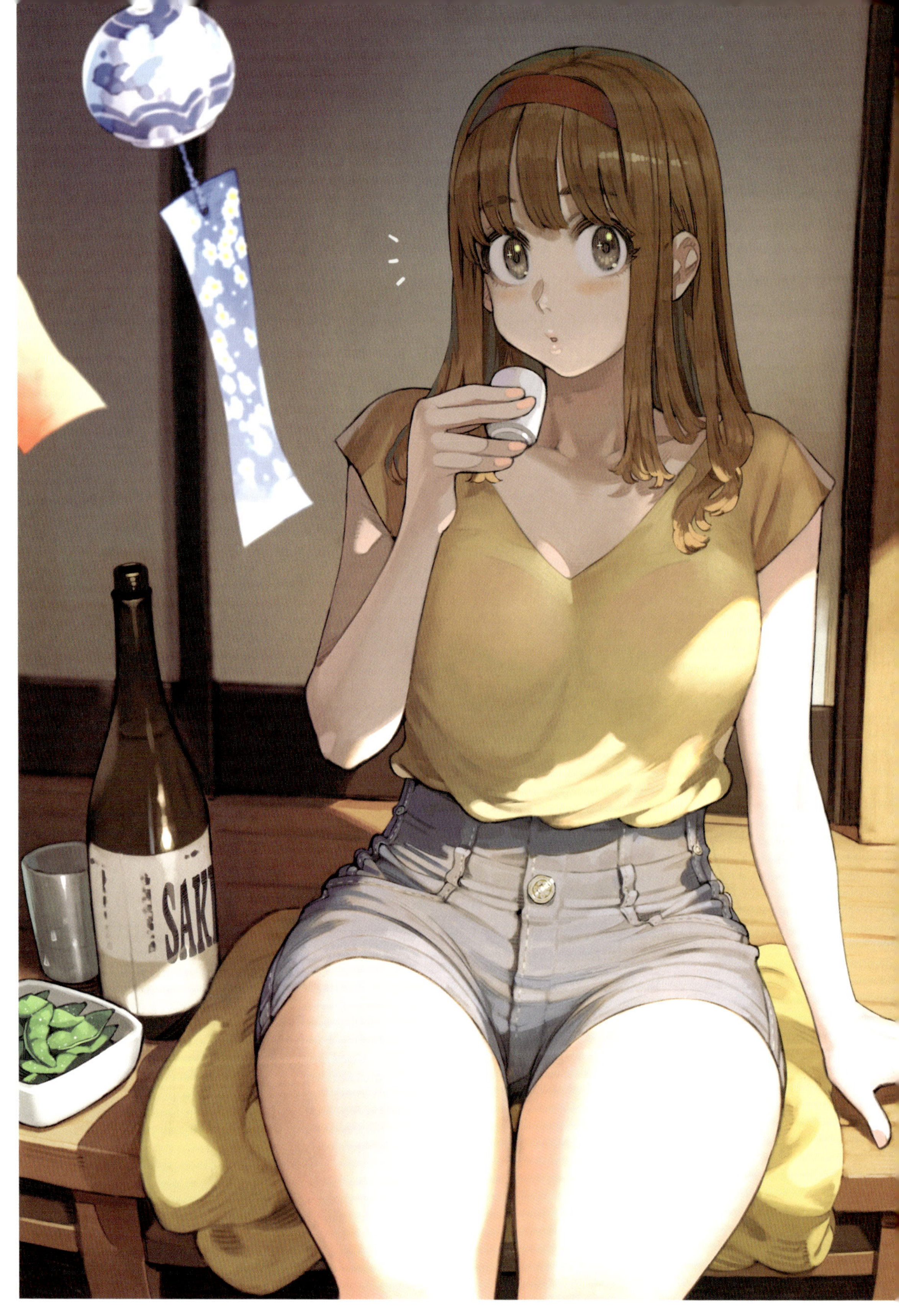

TITLE

"Don't just Stand There"

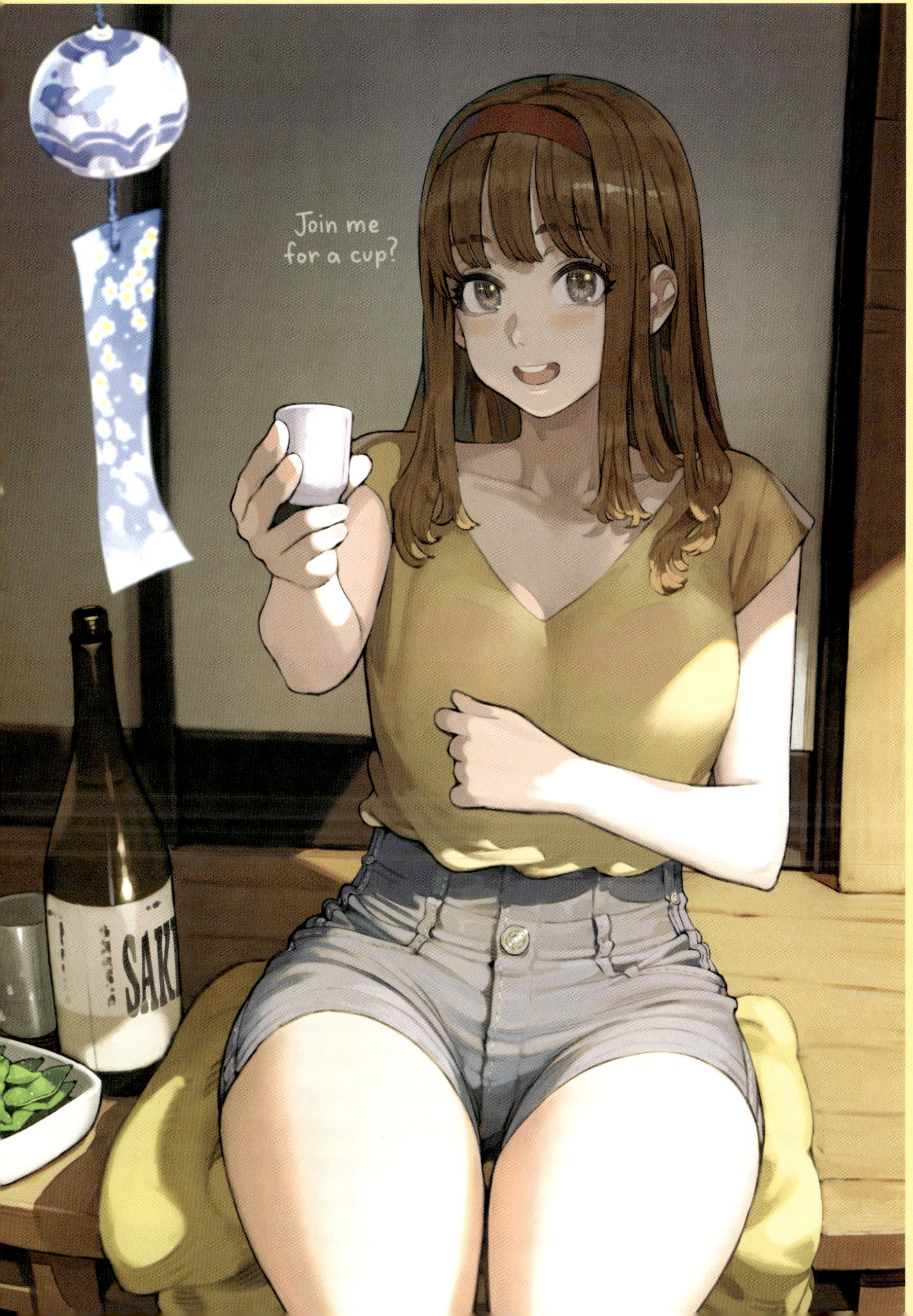
Join me
for a cup?
SAKE

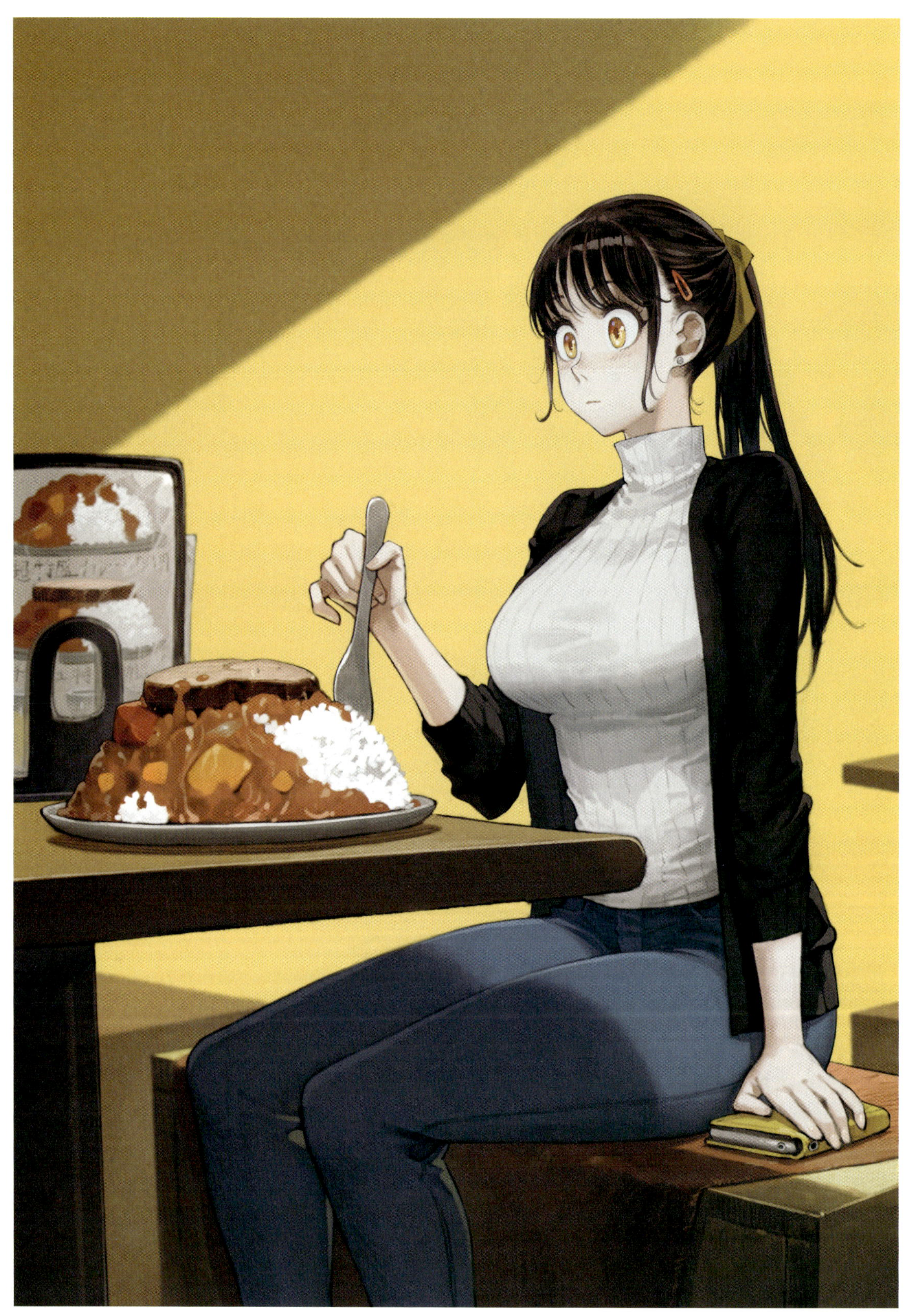

TITLE

"Curry"

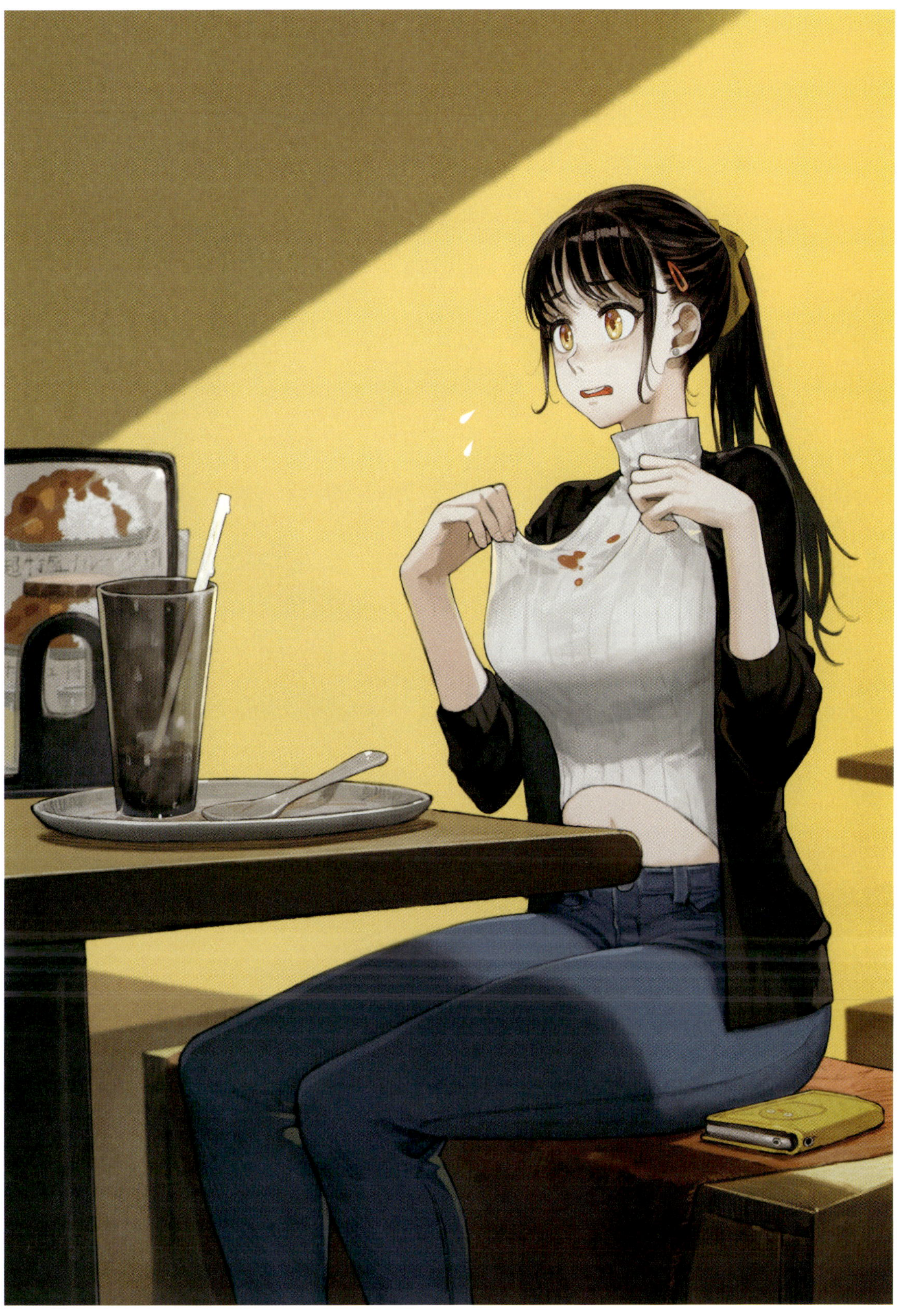

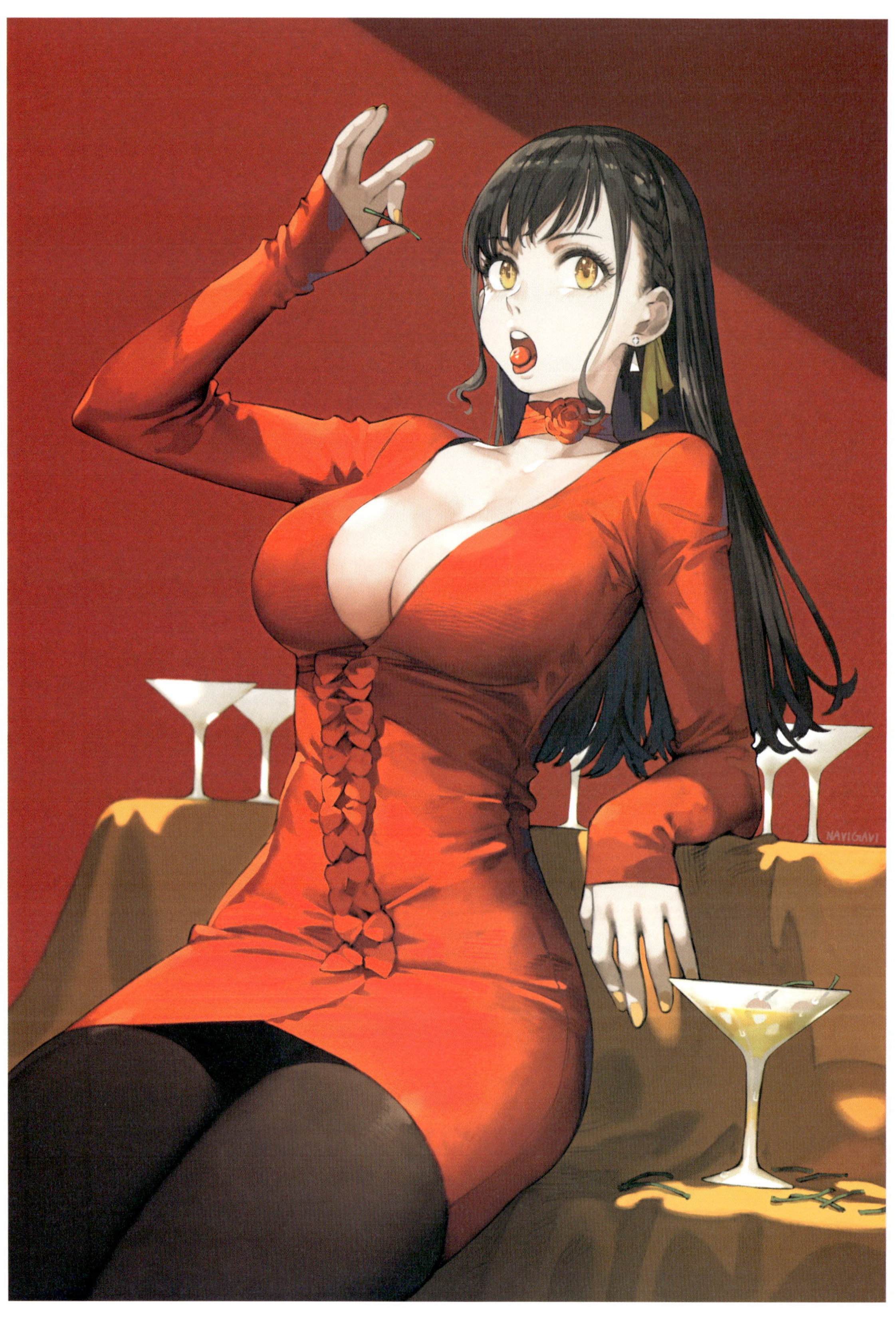

TITLE

"Cherry"

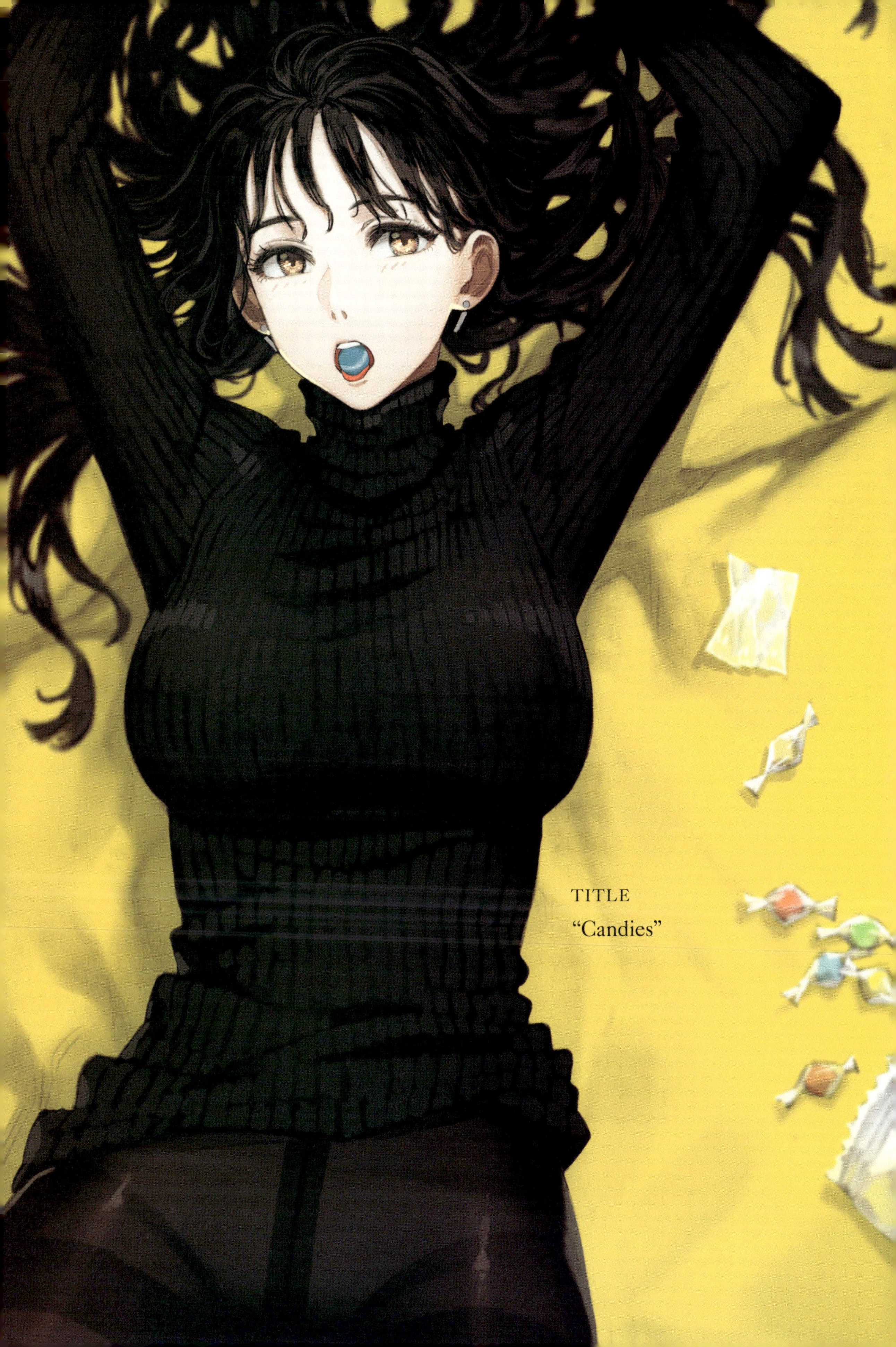
TITLE
"Candies"

TITLE
"I'll Just Have One…"

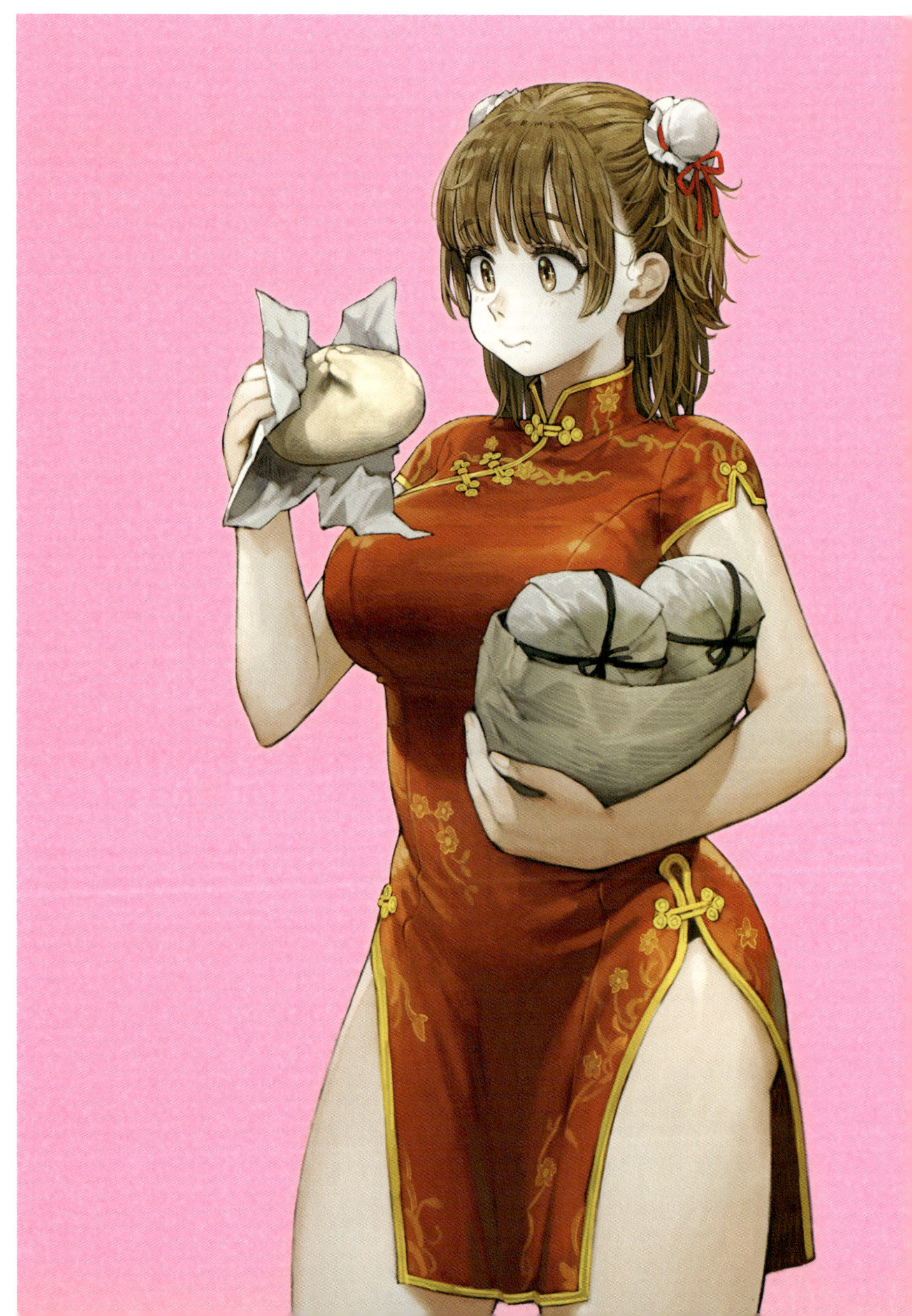

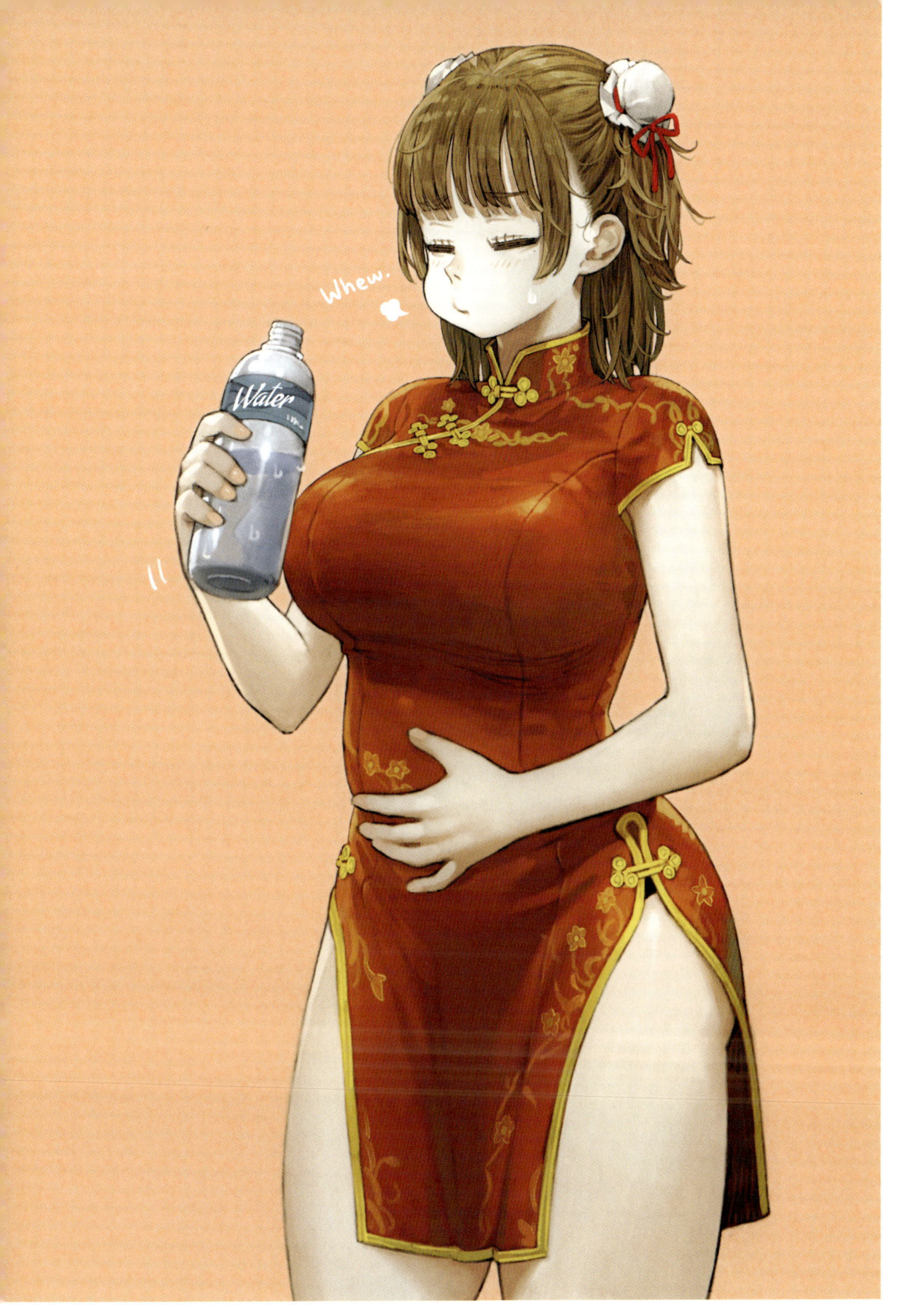

Whew.
Water

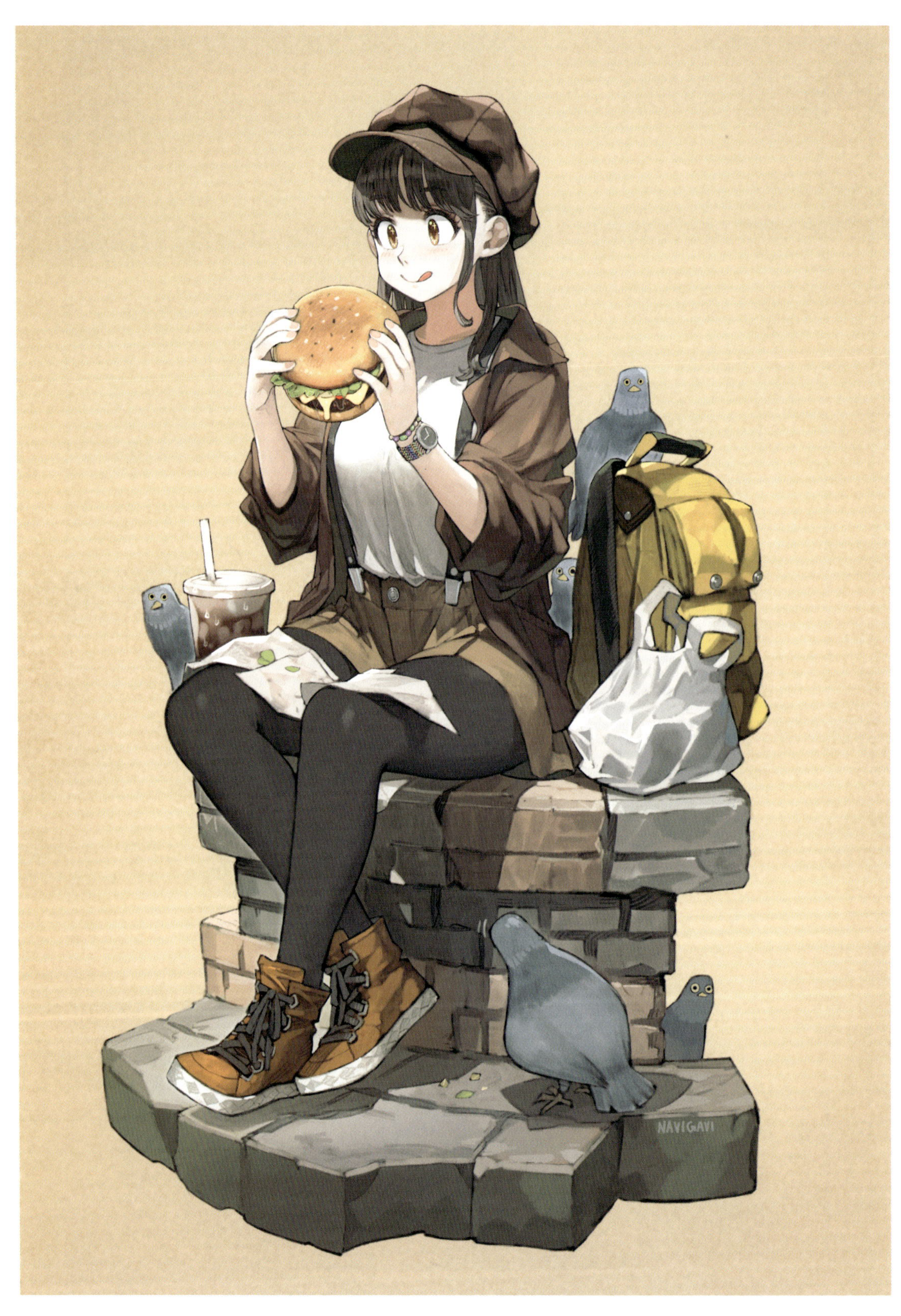

TITLE
"Coo Coo Coo Coo"

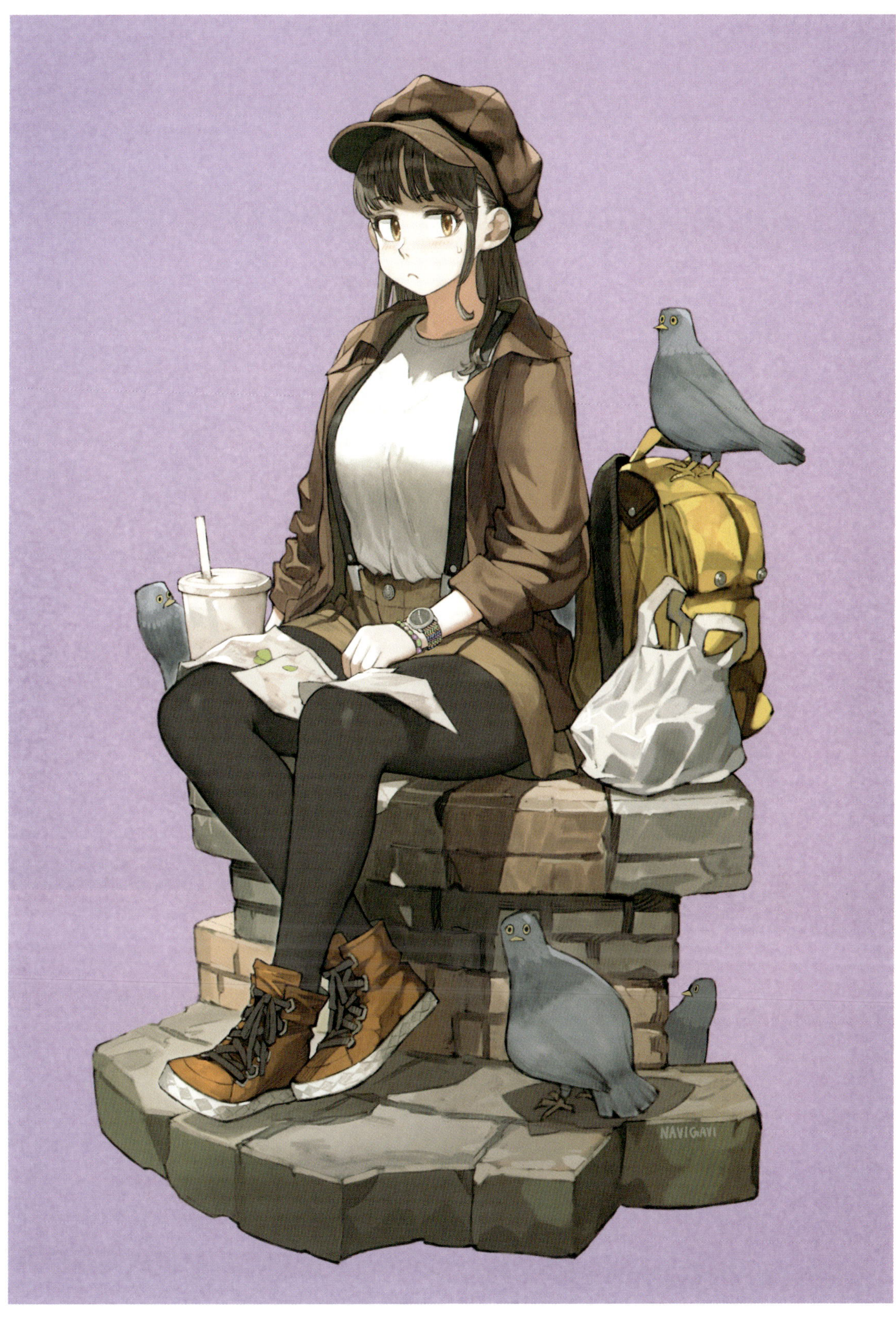

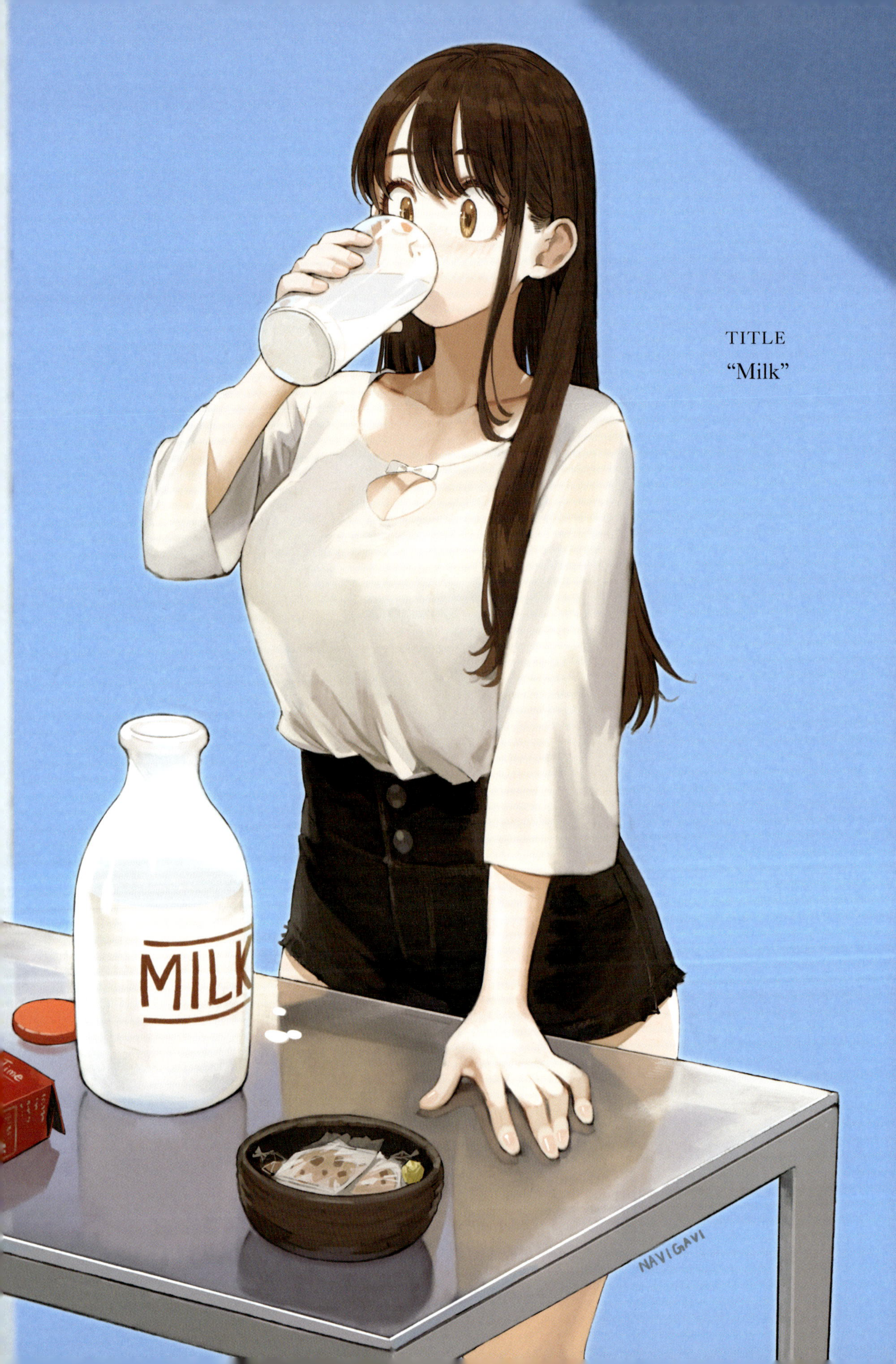

TITLE
"Milk"
MILK
NAVIGAVI

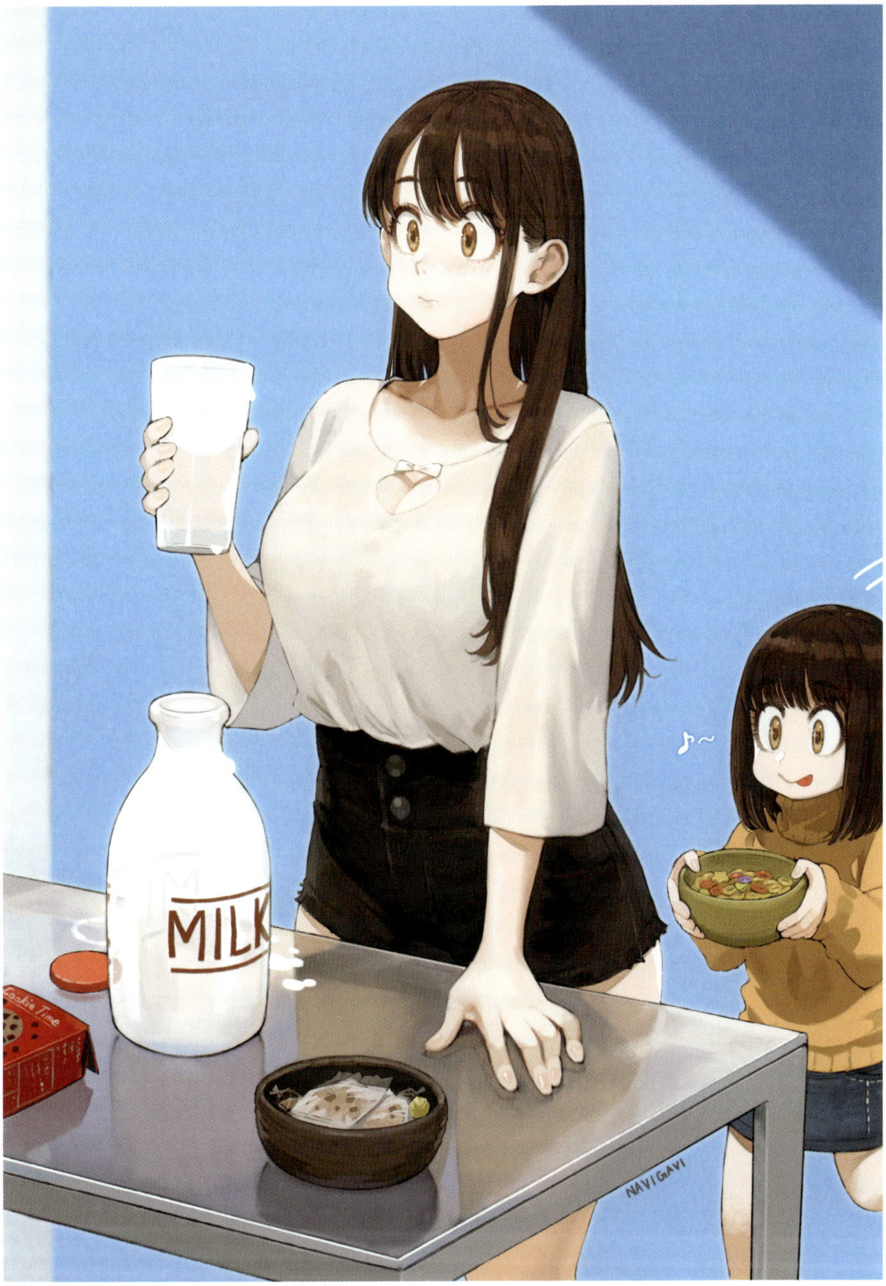

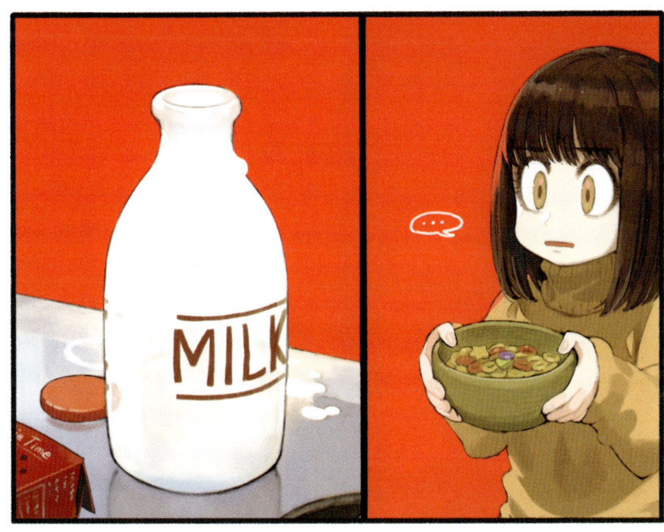
MILK
Cookie Time
NAVIGAVI

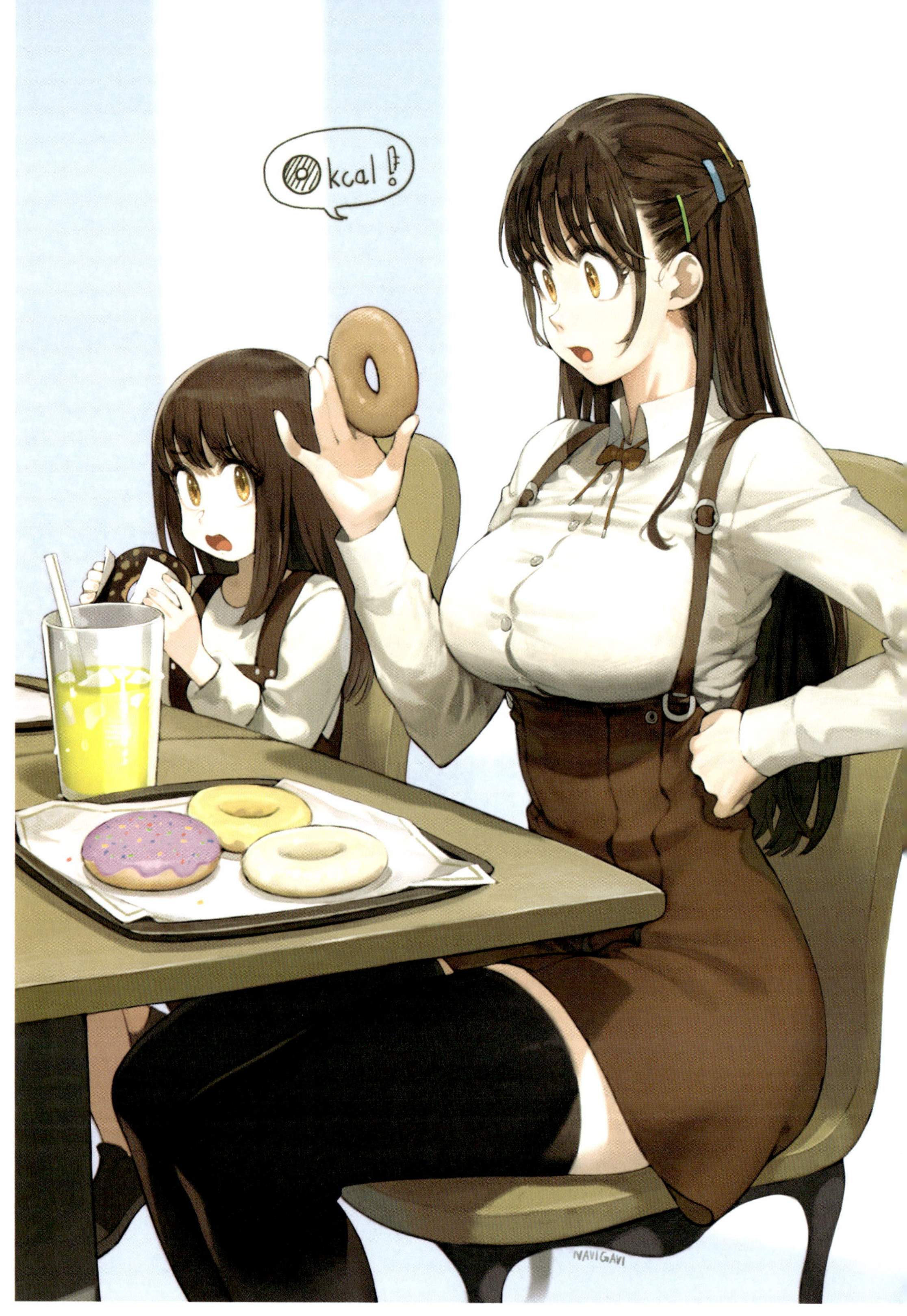

TITLE
"Donuts"

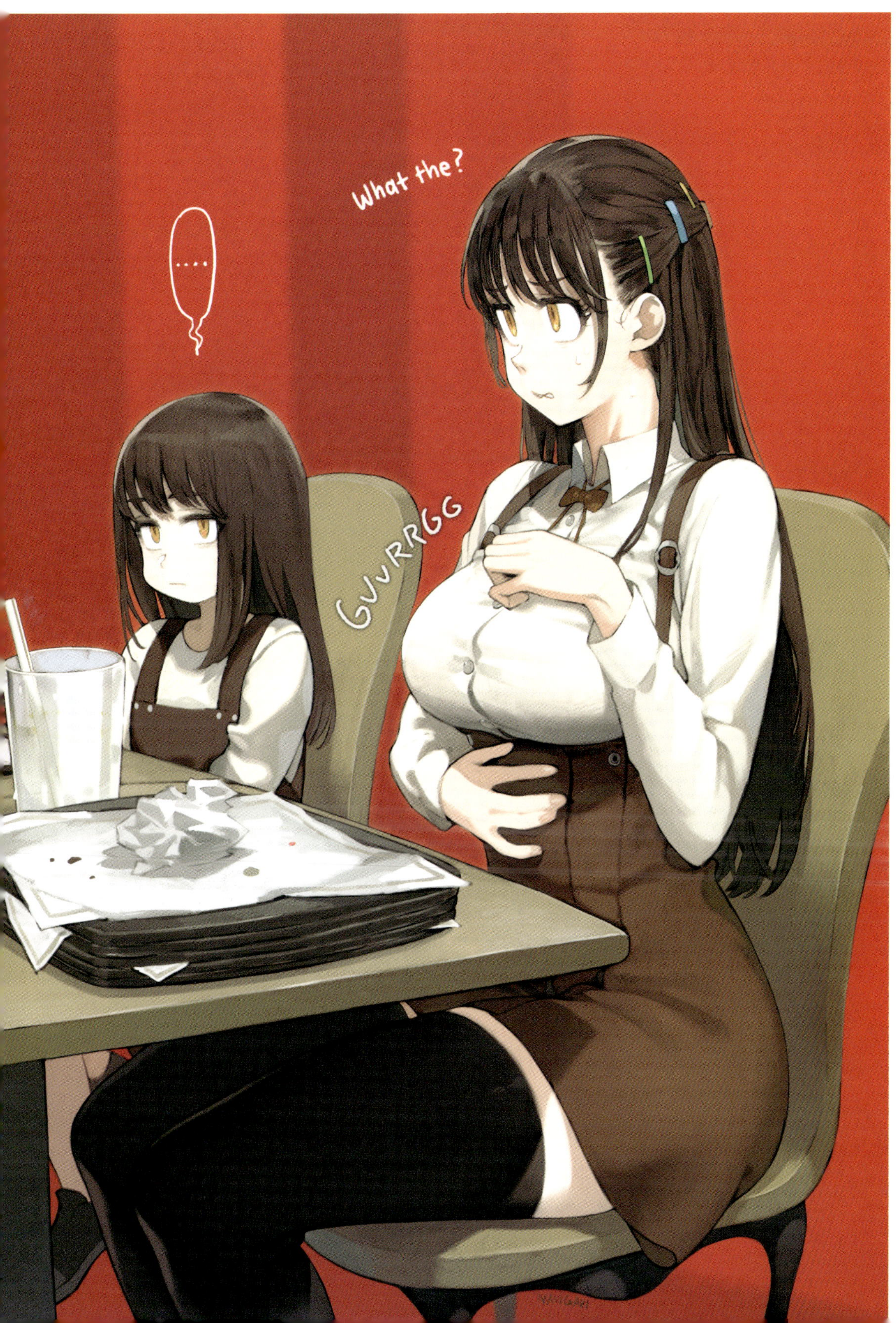
What the?
….
GVVRRGG

TITLE
"Sushi"

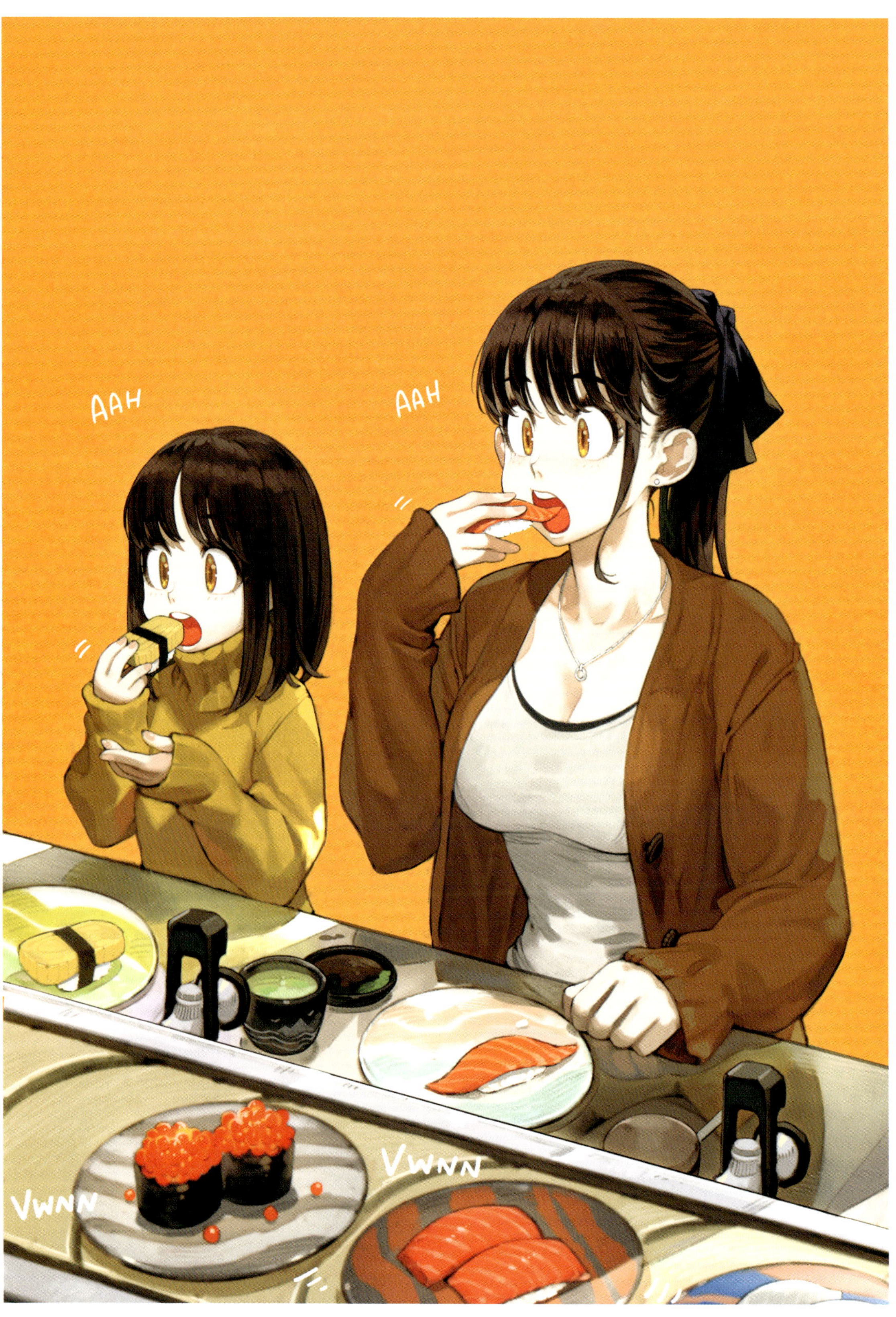

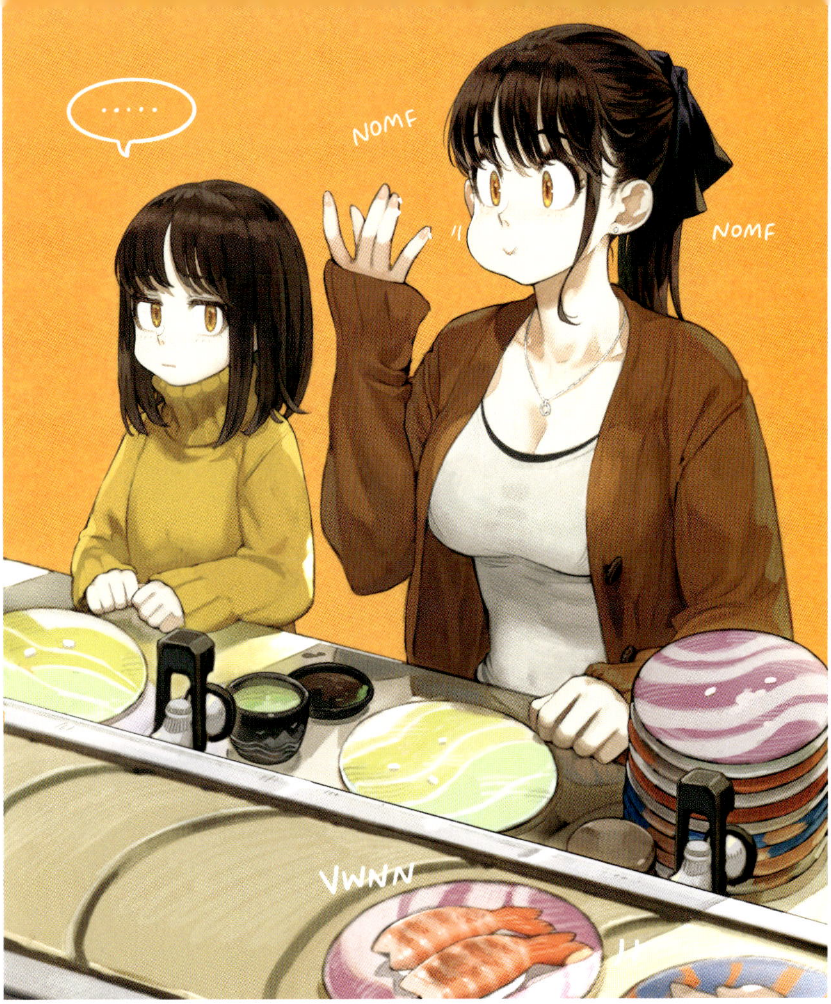

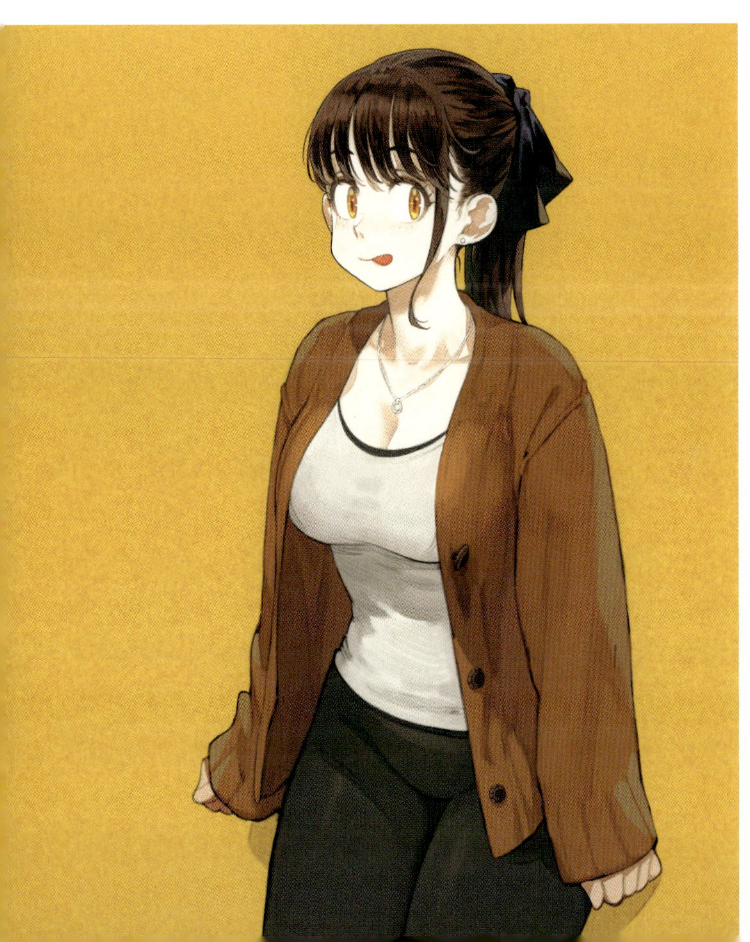

· · · ·
NOMF
NOMF
VWNN

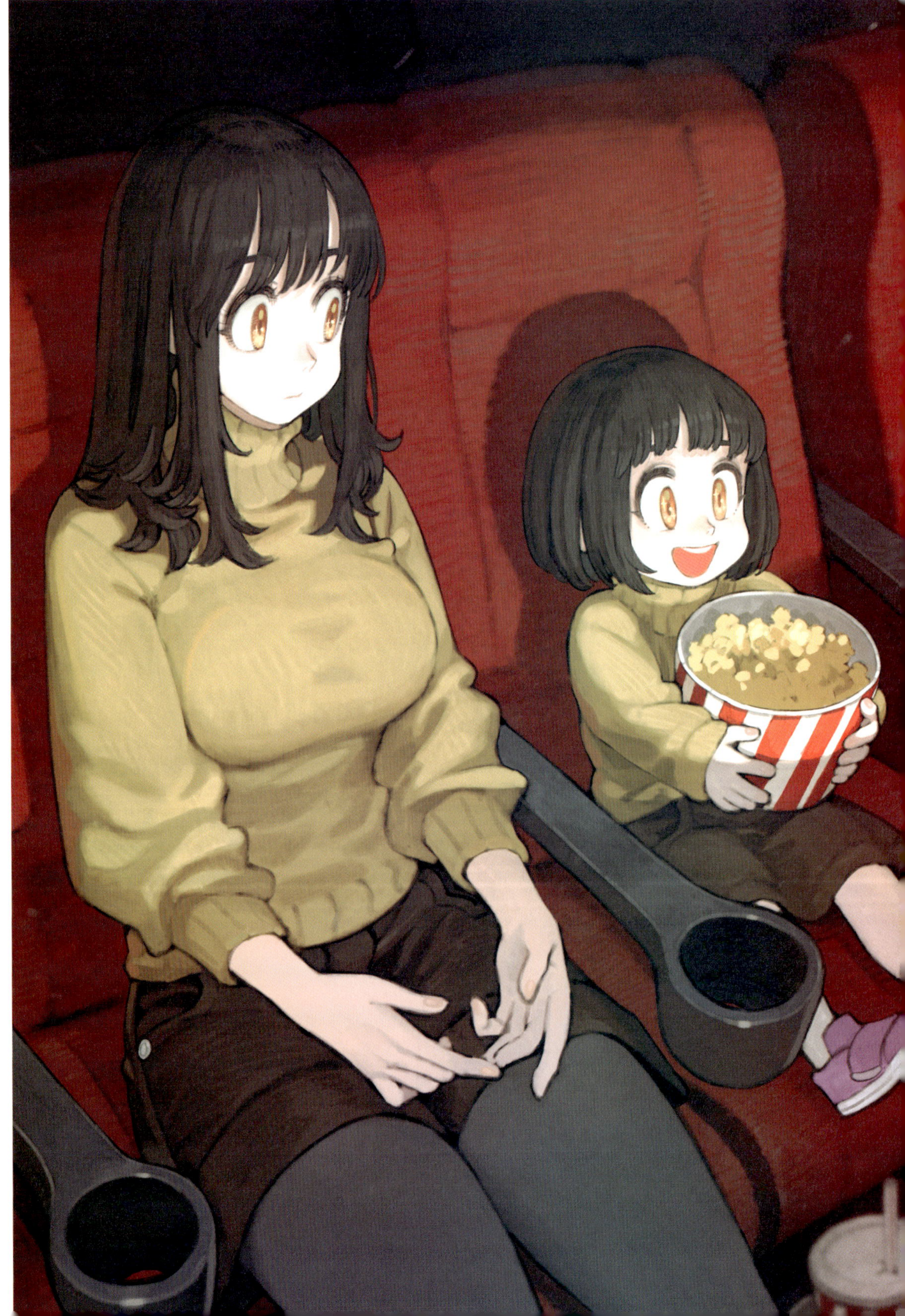

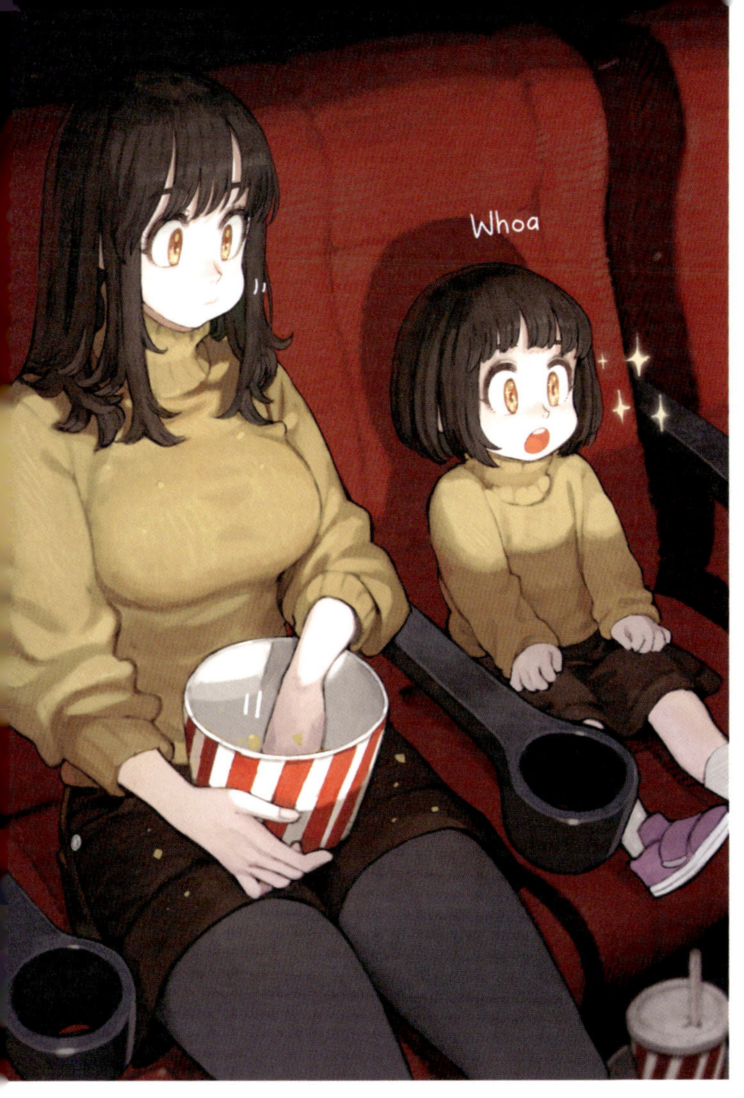

Whoa

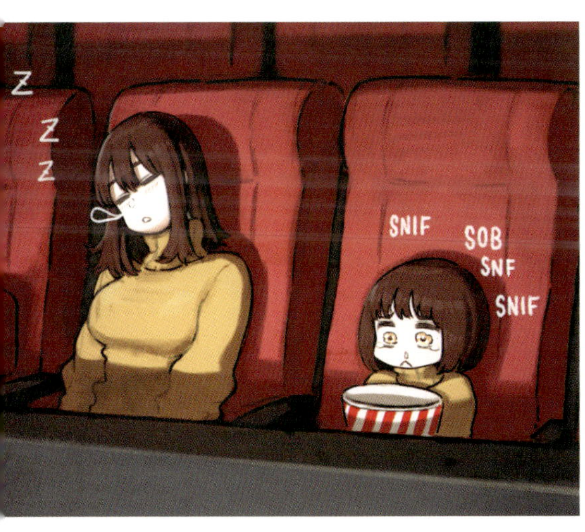

Z
Z
Z
SNIF
SOB
SNF
SNIF

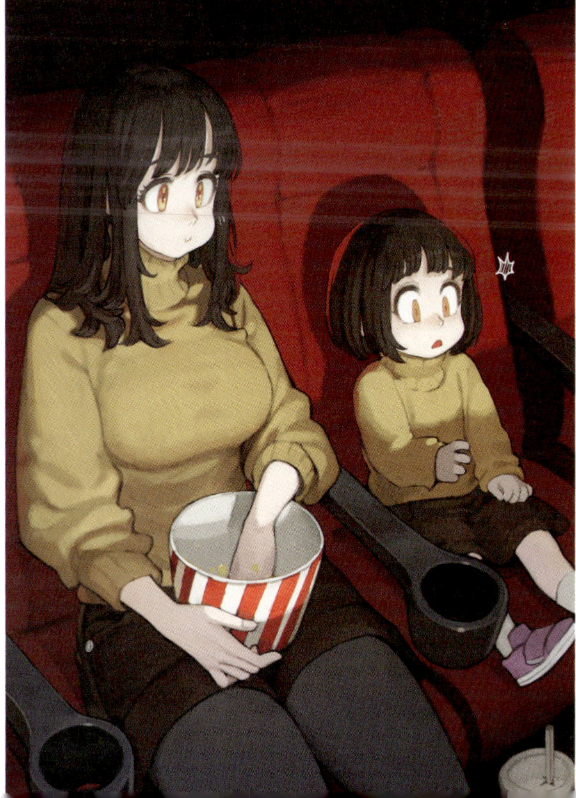

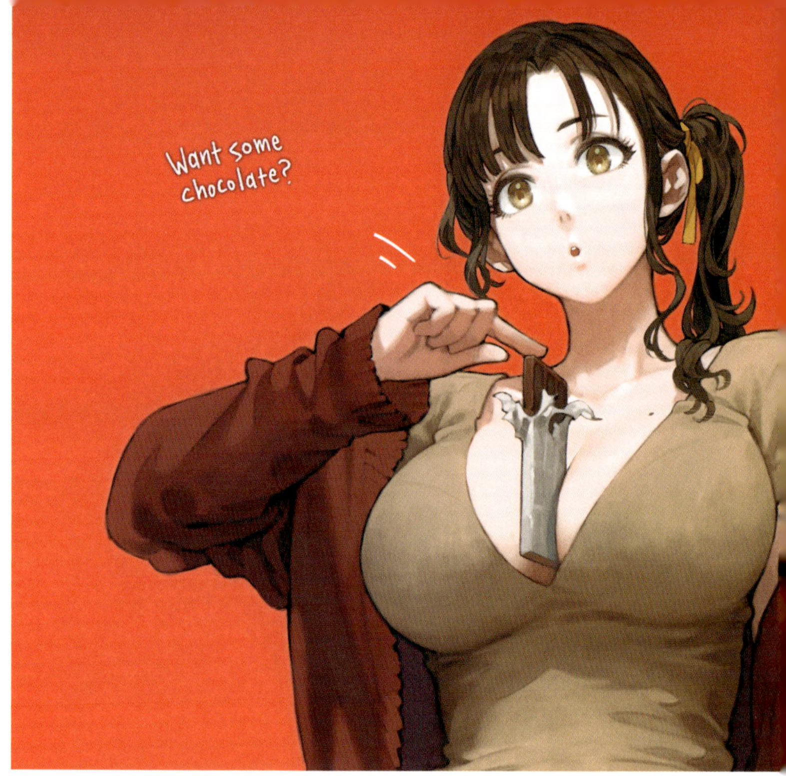

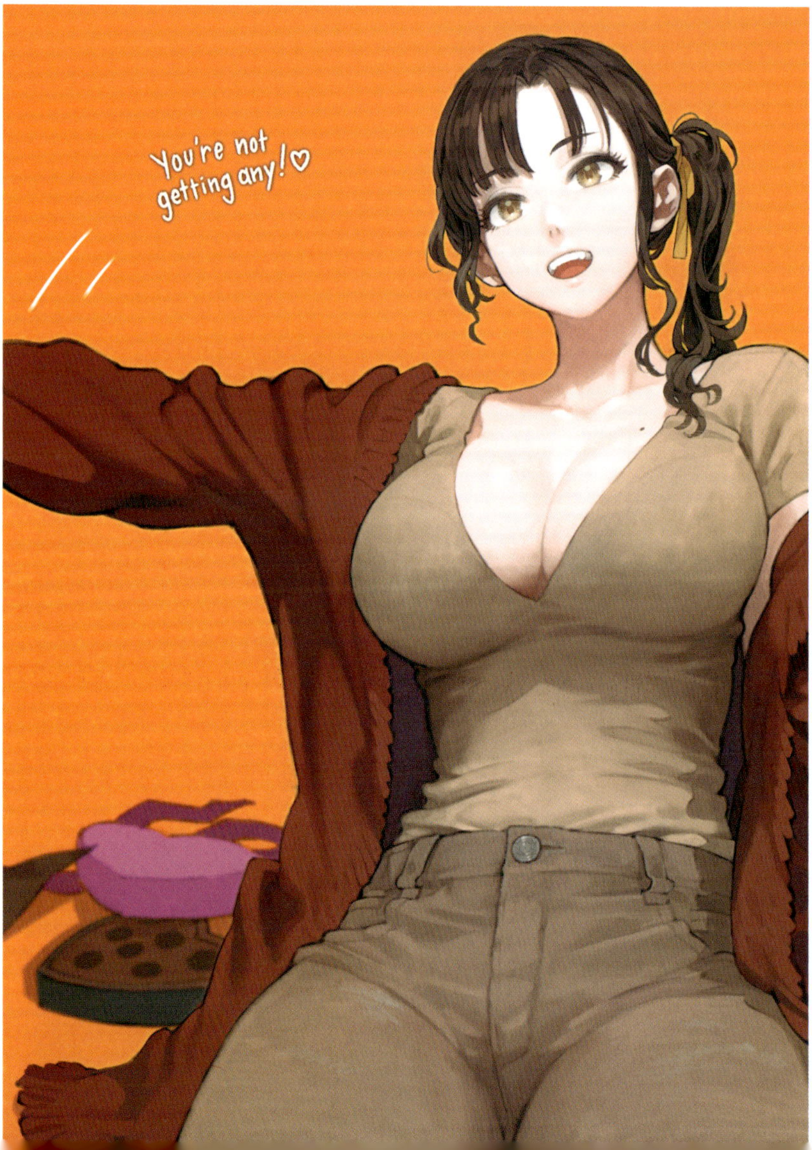

TITLE

"You're Not Getting Any"

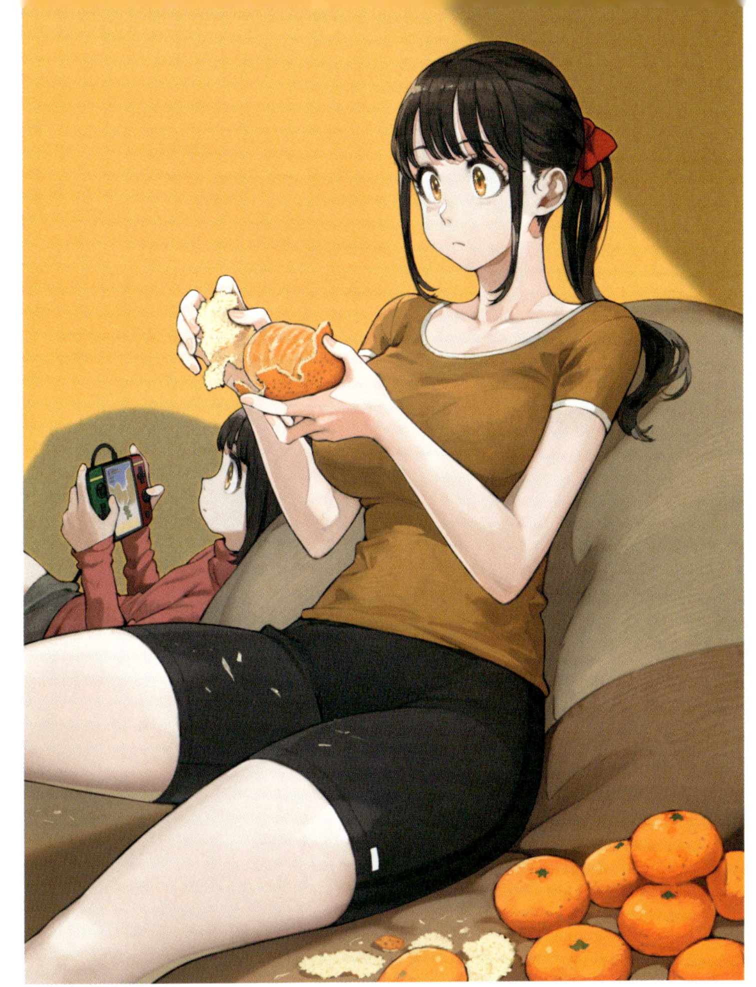

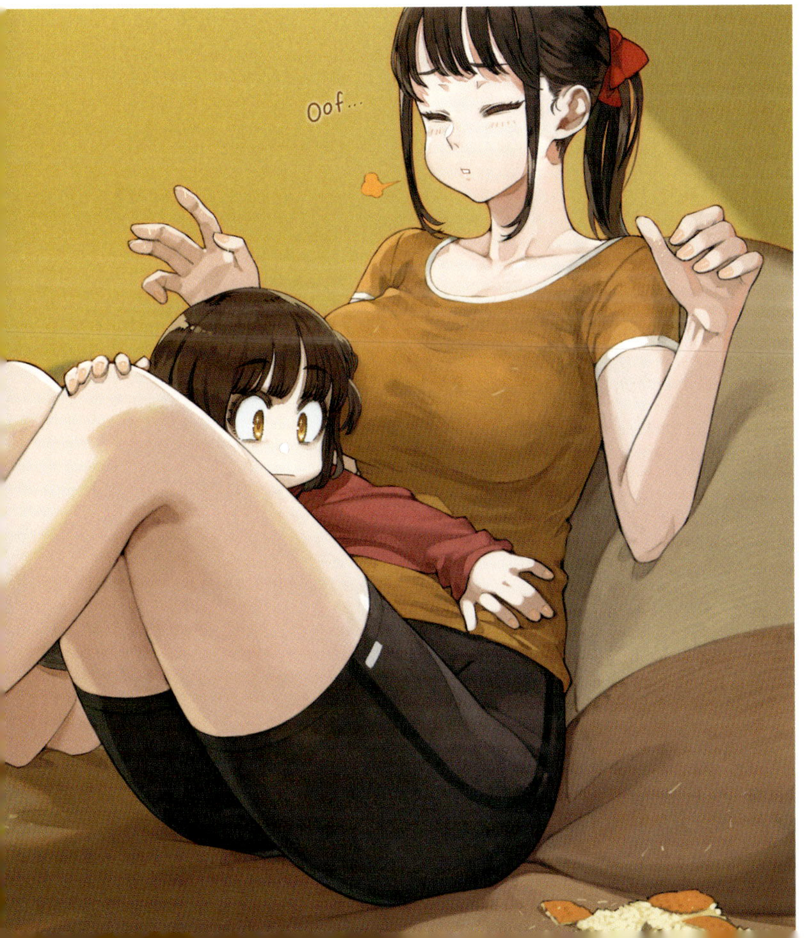
Oof...

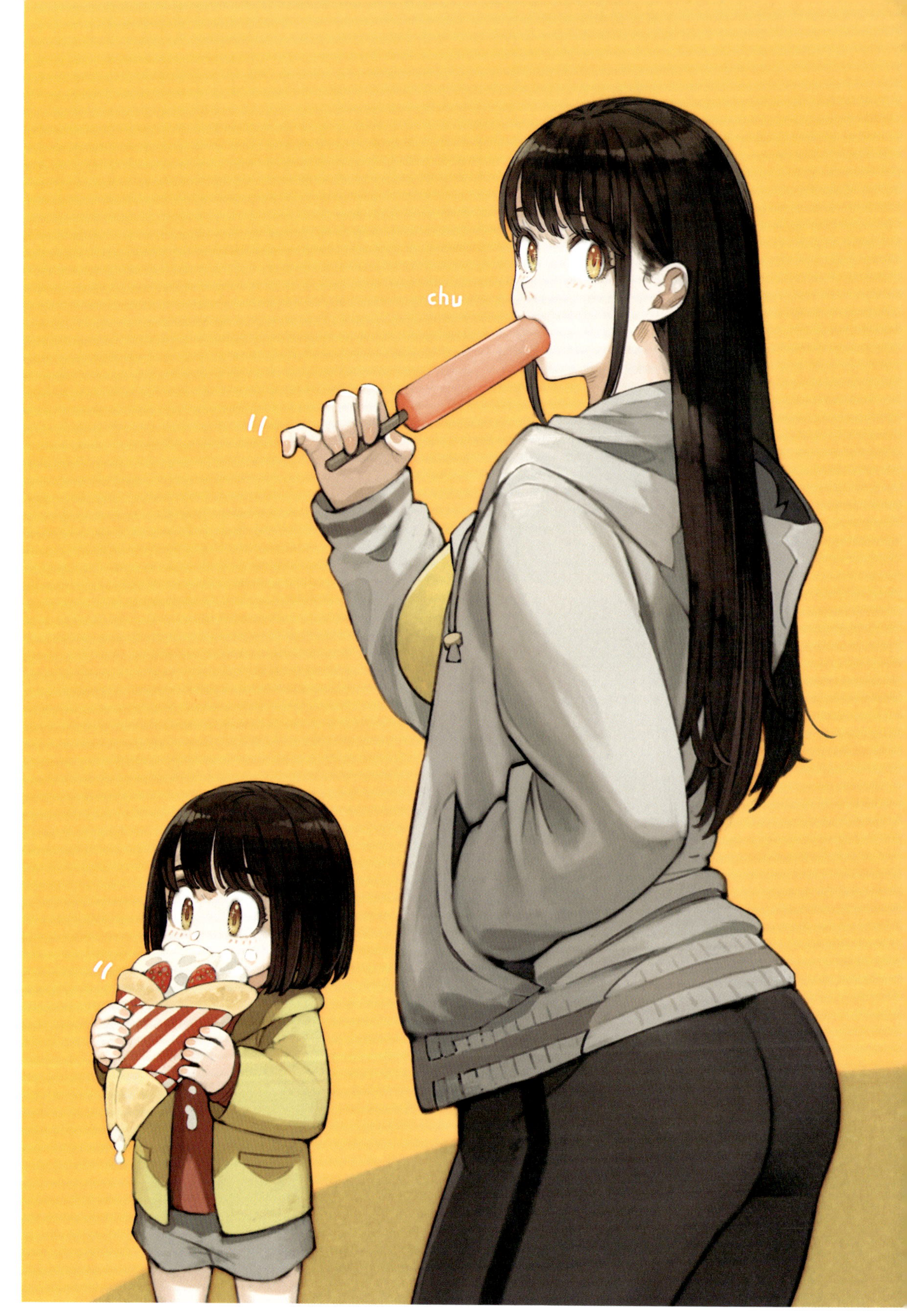

chu

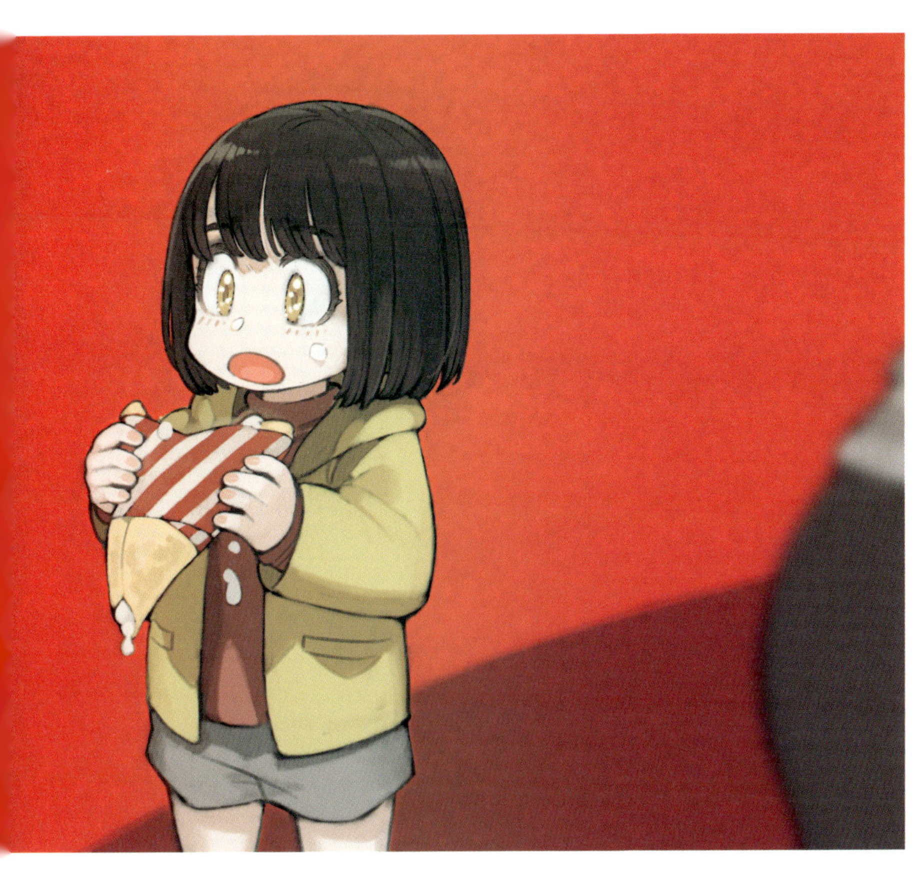
GRARARARAR

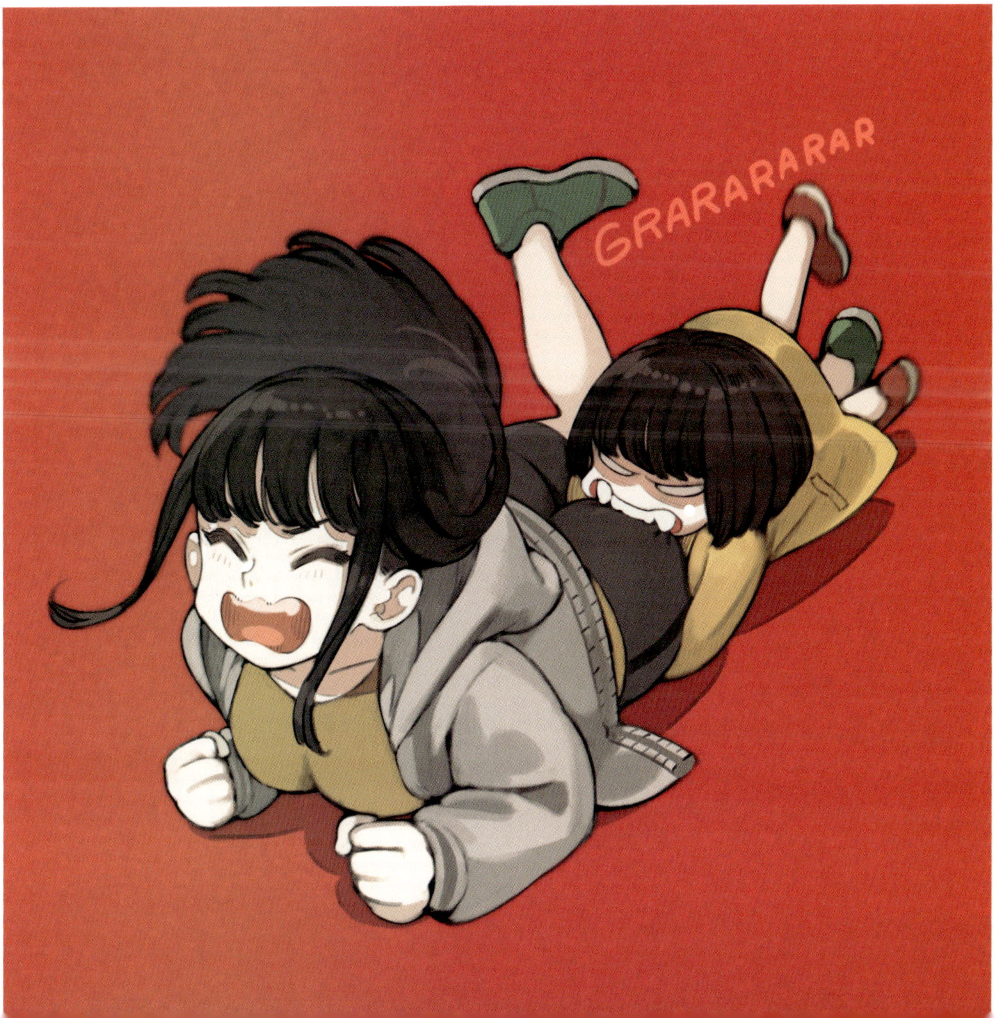

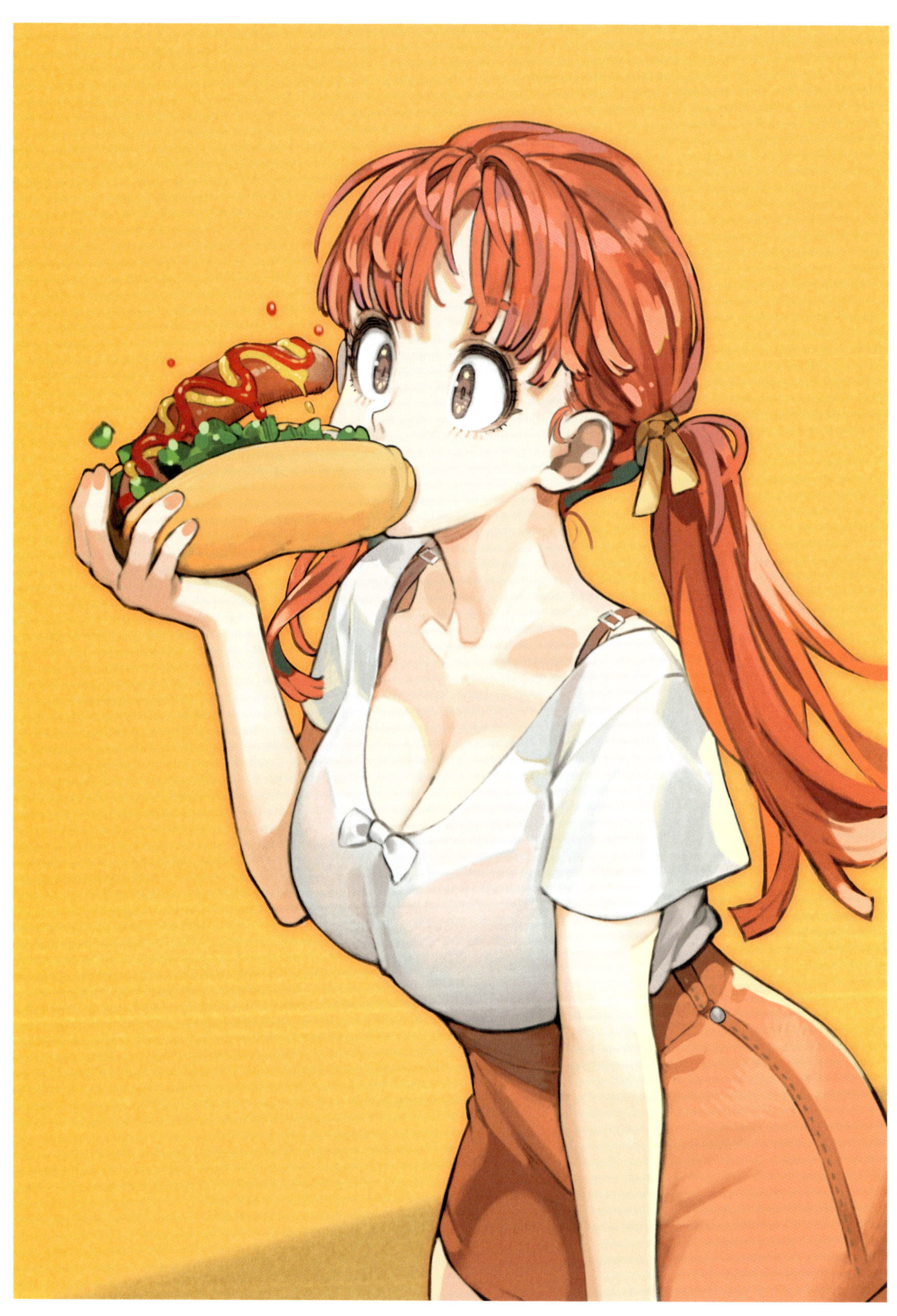

TITLE
"Tragedy"

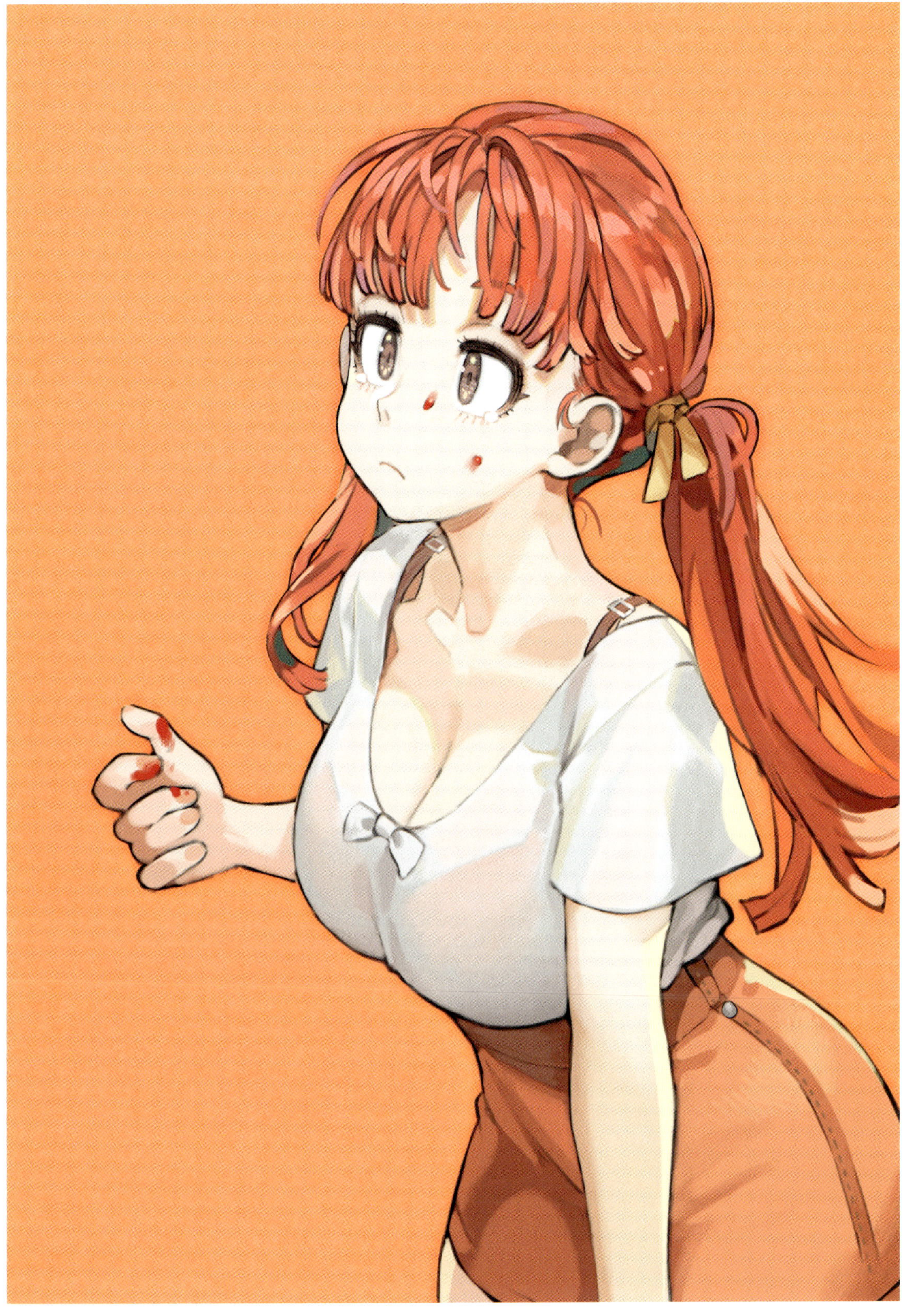

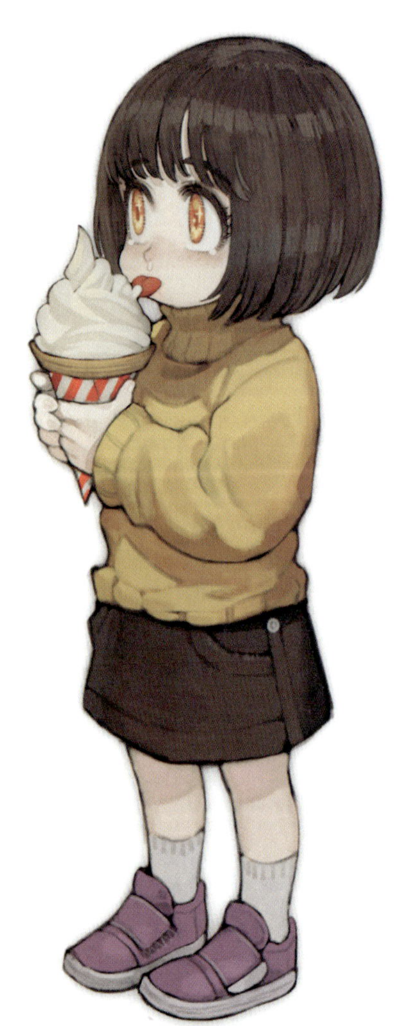

CHAPTER 2

"CUTE GIRL"

Besides the Tabegirls, Jun also created many illustrations of cute, sexy, and powerful girls.

Here we present several illustrations from among those, selected by Jun as particular favorites. Included are girls in various states such as bursting smiles, bashful expressions, and moments of ennui.

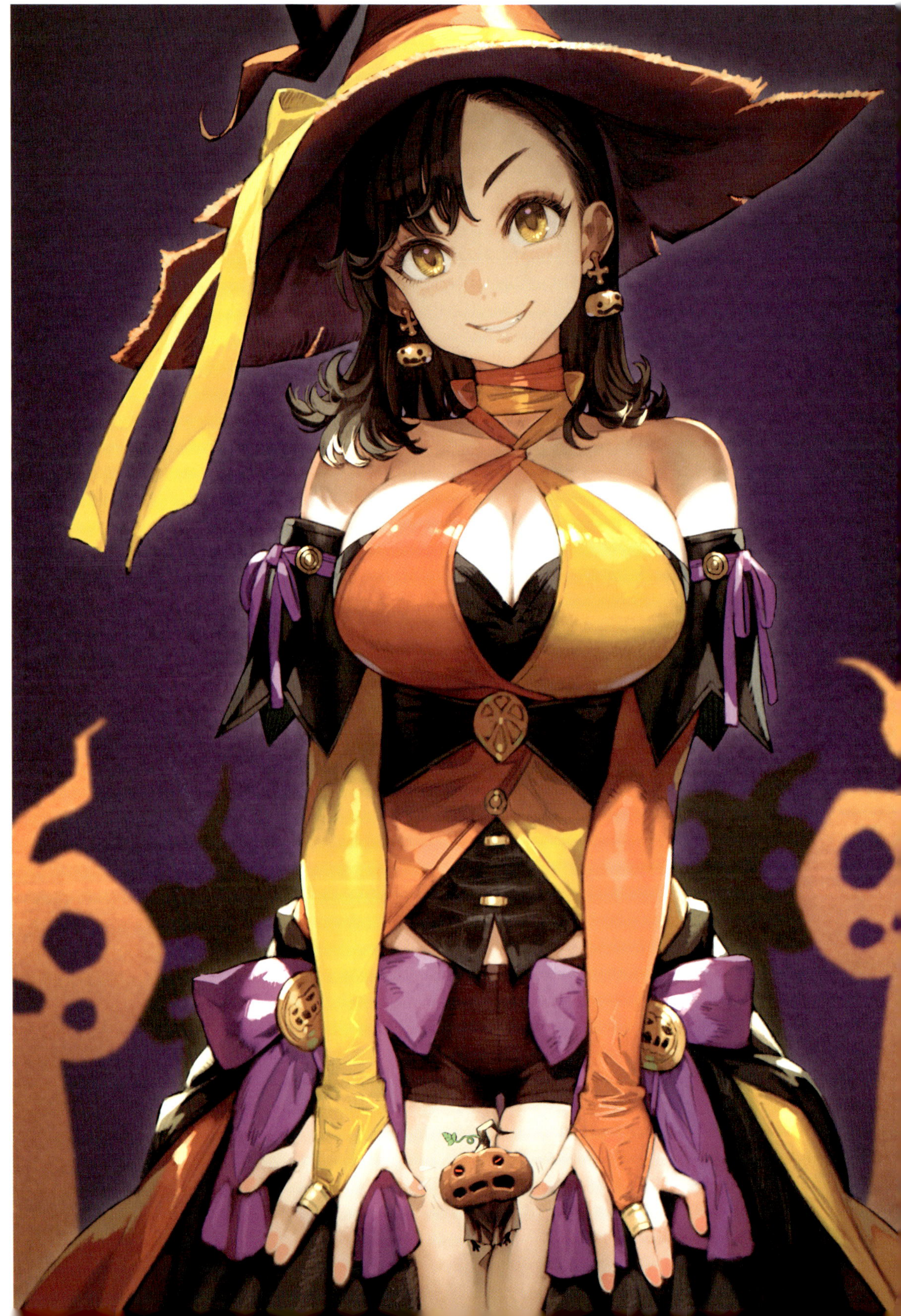

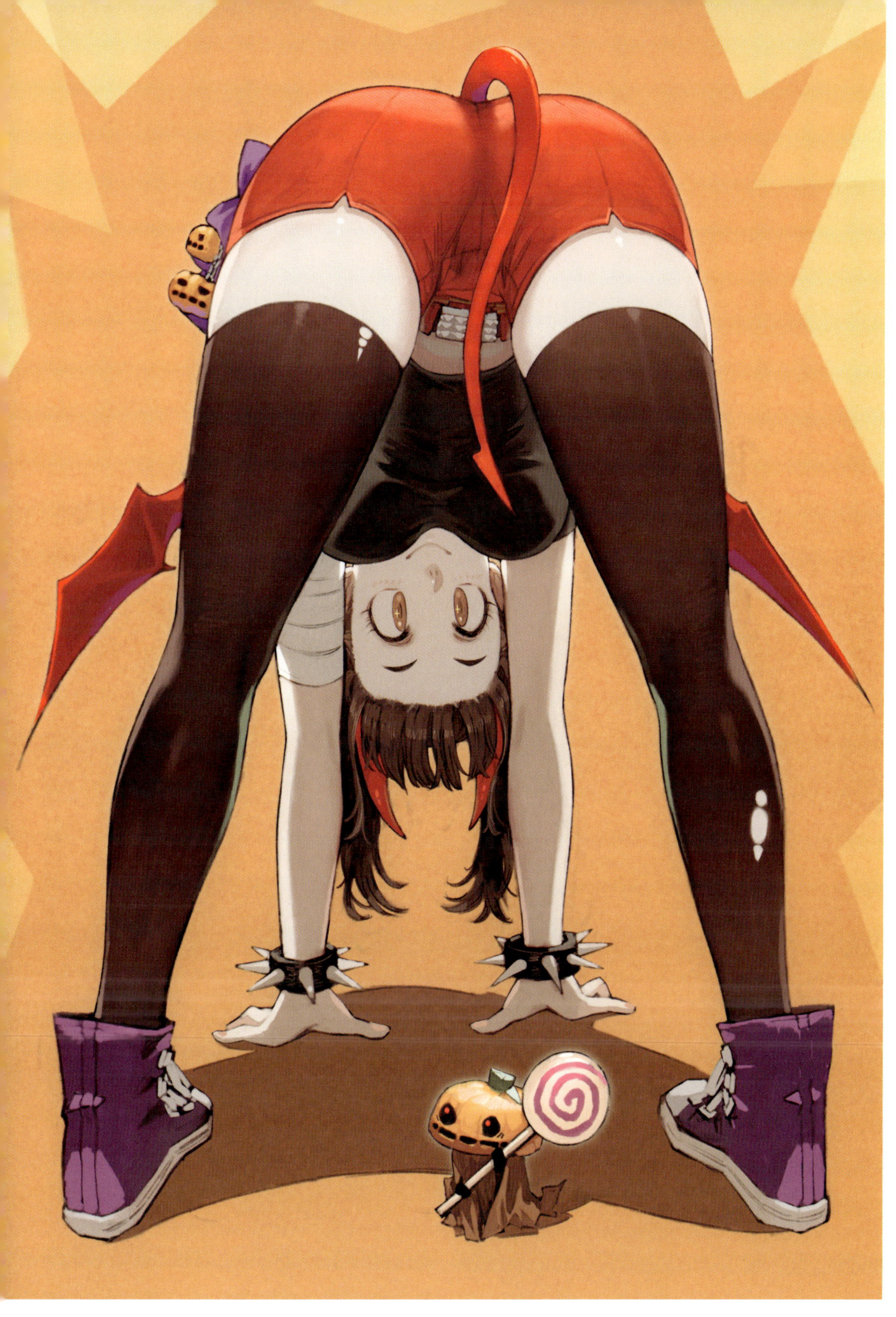

TITLE

"Found You!"

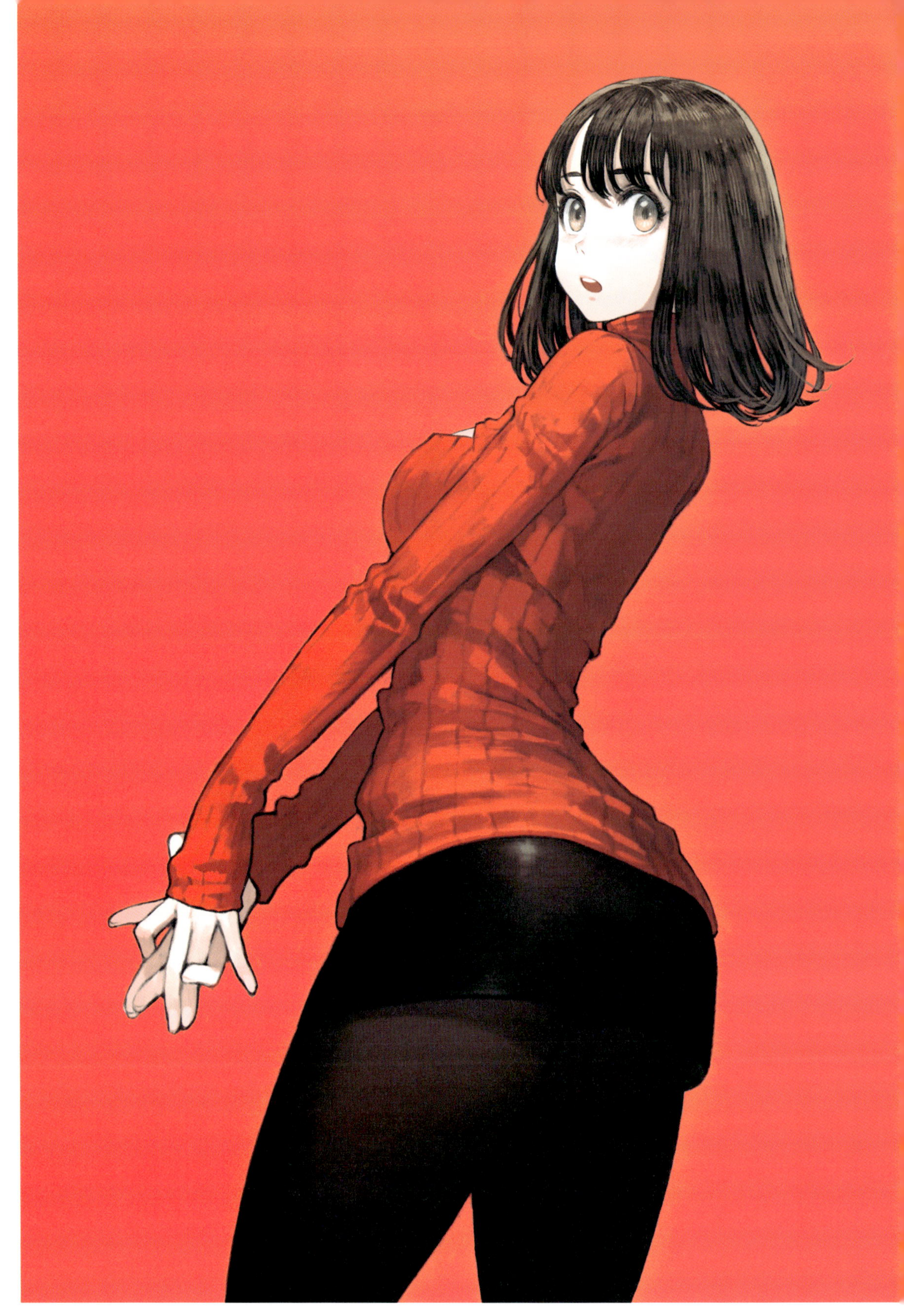

TITLE

"Sweater 1"

TITLE
"Sweater 2"

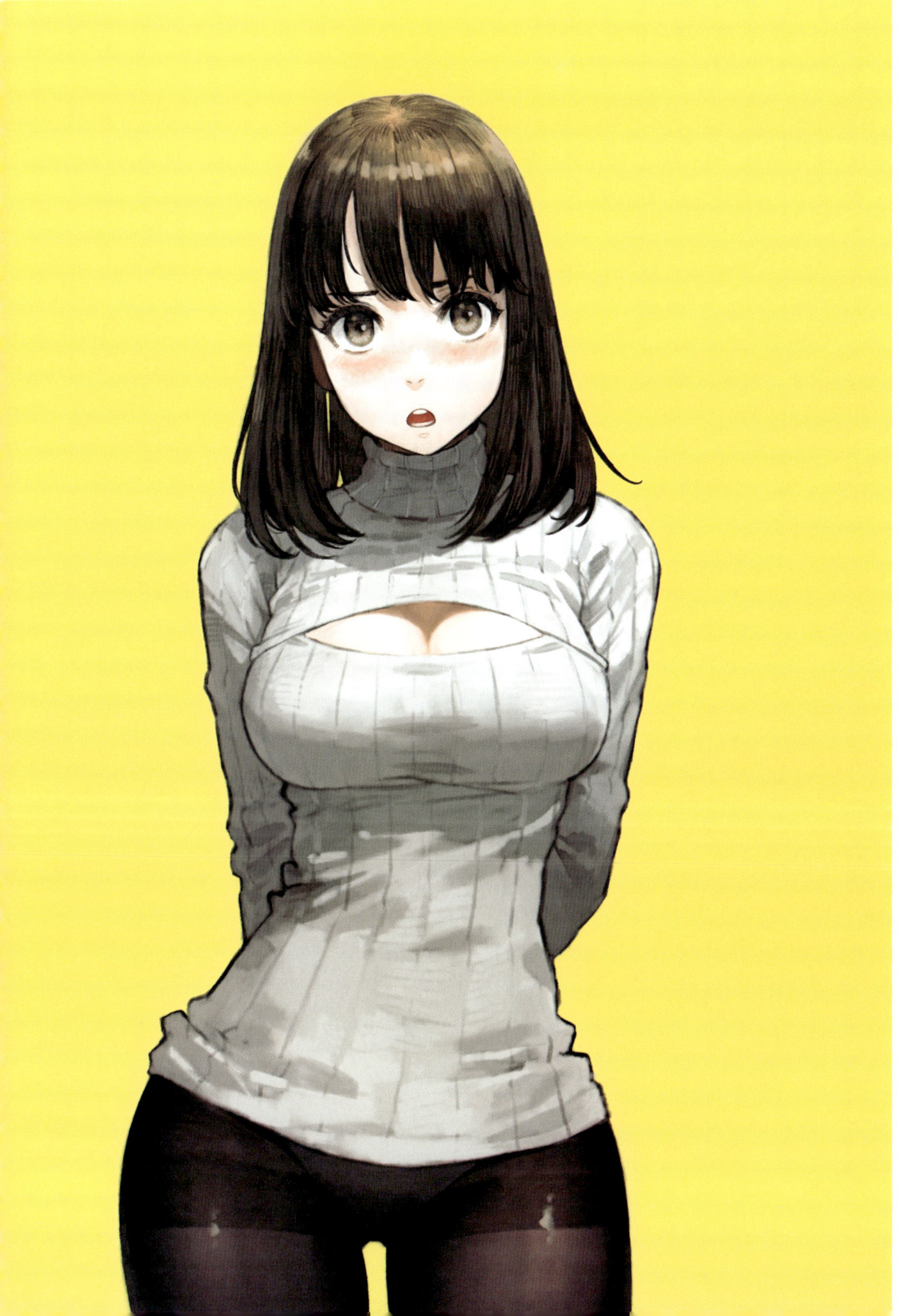

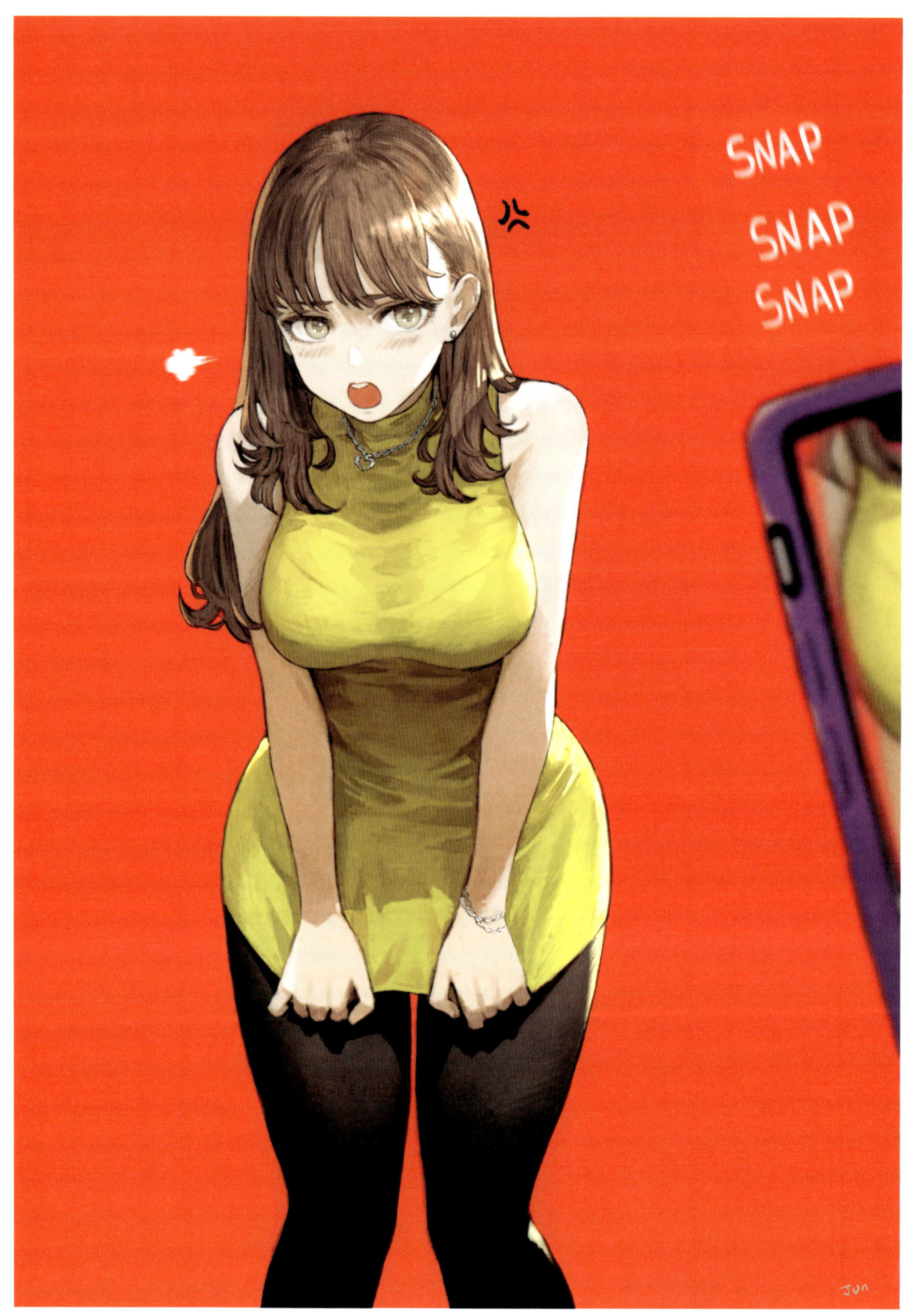

TITLE

"Because I'm Embarrassed"

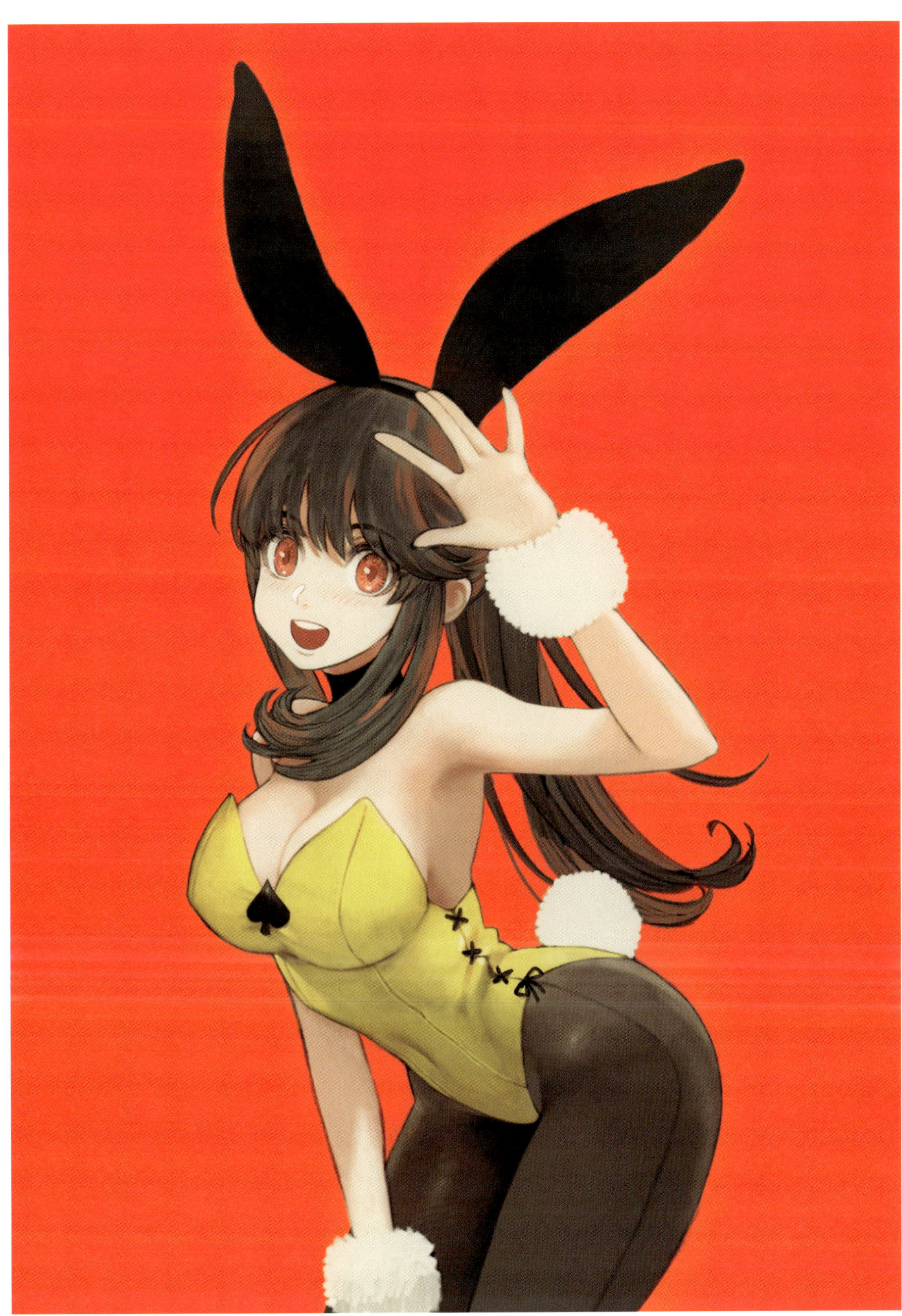

TITLE

"Bunny"

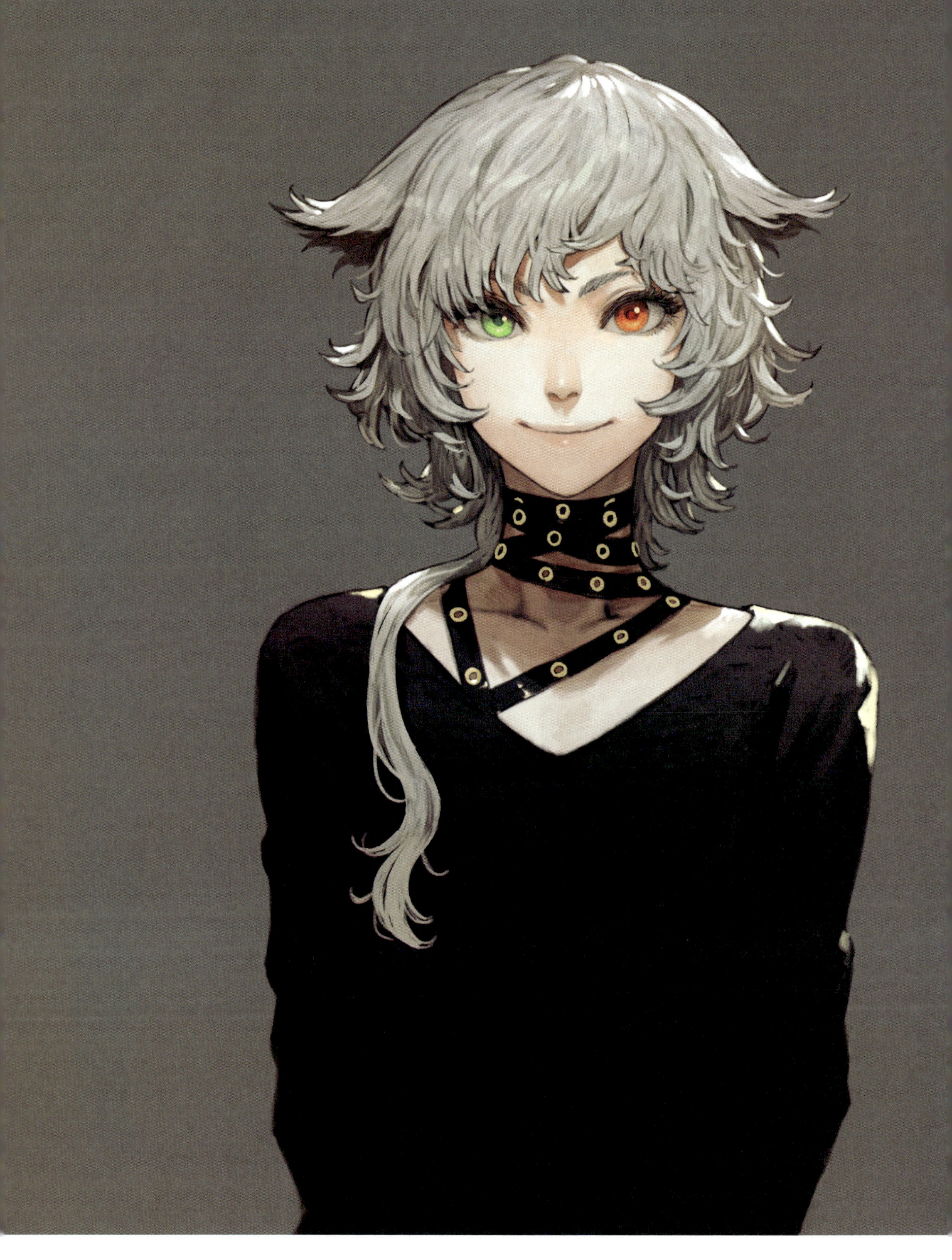

TITLE

"Odd-Eyed"

TITLE
"Sweater 3"

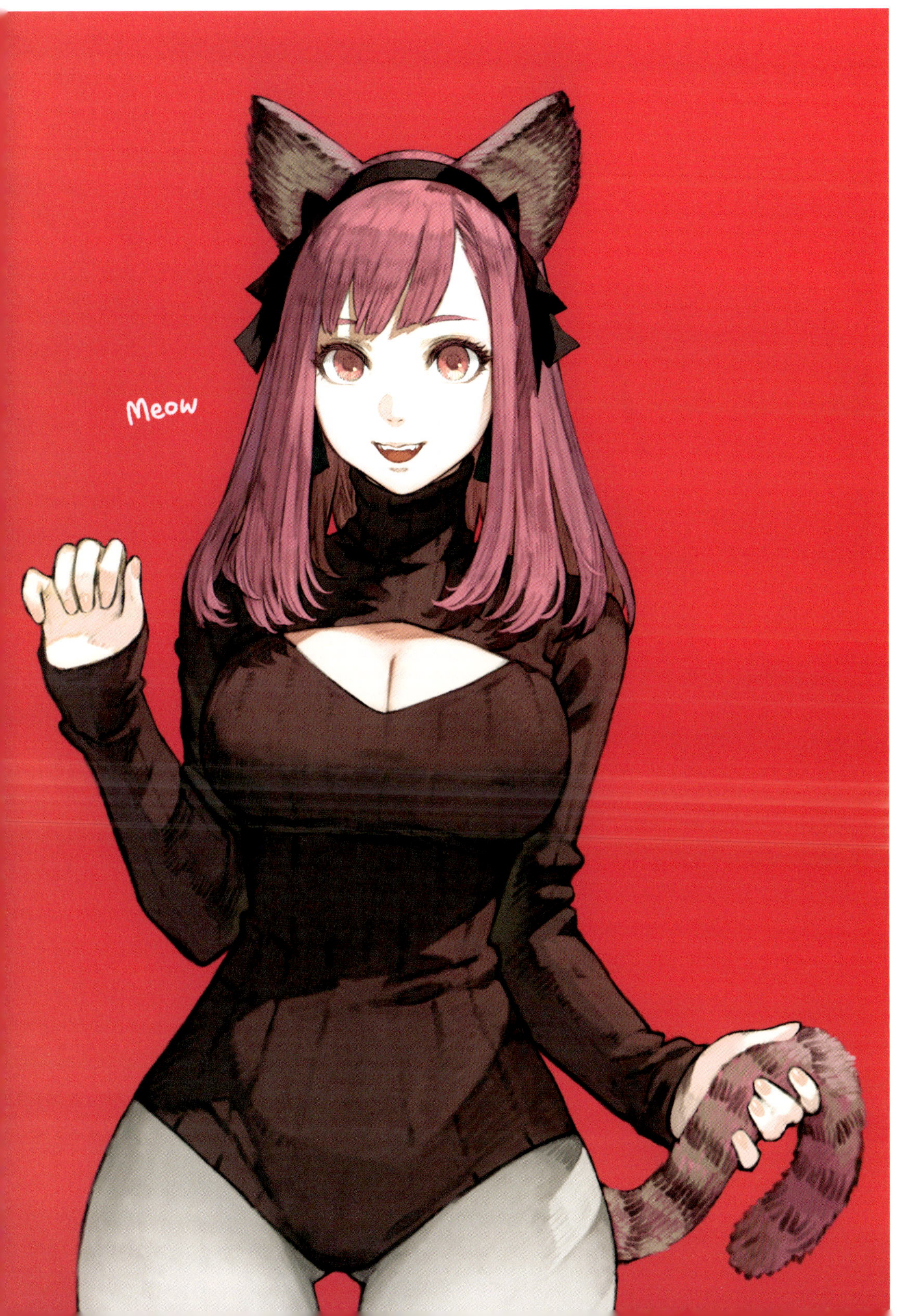

TITLE
"Feburary 14th"

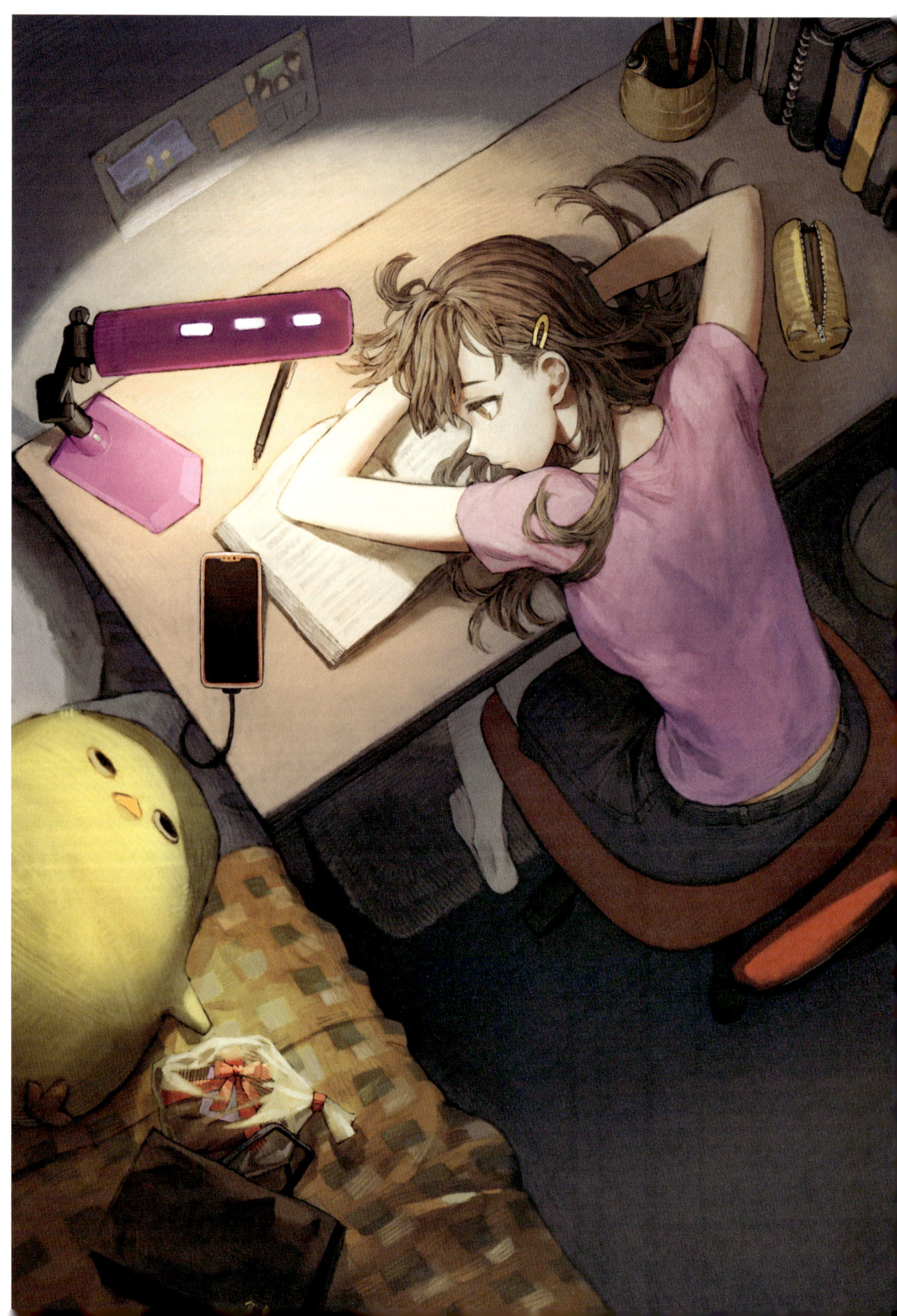

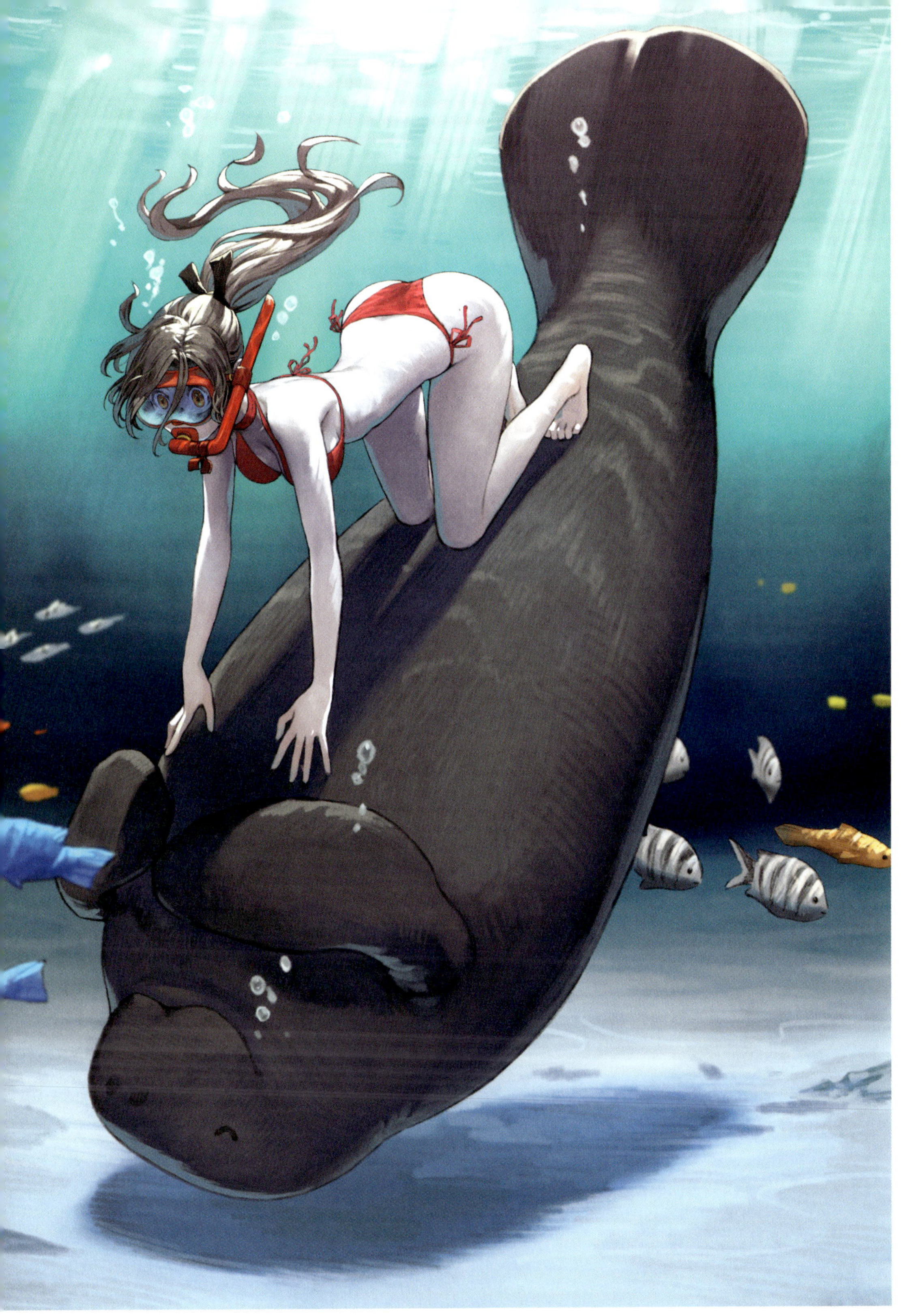

TITLE

"Manatee"

TITLE

"Headache"

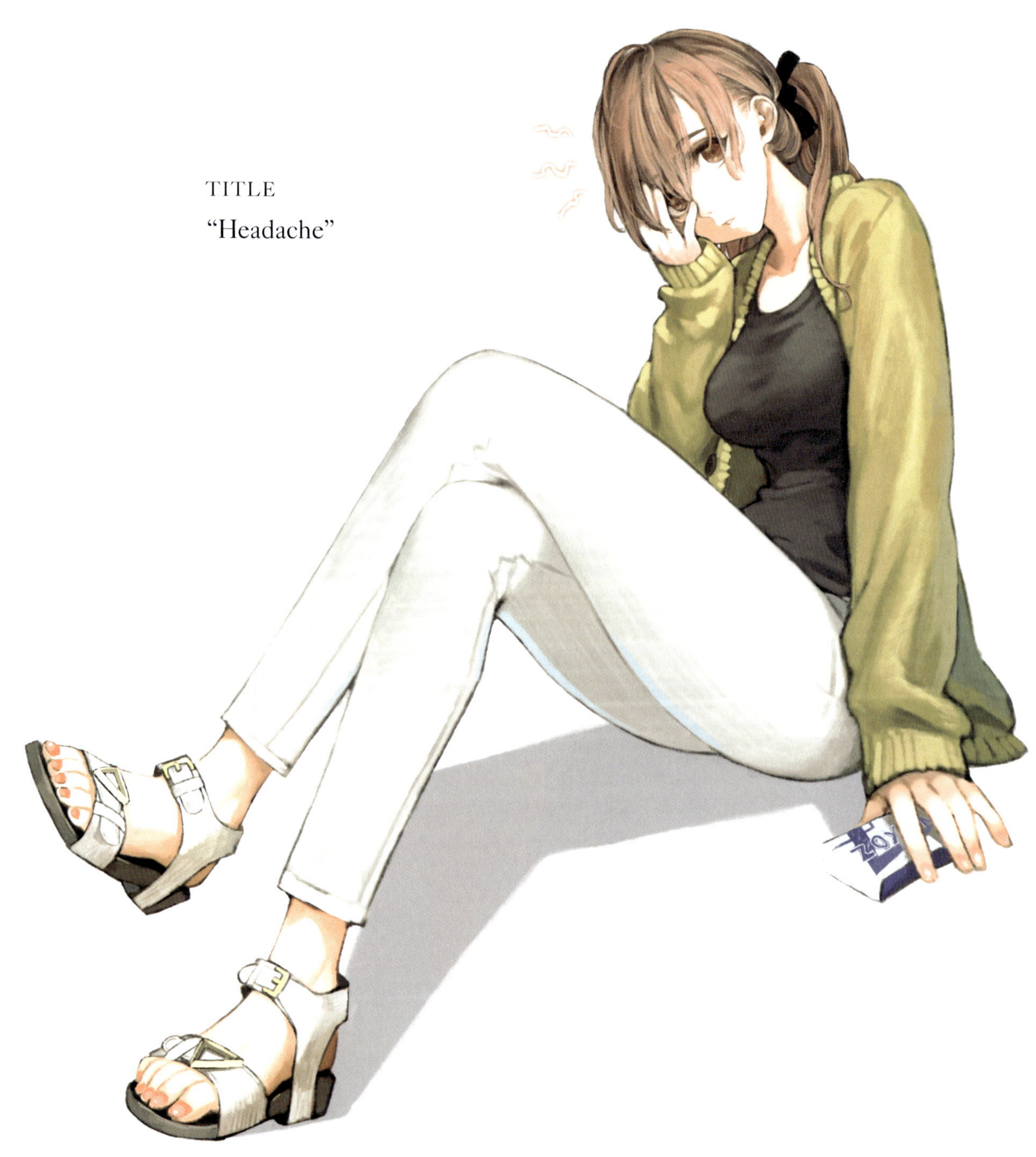

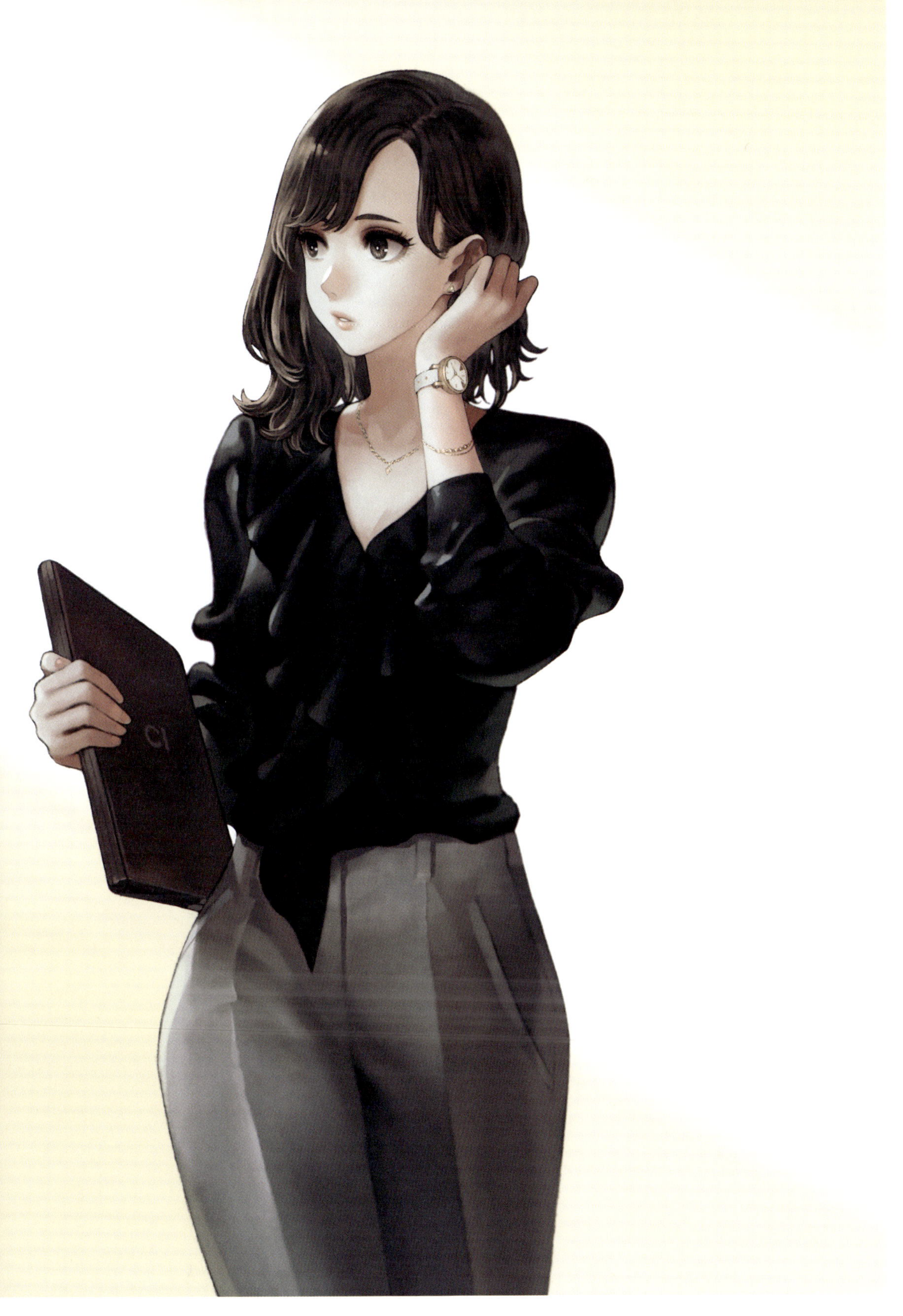

TITLE

"Office Lady"

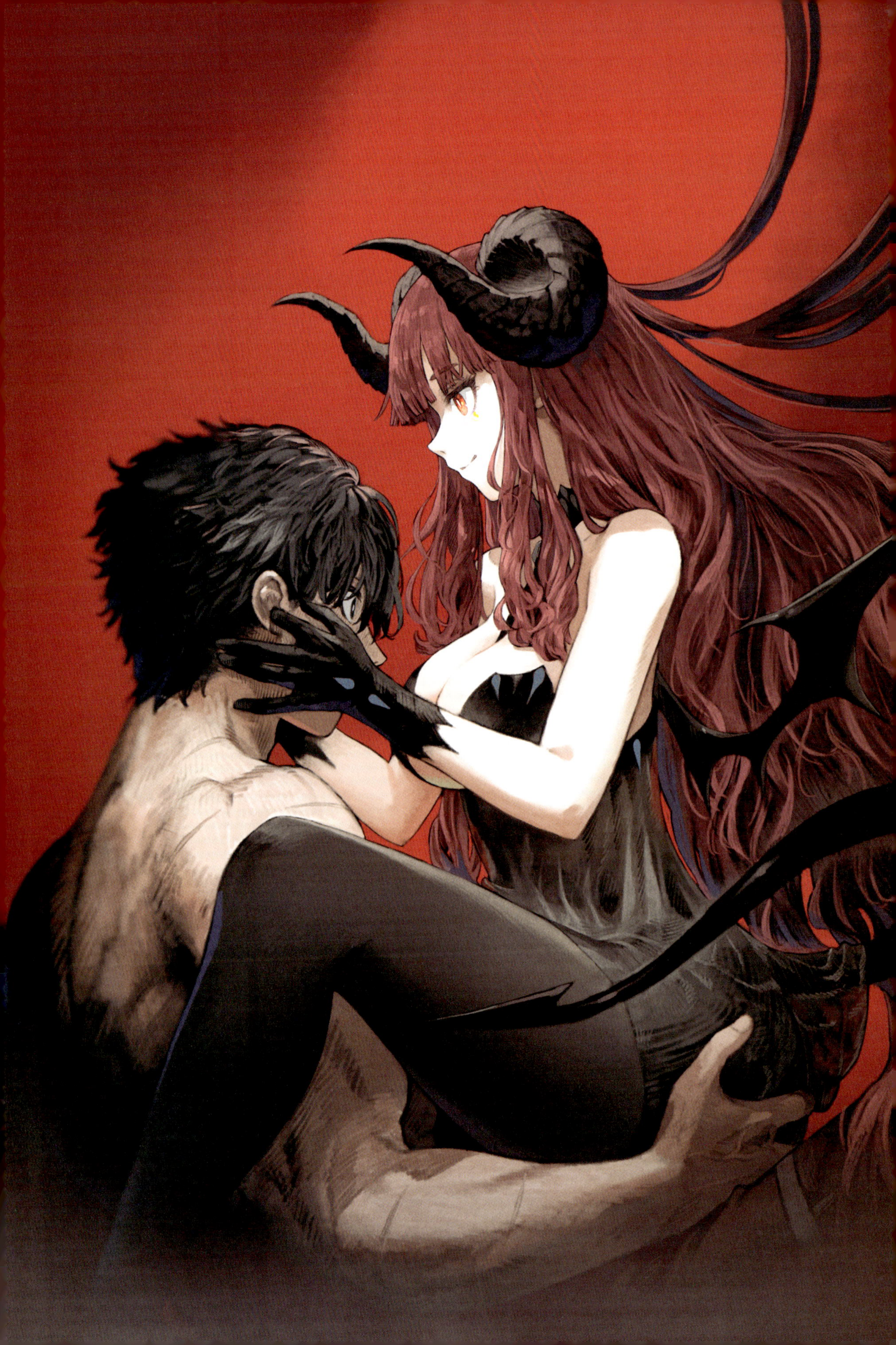

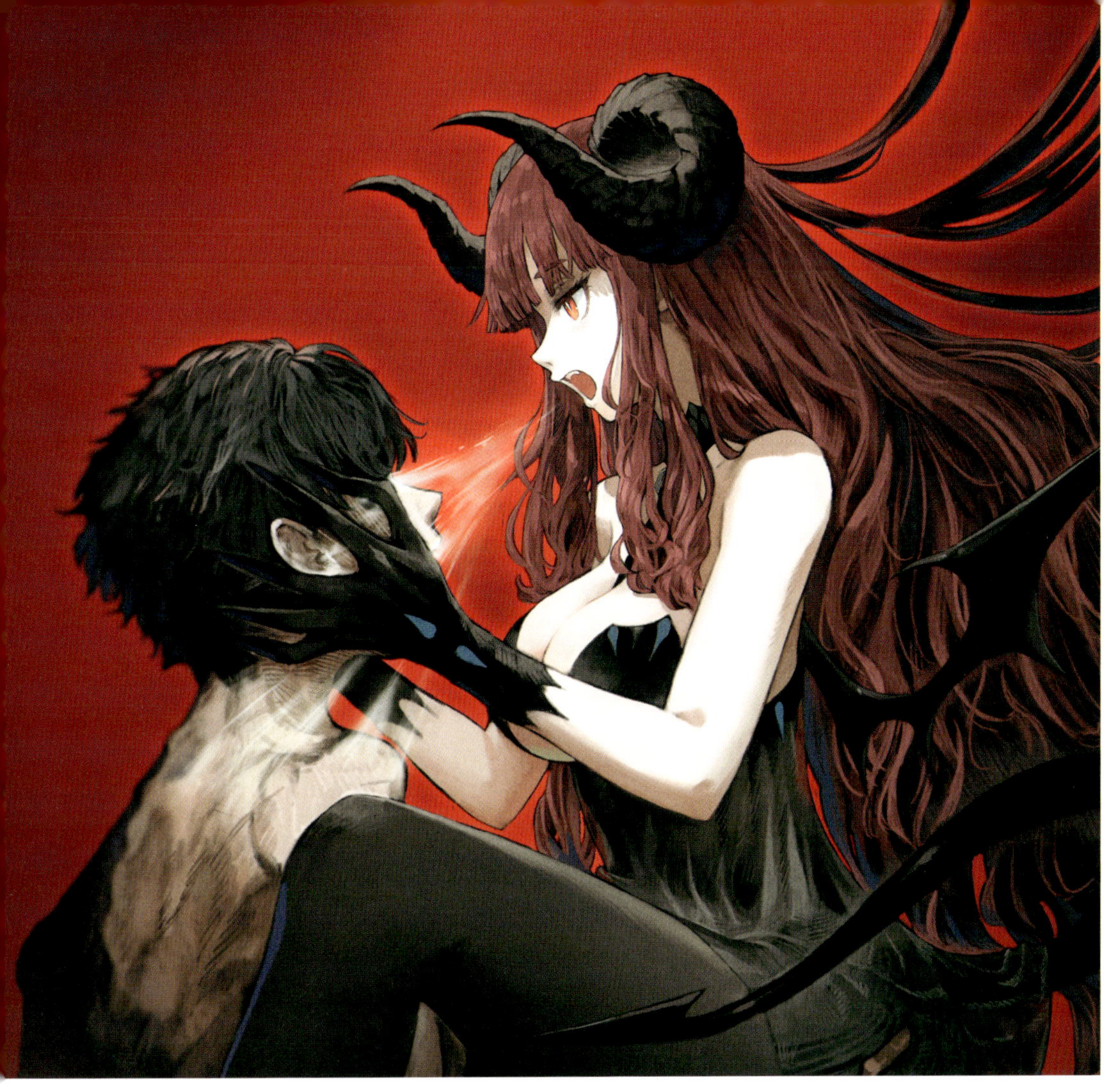

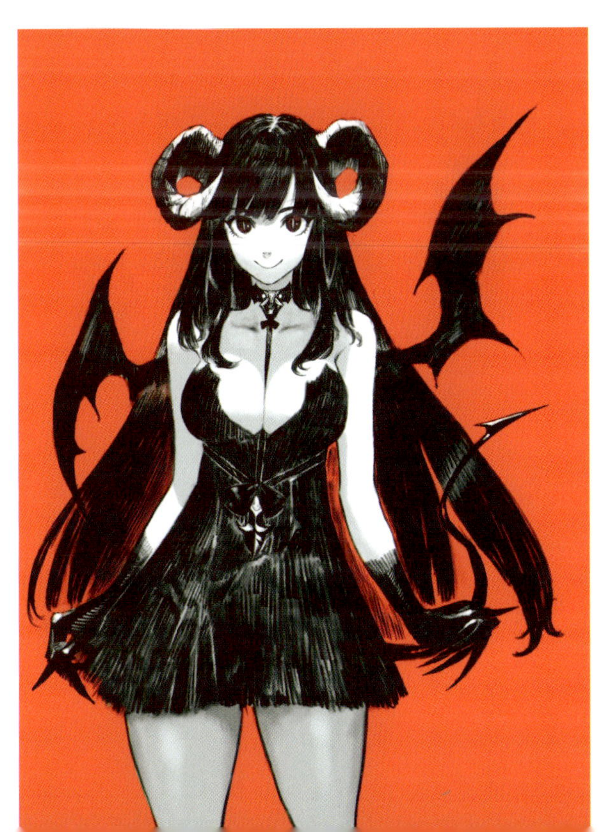

TITLE

"Succubus"

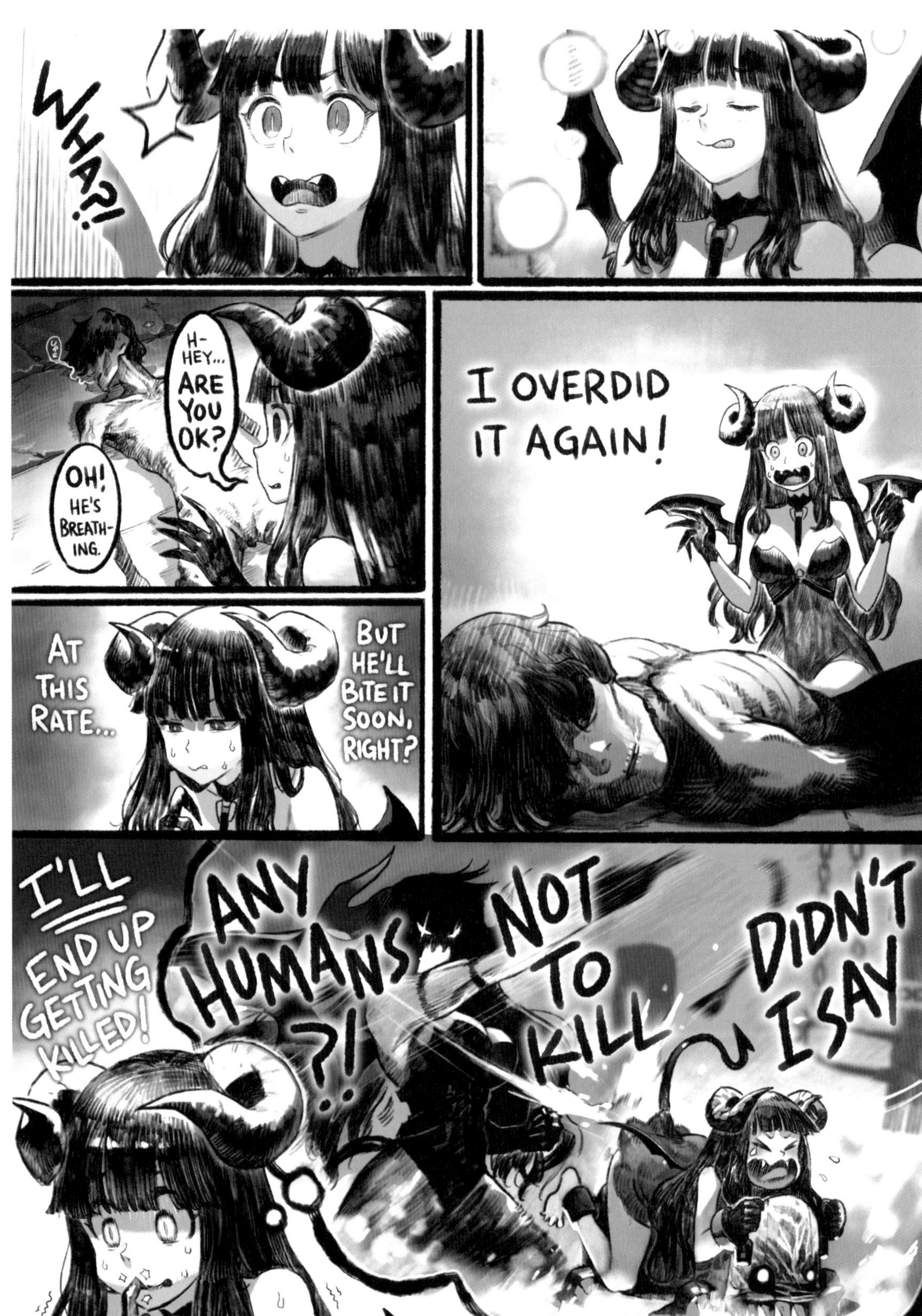
WHA?!
H-HEY... ARE YOU OK?
OH! HE'S BREATH-ING.
AT THIS RATE...
BUT HE'LL BITE IT SOON, RIGHT?
I OVERDID IT AGAIN!
I'LL END UP GETTING KILLED!
ANY HUMANS ?!
NOT TO KILL
DIDN'T I SAY

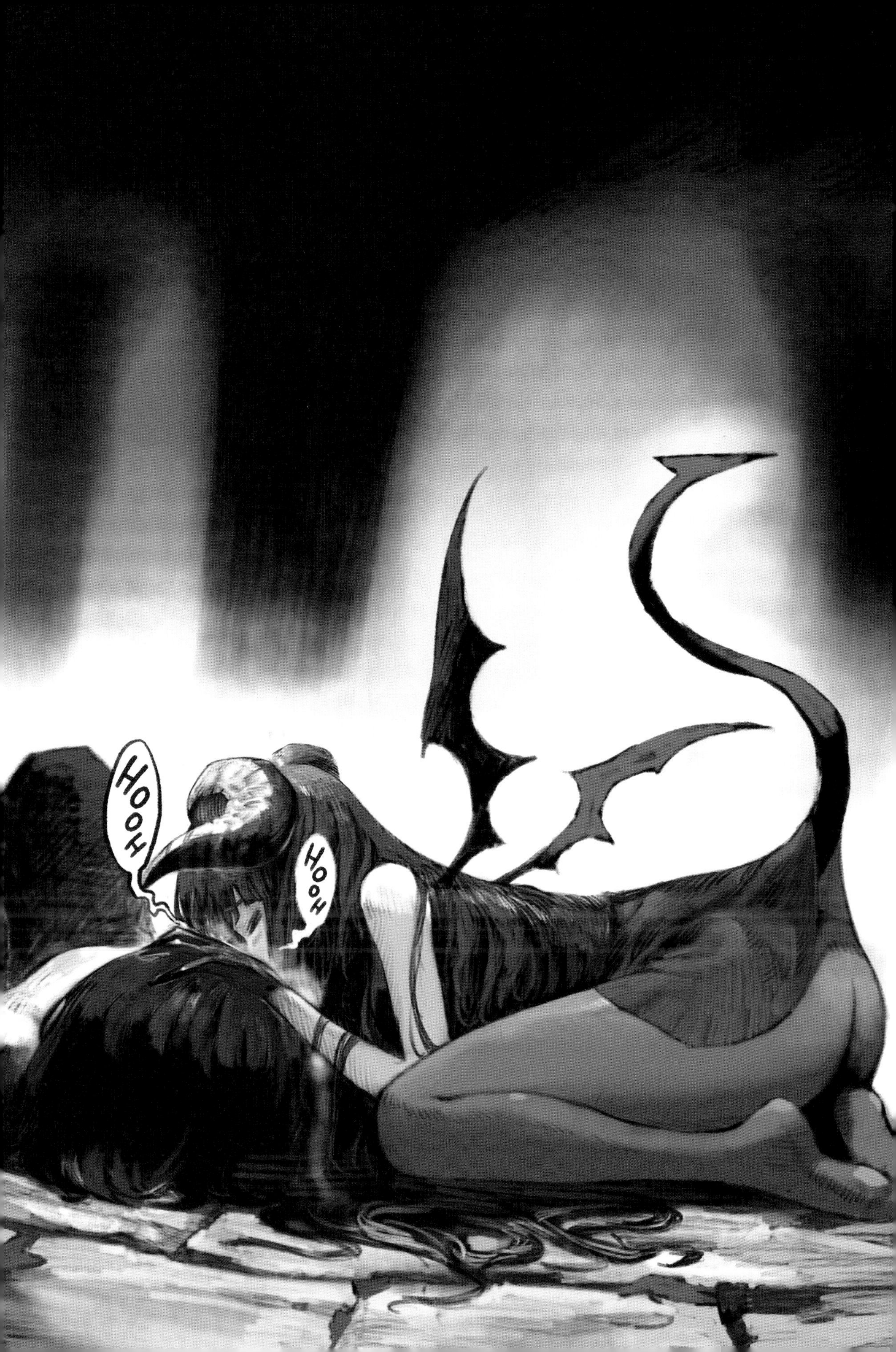

HOOH
HOOH

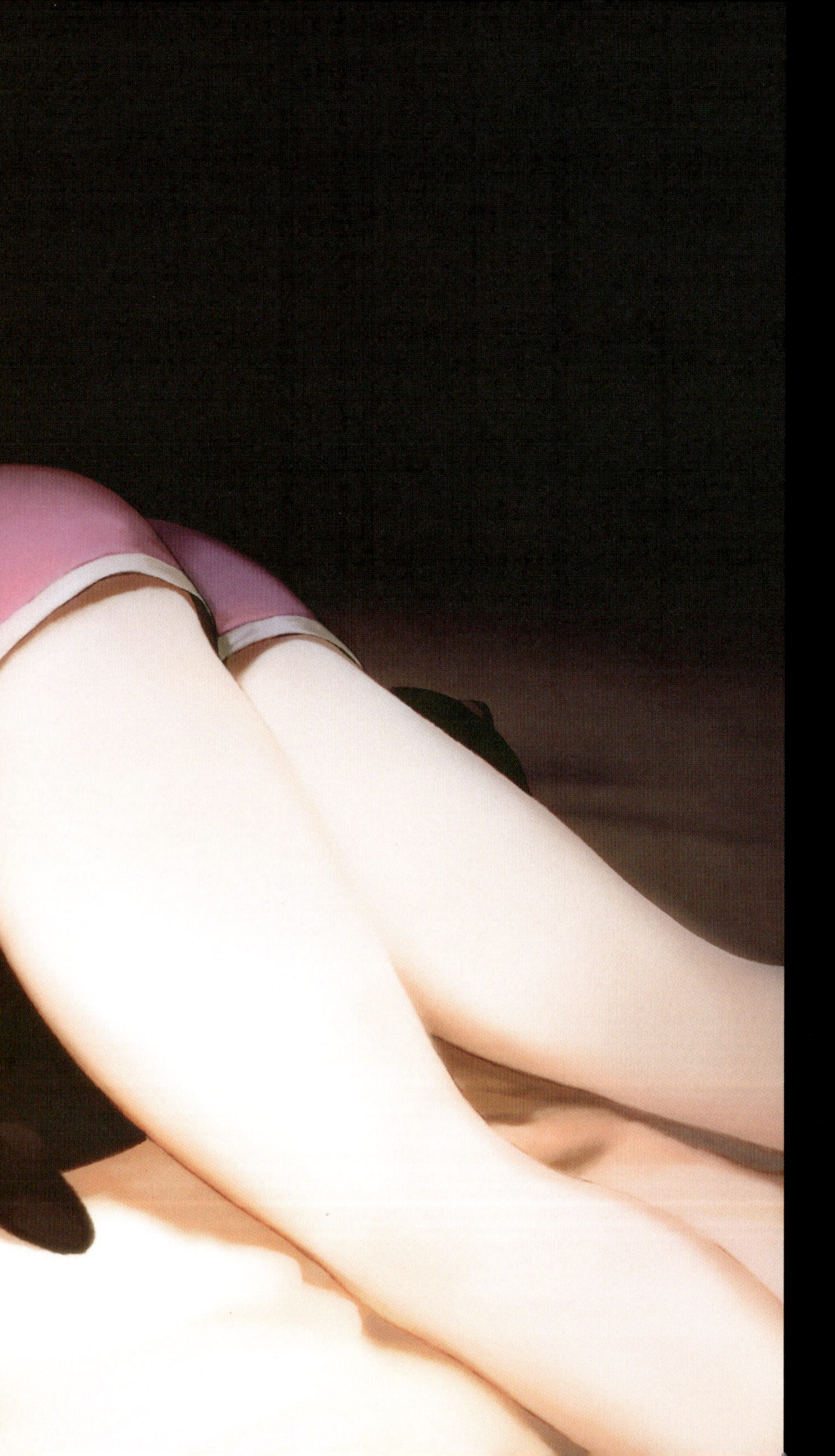

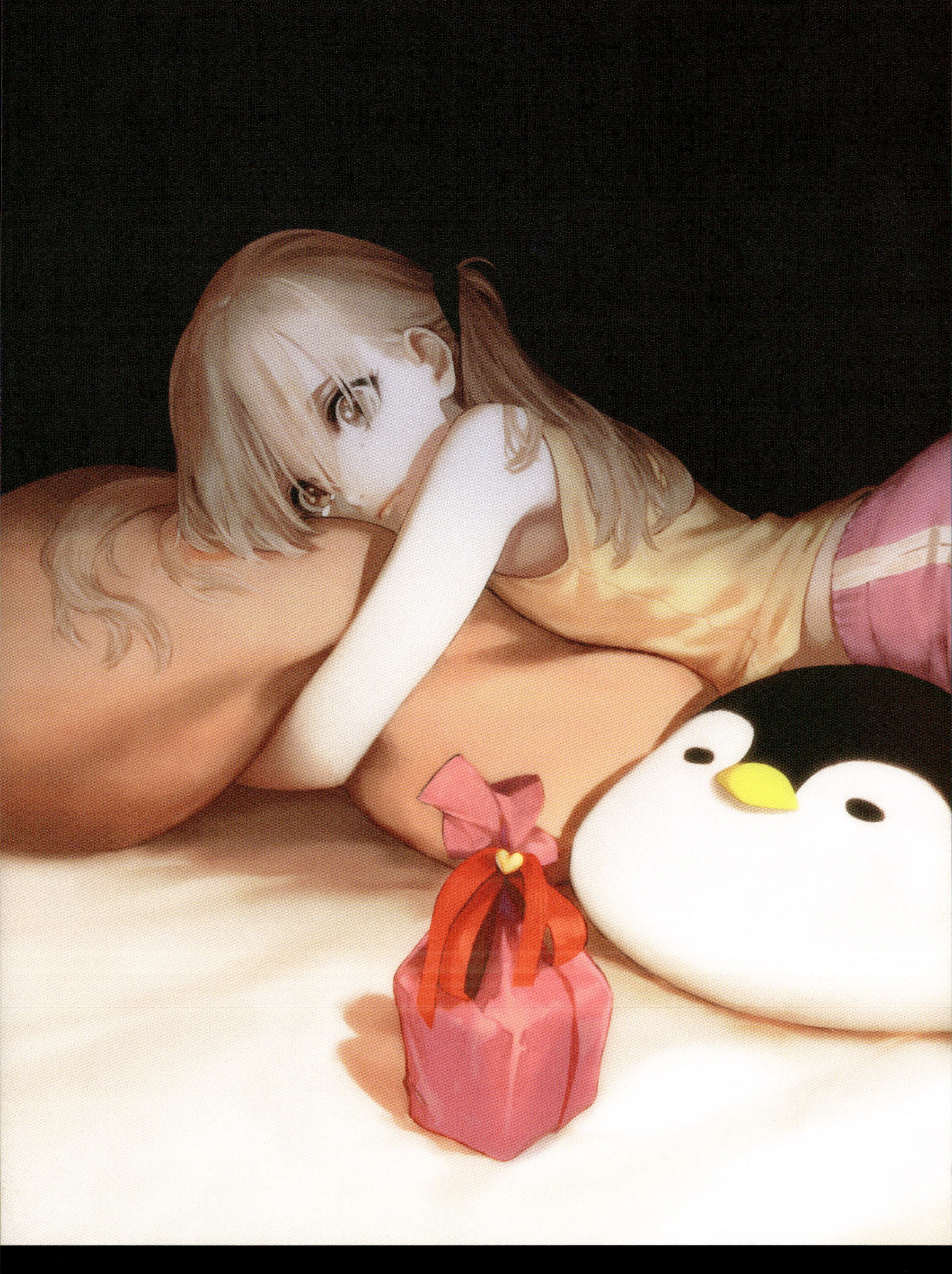

TITLE
"I Couldn't Give It"

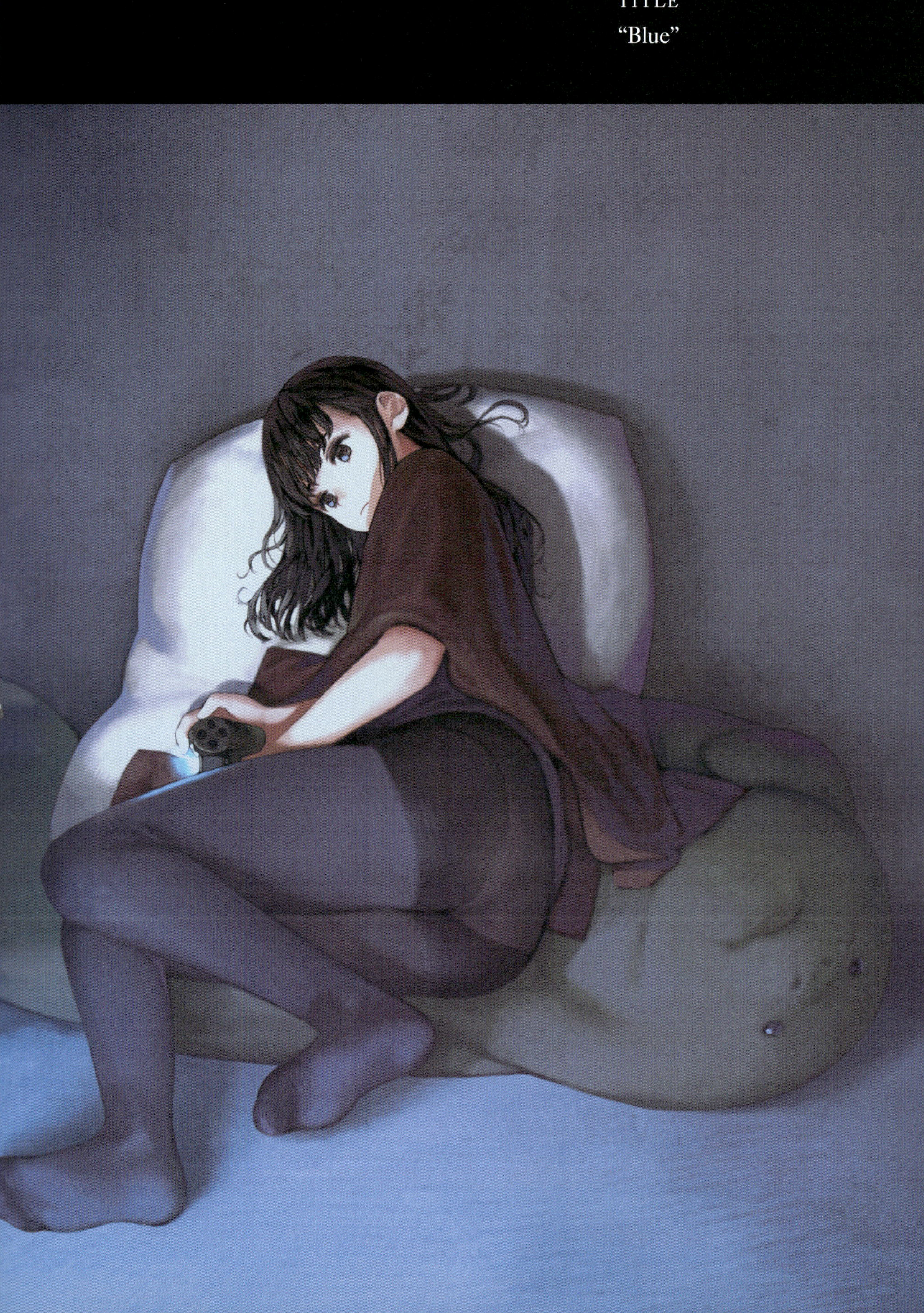

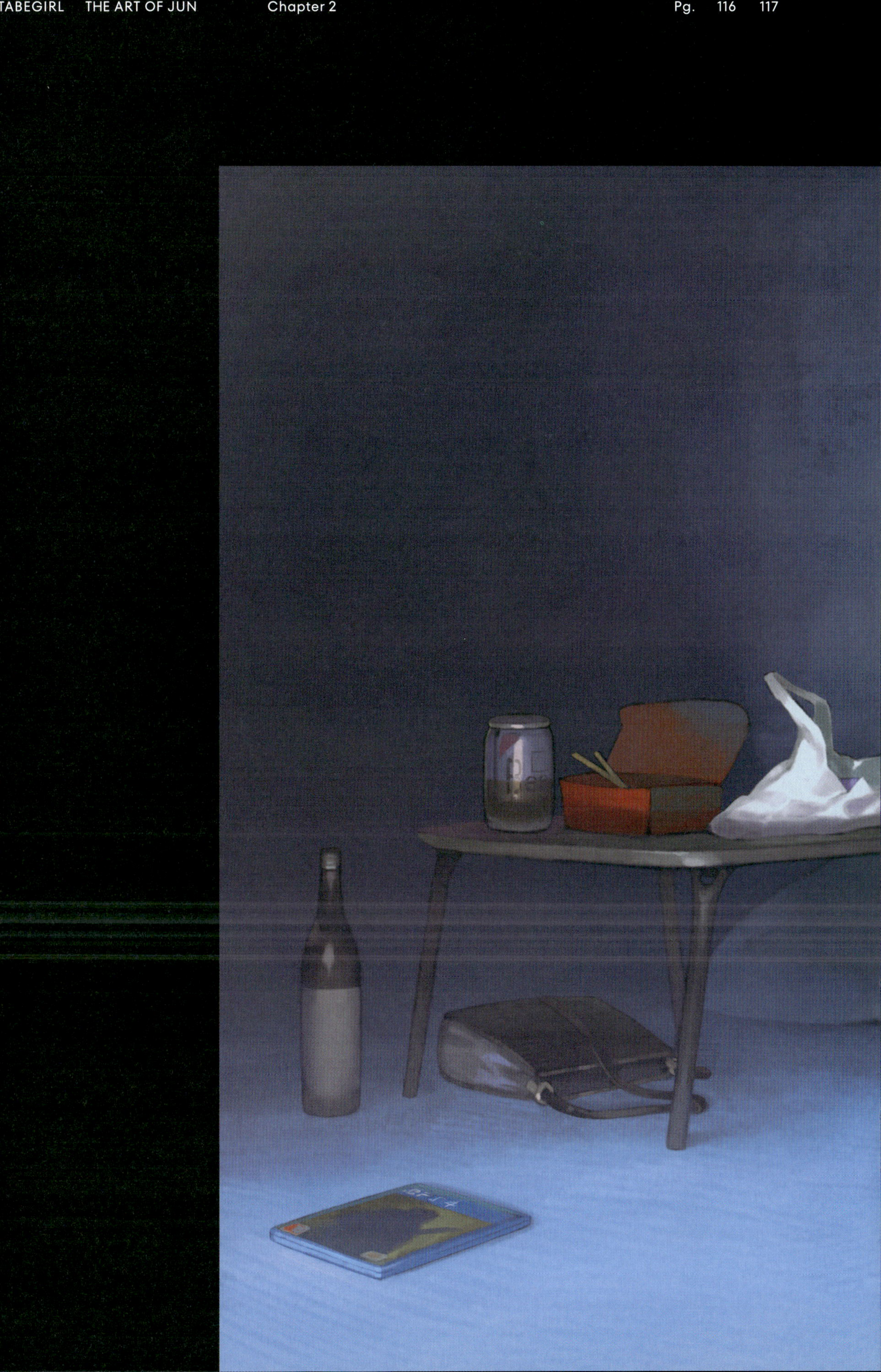

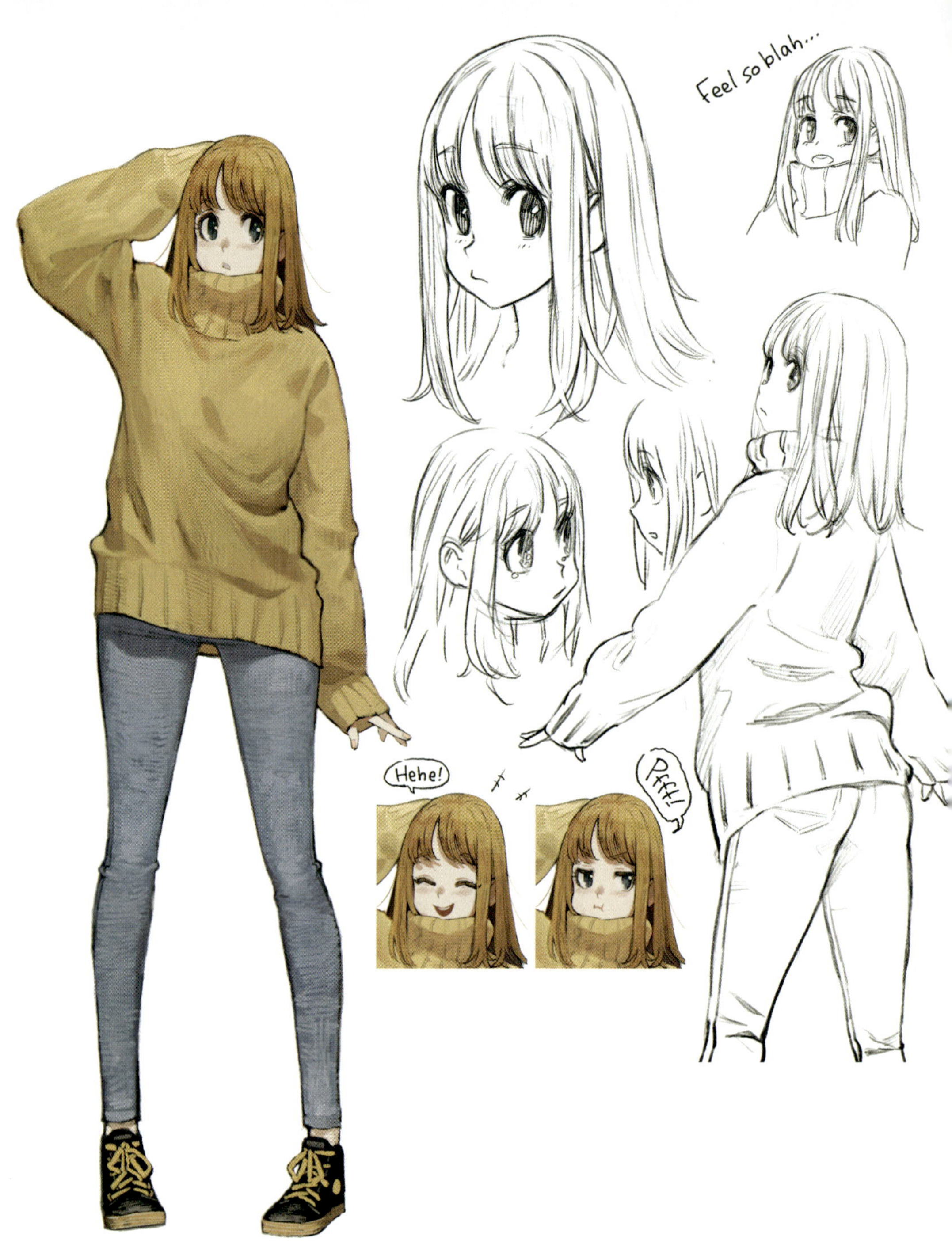

TITLE

"Character Designs 1"

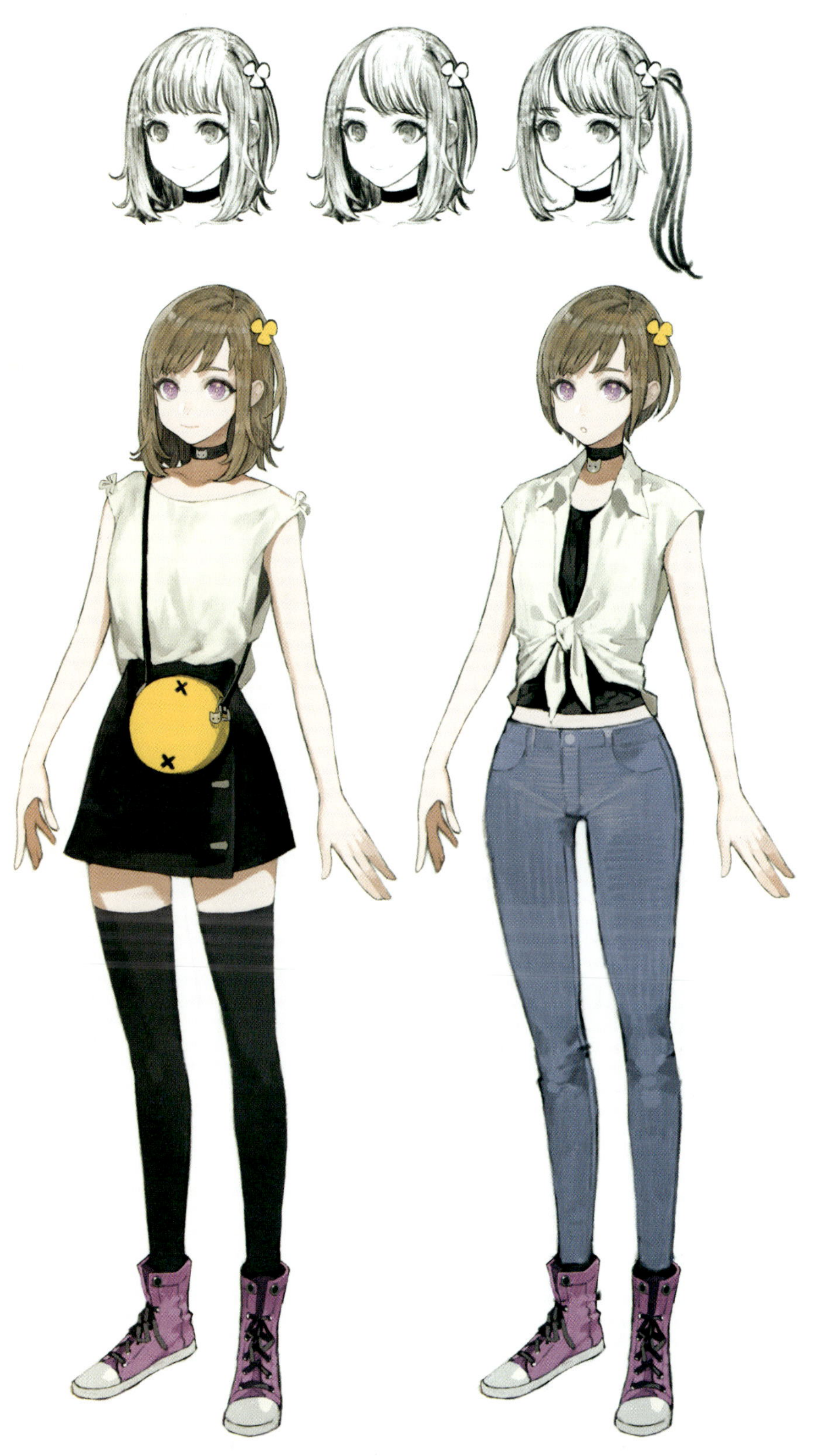

In my case, when I pour my energy into several drawings after I see an interesting work, I'll certainly fall into a slump later. When that happens, the simplest solution for me is to go to sleep early that day and draw the next morning. If I'm still in a slump after that I think the most important thing is to believe that right now I can't draw for some reason, but I will be able to again for sure. I think skilled illustrators all have times when they can't draw well, so I think it's important to look at myself objectively and figure out quickly when the downturn is going to come and where it's going to come from.

That's a difficult question (laughs). Honestly, there are many people with astonishing skill in the industry, and I don't think my own abilities are that exceptional. But looking back on how I've continued drawing so far, I'd recommend first drawing a lot. I'm an otaku to the core, and I remember worrying every day about how to draw fan art of a property I liked in a way that it would look lovely to its fans. Those layers of love for various properties are there in my work now, I feel.

In my own experience, rather than trying to be conscious of honing the fundamentals and drawing well, it was more important to first come up with a realistic scheme to be able keep drawing and having fun. The time to take on the challenge of trying to go pro is different for everybody, but I think those days that you keep drawing slow and steady and keep gaining that experience will eventually lead to becoming a professional.

If time allows, I'd like to do illustrations bringing together the Tabegirls and fantasy characters I've done so far. Since I love fantasy, I'd love to focus on fantasy-type illustrations! I'd like to do more illustrations with backgrounds that give you a sense of the world.

My name is Jun, I'm the author. Thank you truly to the fans who always support me, and those who have picked up this art book by chance, for purchasing this book. Thanks to everyone's support, my work is in book form for the first time and is out in the world. I appreciate it from the bottom of my heart. I'll continue to release work on social media, so I look forward to seeing you again into the future.

(Composition: Yoshihiro Goto [C-Garden])

The interview with Jun starts on page 125 and ends on page 122.

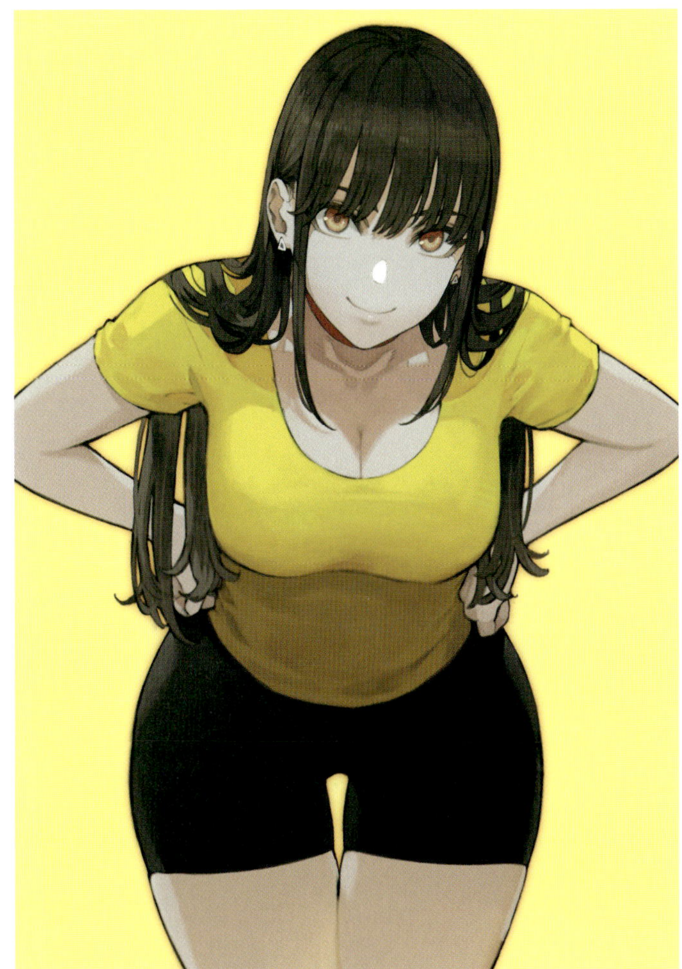

You say drawing faces is your main focus, so how do you make them cute?

This may be an obvious answer, but I think when it comes to the faces and poses it's important to draw them when my drawing's at its best. If it won't come out right no matter what I do, then I think it's good to stop for a while and just have a nap. If I draw after a good sleep, I can usually draw that cute face, but if it's still not coming out well, I think the idea as a whole is no good. That's when I give up any attachment to it and erase the whole thing and start over.

The expressions and atmosphere of your characters' are really appealing. What are you conscious of when drawing them?

It differs depending on the illustration, but what I always want to express in my illustrations is a balance of stylishness and cuteness. When those two seemingly opposing elements are expressed well in a drawing I've made, that's the most pleasant feeling for me. I'll keep redrawing it until I feel the conviction within myself that "Ooh, that's cute!" I often rely on my own senses.

Do you ever get stuck in the process?

In my case, I think the biggest cause of getting creatively stuck is tiredness. If I work on personal projects after work for days on end, it'll definitely happen. If I don't squeeze in a moderate amount of play and rest my creative flexibility suffers. That's something I feel I finally understood after become a professional.

using *CLIP STUDIO PAINT*. For pastime illustrations and personal work, I do everything with *Procreate* on the iPad. The biggest advantage of the iPad is that you can draw anywhere, I think. To be honest, I don't think the process is as efficient as on a PC, but personally I feel being able to draw anywhere is a big attraction, so I've tailored my drawing process itself to suit *Procreate*.

Where do you most often get ideas from when making illustrations?

Mostly video games that I enjoy playing, or interesting anime soundtracks. In many cases, I get the mood for an illustration or a sense of the characters from music.

Please talk about genres or themes that you like. Also, what is it you like about them?

The genre I like most is fantasy. I like the freedom of various ideas you can experience in an invented world. I used to enjoy drawing fantasy world weapons and armor, but now I'm most fixated on characters' faces. I keep redrawing them over and over trying constantly trying to figure out how to make them the most cute.

What's the most common feeling among fans of your illustrations? Also, what opinions please you or leave an impression on you?

I feel like a lot of people say, "I wish I could draw like you," not only in Japan but also overseas. Basically, all of their thoughts make me happy, of course, But when they say, "I wish I could draw like you," I feel like others have noticed the effort and passion that went into the work that I myself don't notice. Their words simply make me happy, so every time I see an opinion like that I think, "I'm gonna work even harder!"

Do you do anything to increase your motivation?

This might be simplistic, but I play video games or watch anime. The "enjoyable experience" of playing a game or an interesting anime connects directly to my creativity as motivation. I particularly love passionate stories! Those tend to stimulate my own sensitivities, and memories of them spark my own creative feelings. And when my feelings are heightened, it becomes easy to make illustrations!

Could you talk about any pieces in the book that you particularly like?

If I was to choose something from this art book, the one I'm most taken with is the illustration of the girl eating pizza that I mentioned in my first answer. Maybe it's just a fluke, but I feel like there's something expressed in it that goes beyond the realm of what I was consciously able to draw at the time.

When did you decide you wanted to become an illustrator? Was there something that set you off?

I liked drawing since I was a child, but I was convinced that my drawings were different than the style that was currently popular, so I never thought that I would actually be able to become an illustrator. I finally genuinely made the decision in 2014. After graduating from university, I went to a trade school for illustration, and a professor there introduced me to some jobs and that was the start of it. So I did several jobs at that time, and even though I thought even if it's impossible right now, maybe someday I will be able to become an illustrator… and I just kept on drawing.

What's the origin of your pen name?

It comes from my real name.

What kind of practice did you do to learn to draw?

I remember in elementary school I used to copy characters from *Dr. Slump* and *Dragonball* a lot. Thinking about it now, that may have been the first step in learning to draw. Even in junior high, I continued copying and doodling, but from eleventh grade, I started seriously studying drawing, and I think that was extremely useful to this day. At the time, I hated studying, so being placed in a private art school environment where I "had to do it" was very useful, I think. After graduating from university I worked part time at an art school and did three-minute sketches with the students for about a year.

Can you talk about motifs that deeply impressed you when you from studying drawing in eleventh grade, and in what ways the three-minute sketches are useful to you even now?

I wouldn't say there were any deeply impressive motifs, but I drew plaster busts a lot. There were a lot of motifs for my university entrance exam. The three-minute sketches serve as training in observing the outlines of a subject in a short amount of time and that's one of the foundational abilities for drawing illustrations. Even now, sometimes when my pen stops while I'm working, I remember my experience from back then, and I become able to draw the illustration that I couldn't before. So I think it's a good thing I did that rough sketch work.

Looking back on your creative activity so far, what are your own feelings about it?

As you'd expect, I love the act of creating art. Like most illustrators, from childhood I just doodled naturally (laughs). There was no one thing in particular that you could say made me like art, but I won top prize in a local high school student art show. I still can't say that like studying drawing, but thinking about it now, that was my first experience of my abilities being recognized by those around me. That was

when I came to think, "I want to get even better at this." That said, in my university days, I was totally obsessed with online games and I completely stopped doing illustrations as a pastime (laughs). I think my being able to keep drawing like this now is because I wholeheartedly love drawing.

Can you explain the reasons for your interest in popular forms of entertainment?

It's the influence of all the anime I've watched since I was little. The first thing that had an impact on me was the OVA *Mobile Suit Gundam 0083 STARDUST MEMORY* which I rented from a video shop. That's when I first learned about the existence of *Gundam*. That anime of such incredible quality existed in the world really affected me.

Can you tell us about works or creators that influenced you?

Berserk which I read from the time I was a kid! My taste for degree of detail, hatching, and powerful action all came from that series. That's what started my interest in fantasy as a genre.

How did you start posting art on *Twitter*? Also, are there any posts you have a special attachment to?

When I started at the trade school, everyone around me was using *Twitter*, so I started posting on there too. The posts I feel attached to are the *Dragon Quest XI: Echoes of an Elusive Age* fan art. That was when I first experienced a buzz and thought, "*Twitter* is interesting!!" My phone kept ringing with notifications all day, and it made a big impression on me.

In July 2020 you were part of a live event in front of students. What are the differences drawing live versus how you usually work?

I'm not that reluctant to talk while I draw, so it wasn't that different than usual, but recently I've started by preparing roughs. Even if it's a short live event, that way I often end up with a decent piece.

What pieces have you worked on that left a particular impression?

I did multiple drawings for a game called *World of Final Fantasy* for Square Enix. It was my first time to be involved with a famous title. The process was really fun, and I drew for days listening to *Final Fantasy* music and hardly sleeping or resting.

What parts of the process of creating an illustration do you like?

I often go straight from creating sketches to coloring. If I'm assigned an illustration job, I often do a tight line drawing. The part I enjoy the most is coloring. Seeing the process as it nears completion is nice.

What tools do you use for your art?

For illustrations for work, I used to draw in *Photoshop*, but since I became an illustrator the year before last I've been

INTERVIEW

Profile

A popular illustrator that creates under their original hashtags #tabegirl and #BushiHimeWeapons (#武姫Weapons). Jun is greatly supported by fans both domestic and abroad, and as of September 2022, they have 680,200 *Twitter* followers and 280,000 *Instagram* followers (as of October 2022).

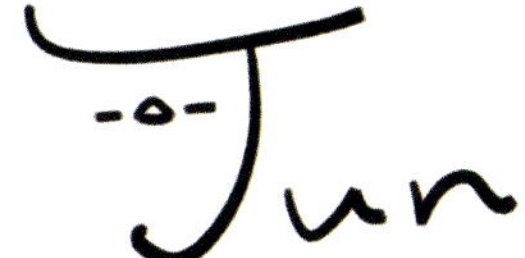

What was the genesis of the Tabegirl (girls eating) theme?

It started about four years ago while I was taking a breather from doing a lot of fantasy illustrations. An illustration of a girl eating pizza (page 18) caused some buzz, and I thought more might catch on so I kept drawing them.

What was the thought process that brought you to the name "Tabegirl"?

Certain things that were trendy in Japan for a time like "Forest Girl" and "City Boy" made me think of it.

What do you think is the appeal of "Tabegirl"?

The theme of "Tabegirl" is characters who have outstanding style even though they consume an amount of food that would normally be unthinkable. In a sense it's a fantasy. I don't eat that much myself, but when I first started drawing it, the fans enjoyed it. Based on everyone's responses, I thought it would be interesting to have the slightly ironic themes of "junk + gluttony", the opposite of health. I just wanted to have fun on social media, and didn't think about it too deeply. So, it made me happy that there were so many people out there who shared my feelings.

Is there anything you're particularly careful about or conscious of when doing "Tabegirl" illustrations?

I think the most important thing is to depict the food in a way that makes it seem tasty. Personally, I don't have that many favorite foods, so I try to draw each one so it looks as delicious as possible.

How did you come up with the sister main characters?

At first it was just the older sister. But to increase the narrative quality of it, I needed a side character so I created the kid sister. People sometimes ask, but I actually have a sister that's five years younger. But she's quite tough and not at all the small little weakling type like the one in "Tabegirl" (laughs).

Could you talk about any of the background of each sister? What about things behind the scenes that aren't depicted in the illustrations?

The sisters live together. The younger sister is in elementary school, while the older one basically works at some company. Incidentally, their ages change depending on the illustration. Sometimes the kid sister gets bigger, or the older one gets younger. There may be other characters turning up in the future too.

Since you started "Tabegirl", many other illustrators have drawn "Tabegirls" and it's become a movement. As the founder of it, what do you make of its popularity? Also, do you have any thoughts about the "Tabegirl" illustrations done by other artists?

I suppose it goes without saying, but it makes me happy. All these people drawing under a hashtag that I came up with! It feels like when we were kids and we'd all draw pictures together. It's super fun! I think everyone else's Tabegirls are so lovely and they're just the best!

What are some of the differences between drawing fantasy versus something in the modern day like "Tabegirl"?

Maybe the way you focus your energies. Fantasy can be kind of a cool genre that's stylish and clean, and I draw it with a lot of oomph. But I draw Tabegirls with the soft and fluffy feelings of tastiness and cuteness.

What were your feelings when it was decided to put together an art book? Also, do you have any comments about the new illustrations done for this volume?

Naturally, I was overjoyed. But when I thought about the volume of art I would have to draw, completion seemed quite a long way off, and I figured I had a real struggle ahead of me (laughs). I worked hard on the new illustrations for the all the people that would be buying the book!

TABEGIRL
The Art of JUN

Translator: Kumar Sivasubramanian
Production: Nicole Dochych

TABEGIRL
©Jun 2021
First Published in Japan in 2021 by KADOKAWA CORPORATION, Tokyo.
English translation rights arranged with KADOKAWA CORPORATION, Tokyo
through TUTTLE-MORI AGENCY, INC., Tokyo.
Published in English by Denpa, LLC., Portland, Oregon, 2023.

Originally published in Japanese as *Tabegaaru Jun Gashu*
by KADOKAWA CORPORATION, 2021.

This is a work of fiction.

ISBN-13: 978-1-63442-828-6
Printed in Hong Kong, China

First Edition published October 2022.

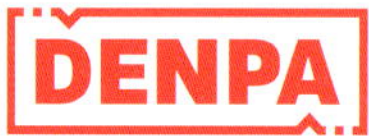

Denpa, LLC.
625 NW 17th Ave
Portland, OR 97209
www.denpa.pub

I'm Done.

PORNEIA

PORNEIA

PORNEIA

Movimento de Arte Pornô

1980–1982

Porn Art Movement

EDUARDO KAC

PORNEIA

Nightboat Books
New York

EDUARDO KAC

ISBN: 978-1-64362-026-8

Design and Typesetting by Rissa Hochberger
Typeset in Bank Script and Akkurat

Photo credits
Cover: America Cupello
Introduction: Belisário Franca
Performances: Belisário Franca (exceptions: photonovel on page 18 by Marco Rodrigues; photo on page 19 by Marcos Abel; photos on pages 20-21 by America Cupello).
Graffiti: Eduardo Kac (exception: *Overgoze* graffito with bus on page 89 by Belisário Franca.)
Filosofia t-shirt (page 94): Ricardo Elkind
Filosofia sticker (page 95): Ben Pegram

Cartoon (flap): Ota

Cataloging-in-publication data is available from the Library of Congress

Nightboat Books
New York
www.nightboat.org

Contents

Introduction

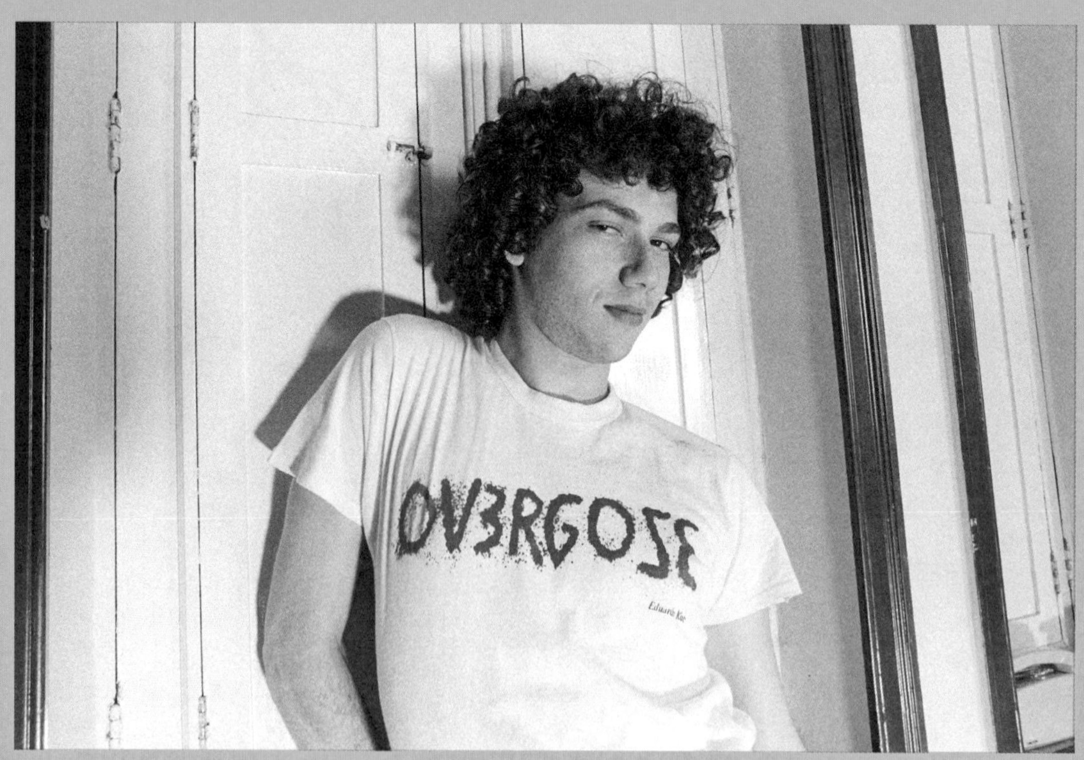

Eduardo Kac wearing his
one-word poem t-shirt
OVERGOZE, 1981

I created the performances, poems, visual works and multimedia projects collected in this book between 1980 and 1982, all in the context of the Movimento de Arte Pornô. During this period, I lived in Rio and traveled regularly to São Paulo to meet friends and see exhibitions, to strategize and promote the movement, and to carry out performances and public interventions. I often worked with ephemeral media not only to explore aesthetic elements of immediacy, intersubjectivity, reproduction, circulation, and unauthorized public action, but also to activate the expressive potential of ephemerality to evoke urgent issues, such as gender, desire, pleasure, power, agency, and the transformative potential of the individual. In this two-year period, which I lived intensely, I worked with media and materials as diverse as audio tapes, film, multiples, garments, rubber stamps, flyers, posters, makeup, correspondence, zines, t-shirts, postcards, drawings, poems, mailers, books, and photographs. I also invented unique artistic forms such as *Pornograms* (works that call for the body to be not only seen but read), flatographic poems (euphonic pieces predicated on the flatal flow as compositional unit), and 3D graffiti (the creation of graffiti not on flat walls but on volumetric intersections). For me, pornography was more than a technical device. A mode of perception that reflected and imposed an ideology, if given new directions it could express a diversity of forms and ideas; it could combine the fleeting with the perennial and capture the complexity of life.

In my *modus vivendi*, I frequently wore a pink miniskirt both in performance and in carrying out ordinary chores, such as going to the supermarket. To me, it was about ungendering fashion. I never intended this intervention to be drag or cross-dressing; it was always about self-fashioning in a way that denaturalized norms (i.e., claimed the right of men to wear skirts) and about socially projecting an entirely different notion of what a man is or can be. I meant my pink miniskirt to be what in the twenty-first century we would call a "non-binary object." Within its pansexual agenda, the Movimento de Arte Pornô embraced a general refusal of stable categorization. While it undoubtedly privileged gender-nonconforming expression, it also gave voice to cismen and ciswomen artists who rejected the imposition of rigid, received binary expectations of what constitutes masculinity and femininity. Unmoored from the restrictions of state and religion, such as heterosexual marriage and reproduction, the movement respected and embraced those for whom these were a matter of sexual identity or personal choice.

The work I produced during this period reflected an understanding that art and poetry are instruments not only of aesthetic stimulation and formal inventiveness, but also of resistance to the subjugation of language and visuality by the political and social forces that maintain the status quo. The Movimento de Arte Pornô was fully cognizant of the fact that the ruling class uses language to isolate, classify, contain, and control undesired social groups perceived to threaten its worldview and hegemony. Through language, the establishment carries out an assault on all those it wishes to suppress due to their cultural or transgressive difference. The use of a stigmatizing lexicon segregates non-dominant groups from the social order, ascribing to them instead an inferior status and relegating them to the realm of abnormality. To counter this hegemonic use of language, I developed strategies to unhinge syntax from the high/low bind and remapped semantics to serve emancipatory imperatives. Often with a liberating sense of humor, the poems I wrote undermined this process of stigmatization by creating a context in which conservative expressions (such as those ascribing animality to humans, or using sex acts or body parts aggressively) would be restored to positive and healthy meanings. I knew that to change life it is necessary to change language itself by stopping the usage of certain words, changing the meaning of others, and, when needed, coining new words or phrases to name new realities, whether *de facto* or wished forth. These poems, performances, and visual works deal with the transgression of boundaries of the body as assigned destiny (activism) and the emerging consciousness of new possibilities of the body as a sign system (semiotics). Ordinarily the body is represented by language and images; in the Movimento de Arte Pornô, the body also presented itself to be seen, read, and heard.

> The selected poems in this volume are neither rants nor confessions; they are carefully constructed verbal objects that may or may not have any relation to my direct personal experience. They emerge from and contribute to a conscious program that deliberately exposes bourgeois hypocrisies, operates an unyielding political critique, subverts the stigmatized meanings of words imposed on an underrepresented population, and promotes a pansexual agenda. Both a Cinelândia Square performer by night and a "boy from Ipanema" by day, in writing these poems I drew from the devalued argot of rentboys, jailbirds, call girls, *malandros*, go-go dancers, street youth, informal workers, *cachaceiros*, junkies, hawkers, drag queens and kings, pamphleteers, favela kids, hobos, hinterland troubadours, déclassé market performers, *transformistas*, and a whole plethora of subcultures that make up the invisible side of society. These poems employ humor, semantic contortions, parody, exuberance, misspellings, unexpected associations, and other techniques to elevate this vocabulary and, in so doing, turn upside down a value system that, for too long, had subjugated both a population and a worldview.

A common mistake about the Movimento de Arte Pornô is to think of it as a reflection of its environment, namely Brazil in the early 1980s. This oversight is predicated on dangerously calcified colonial tropes. Contrary to the Carnival cliché of scantily clad women dancing samba, the reality of Brazil is that this mostly Catholic country (with an increasing Evangelical population) is largely composed of people of modest means who do not necessarily share liberal moral values. The art deco-style Christ the Redeemer statue, with its outstretched arms spanning 92 feet, towers noticeably above Rio's cliffy landscape. This indelible, visually ubiquitous monument to a single, dominant faith is a permanent reminder, encrusted high above the city, of the conservative values that guide Brazilian society and the permission that dominant groups give themselves to impose their beliefs over the rest of society. This is to unambiguously state that the Movimento de Arte Pornô was not reflecting a social circumstance, but working to create a new reality.

> I coined the phrase *Arte Pornô* to produce cognitive dissonance by bringing together what was then understood as sublime (art) and abject (pornography). Further, as there was no legal pornography in the country, the word "porn" made reference to something that did not exist openly in society. While in the USA a porn industry boomed in the 1970s, during the same period Brazil was immersed in the worst, most brutal period of its dictatorship, which suppressed all personal freedoms. The Brazilian Penal Code of 1942 was still in force in 1980. It considered a crime "to make, import, acquire or possess, for purposes of trade, distribution or public display, any obscene writing, drawing, painting, print or object." The *Movimento de Arte Pornô* flaunted the dictatorship's prohibition against pornography at a time when the horror of the "lead years" was still a fresh wound, which made the transition to democracy from the 1964 military coup feel extremely slow—direct presidential elections would only take place in 1989.

With an eye towards the future, it was necessary to challenge the conditioned reflex that led audiences to believe that bodily manifestations should automatically be interpreted according to known historical antecedents and established standards, both invariably understood through the pathologizing antinomy normal-deviant. The Movimento de Arte Pornô sought to dismantle and reassemble the conventions of art and poetry—author identity, book or canvas as privileged media, silent reading or contemplation as modes of engagement— to create new bodycentric experiences. The poetry of the Movimento de Arte Pornô is predicated on the bodily enunciation of performance and the affective power of multimediality on the audience through image, sound and object. I created these pornpoems and artworks out of a wide array of graphic sources, including typographic signs, full words, letters, logos, pictograms, and glyphs. These works elicited a multisensorial reception, conjuring up a future in which media diversity went right along with cognitive and sexual diversity. Ultimately, the movement affirmed the possibility of remaking the world in the image of its joyous and rebellious spirit, of its pansexual values, of plurality, and coexistence.

Eduardo Kac, 2021

Performances

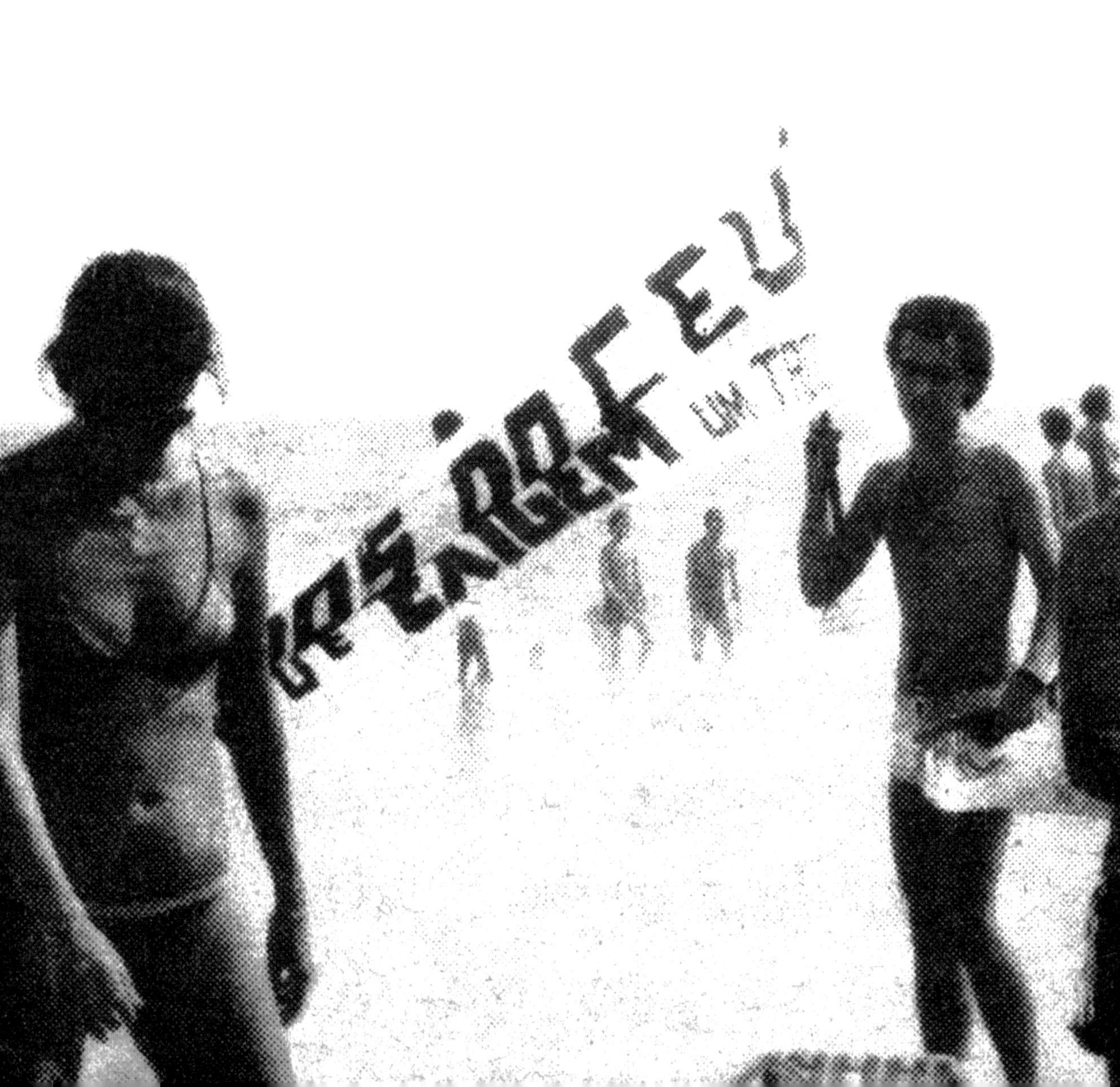

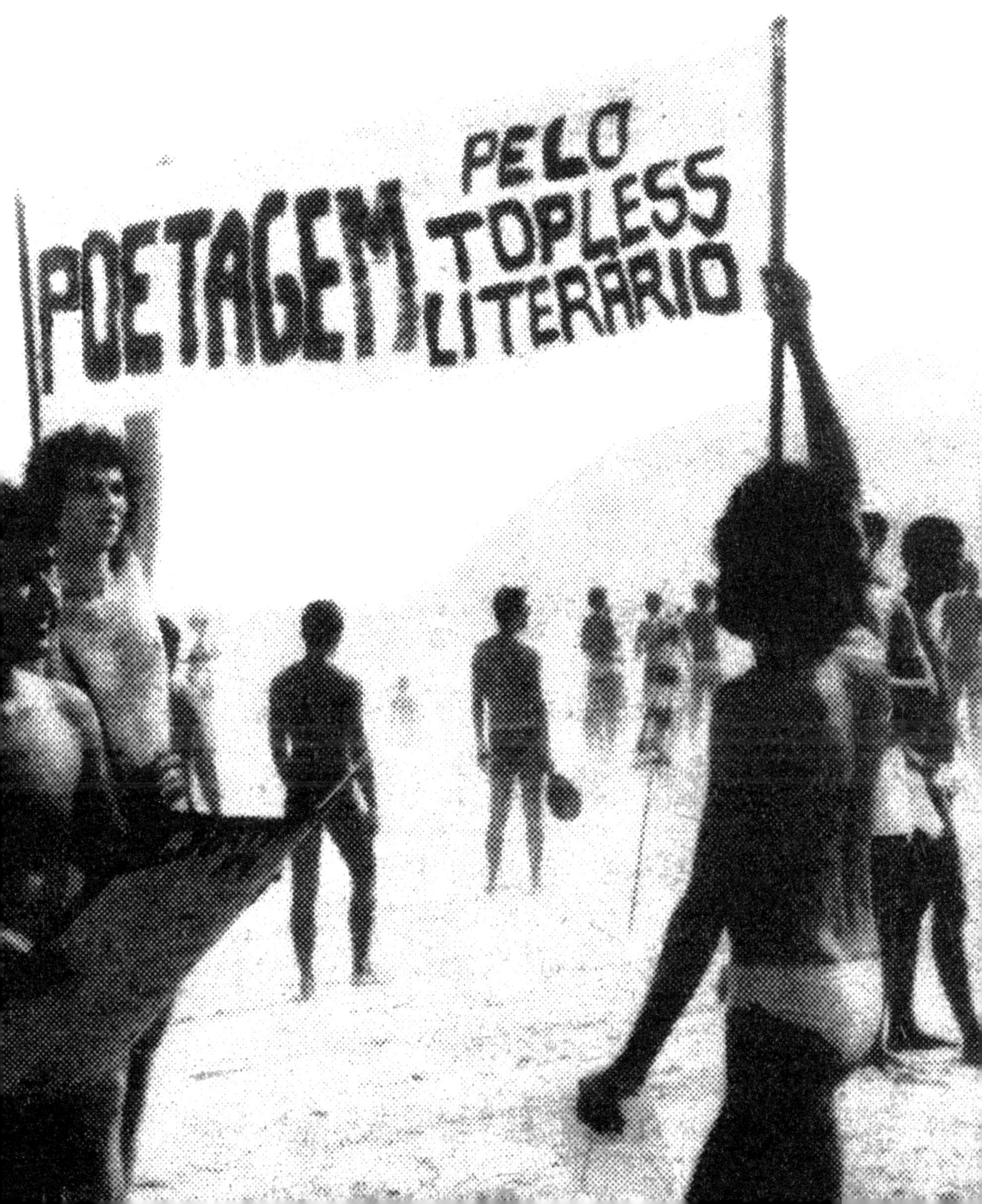

Topless Literário [Literary Topless]
Ipanema Beach, Rio de Janeiro,
February 1980

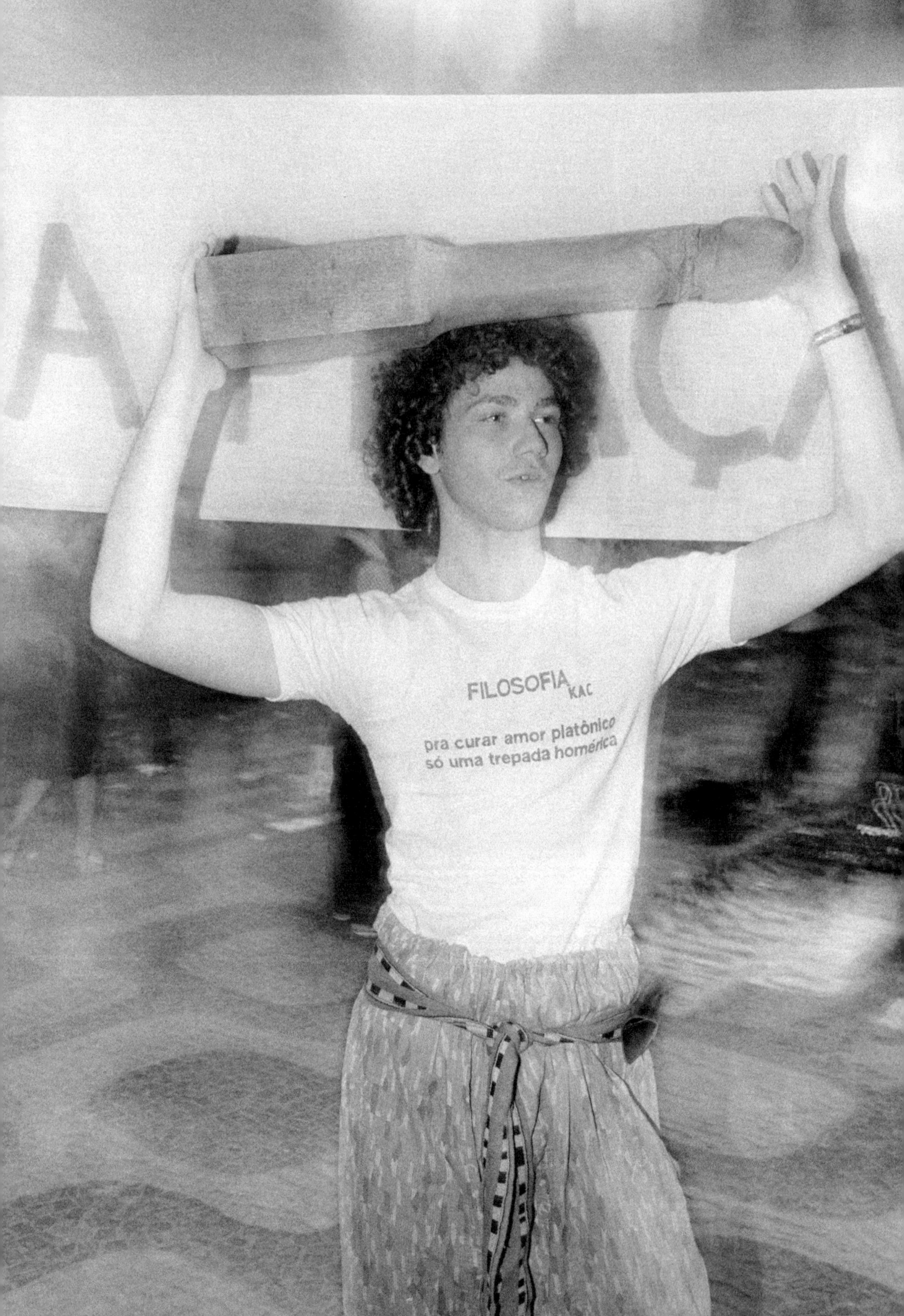
FILOSOFIA KAC
pra curar amor platônico
só uma trepada homérica

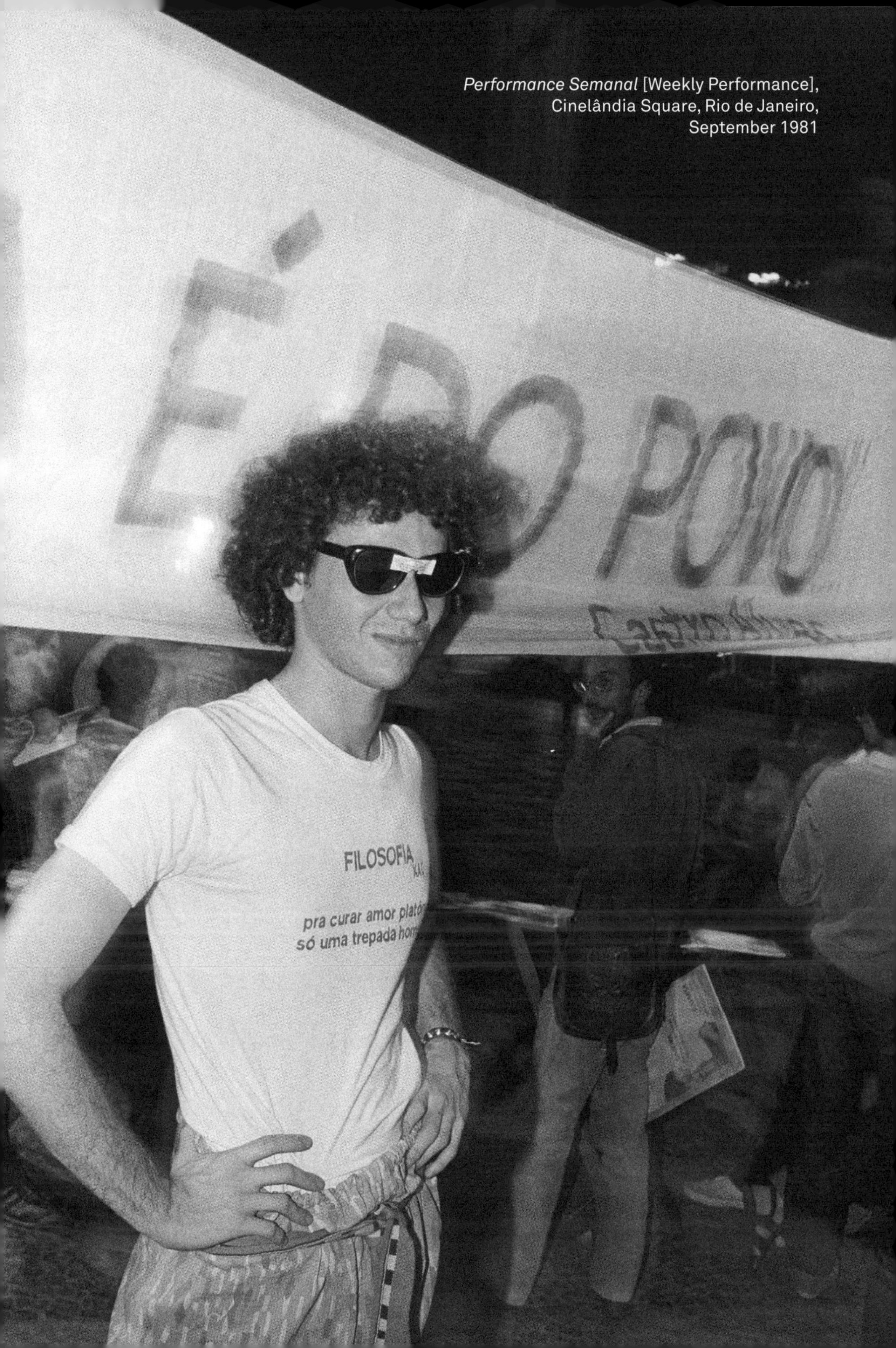

Performance Semanal [Weekly Performance],
Cinelândia Square, Rio de Janeiro,
September 1981

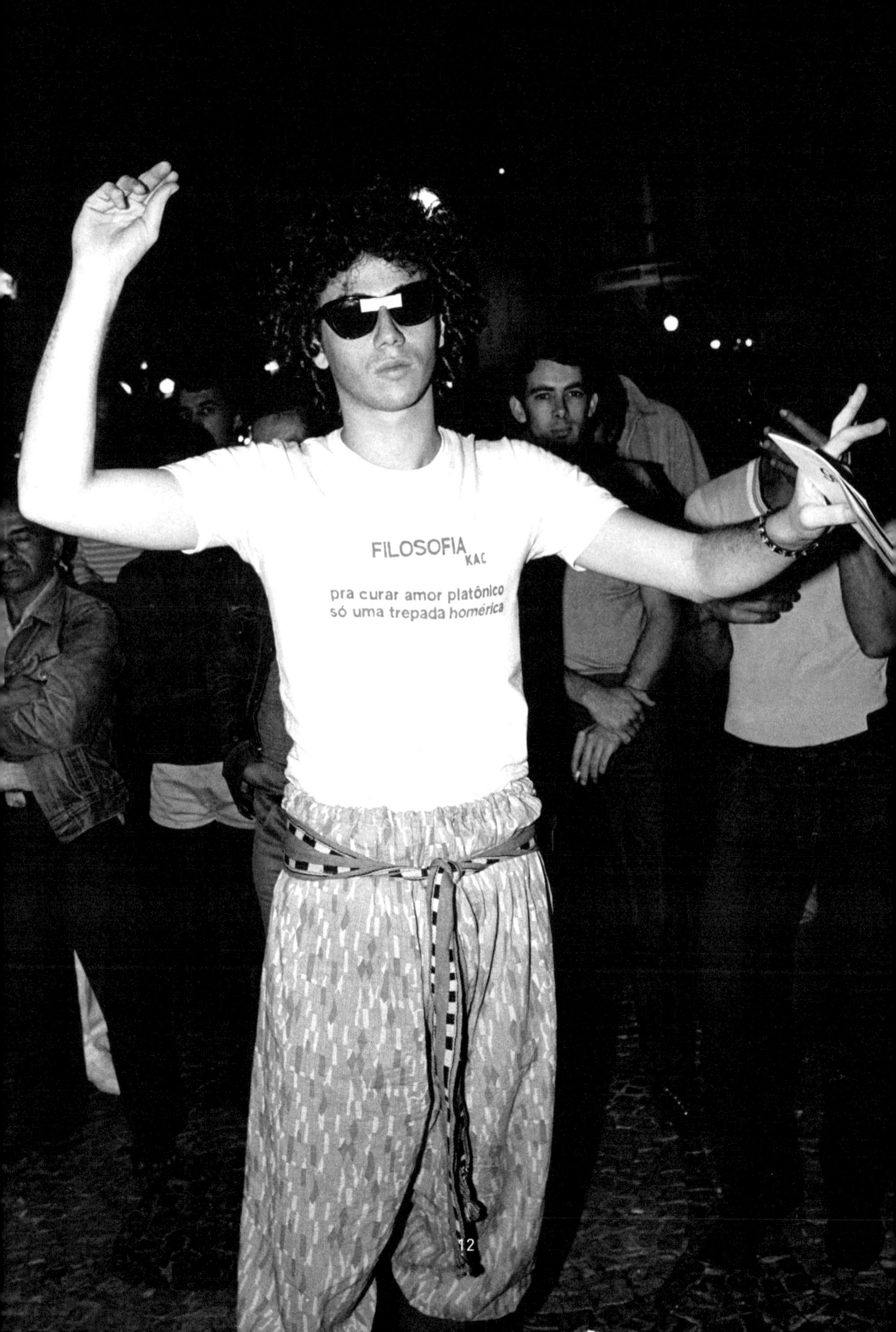

FILOSOFIA KAC
pra curar amor platônico
só uma trepada homérica
12

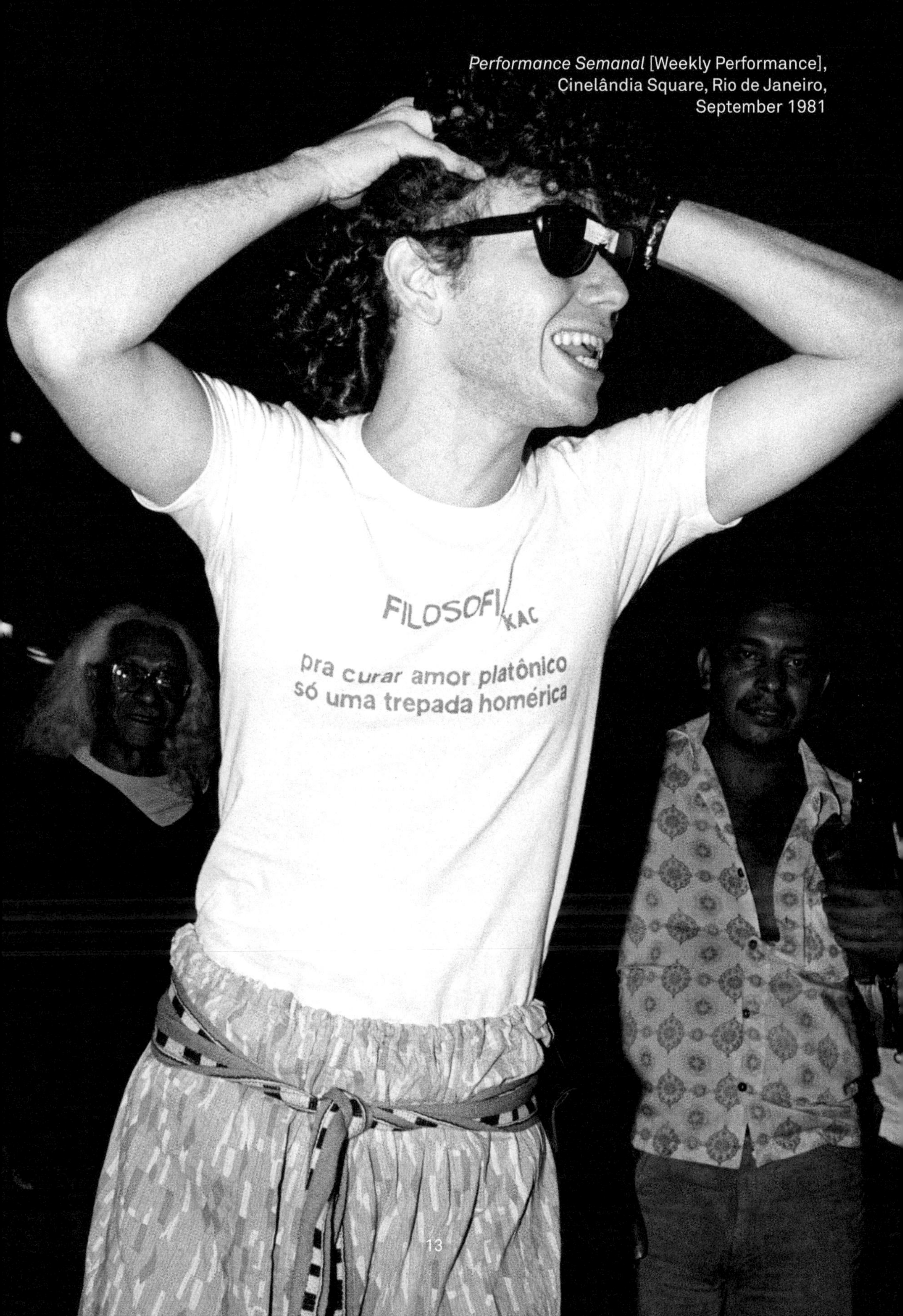

Performance Semanal [Weekly Performance],
Cinelândia Square, Rio de Janeiro,
September 1981

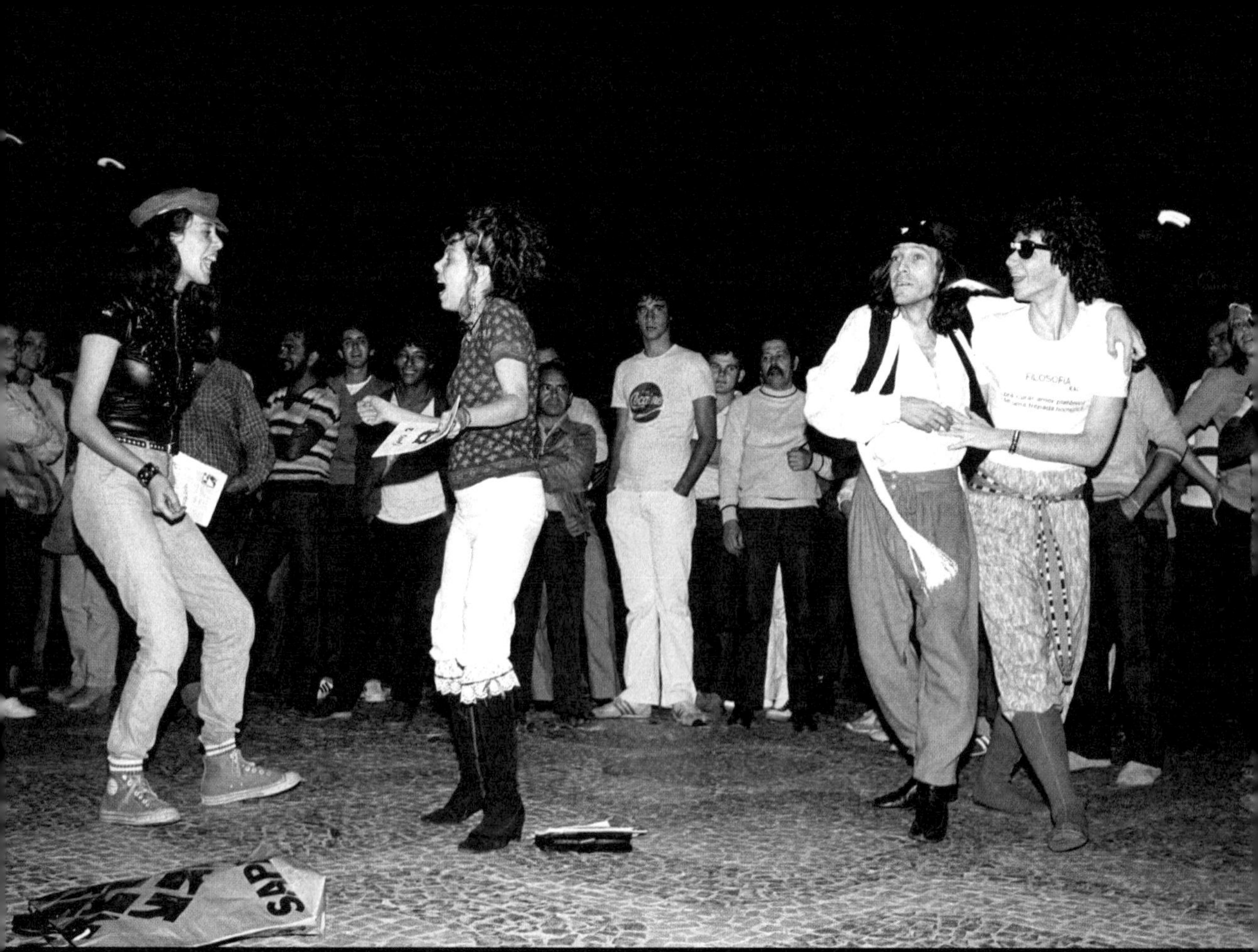

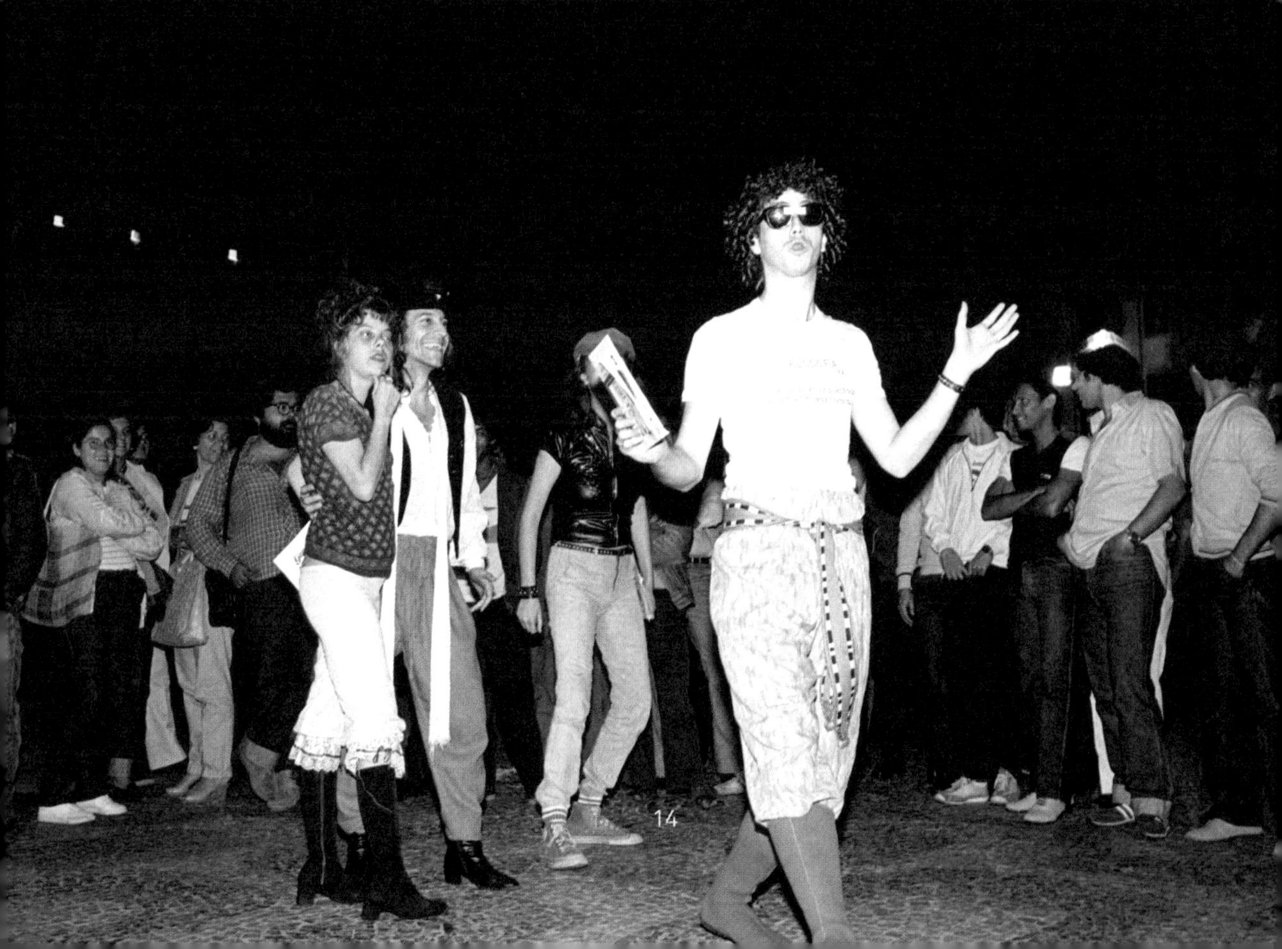

Performance Semanal [Weekly Performance], Cinelândia Square, Rio de Janeiro, September 1981 (left); *Entr'acte*, Teatro Rival, Rio de Janeiro, October 1981 (right)

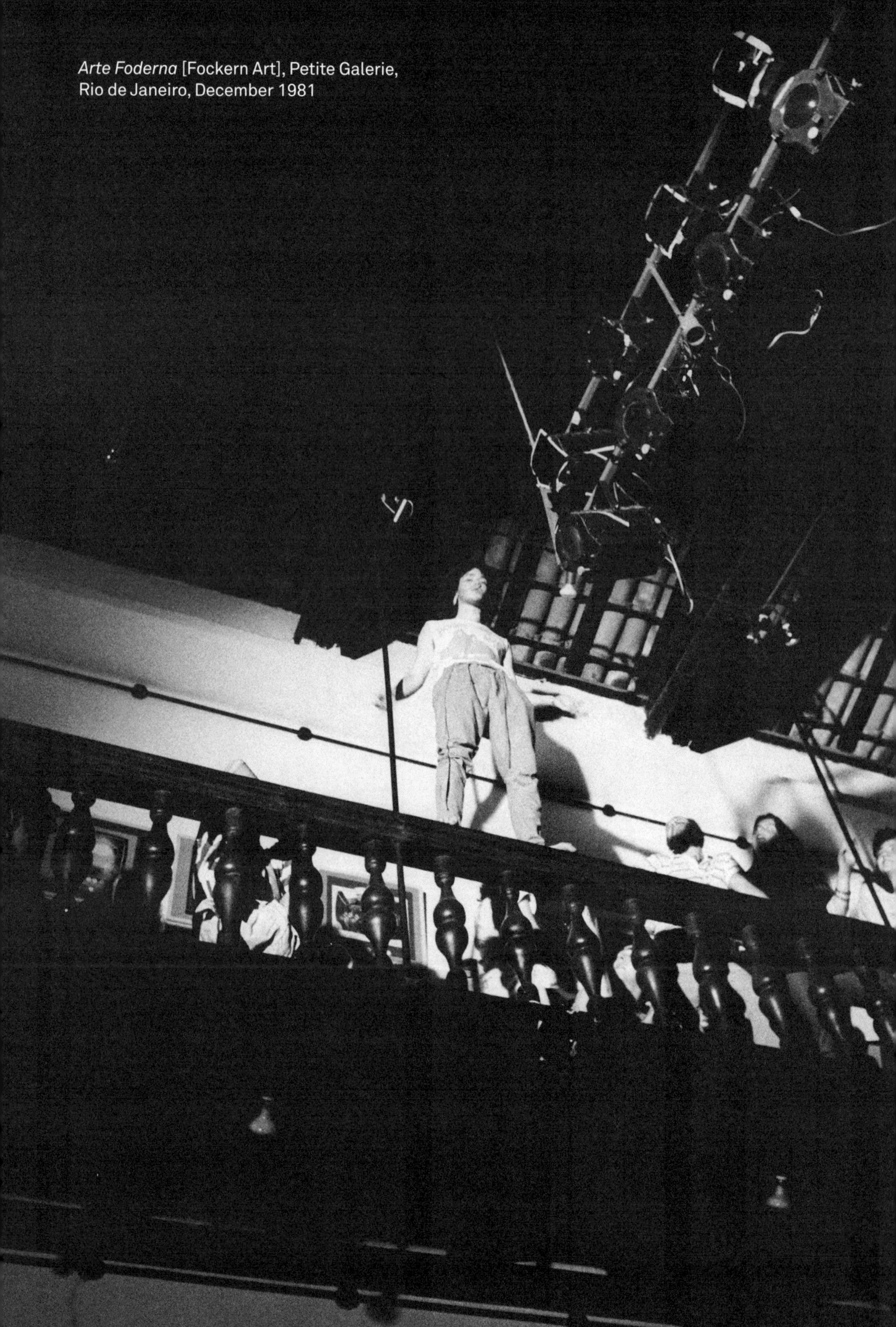

Arte Foderna [Fockern Art], Petite Galerie,
Rio de Janeiro, December 1981

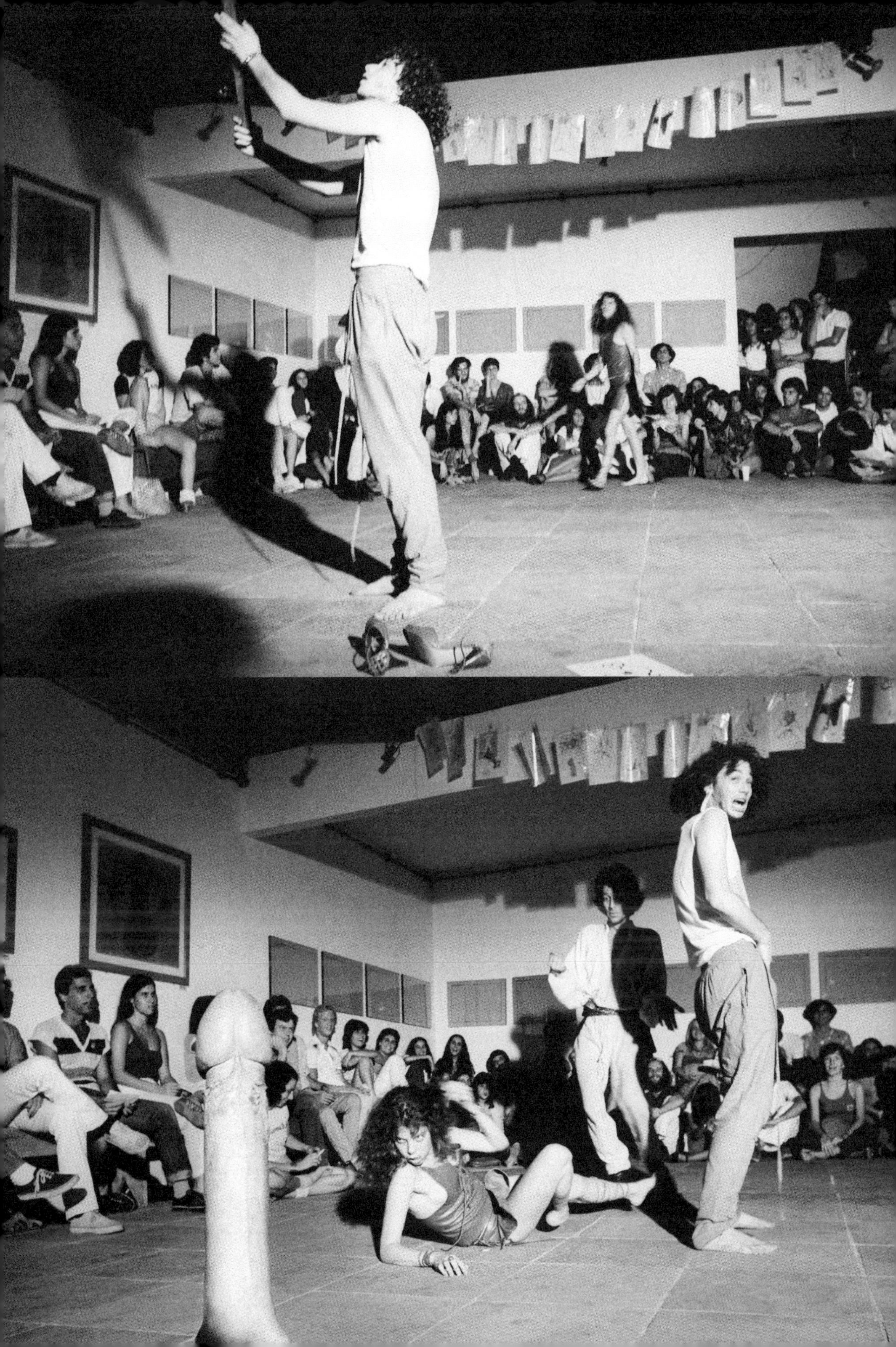

AS AVENTURAS DA GANG!

Estrelando: Kac, Teresa, Sandra, Kairo

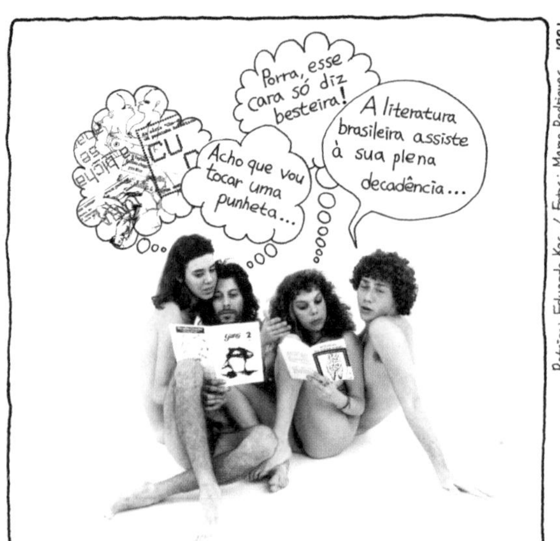

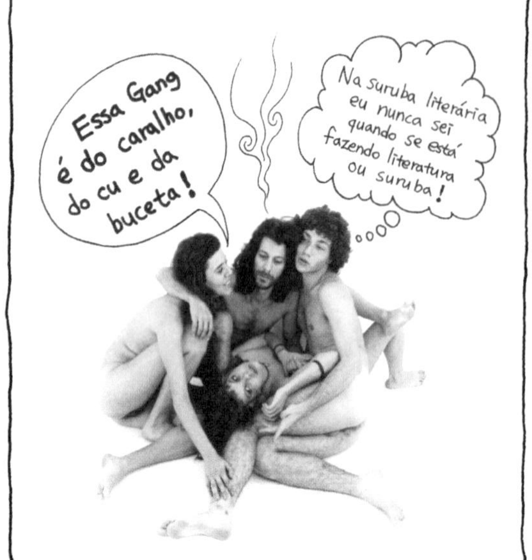

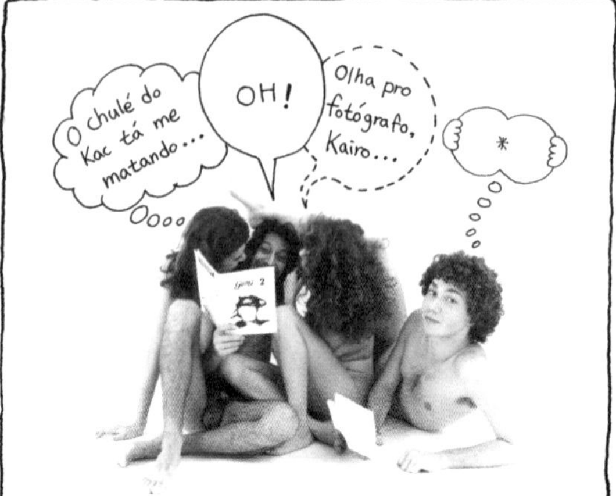

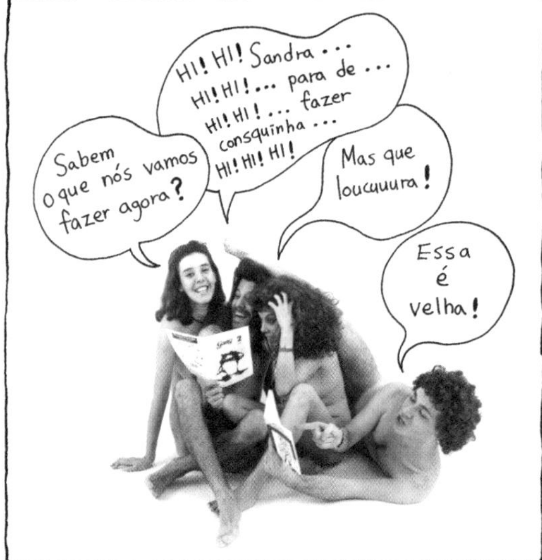

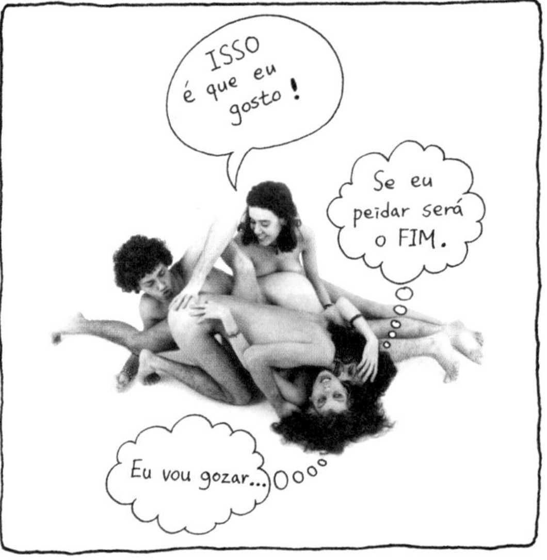

As Aventuras da Gang [The Adventures of The Gang], Rio de Janeiro, July 1981 (left); *Interversão* [Interversion], Ipanema Beach, Rio de Janeiro, February 1982 (right)

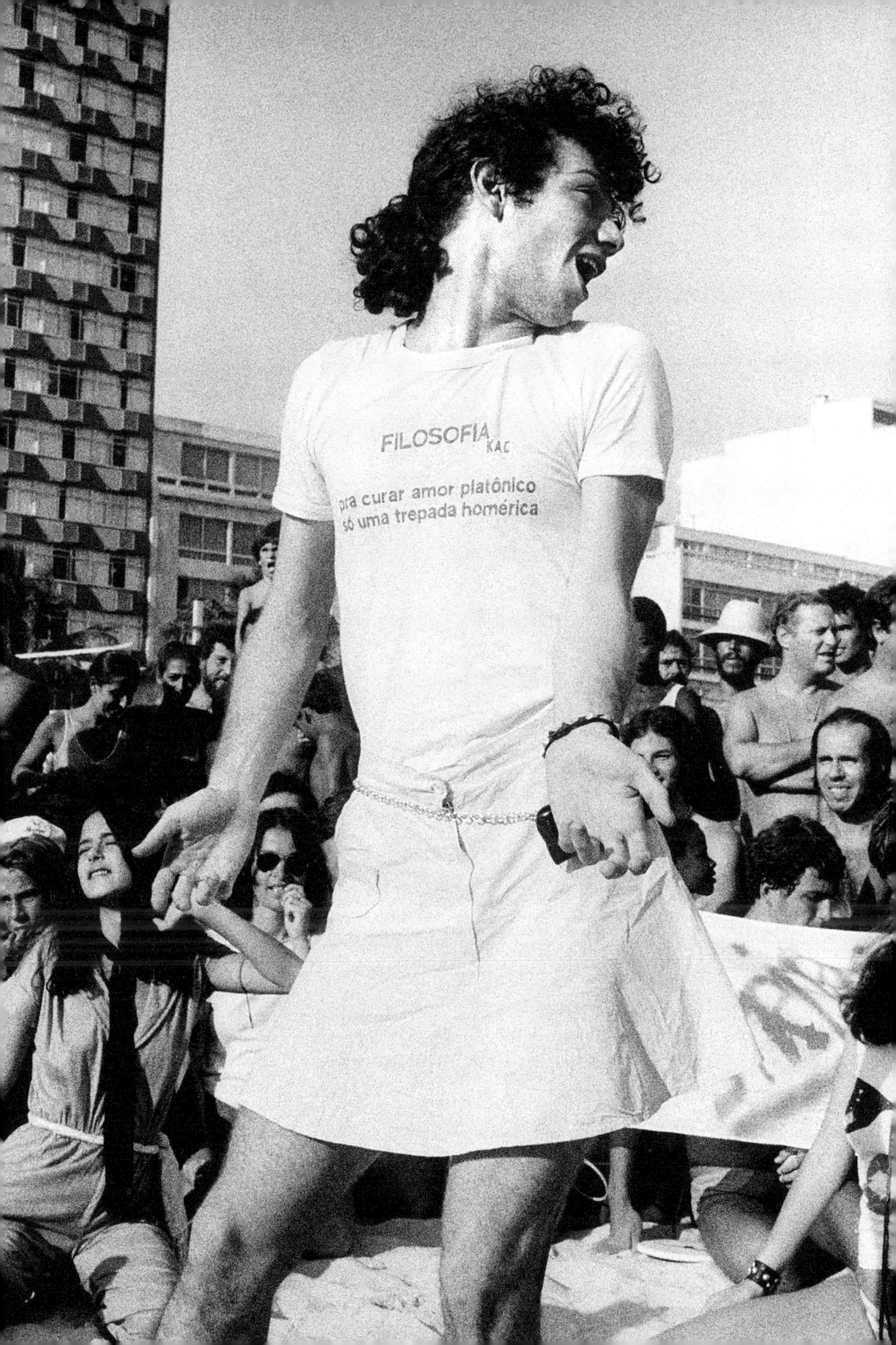

FILOSOFIA KAC
pra curar amor platônico
só uma trepada homérica

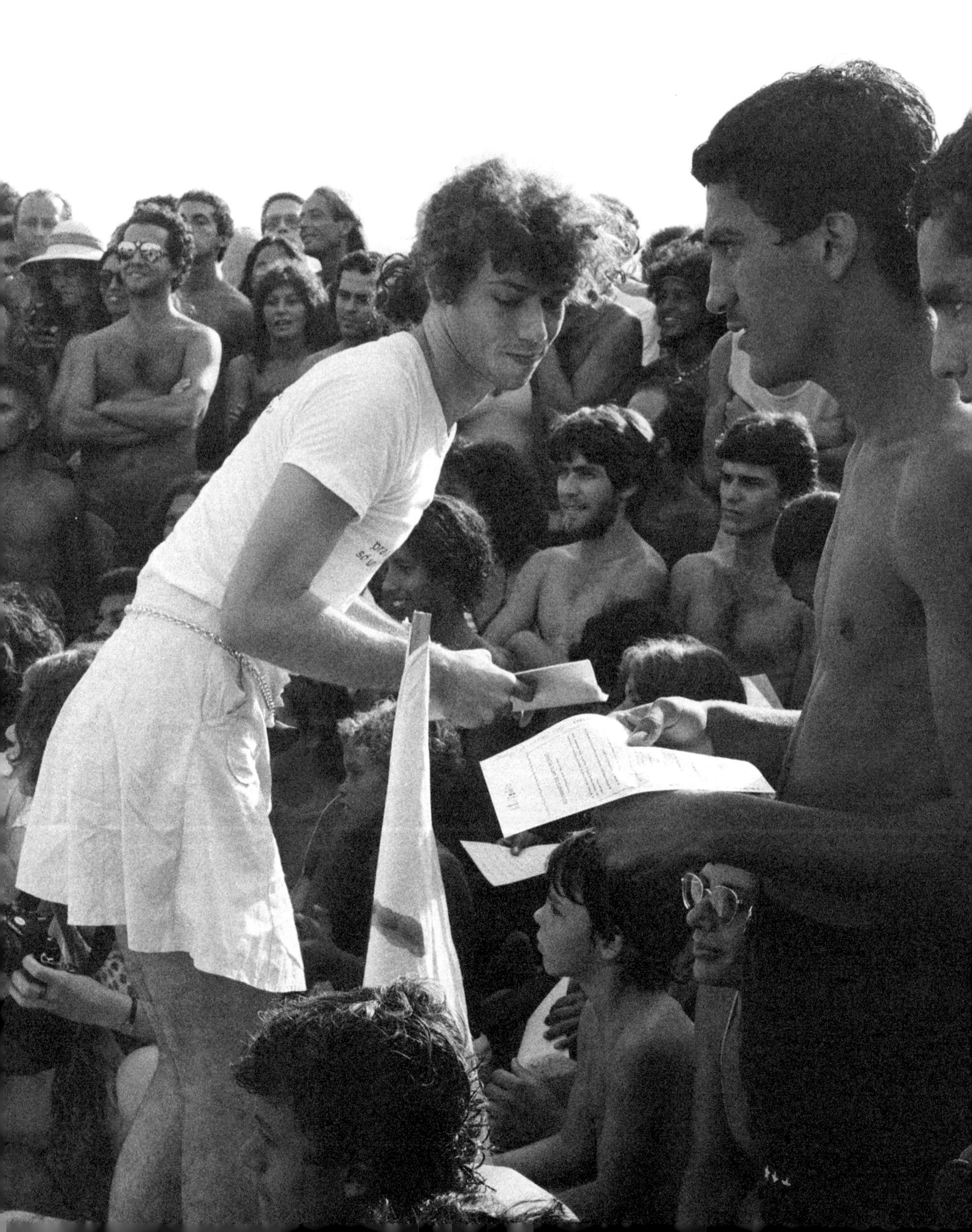

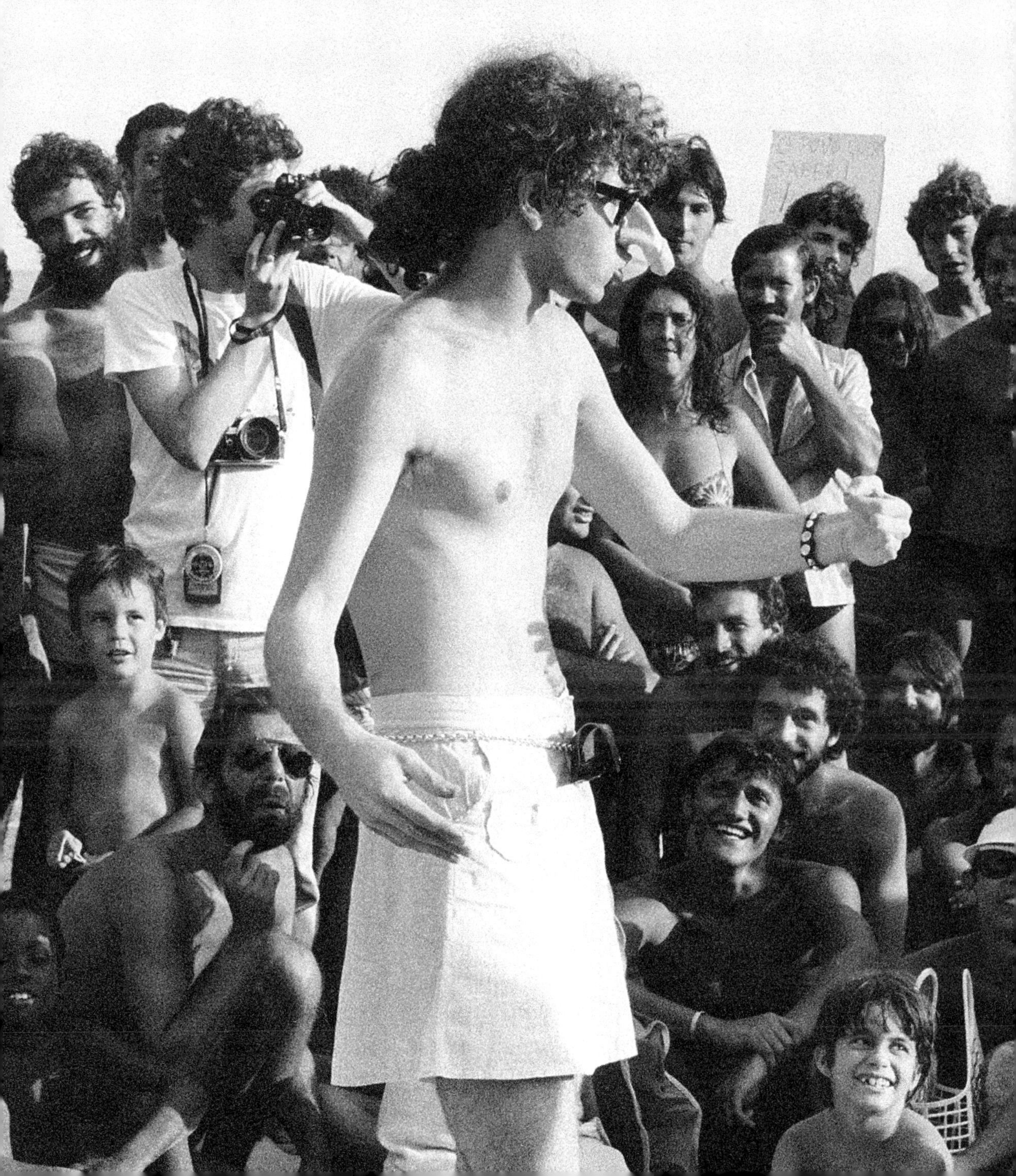

Interversão [Interversion],
Ipanema Beach, Rio de Janeiro,
February 1982

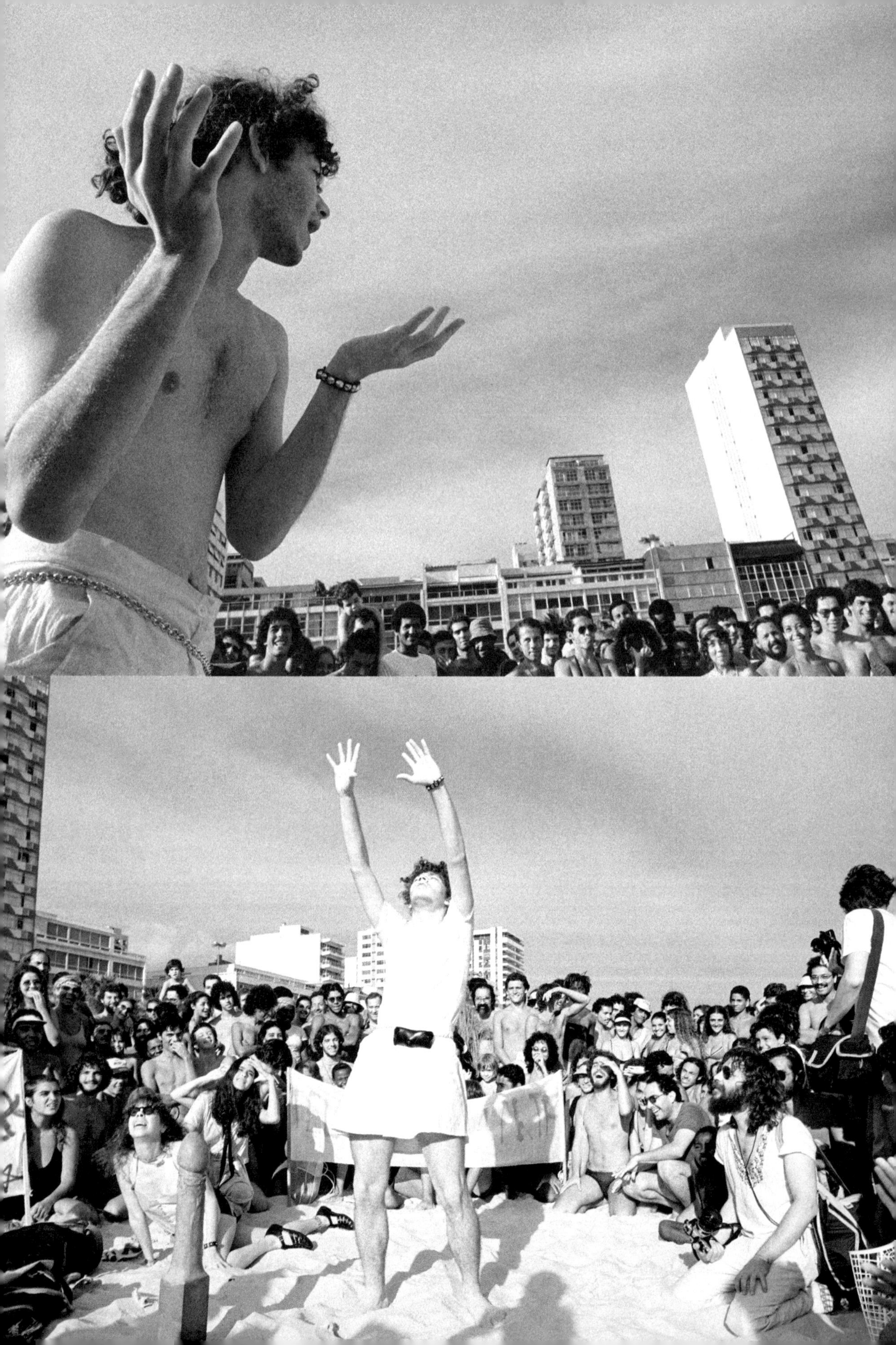

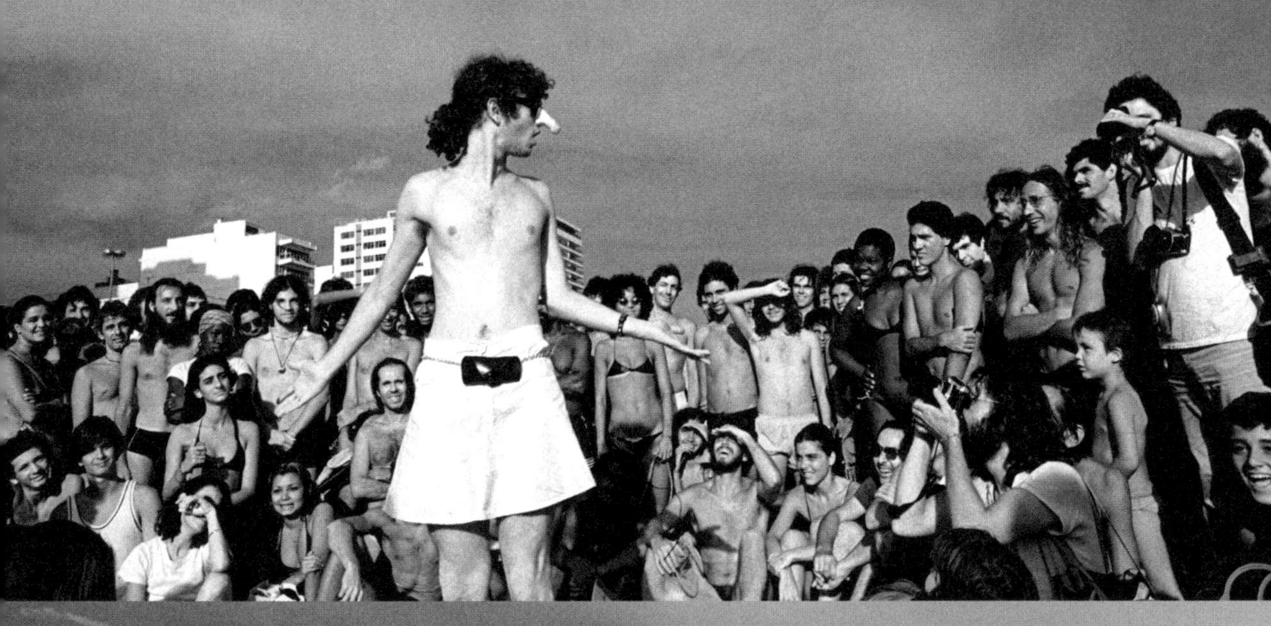

Interversão [Interversion],
Ipanema Beach, Rio de Janeiro,
February 1982

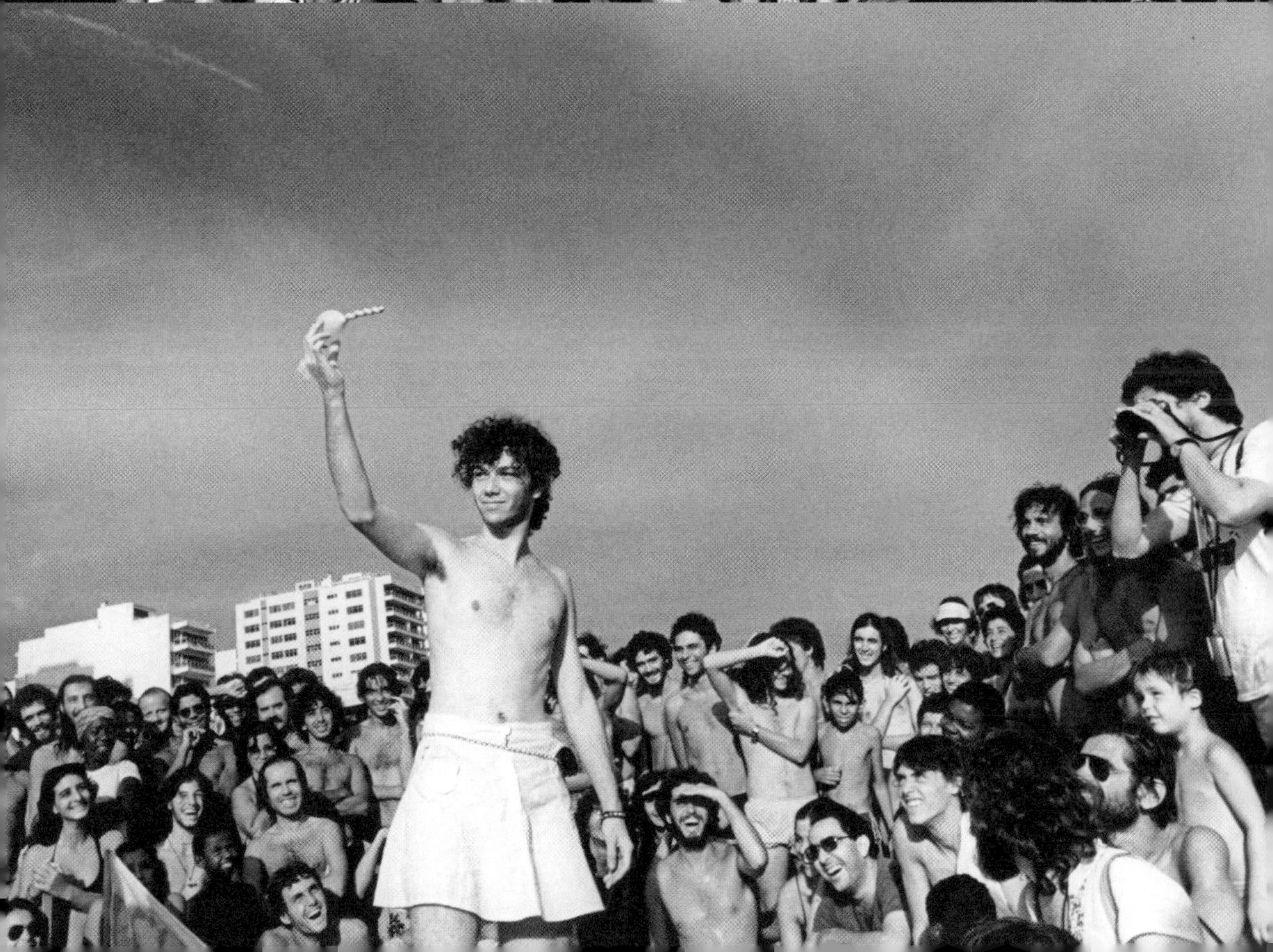

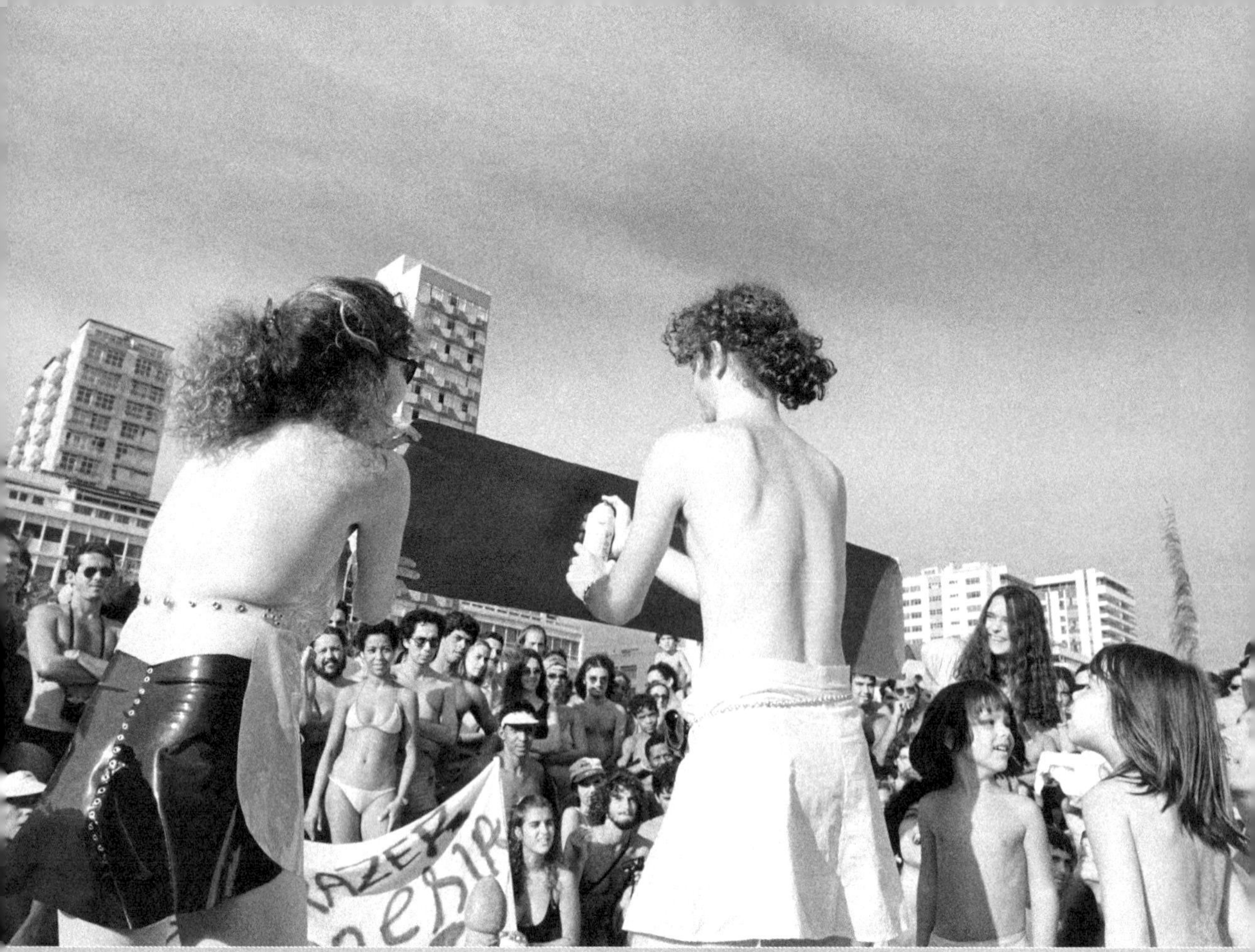

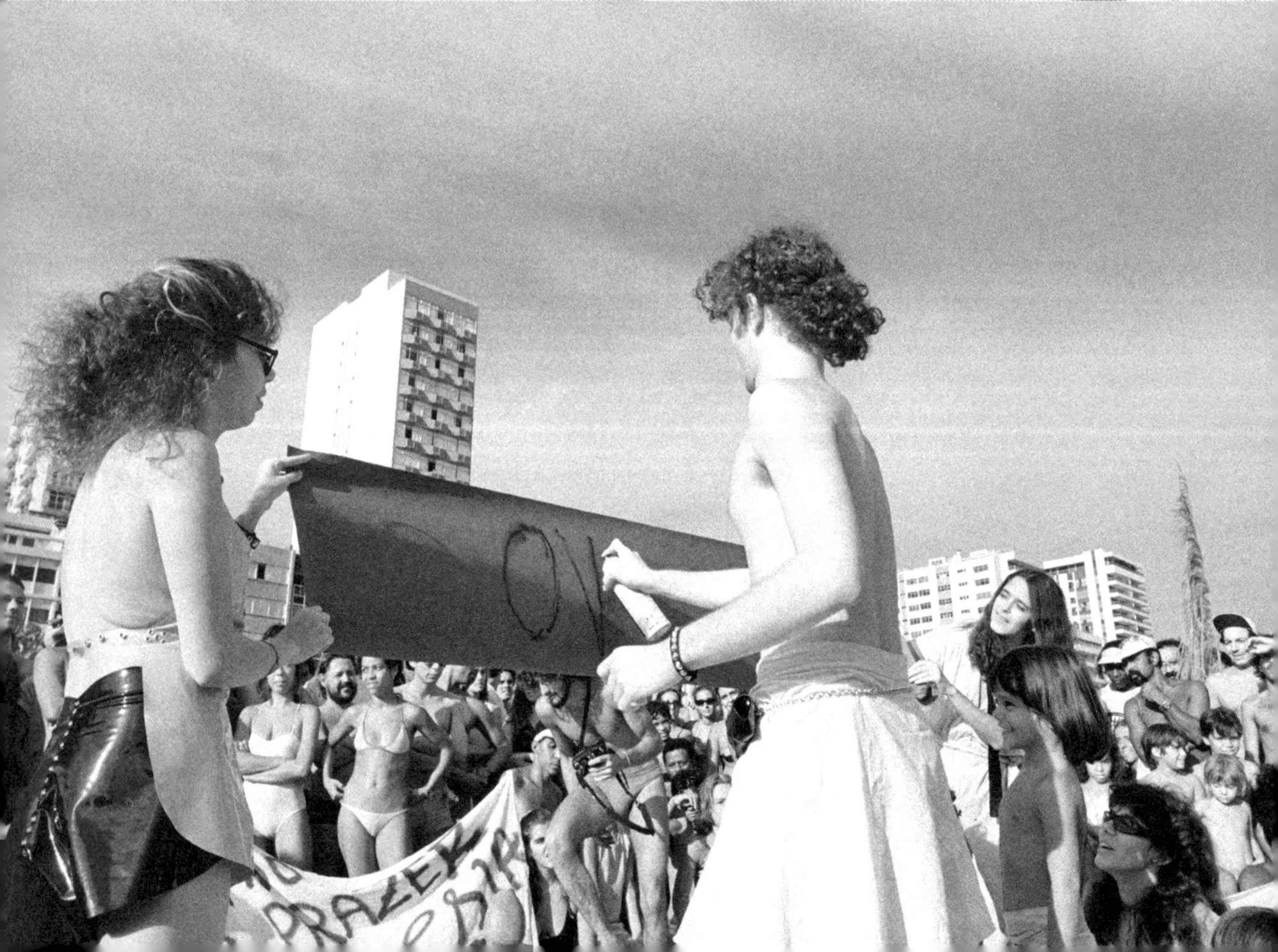

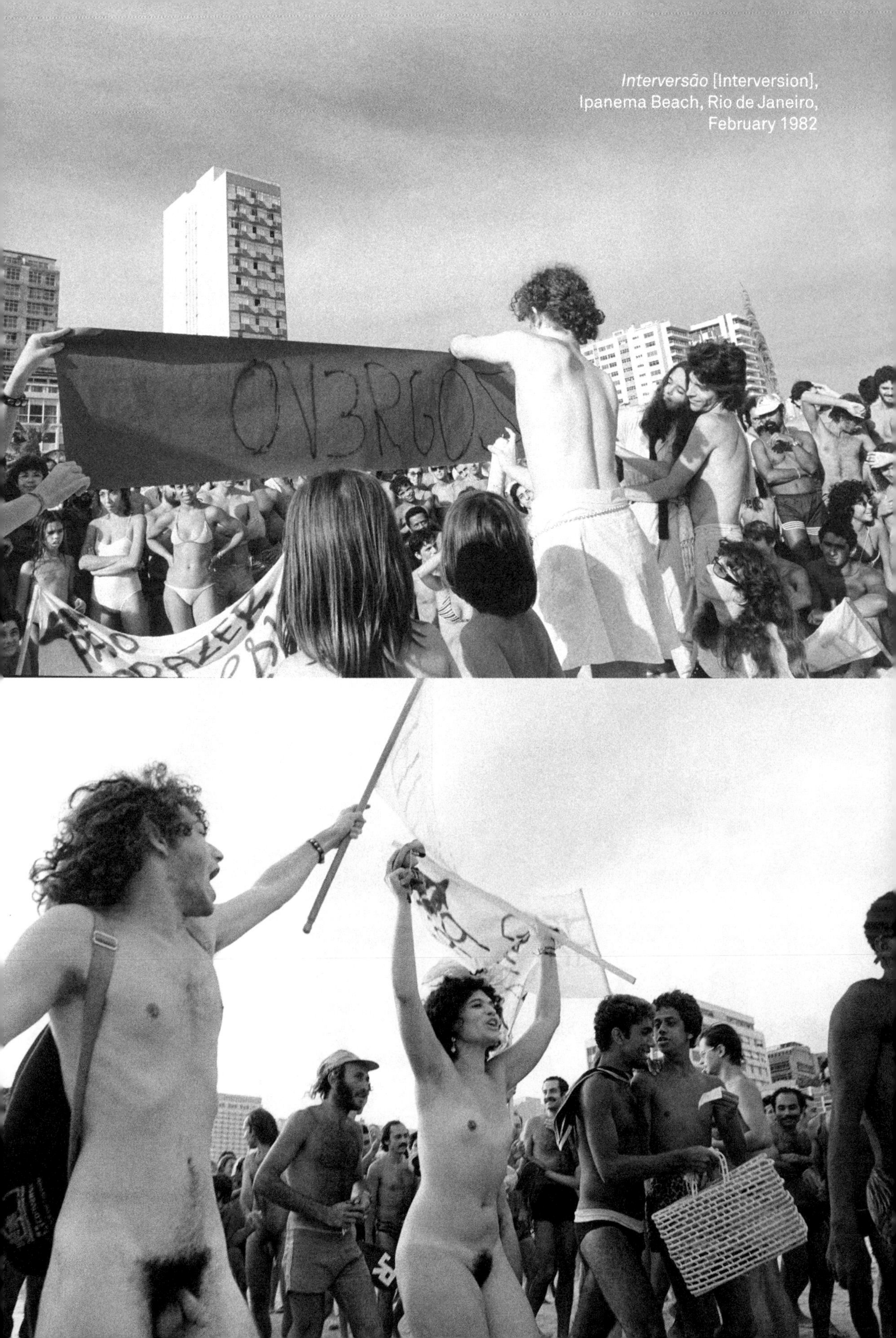

Interversão [Interversion],
Ipanema Beach, Rio de Janeiro,
February 1982

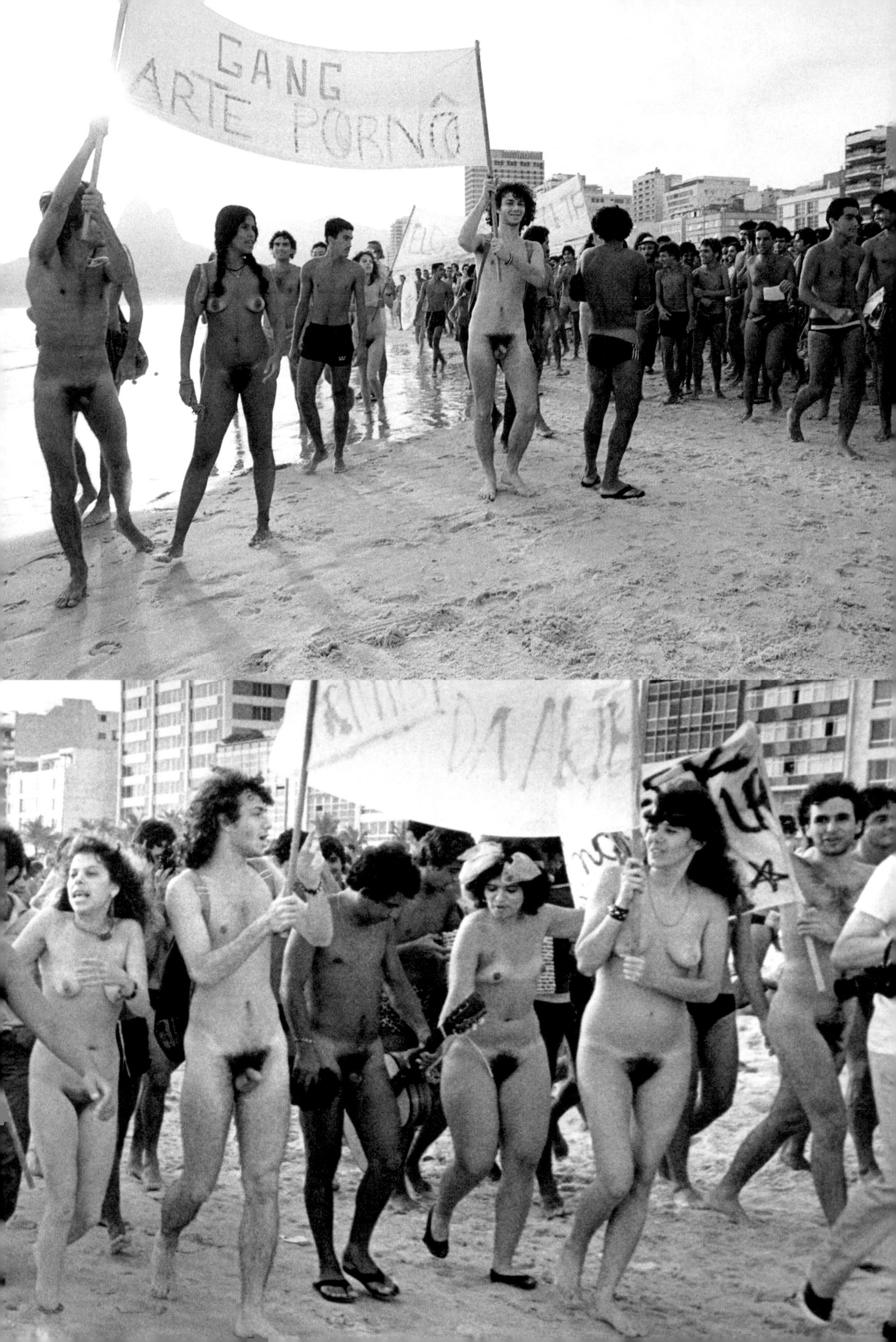
GANG
ARTE PORNÔ

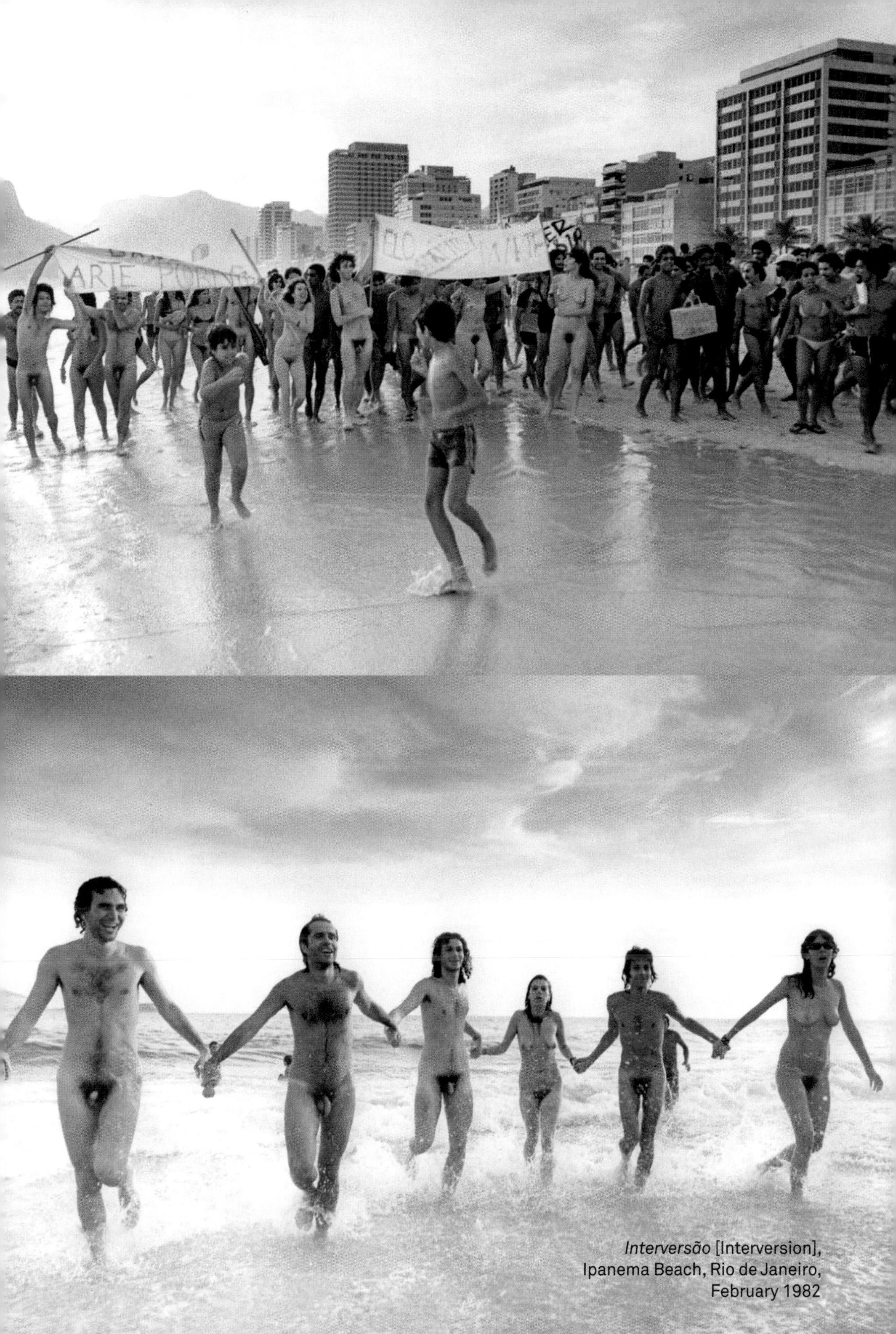

Interversão [Interversion],
Ipanema Beach, Rio de Janeiro,
February 1982

Manifestos

Em caso de incêndio não chame os bombeiros

o erotismo em voga atenta contra a moral
e os bons costumes
porque o pornográfico é o elemento incômodo
    diante da hipocrisia vigente
ondas de calor para queimar bases idiotas

e criar novas: poema=arte : poesia=tesão : poeta=artesão
implodir a pornografia) (explodir a impostação de um falso significado

nenhuma palavra jogada
quer no espaço em branco ou preto
da página feita para   rasgar e nunca pôr na
estante prisão   geladeira q congela
a vida inteira   o calor do novo
em forma nada cria tudo

copia e muito transforma que é da poesia transformar sempre
arde o grito contra a bota o beato o tabu / saquem : ajam : sempre

arde a resposta pelo enfarte do fato não
arte, pelo artefato
político em essência artístico em consistência
como uma bomba de indecência que mata
a inocência

In case of fire do not call the firefighters

the stale eroticism in vogue is a blow to morality
and good manners
because the pornographic is the uncomfortable element
        against the prevailing hypocrisy
heat waves to burn stupid foundations

and create new ones: poem=art : poetry=heat : poet =hot artist
implode pornography) (explode statements with false meanings

                    no thrown words
        either in white   or black spaces
    of the page made to be   torn and never be put on
        the shelf-prison a   refrigerator that freezes
            all of life the   heat of the new
        is the nothing that creates everything

copies and transforms because poetry always transforms
fiery yells against the boot the devout the tabu / act : now

            ablaze is the answer to the infarct of the fact non
                                    art, for the artifact
                    political in essence artistic in consistency
                        like a bomb of indecency that kills
                                        innocence

InterVerSão

MOVIMENTO DE ARTE PORNÔ

(manifesto feito nas coxas)

★ Antes de dominar a palavra escrita, o homem já desenhava sacanagem nas paredes das cavernas.

★ Masturbação literária não gera porra nenhuma.

★ Arte é penetração e gôzo.

★ Trepar, parir e criar fazem parte de um mesmo processo.

★ O Pornopoema vai por no poema.

★ Os caras do poder baixam o pau com medo de baixar as calças... e acabar levando pau.

★ A rapaziada tá cagando prá Literatura Oficial.

★ Pela suruba literária: um processo concreto da praxis marginal na sacanagem tropical e o escambau.

★ O Poema Pornô taí prá abrir as pernas e as idéias.

★ Viva o BUM da poesia em toda arte, em toda parte.

maio de 1980

TODO MUNDO NU

GANG
Rio, 13-2-82

PELA PAZ PLANETÁRIA

Tesão Permanente

ABAIXO AS CALÇAS

Luzia G Frazão São

OVЗRGOZ3 NÃO MATA

PELO STRIPITIS DA ARTE

PORN ART MOVEMENT
(quickie manifesto)

• Before mastering the written word, humans already scrawled sexy doodles on cave walls

• Literary masturbation hasn't got the spunk

• Let's make art and come

• Fucking, birthing and creating are part of the same process

• The pornpoem fucks with poetry

• The guys in power take off our pants and kick us in the groin because they're afraid to drop their pants and kiss us in the groin

• Our homies don't give a shit about official literature

• For a literary orgy: a concrete process of marginal praxis in the down and dirty tropics

• The pornpoem opens legs and ideas

• Let poetry SPREAD everywhere and in every form of art

Manifesto Fale Cu

• Depois de toda sacanagem, Adão e Eva descobriram o paraíso. Estava socializado o gozo.

• Chega de eufemismos! A arte nasce nua e crua. Só uma excelente trepada pode desviá-la de um mau caminho.

• A vida transcende a mediocridade — alcança o equilíbrio.

• Façamos o Poema Fálico; curto e grosso, como o diabo gosta.

• Falemos de silêncio. Se não falo no cio, silencio.

• O poeta tem um papel na sociedade: o higiênico.

• Limpar o olho do cu é enxergar mais longe.

• Viva o lirismo! Liberdade, abre as pernas, meu amor...

• Cada poema é uma cama; só sobrevive quem ama.

• Vamos destruir para construir. Invento a poesia com o nome Vida e o sobrenome Arte.

Buttiful Manifesto

• When they got laid, Adam and Eve discovered Paradise. There! The orgasm was socialized.

• No more euphemisms! Art comes into this world butt naked. Only a megafuck can get it on the right track.

• Life has to overcome mediocrity and achieve balance.

• Buttiful poems: to the point, as the devil likes them.

• When I stick it up, I speak up. When I don't, I shut up.

• I wrote it in the crapper: the poet's social role is paper-thin.

• To wipe the brown eye is to see ahead.

• Long live lyricism! Freedom, spread your legs, babe…

• Every poem is a bed; only the lovers survive.

• Let's destroy it all to build it over. I hereby introduce you to a new poetry; first name: Life; last name: Art.

Já 'n hora!

Che gay pra pivur
CINELÂNDIA a esquerda
e virar a direita CU OO MUNDO
U MOVIMENTO PORNÔ é
UM TRÁFICO DE IDÉIAS
FEIJOADA & POESIR
— MALARMELADA SACANA
O POETA COM O CU NA RODA A
POESIA É BOA di CAMA
DIRETA COM a relação OLHO DO POETA
CORAÇÃO e o olho DO PÚBLICO
A MÁGICO SURGE DE repente!!!

EK 81

It's Time!

To queer the left

CINELANDIA

SQUARE NOT FOR SQUARES

and TURN THE RIGHT

UPSIDE DOWN

GAY MOVEMENT

EVERYONE IN HEAT

TRAFFICKING

† FEIJOADA & IDEAS

— MALLARMELADE SEXY

THE POET'S ASS IS ON THE LINE POETRY

POETRY'S PLACE IS IN BED

FORWARD as when the POET

RIGHT into THE EYE of PUBLIC LOOKS

AS WHEN your the HEART

SUDDENLY APPEARS!

EK 81

levantamento rápido

,o movimento do poema pornô começou com a passeata pelo "topless literário", em fevereiro de 1980, na praia de Ipanema. O uso da palavra "pornô", em associação com a palavra "poema", recontextualiza ambas, e sugere uma nova síntese. Uma das faixas dizia: "Barulho: Poetas Trabalhando". O Manifesto Pornô, escrito em 14 de maio de 1980, foi lido pela primeira vez em praça pública, na Feira de Poesia, na Cinelândia, em 6 de setembro de 1980. Na mesma data, a revista Gang, veículo principal do movimento, foi lançada na Feira. Participam do poema pornô Kairo Trindade, Glauco Mattoso, Leila Míccolis, Bráulio Tavares, Teresa Jardim, e muitos outros.

,nós, os poetas do movimento pornô, valorizamos a política do corpo no que esta pode ser útil na elaboração de uma nova atitude estética. Mas, enquanto muitos perdem tempo em discutir se trazemos ou não uma atitude revolucionária, nós vamos fundo. Portanto, leia e goze conosco. Nossas camas são verdadeiros laboratórios de criação, onde curtimos a suruba literária. Assim, num sopro de pensamento peidamos o poema/prosexo, o hai-cu, o pornopoema concreto, o someto e toda a sacanagem da pesquisa de linguagem. E se muitos ficam só na sacanagem, conosco o buraco é mais em baixo.

,na ponta da língua: o discurso estigmatizado que se cagava foi subvertido. Como também foram repelidas posições incômodas e atitudes brochantes. Damos lugar aos binômios: espontaneidade-tesão, sinceridade-prazer e felicidade-gozo. Eis o que talvez haja de mais radical na merda que escrevemos. E os palavrões? Tanto os cagamos por toda parte que não fedem mais. O que era merda virou perfume. Atenção: a merda é vendida em frasquinhos de fragrâncias. A merda é indispensável à vida e, exatamente por isto, nossa linguagem de merda pode ser revolucionária.

,não somos Vanguarda. A Vanguarda está sempre à frente e nós estamos, muitas vezes, bem atrás. Também não somos "poetas marginais". Penetramos em todos os buracos e seguramos todas, desde o prelo da editora à manivela do mimeógrafo (movido a álcool). Não somos escola porque não temos mestres nem discípulos; corrente menos ainda, já que dispensamos grilos e grilhões. Estamos em movimento (de vaivém, como diz o Glauco). Jogamos aberto, segundo Teresa. Somos poetas sem classe, desclassificados em qualquer pelada oficial. Membros espermanentes do PUTA (Partido Universal dos Trabalhadores Anarquistas), uma criação de Kairo. Um hino ao ânus e uma bandeira hasteada, nunca a meio-pau, nos representam.

,se no começo do movimento assumimos uma atitude panfletária e radical diante do discurso poético tradicional, hoje buscamos a síntese pela abolição de entrelinhas e incorporamos poesia a tudo que é adjetivado de vulgar e obsceno. Frequentemente utilizamos a rima como recurso rítmico e até pedagógico. Reformulamos a linguagem mais imediata do cotidiano no que ela é manipulada pelo rígido discurso do poder. E quando em nossos poemas revelamos a sexualidade dentro de um contexto simbioticamente politico, o fazemos sem os adornos e subterfúgios que costumam deformar o sentido natural do sexo, exorcizando a vergonha do corpo e combatendo a aplicação ambígua do rótulo pornográfico. Nós, os poetas do movimento pornô, não traduzimos a linguagem da abertura e sim a abertura da linguagem.

quick assessment

,the porn poetry movement began with the "literary topless" demonstration, in February 1980 at Ipanema Beach. The use of the word "porn" in association with the word "poem" recontextualizes both and suggests a new synthesis. One of the banners stated: "Noise: Poets at Work". The "Porn Manifesto", written on May 14, 1980, was read for the first time at the Poetry Fair at Cinelândia Square on September 6, 1980. On the same date, the zine *Gang*, the main vehicle of the movement, was launched at the Fair. Participants include Kairo Trindade, Glauco Mattoso, Leila Míccolis, Braulio Tavares, Teresa Jardim, and many others.

,we, the porn art movement poets, value body politics, which can be useful in developing a new aesthetics. But while many waste time discussing whether or not we bring a revolutionary attitude, we go deeper. So read and cum with us. Our beds are creation labs, where we enjoy a literary orgy. Thus, in a blow of thought we fart the *poema/prosexo*, the *hai-cu*, the *pornopoema concreto*, the *someto* and we fuck with poetic language research. While many stop half-way, we can go at it all night.

,at the tip of the tongue: we subverted the stigmatized speech that was defecated by society. We repelled uncomfortable positions and limp attitudes. We make room for the binomials: hornyness-spontaneity, sincerity-pleasure, and happiness-orgasm. That may be the most radical dimension of the shit we write. What about cursing words? We shit them everywhere so that they don't stink anymore. We turned shit into perfume. Watch out: shit is now sold in fragrance flasks. Shit is indispensable to life. That's why our shitty language can be revolutionary.

,we are not avant-garde. The avant-garde is always ahead and we are often well behind. We are also not "marginal poets". We penetrate every hole and handle everything, from the (alcohol-driven) mimeograph to the book publishing house. We are not a school because we have no masters or disciples; even less a current, even though we are wired. We are always moving (back and forth, as Glauco says). We play openly, according to Teresa. We are classless poets, unclassifiable, disqualified in any official class. Spermanent members of PUTA (Universal Anarchists Toilers Party), a creation of Kairo. We are represented by a hymn to the broken hymen and our pole doesn't raise a flag.

,if at the beginning of the movement we assumed a radical and pamphleteering attitude toward traditional poetic discourse, today we seek a synthesis to abolish subtexts and we incorporate poetry to all that is deemed vulgar and obscene. We often use rhyme as a rhythmic and even pedagogic resource. We redesigned everyday language because it is manipulated by the power discourse. And when in our poems we reveal sexuality within a symbiotically political context, we do it without the ornaments and subterfuges that usually distort the natural meaning of sex. We exorcise body shame and fight the ambiguous application of the pornographic label. We, the porn poets, do not bring the language of the "opening", but the opening of language.

POECIA FLATOGRÁFICA
— coprojeto didáticu —

§ A Poecia: um truque clássicu
§ O Poema: um traque típicu
§ O Poeta: um treco críticu

1 * A poecia, mais q tudo, é o alterego da flatulência intestinal e cultural. Do mesmo modo q o peido alheio é extremamente repugnante a cada um, o seu lhe é até agradável e, na pior das hipóteses, tolerável. O mesmo ocorre com a poecia, cuja indefinição leva a crer q o critério mais exato para a sua avaliação, enquanto inovadora manifestação de linguagem, é de fato determinado pelo olfato.

2 * O poema é mais q um fato de linguagem, daí o futum de um pum ser como um poema. O ato de peidar socialmente acentua a semelhança entre um poema de vanguarda e um flato, na medida em q um grande poema e um grande peido provocam semelhante reação no público. xeyryllynkuaçem. Já o peidinho é como um poema inodoro, esse q não fede nem cheira.

3 * O q difere os poetas flatográficos daqueles q não o são é, no caso de peidos transcendentais, sua capacidade em respirar fundo um palmo adiante do nariz. Assim exercitam sua técnica e excitam sua imaginação. Os melhores poetas produzem os mais inventivos peidos semióticos e, para tanto, observam a simbiose entre o peido e o poema visual, não deixando de realizar, segundo cada ponto de vista, constantes experimentalismos de olho do cu. De flato, os poetas contemporâneos de vanguarda (entre os quais pintam e despontam os poetas flatográficos) desacatam o peidantismo e se definem por sua capacidade — sem precedentes — de unir o "inútil" (o poema) ao "desagradável" (o peido). GAZES & GOZOS.

FLATOGRAPHIC POECY
— dildactic coproject —

§ Poecy: a classical gag
§ Poem: a typical gas
§ Poet: a critical ass

1 * Poecy, more than anything, is the alter ego of cultural and intestinal flatulence. Just as someone else's fart is extremely repulsive, one's own is even pleasing and, at worst, tolerable. The same occurs with poecy, whose vagueness suggests that the most accurate criterion for its evaluation, as an innovative poetic language, is in fact determined by olfaction.

2 * The poem is far more than a linguistic fact, therefore the fart stink is like a poem. The act of farting socially accentuates the similarity between an avant-garde poem and a flatus, in that a great poem and a great fart cause similar reactions in the public. Ahromandlanguidge. The short fart is like an odorless poem, the one that doesn't give a shit.

3 * What differentiates flatographic poets from others, in the case of transcendental farts, is their ability to take a deep breath inches from their noses. This is how they exercise their techniques and excite their imagination. The best poets create the most inventive semiotic farts; but, in order to do so, they observe the holistic relationship between the fart and the visual poem, never stopping short of butthole experimentations. The flatographic poets are on the cutting edge; they defy arsecademicism and define themselves by their unprecedented ability to unite the "useless" (the poem) to the "unpleasant" (the fart). JIZZ & GAS.

Pornograms

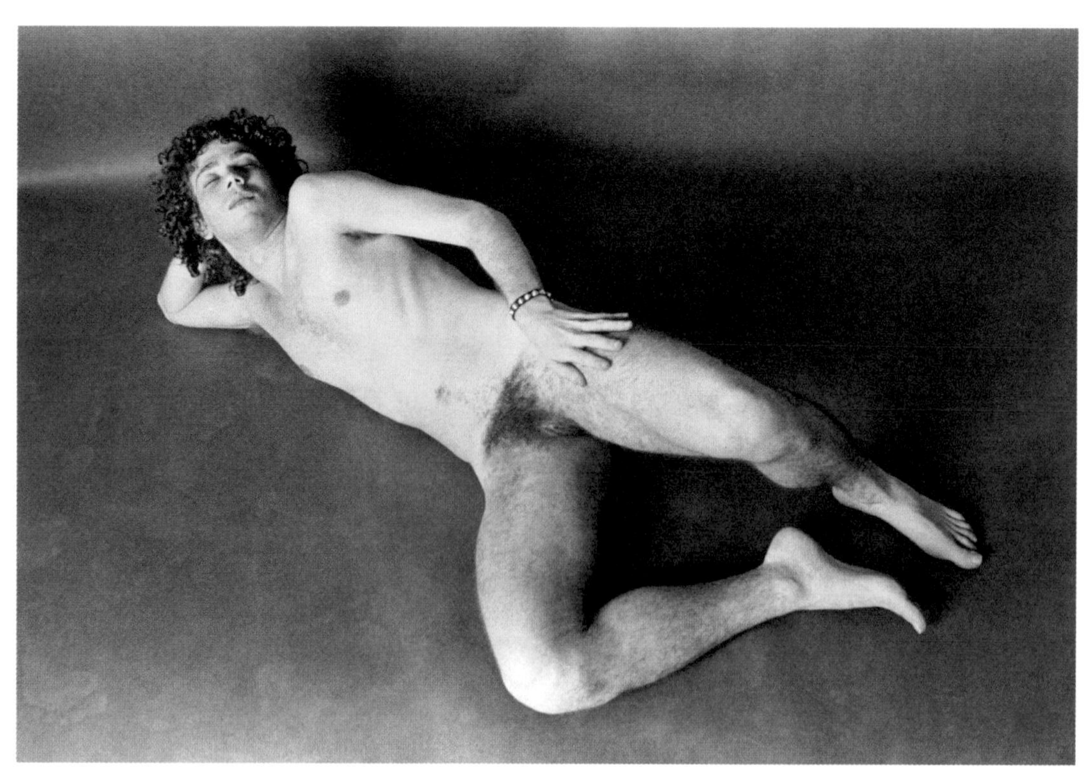

Pornogram I

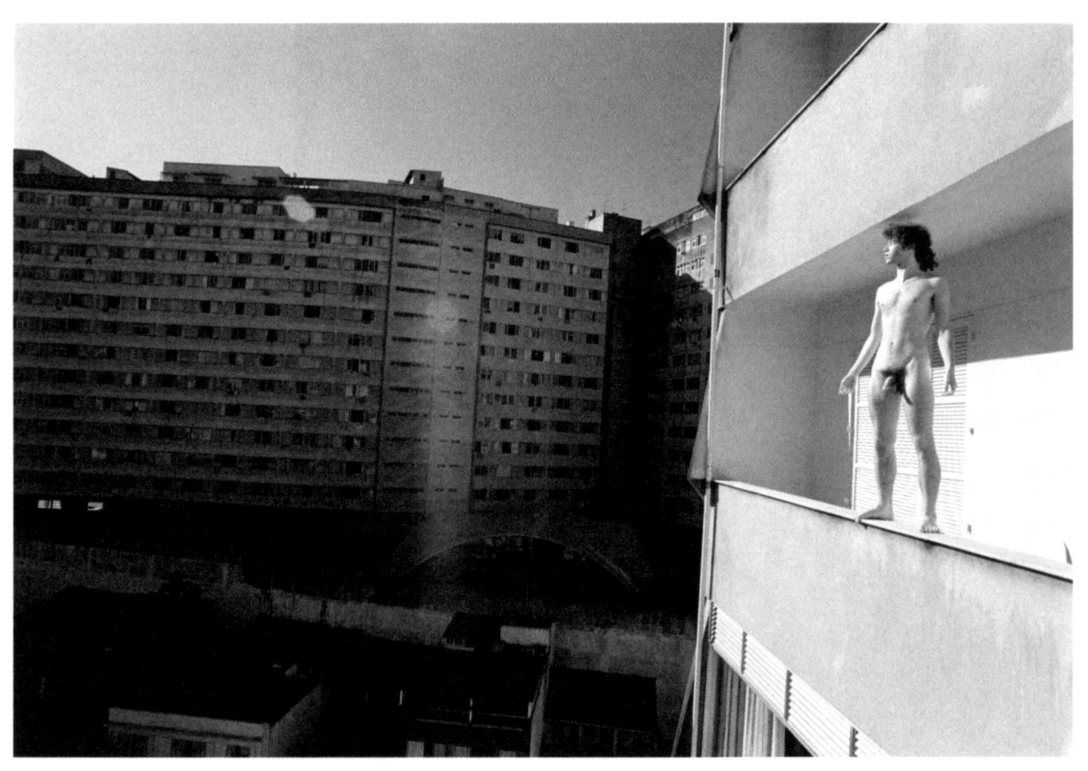

Pornogram II

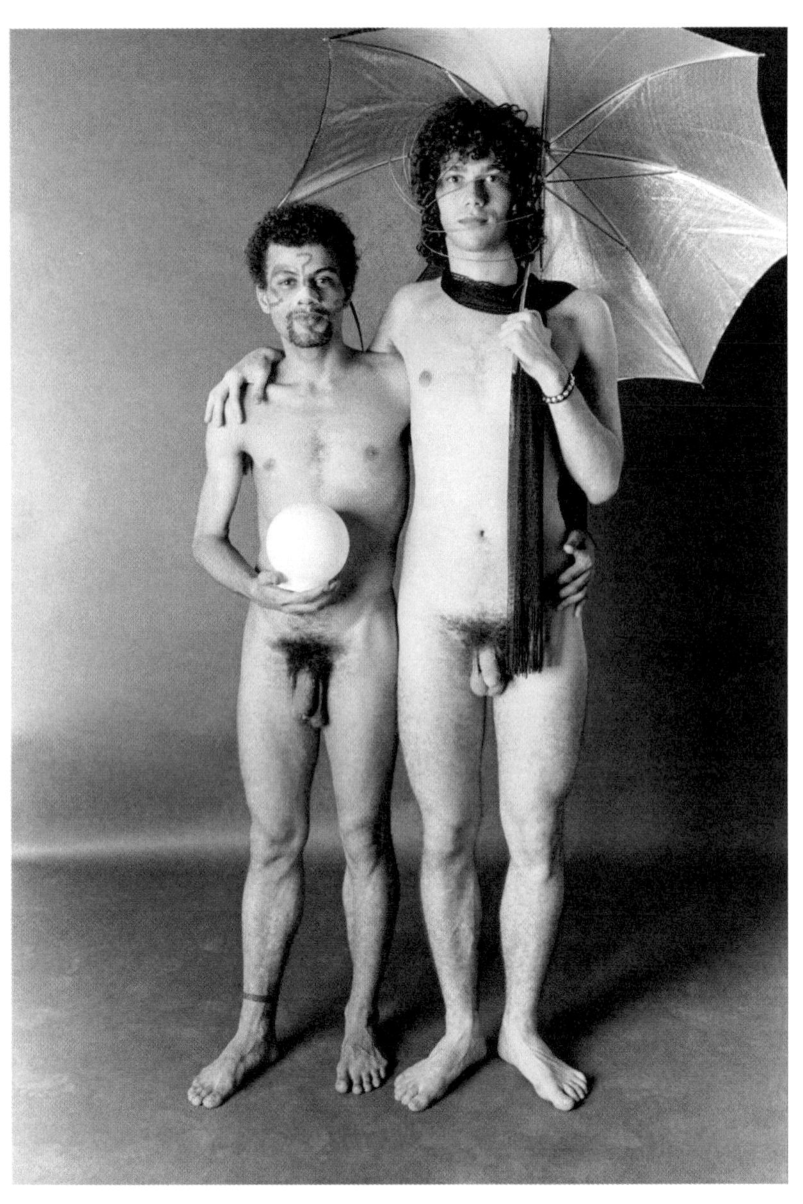

Pornogram III

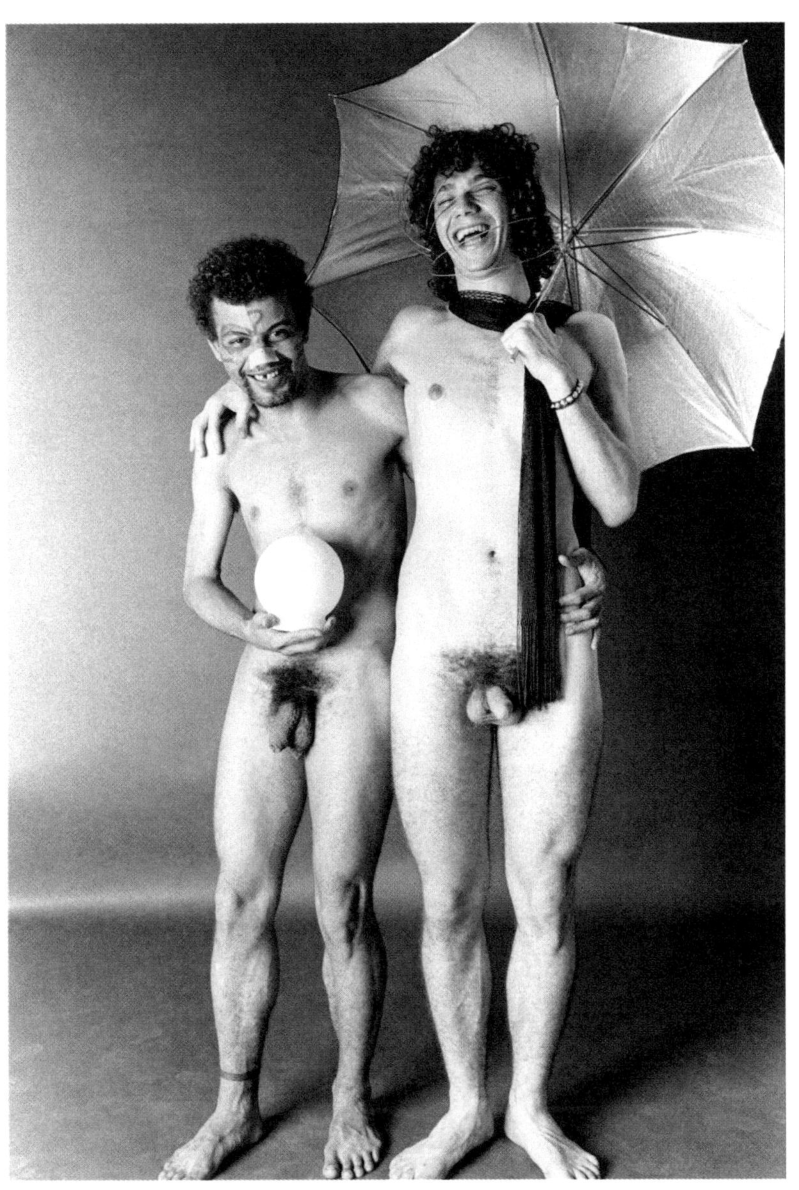

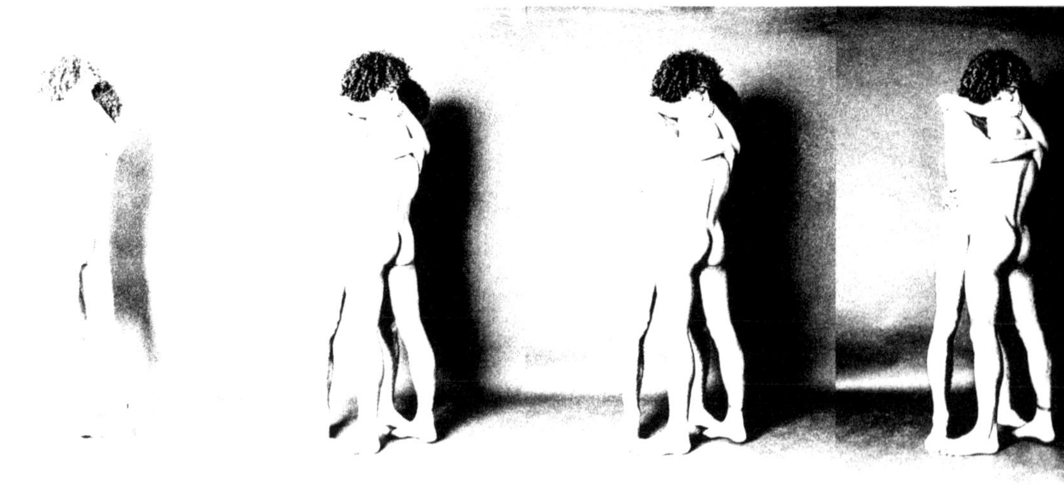

Pornogram IV

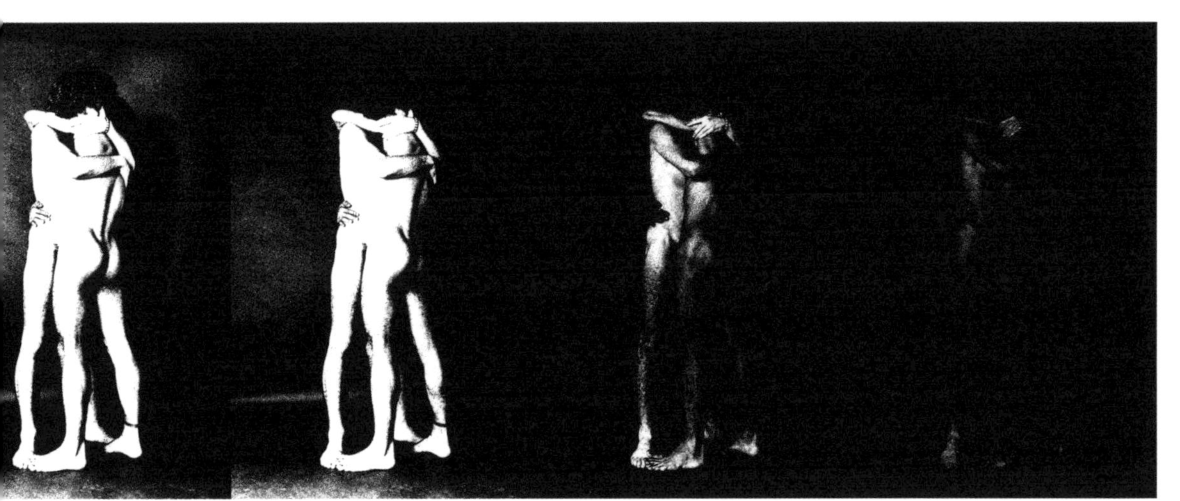

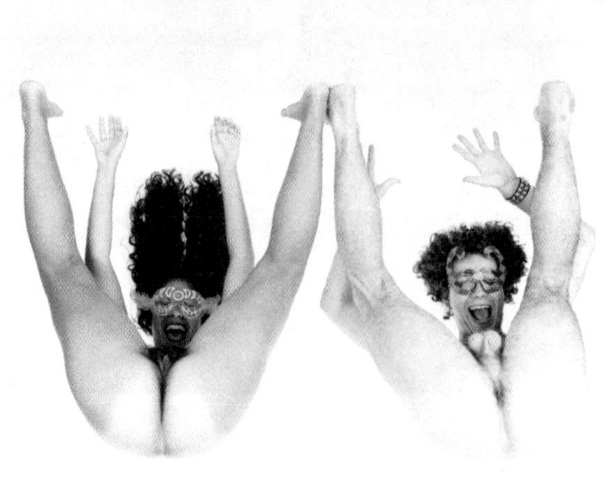

Pornogram V

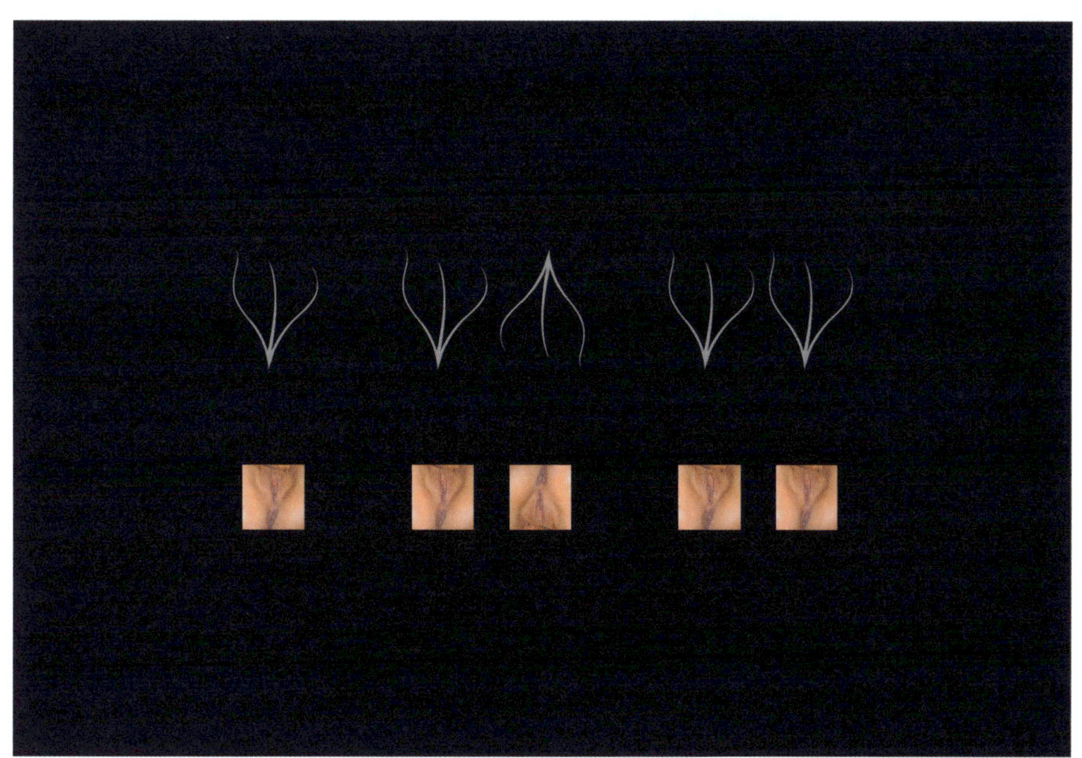

Pornogram VI

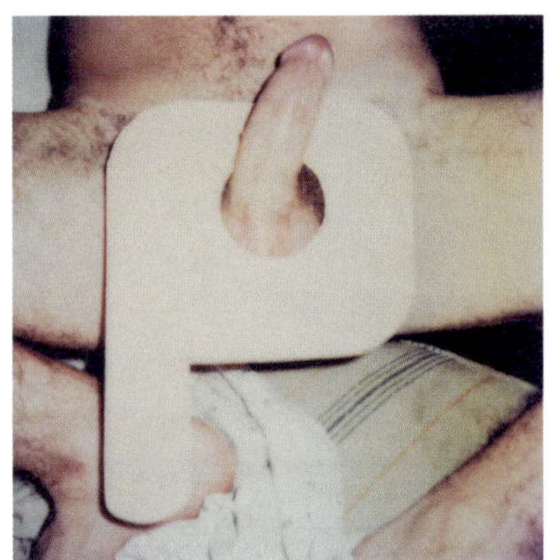
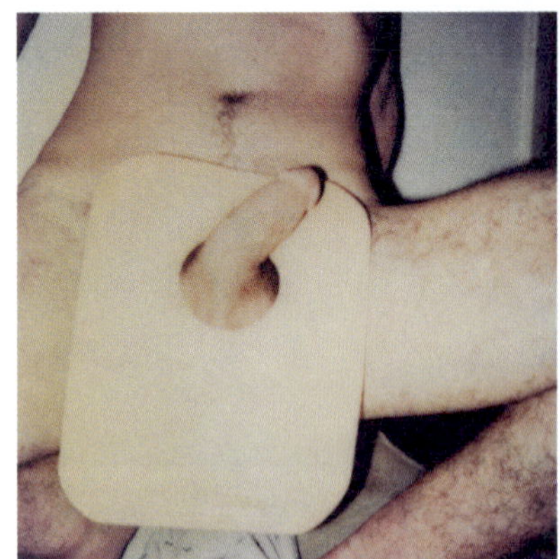
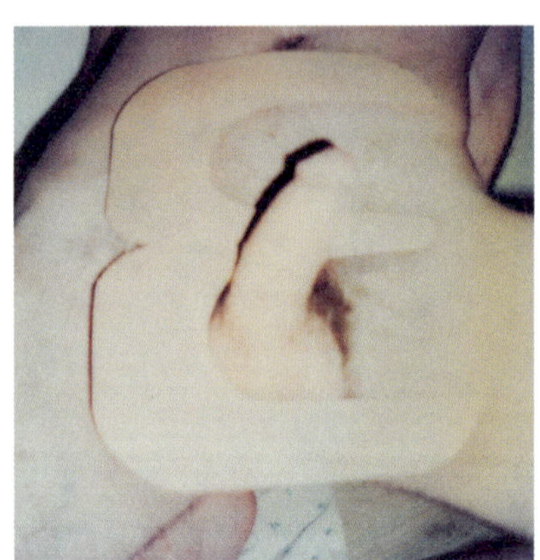
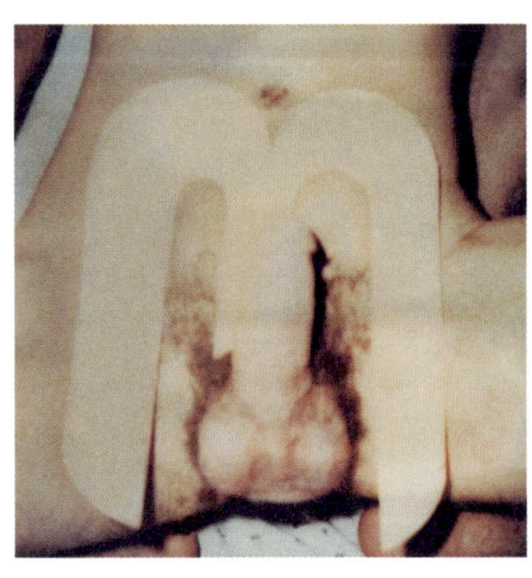

Pornogram VII

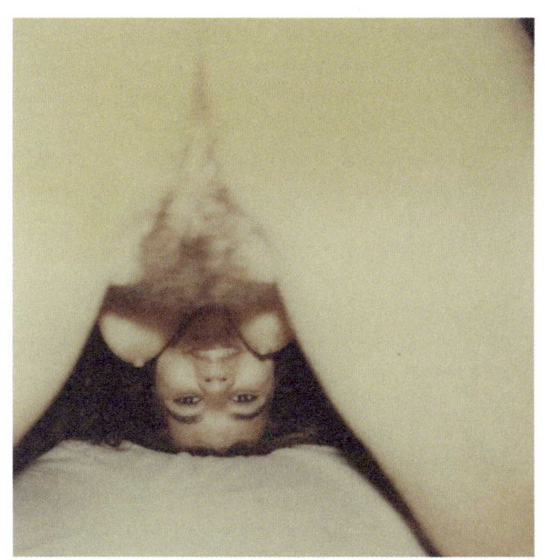 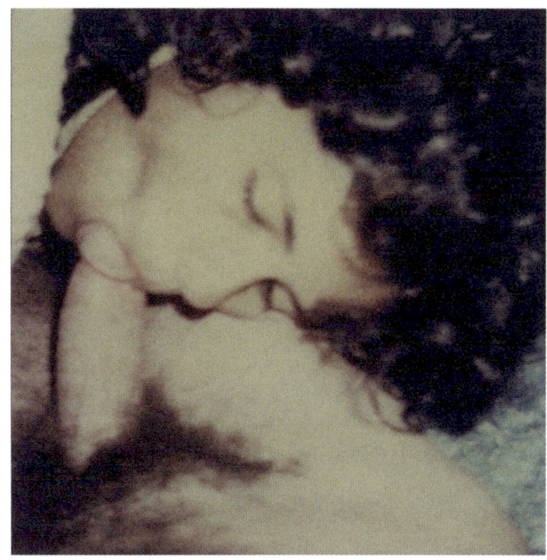

Pornogram VIII

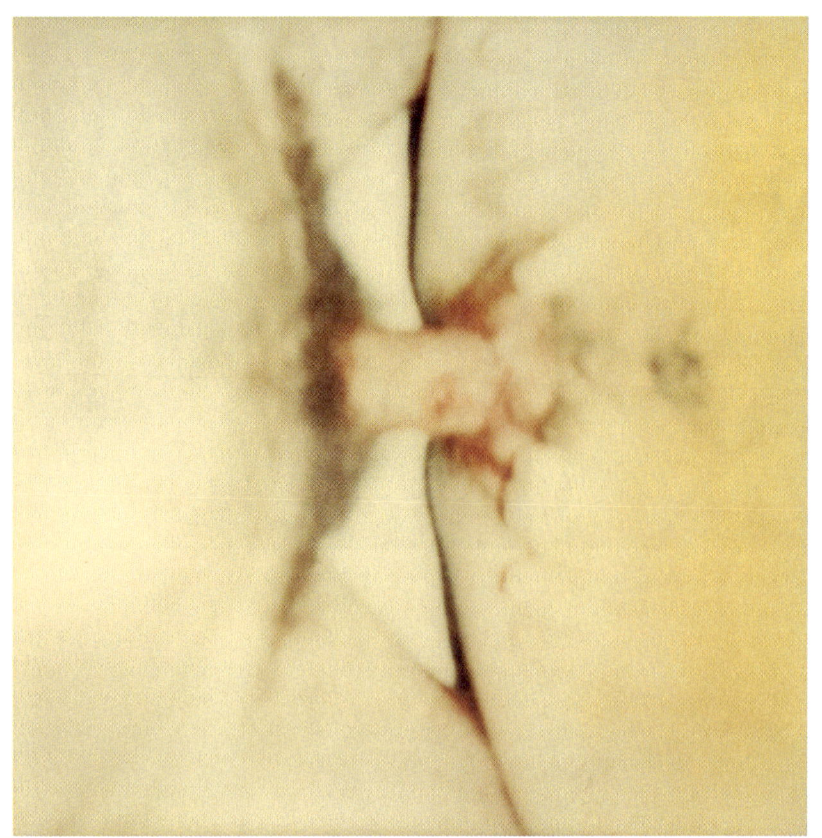

Pornogram IX

Yellpoems

Yellpoems

pra curar amor platônico
só uma trepada homérica

to cure platonic love
only a homeric fuck

a literatura chata não dá uma dentro
a nossa é literatrolha xota
tesão pulsando no texto
que eles coitentam interromper
sem supunhetar
nem ivaginar que tenho pênis
deles que nádegas têm ânus dizer

boring lit doesn't light my clit
ours is high lickerature
throbbing text
tit for tit
that they wood stop
stiff they could
butt they cunt try ass they might

Eclipse

o dia amanheceu tesudo
o mar chupa
a bucetinha do horizonte escancara
um sorriso

                                                                    azul

enquanto o sol de pau duro goza
junto cualua

Eclipse

the day dawned horny
the sea licks
the horizon's pussy gapes
a blue

                                               smile

while the boner sun cums
in the moonass

Encontro

vá se fuder
disse um ao outro

vá se fuder
disse o outro ao um

descobriram a felicidade
em seu lugar comum

Rendezvous

fuck you
said Jase to Joe

fuck you
said Joe to Jase

they found happiness
in its commonplace

[ ] Foda   [ ] Poder
[ ] Caralho   [ ] Tortura
[ ] Buceta   [ ] Fome
[ ] Cu   [ ] Exploração
[ ] Chupada   [ ] Censura

Contra o que você protesta?
Assinale com um X a resposta certa

[ ] Fuck   [ ] Power
[ ] Cock   [ ] Torture
[ ] Cunt   [ ] Hunger
[ ] Butthole   [ ] Injustice
[ ] Blow Job   [ ] Censorship

Against what do you protest?
Mark the correct answer with an X

Batom Marrom

a bosta em minha boca
não me basta
é pouca pra quem gosta
e cara pra quem não gasta
sua tara
nem escancara a sua
cara

Brown Lipstick

the shit in my mouth
is the shit
i want more
i want it with smores
it makes me horny
i want it with honey
honey

O Urubu

eu tocava punheta quando apareceu
um urubu doidão torcendo a maçaneta
agarrou minha bunda e dizia:
"no cu mais, no cu mais"
e a dor era profunda tanto
que de longe se ouviam "ais"
debruçado no meu cu ficou o urubu baco
dizendo a todo instante:
"no cu mais, no cu mais"
tanto me encheu o saco que um dia
o peguei por trás e ele pedia que eu botasse
uma vez mais nunca era demais
depois daquela alegria começamos uma orgia
que não acabou jamais hoje somos
eu e o urubu o mais feliz dos casais

i was jerking off when the vulture showed up
he was wasted and slammed the door
he grabbed my ass and said:
"i want more, i want more"
it was hard and it hurt and my butthole was sore
what a fit i had
then the vulture licked my booty
grabbed my ass and said:
"i want more, i want more"
baby, it's not so hard to find
one day i grabbed him from behind
he said: "i want more, i want more"
oh boy what a joy he wasn't coy
and so goes the tale
of the merry couple and their happy tails

Johnson & Johnson

ei! que tal
depois de chupar o meu pau
e comer o mingau
usar o pentelho
como fio dental?

hey! wanna lube
and suck my cock?
after you swallow the caulk
wanna floss
with my pubes?

Não Ria

eu me fudi
sabe como?
estudei acrobacia

I fucked myself
wanna know how?
I studied acrobatics

Pipiuzinho Vermelho
Gato de Bosta
João Mete Sete
Galinha dos Óvulos de Ouro
Ali Babaca e os Quarenta Ladrões
Putinho Feio

Little Red Riding Ho
Pussy n' Booty
The Brave Limp Tailor
The Golden Eggs Goose That Got Laid
Ali Babe and the Forty Fruits
The Ugly Fuckling

era uma vez uma Pica
essa Pica morava no Reino da Bunda
onde a Bunda abundava
certa vez a Pica picou a Bunda
e desde então
viveram felizes para sempre

once upon a time there was a Dr. Dick
Dr. Dick lived in Buttland
where Mr. Butt was a buttermaker
one day Dr. Dick kissed Mr. Butt
and they happily spread love
ever after

uta e ariu aralho orra uta erda!
udi o u e a uceta!
altou gum lavrão?

other ucker ock ucker hit!
i ucked the unt and the utt'ole!
issing any wear ords?

momentos bucetâneos de verão
pés desbucetados na areia quente
contemplo o mar balbucetando palavras ao vento

água fria com ondas bucetolentas
baseados e sorrisos bucetílicos
penso em nada bucetilhando o movimento

gatas lindas leves loucas embucetadas
os papos mais bucetinados
mergulho no sol esbucetante congelando o tempo

summer cuntastic moments
cuntly feet in hot sand
I contemplate the sea cunting words to the wind

cold water with cuntilinial waves
cuntomic joints and smiles
I think of nothing but cuntoning the scene

crazy gorgeous cuntious girls
cuntsy chats
I dive in the cuntful sun freezing time

Xereca Sapeca

linda puta louca
é o sol tão feminino
em purpurinas de fissura
esquenta o meu sangue de menino

com toda doideira e todo ouriço
rompendo cabaços fazendo cabeças
brilho pelo piço
lanço o grito de alerta

uma menina alegre e inconstante
dentro de mim desperta

beautiful crazy bitch
the sun is so feminine
in cracked glitter it
heats up my boy blood

I'm taken
popping cherries smoking charas
snorting glowing lines
let the world know

a haphazard happy girl
inside me awakens

Graffiti

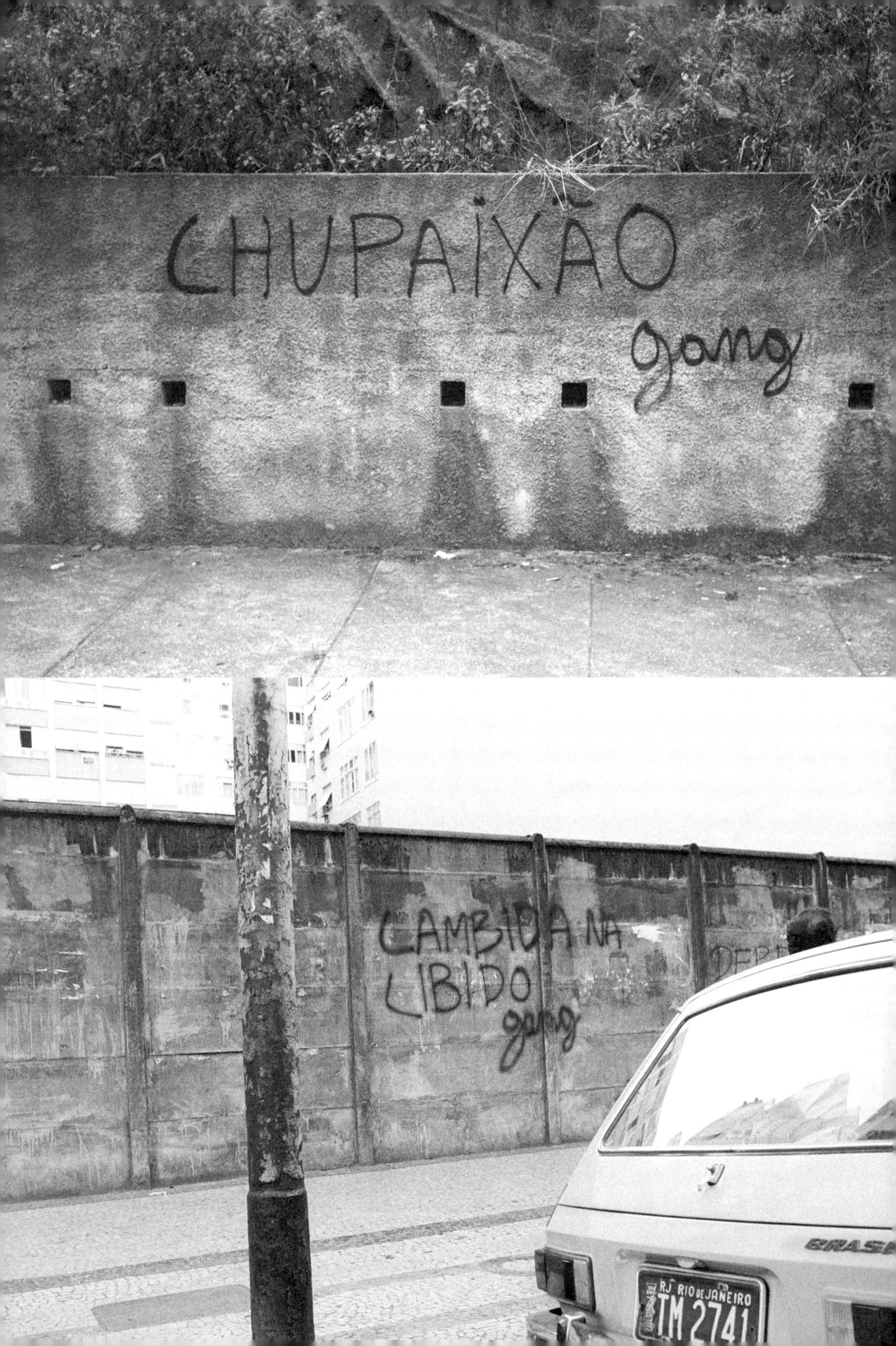

CHUPAIXÃO gang
CAMBIO NA LIBIDO gang
RJ RIO DE JANEIRO
TM 2741

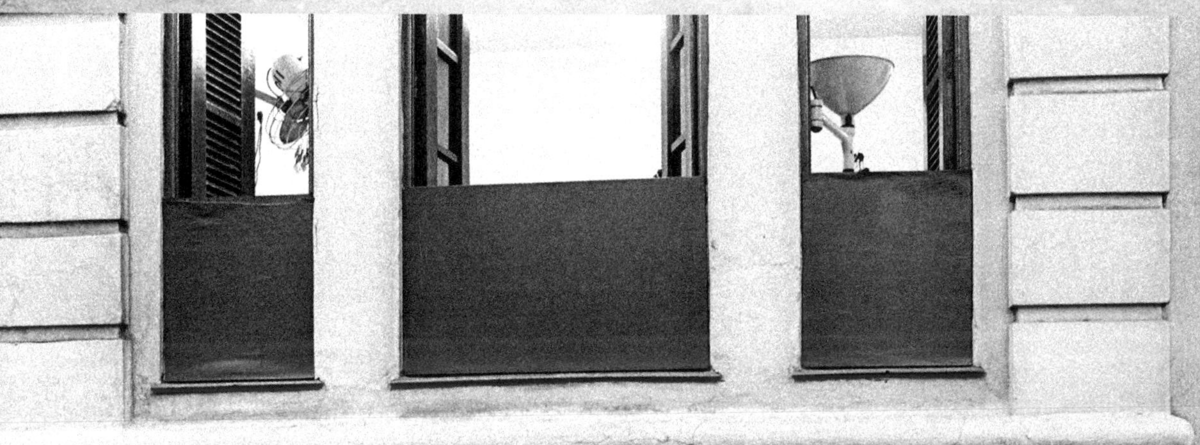
OVERGOZ3 gang
PIKA DIKA DURA PURA
gang
OU3RGOZE

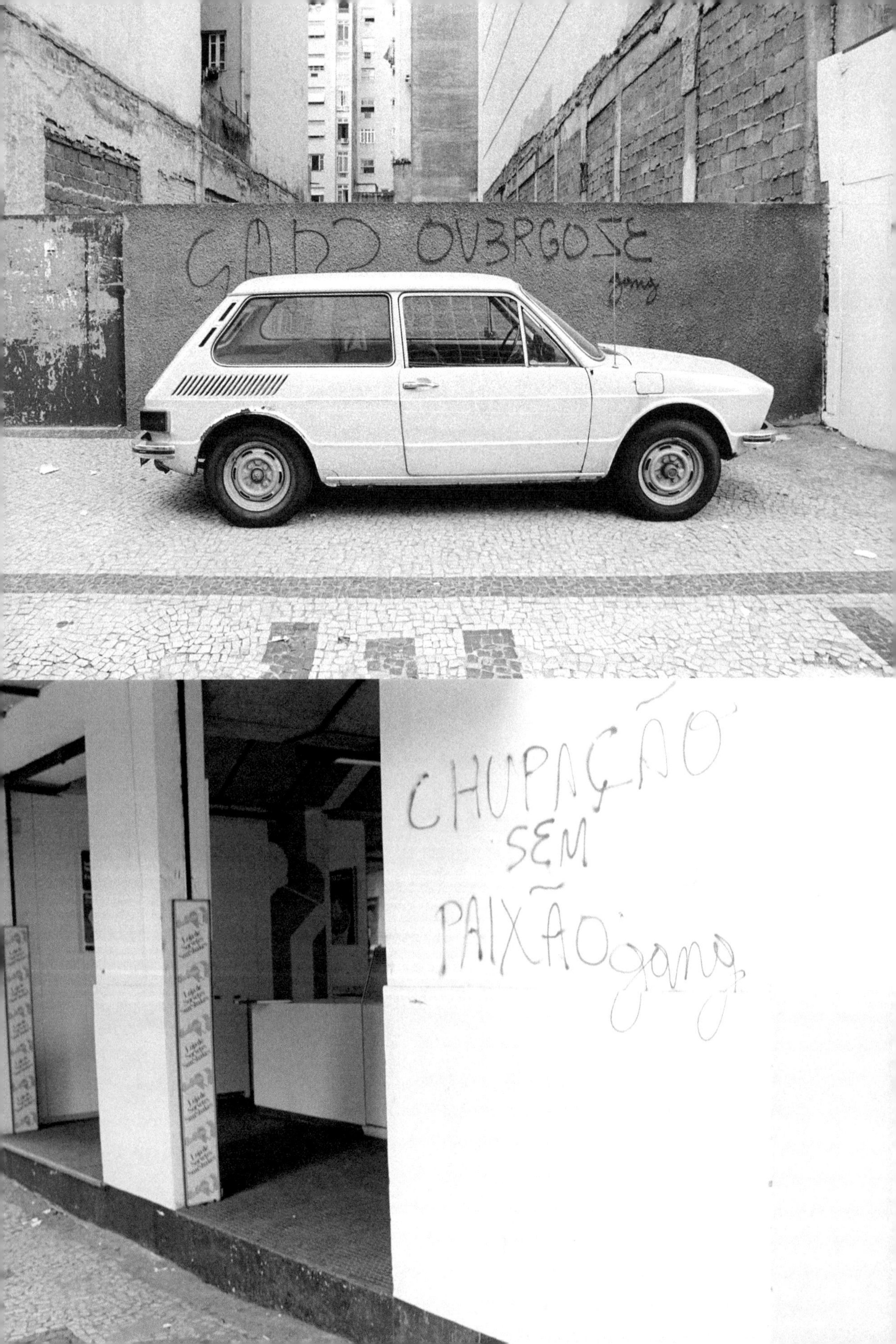
GADZ OV3RGOZE
gang
CHUPAÇÃO
SEM
PAIXÃO gang

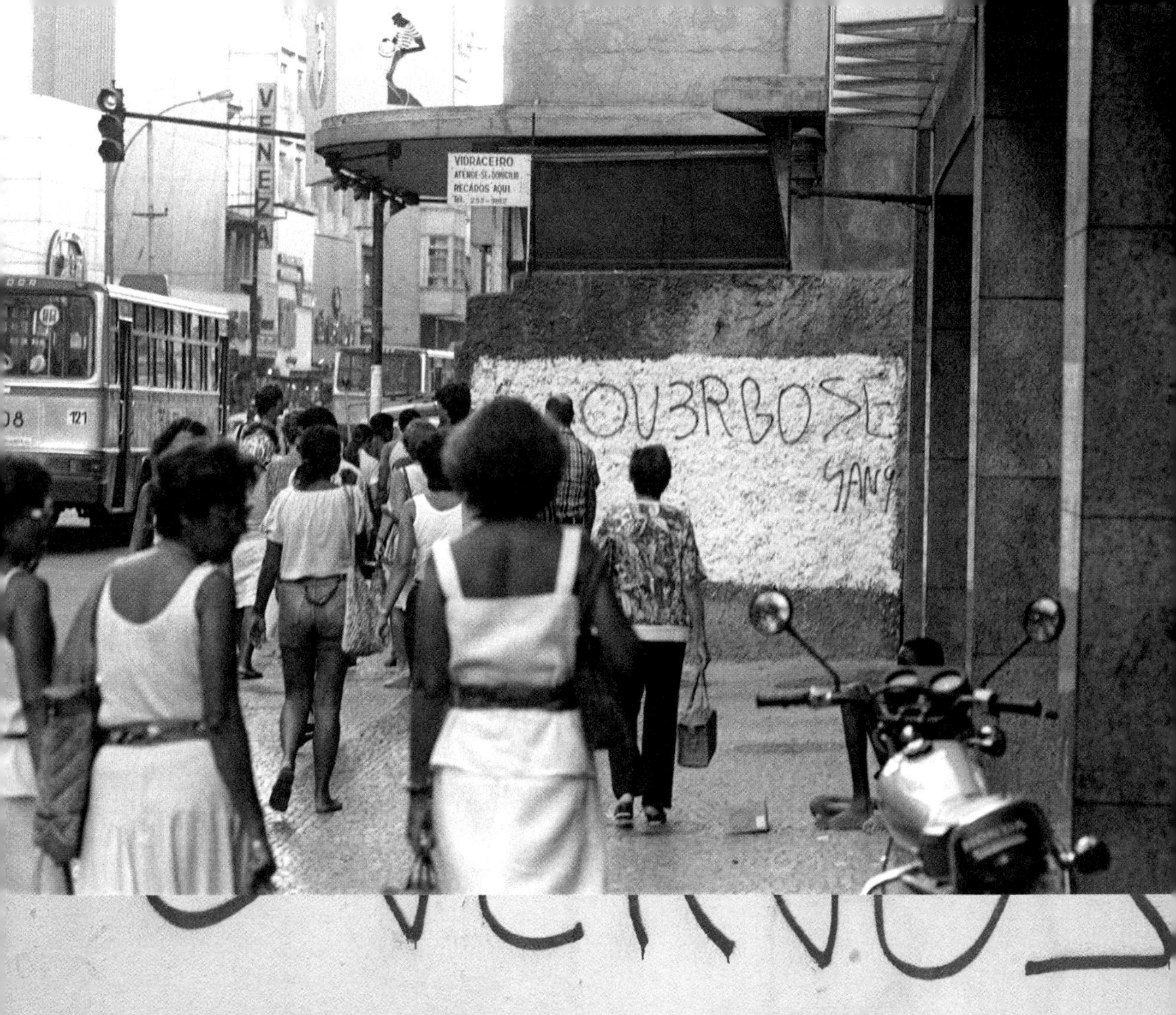

VENEZA
VIDRACEIRO
ATENDE-SE DOMICILIO
RECADOS AQUI
Tel. 253-9857
OU3RBOSE
gang
PIKA DIKA
DURA PURA
gang

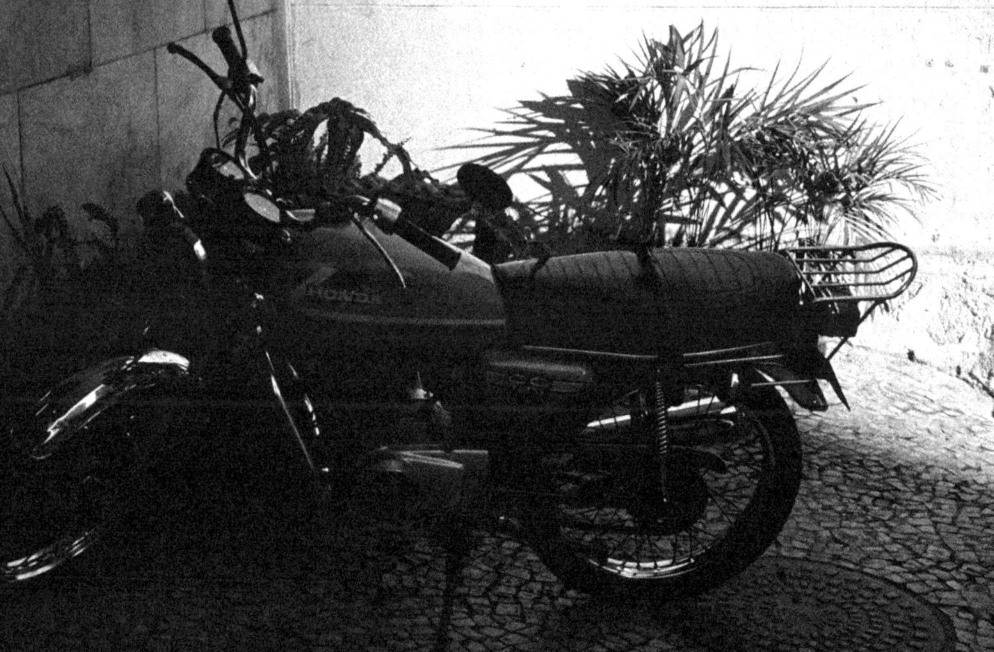

OVERGOZ3
gonoz

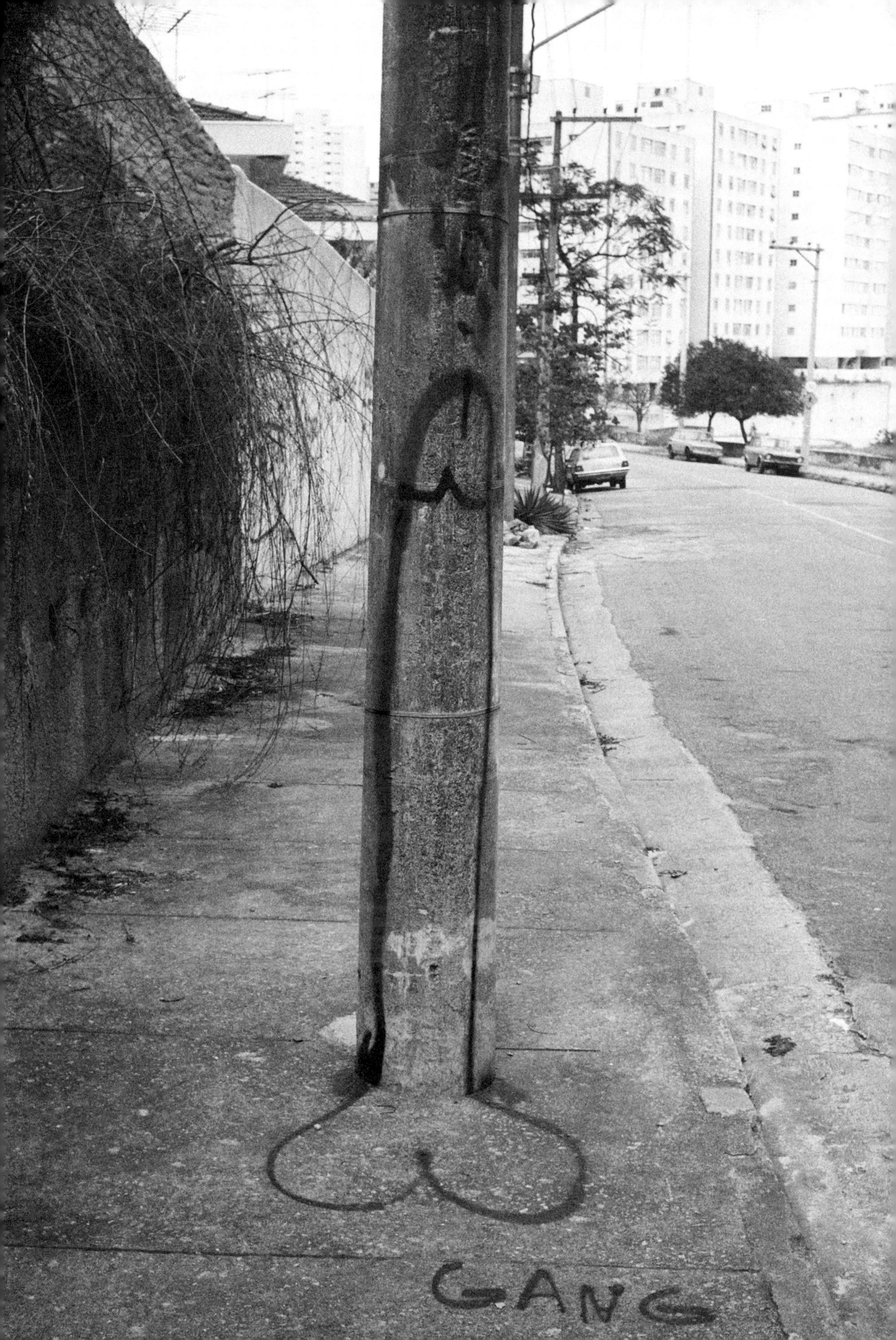
GANG

Visual Works

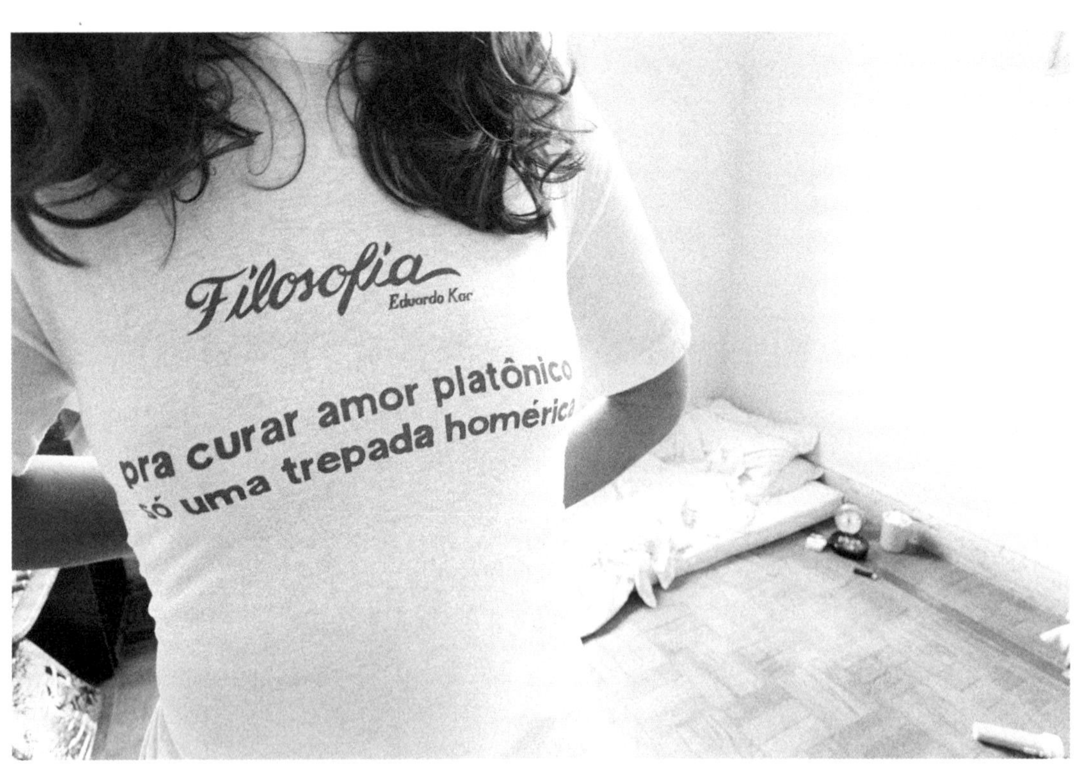

Filosofia
[Philosophy], 1980

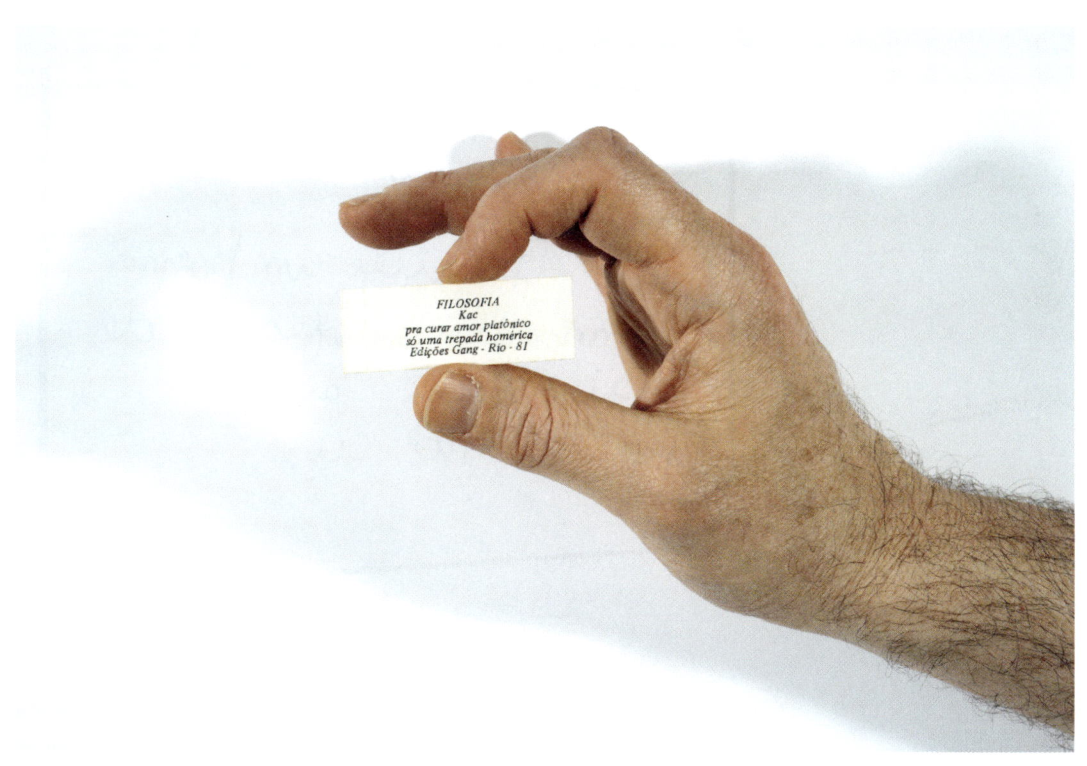

Filosofia
[Philosophy], 1981

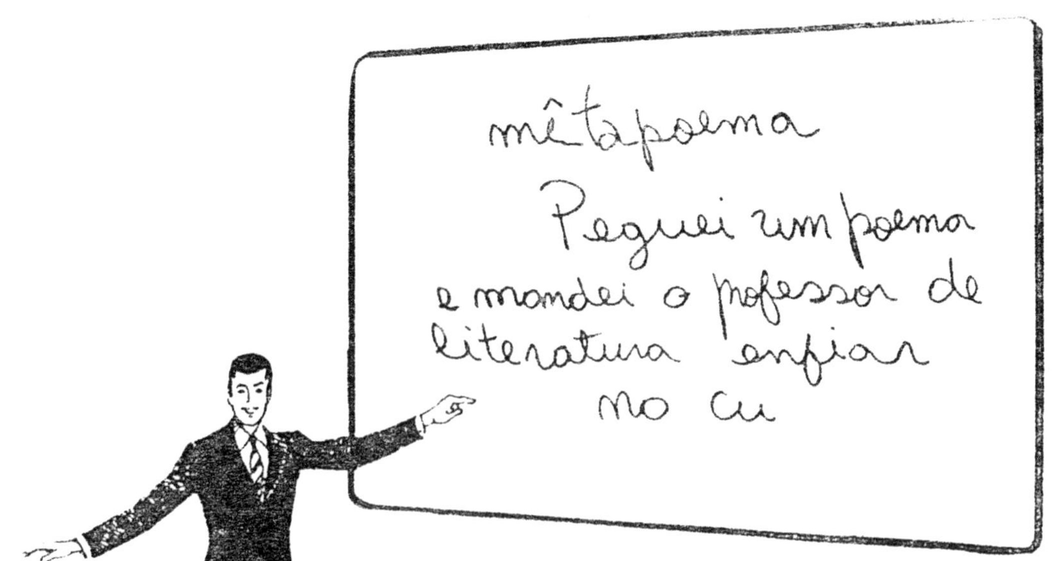

Metapoema
[Metapoem], 1980

metapoem
And then I said to the Lit prof:
take this poem and
shove it up your ass

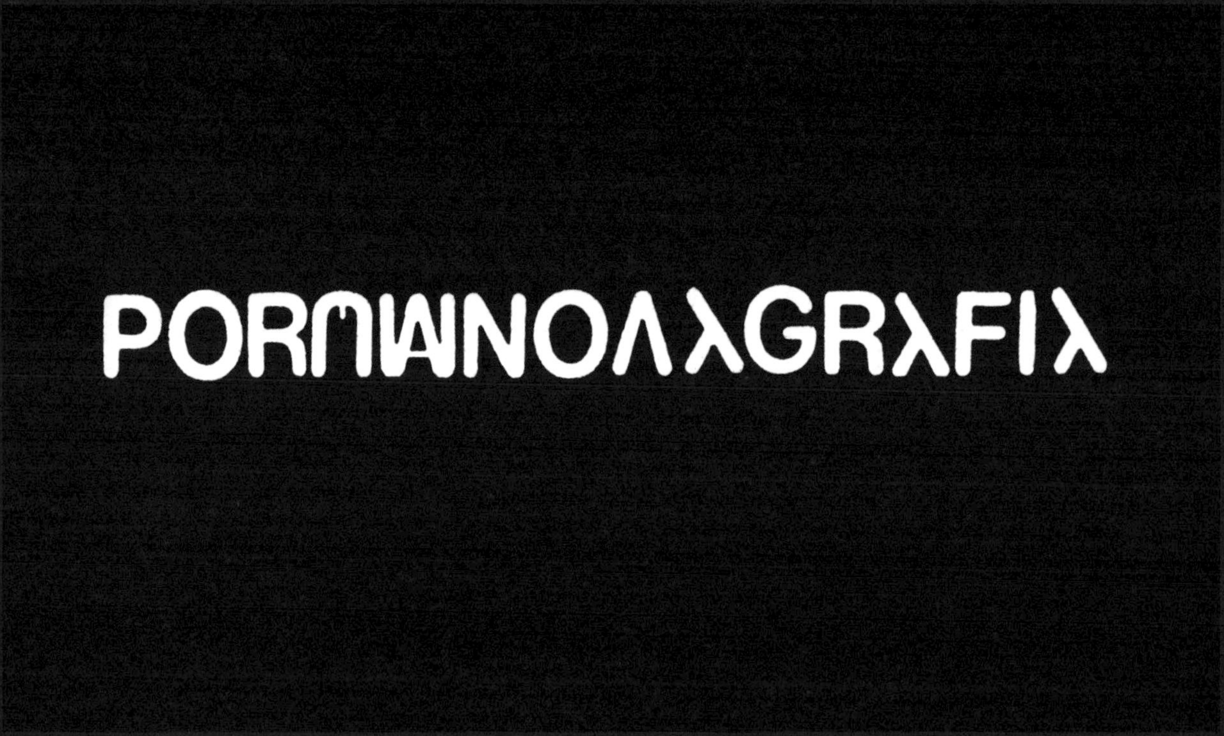

Por uma nova grafia
[For a new spelling], 1981

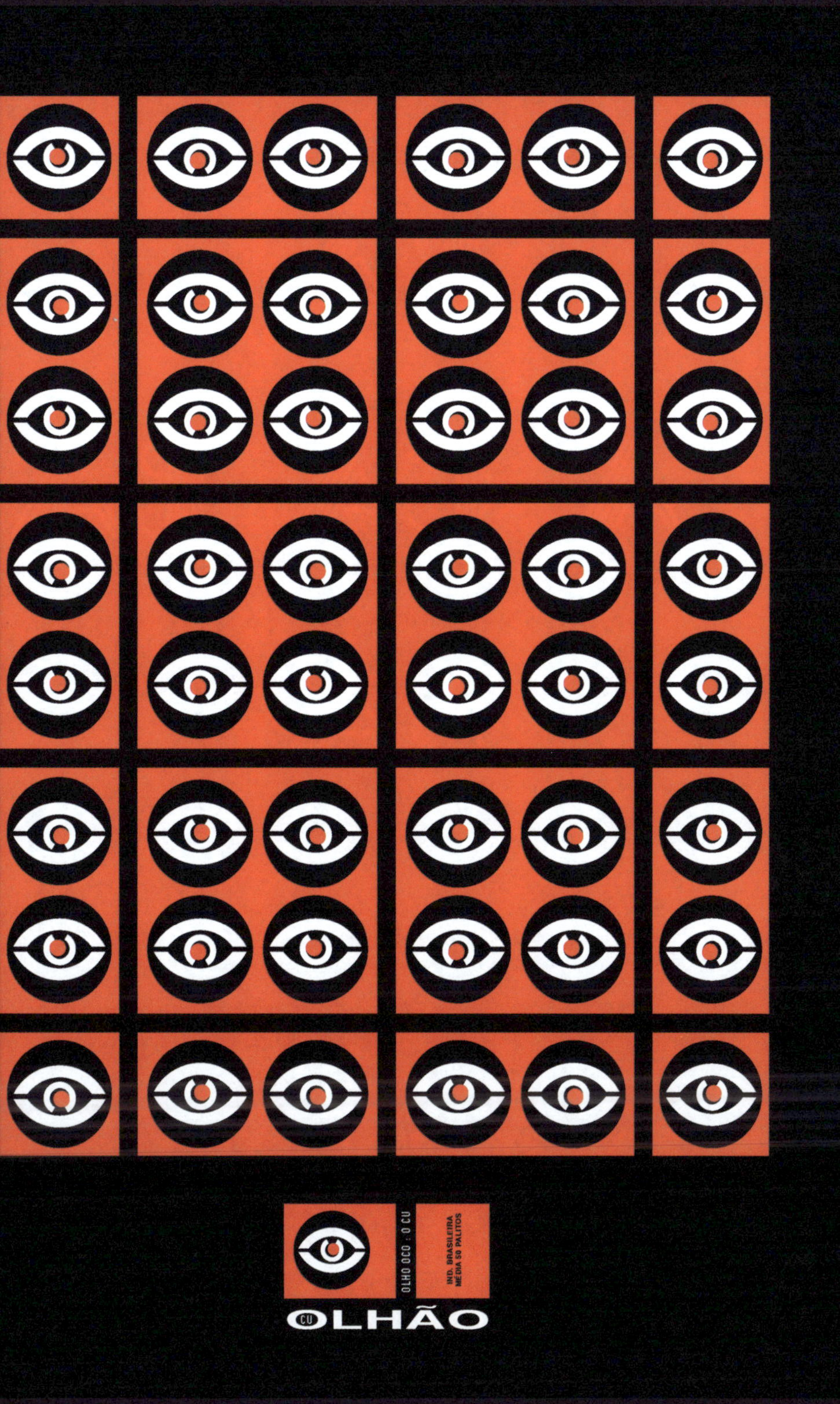

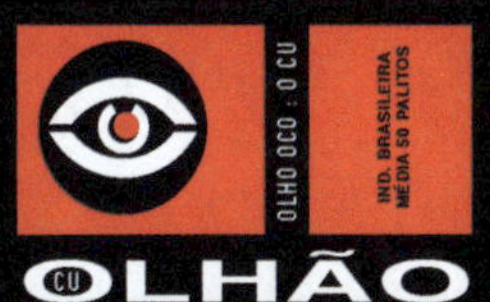

Olhão
1981

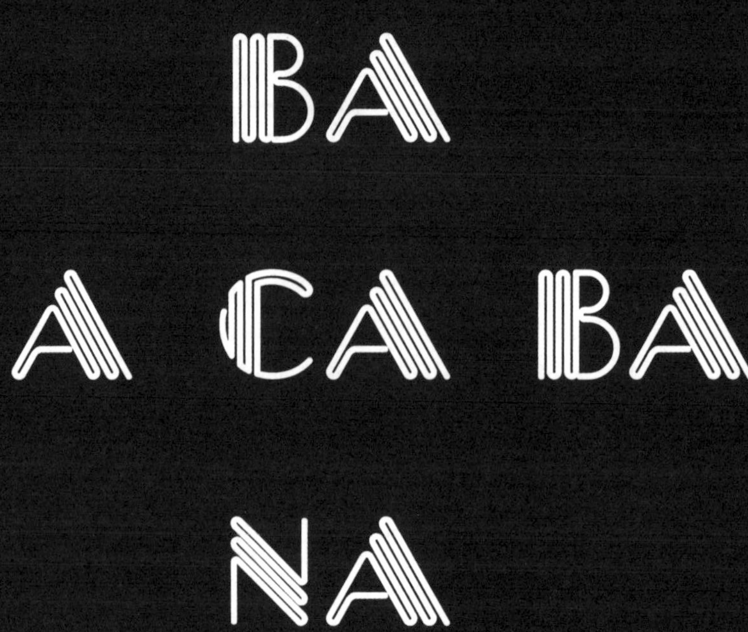

Em Copa
[In Copacabana], 1981/2015

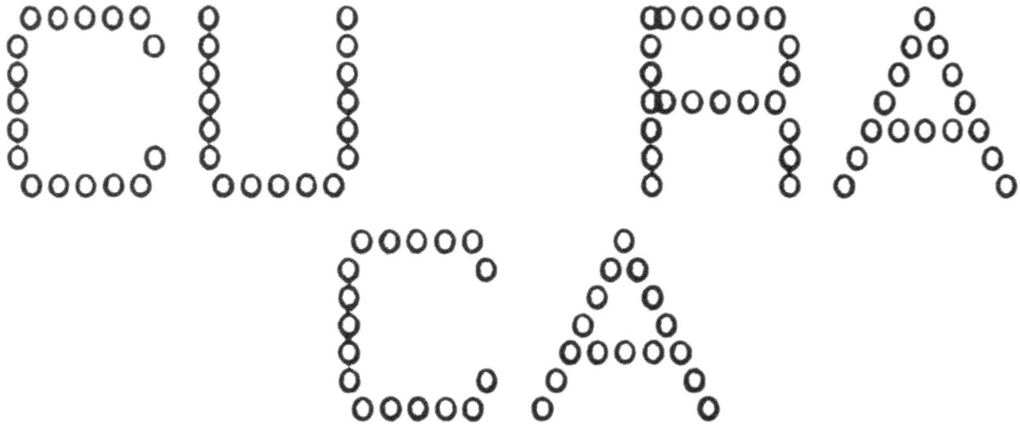

Sem Título (Cu Cura Cuca Cara)
[Untitled], 1981

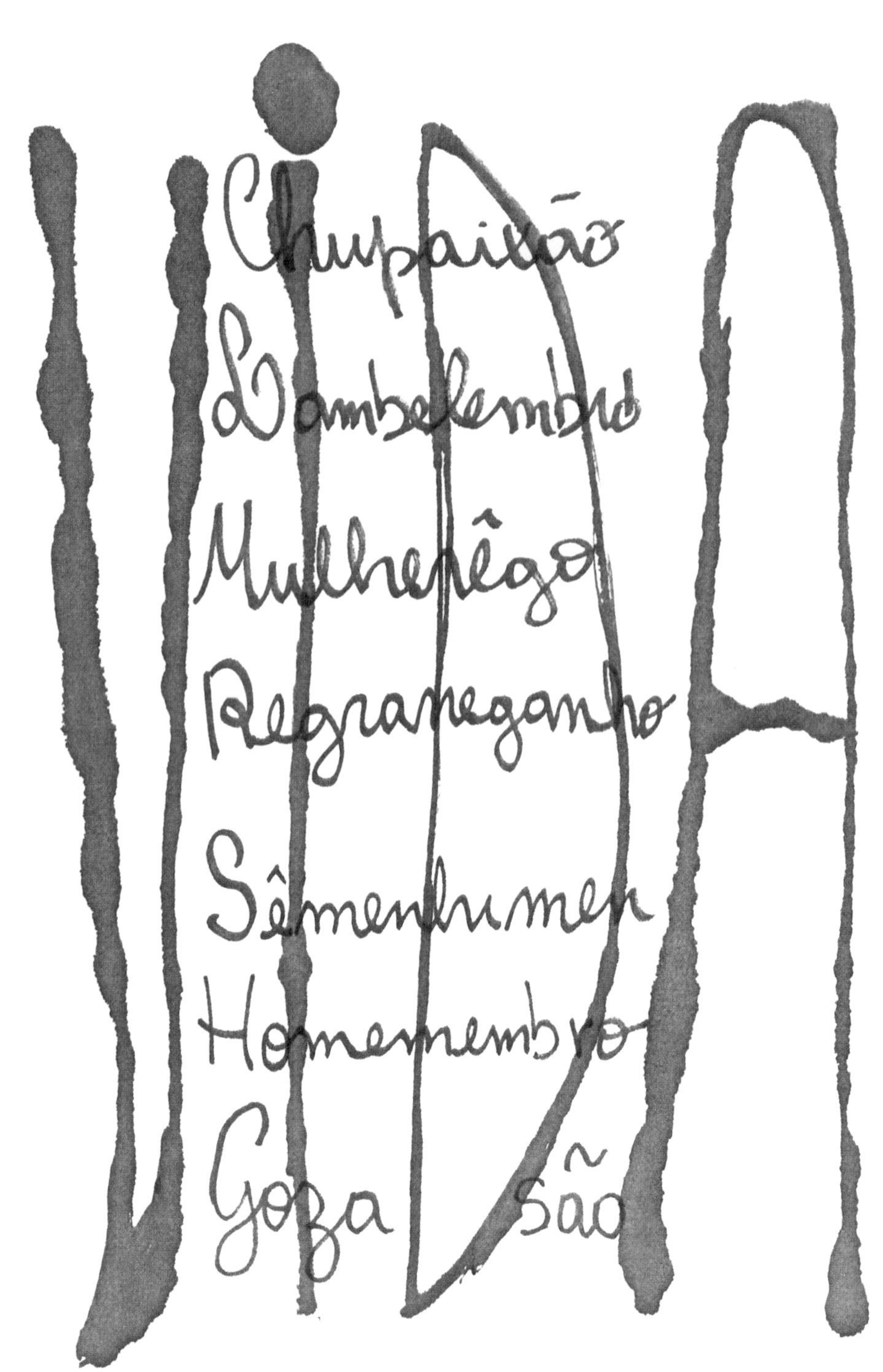

Vida
[Life], 1982

pág. 6

pág. 9

pág. 69

pág. (6=9)

pág. 6&9

pág. 6/9

pág. 6:9

pág. 6)(9

pág. (69)
pág. (6)(9)

pág.)69(

pág. 6(∅)9

pág. 6( )9

pág. 6̶9̶9̶9̶9̶9̶

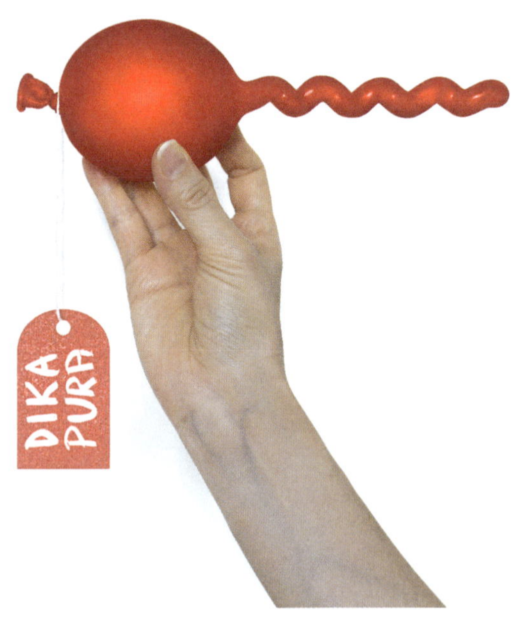

Poemazoide
[Spermpoem], 1981

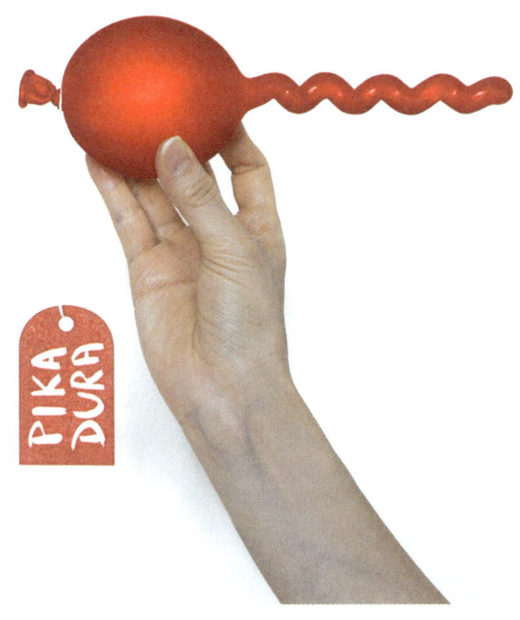

PIKA
DURA

Someto
[Sonaughty], 1981

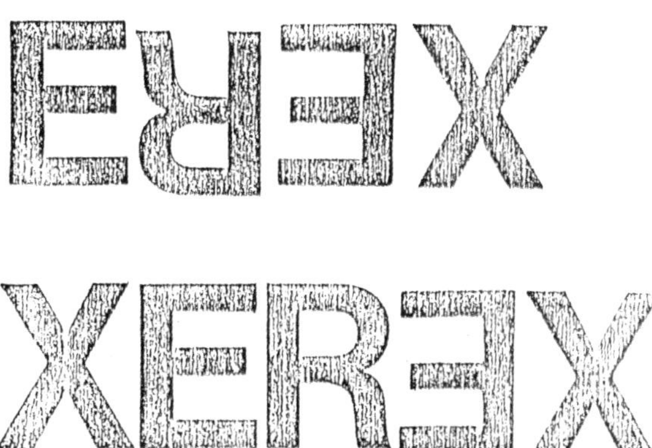

2x3X
1982

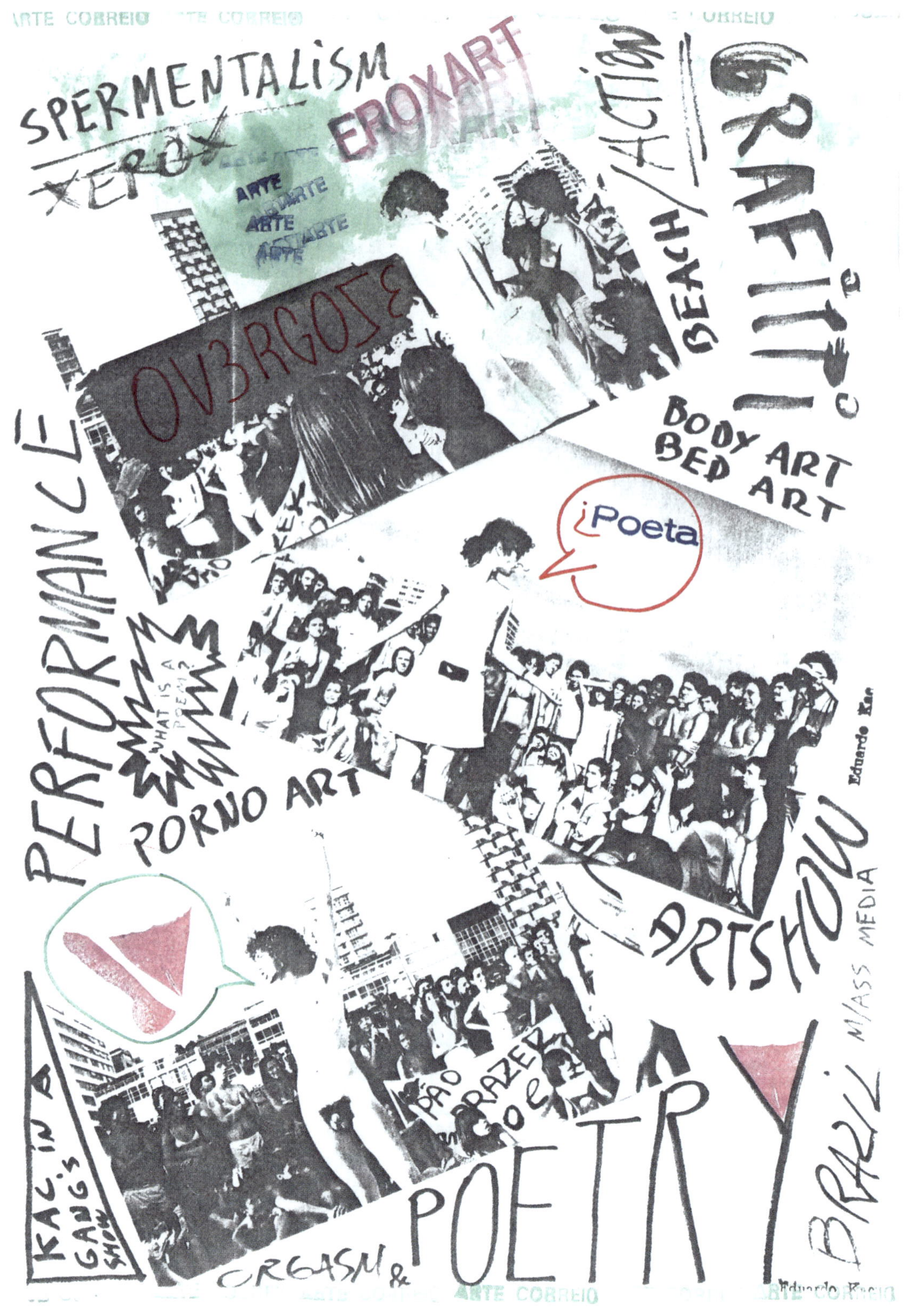

M/ASS MEDIA
1982

PICTOGRAM SONNET

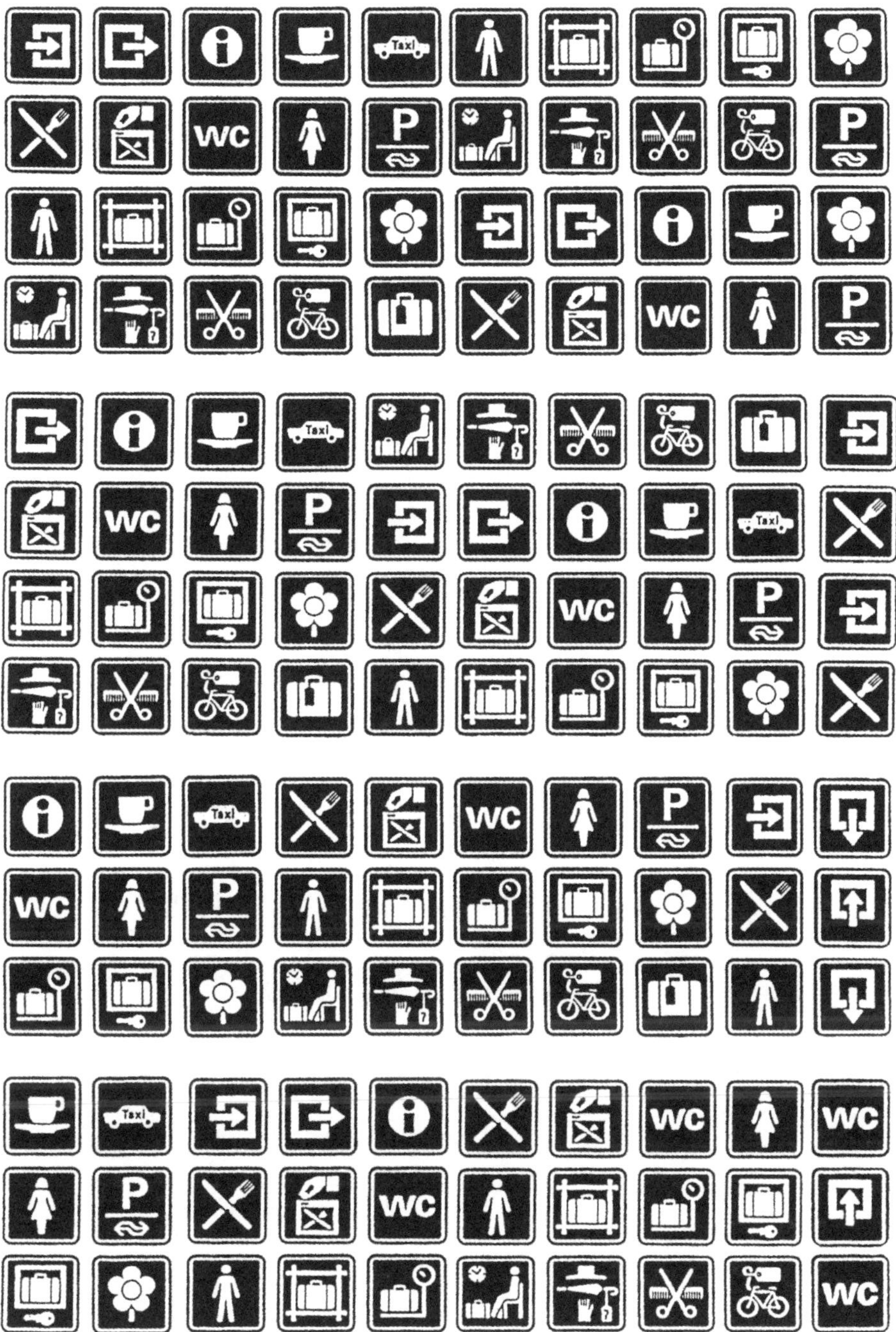

Pictogram Sonnet
1982

Obra

```
b " / § £ _ & ( . )
u =   ) ( ' § o | o
c ) £ § / = & ( . )
e _ / "   § o | o

t ' ( § = / # o-
a -- ) " _ * ~ 00
e £ / " : = ~ o-
c ) ' ( § " / 00

a ' ; / " _ ] { }
r : - , . & . ( * )
a £ : x _ ) ] { }

l ' _ / : ; . ( * )
h : ' _ / " ] { }
o ) £ , : ? . ( * )
```

Obra
[Work], 1981

Work

c " / § £ _ & (.)
o = °) ('§ o|o
c) £ § / = & (.)
k _ / " ° ⚵ § o|o

c ' (° ⚵ = / # o-
u --) "_ * ~ 00
n £ / " : = ~ o-
t) ' (§ " / 00

t ' ; / " _] { }
i : - , . & . (*)
t £ : x _)] { }

a ' _ / : ; . (*)
s : ' _ / "] { }
s) £ , : ? . (*)

Na Veia
1981

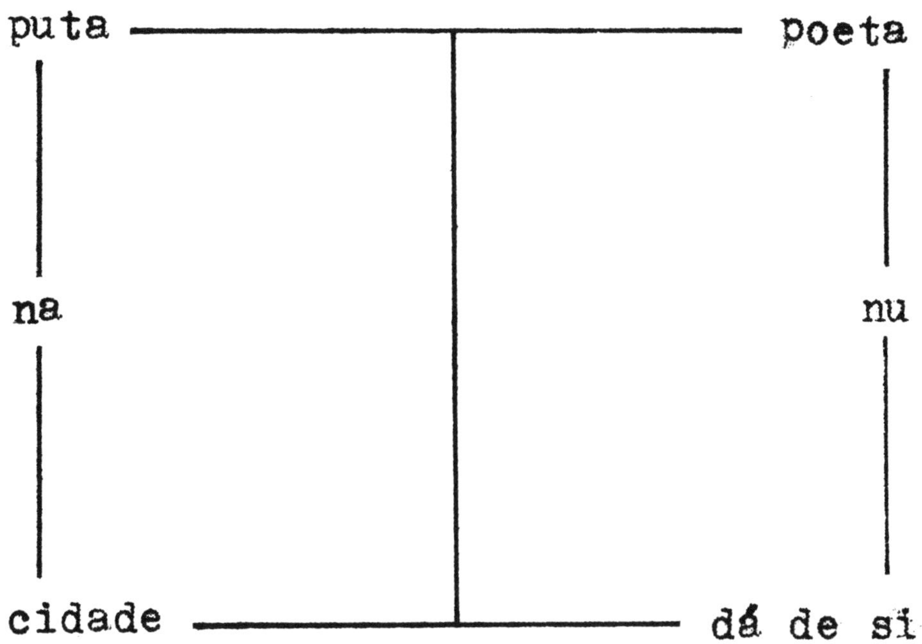

Puta Poeta
1981

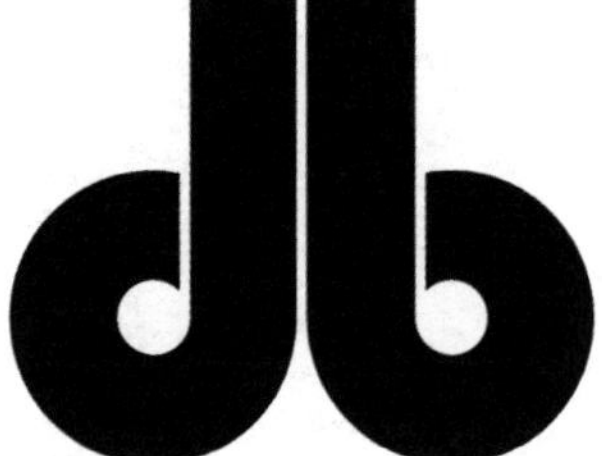

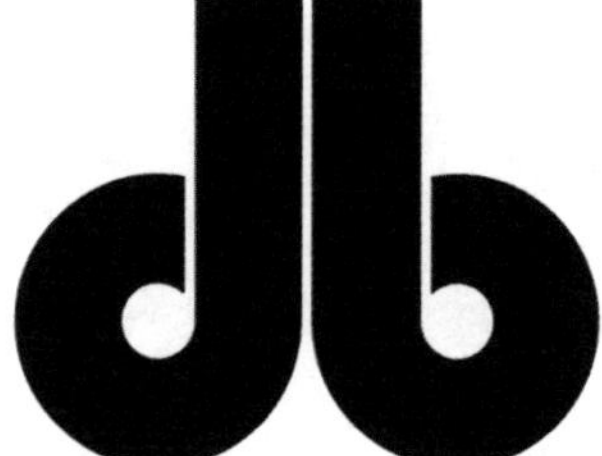

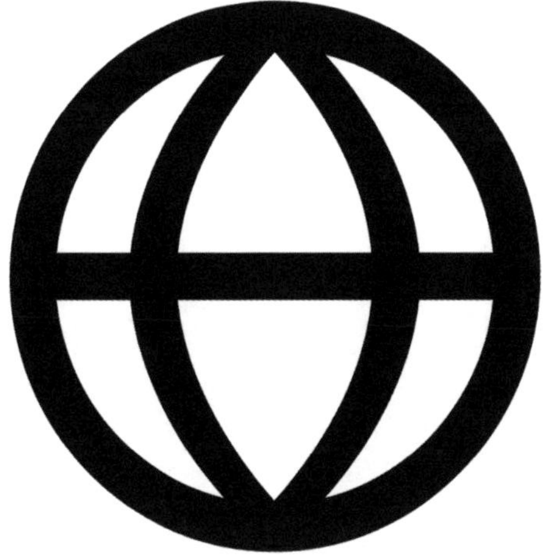

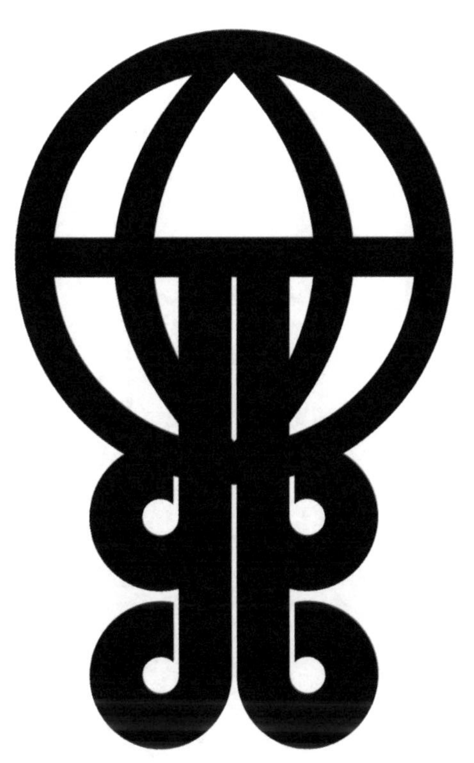

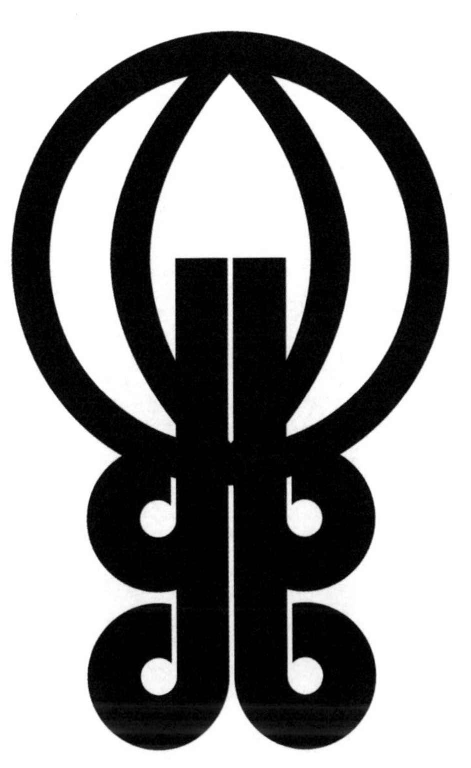

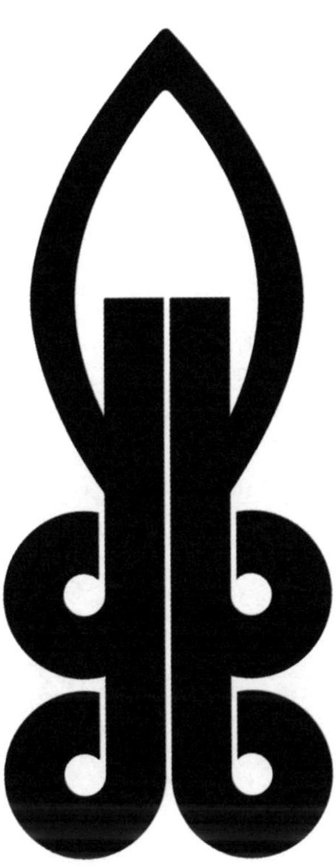

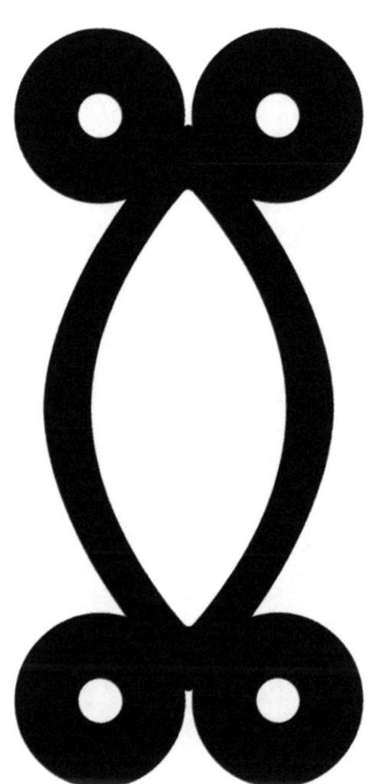

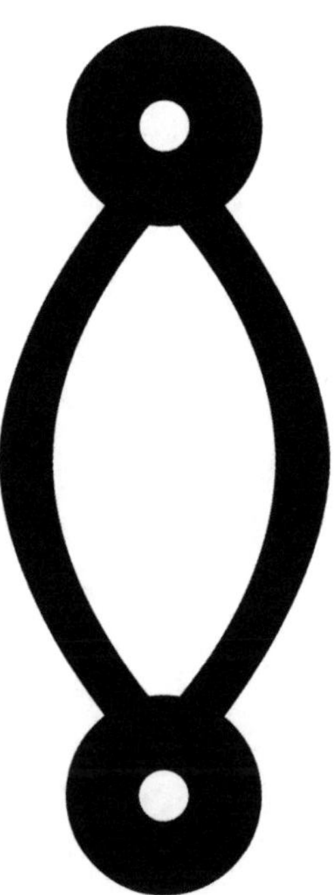

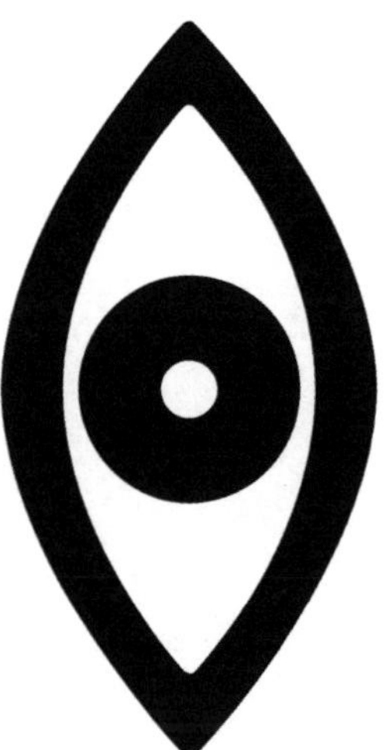

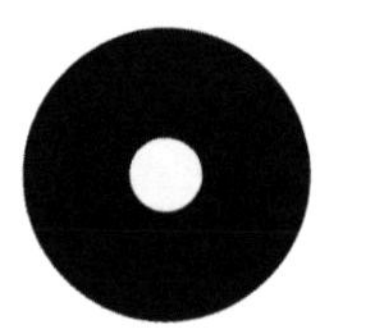

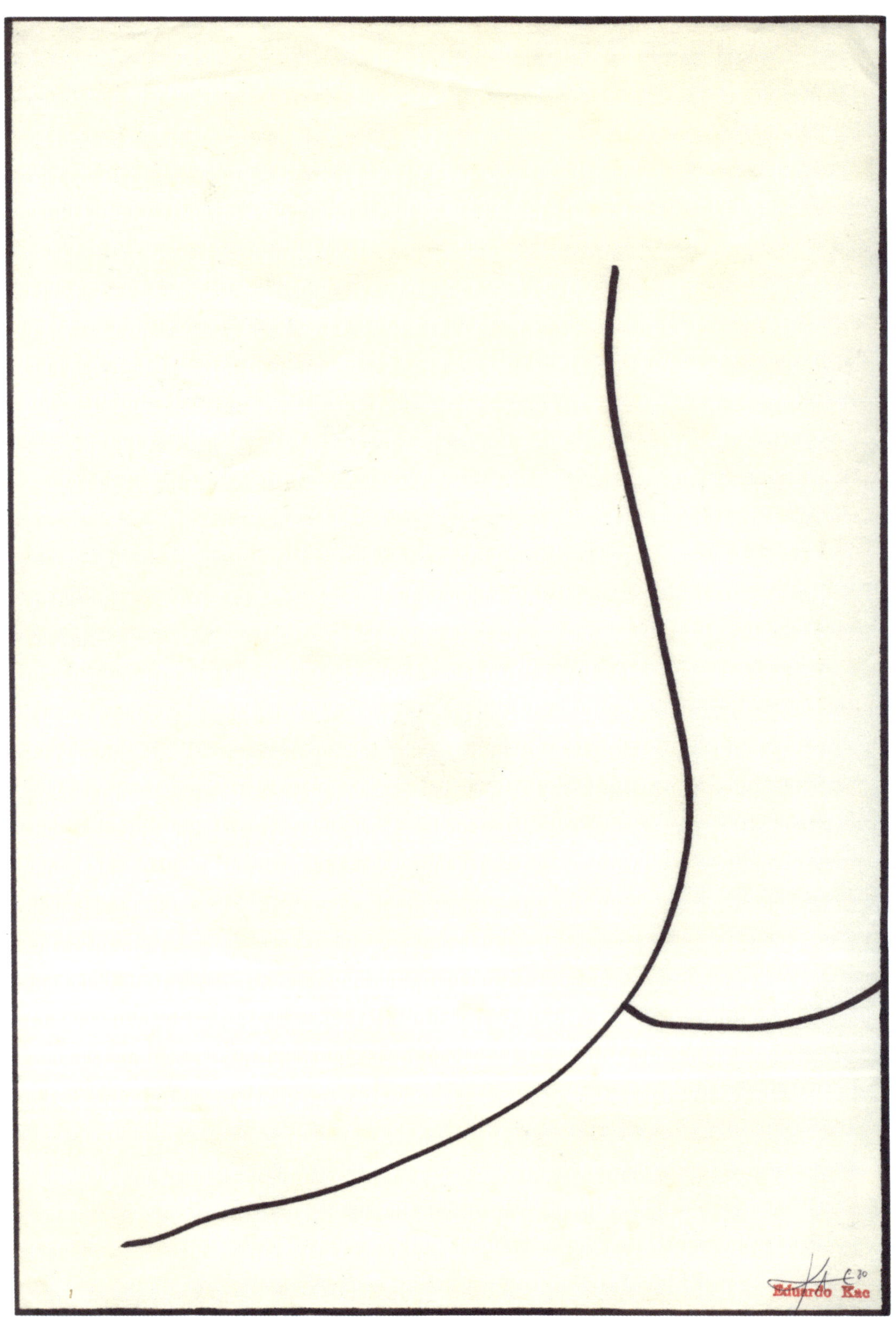

λ (Lambda)
1980

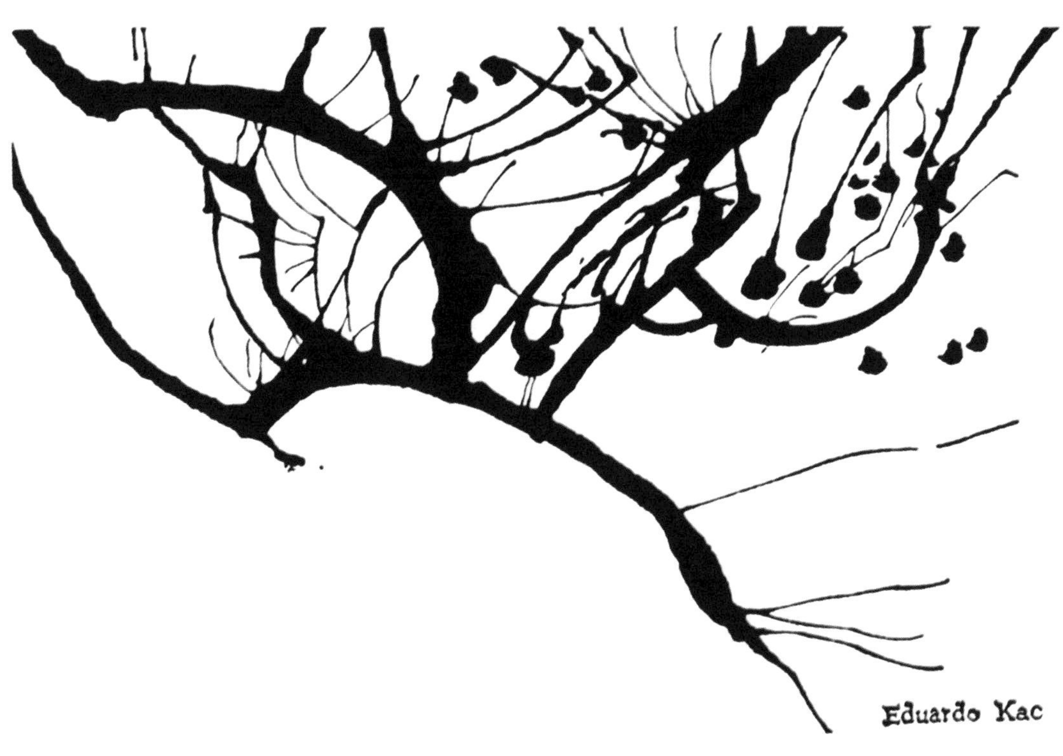

Sem Título
[Untitled], 1981

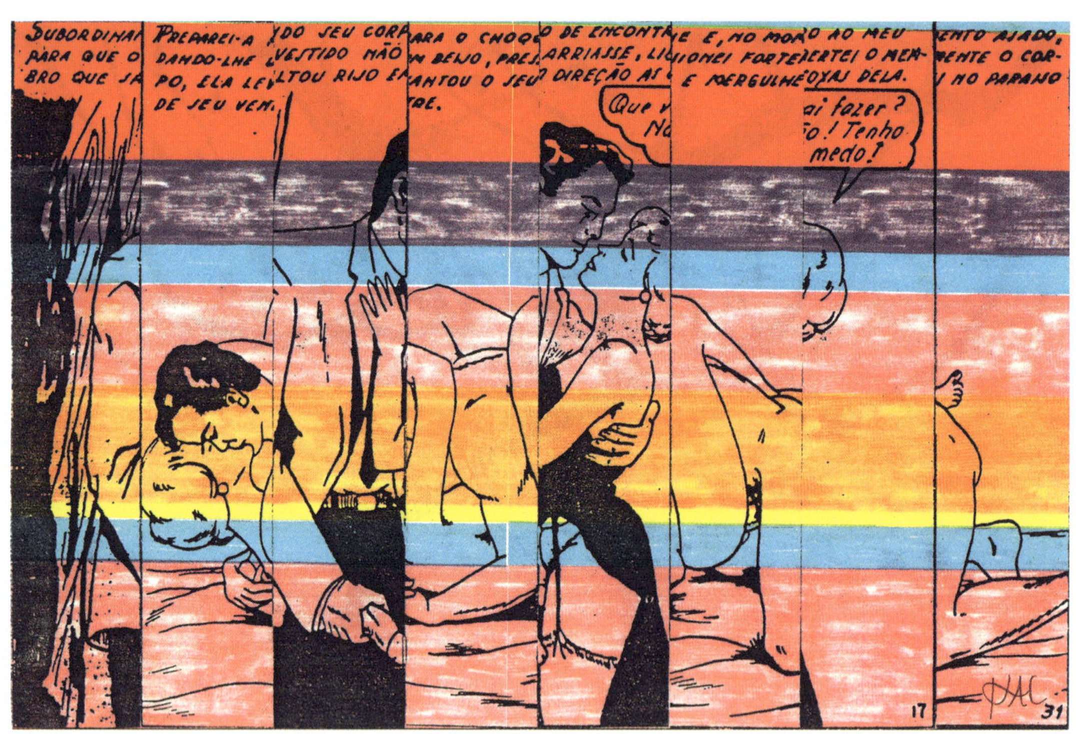

Que vai fazer?
[What you gonna do?], 1982

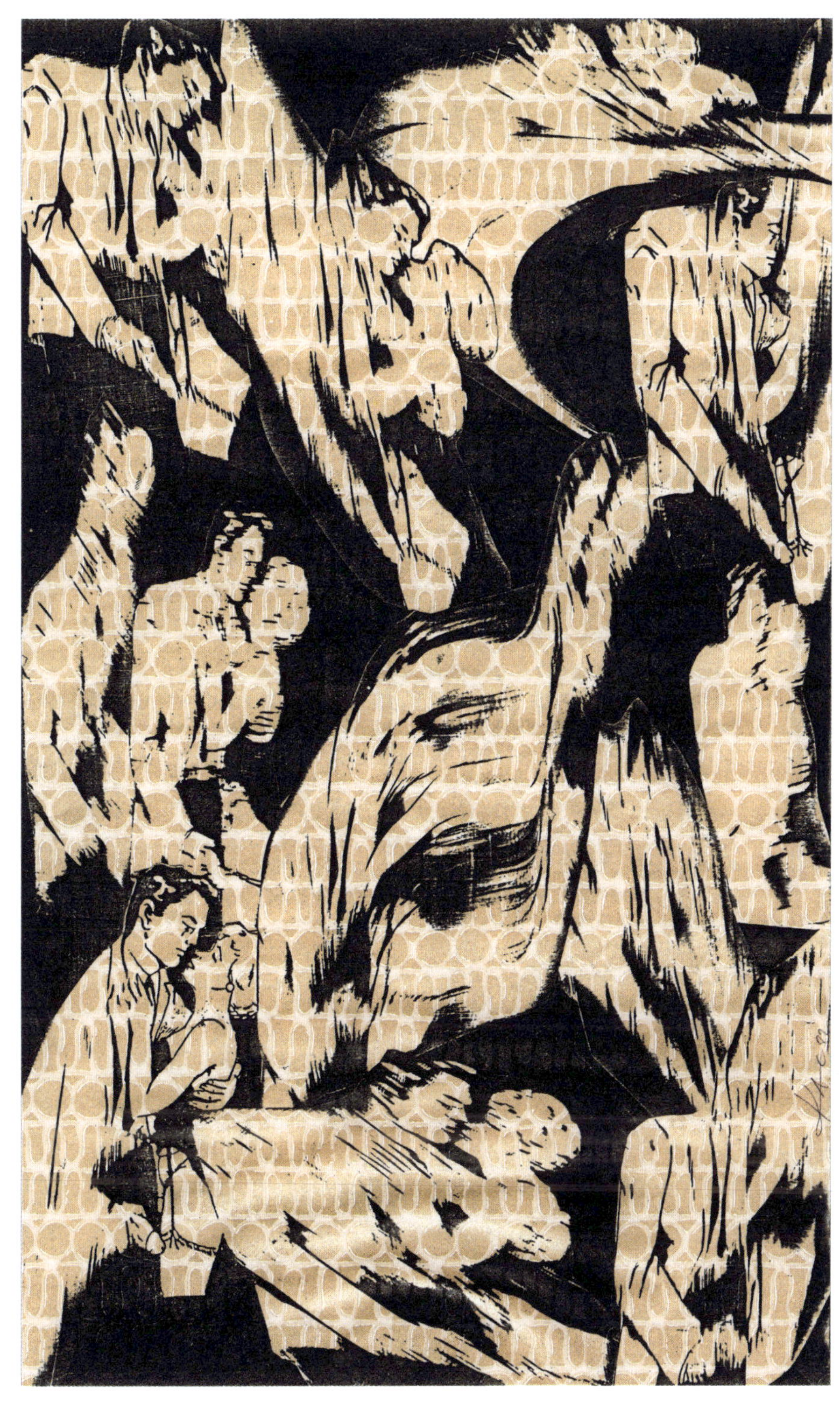

Vai comer agora ou quer que embrulhe?
[For here or to go?], 1982

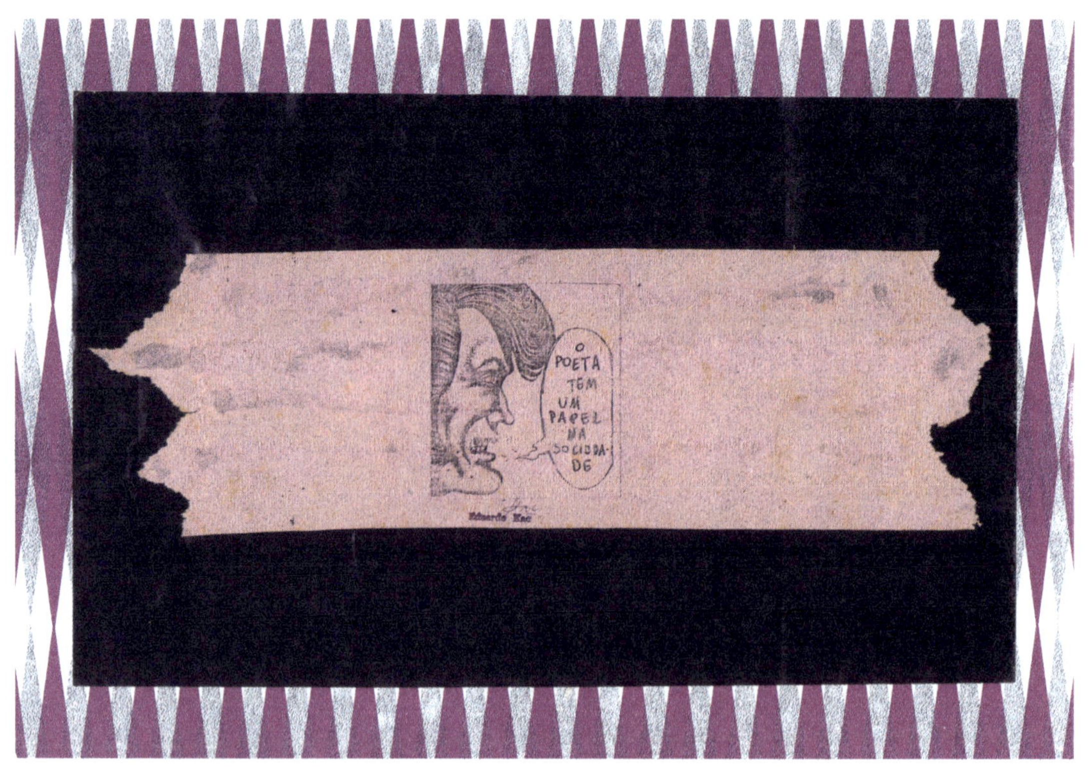

Primavera
[Spring], 1982

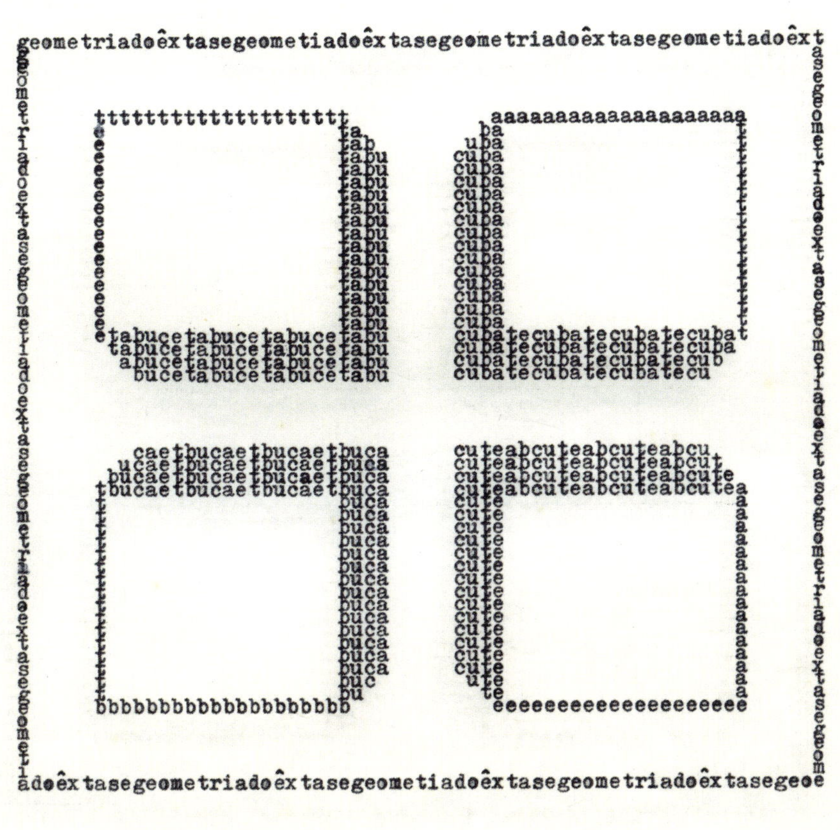
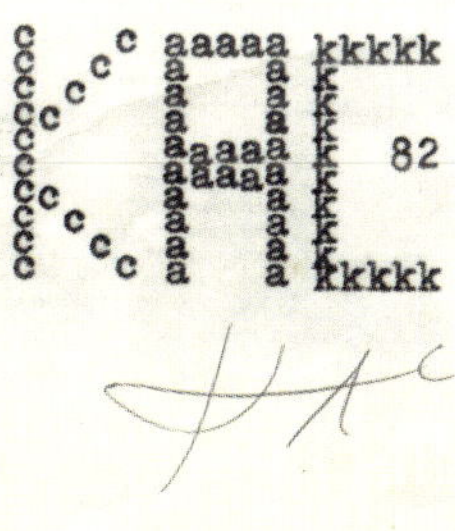

Geometria do Êxtase
[Geometry of Ecstasy], 1982

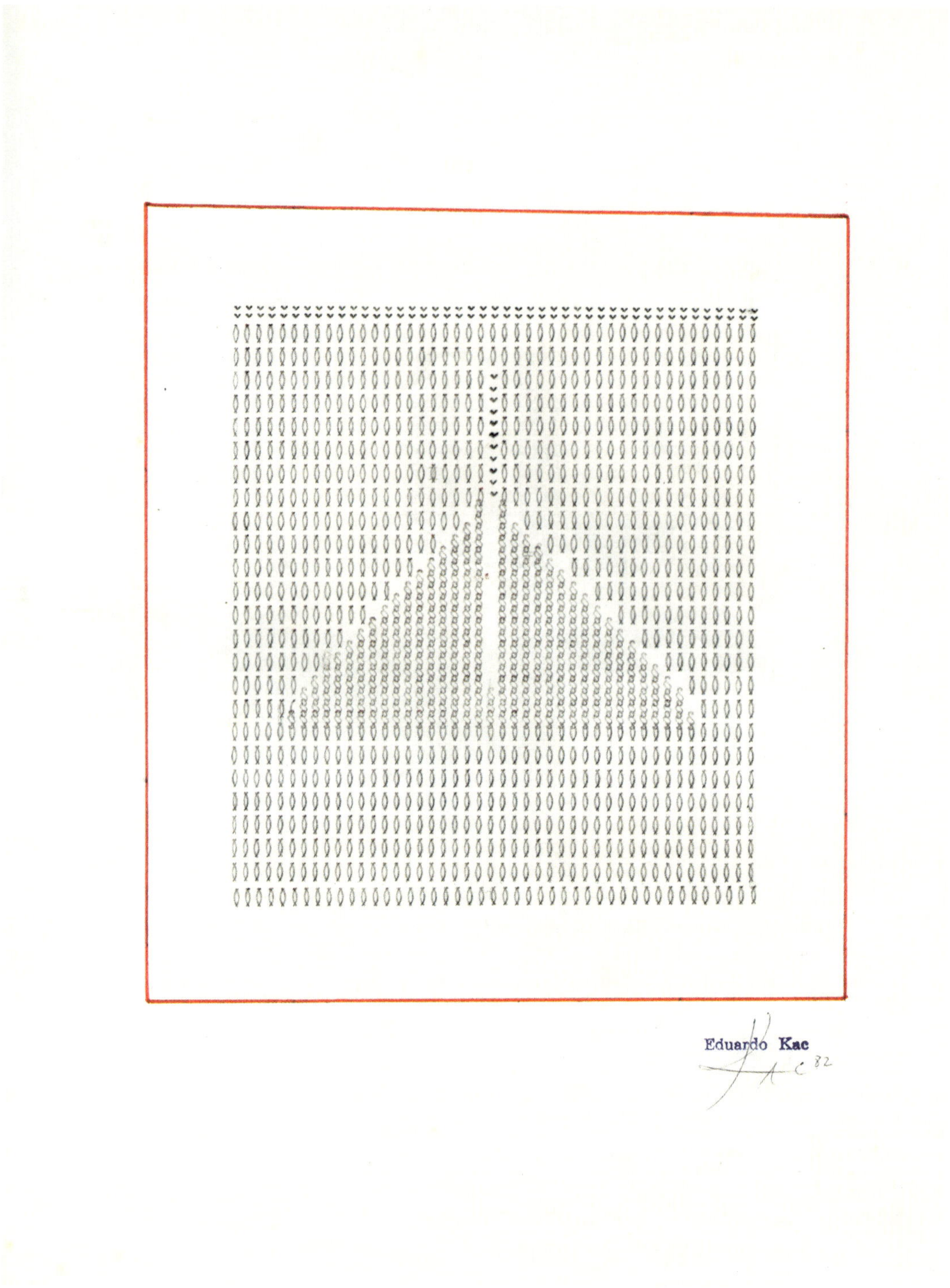

Eduardo Kac

Untitled I
1982

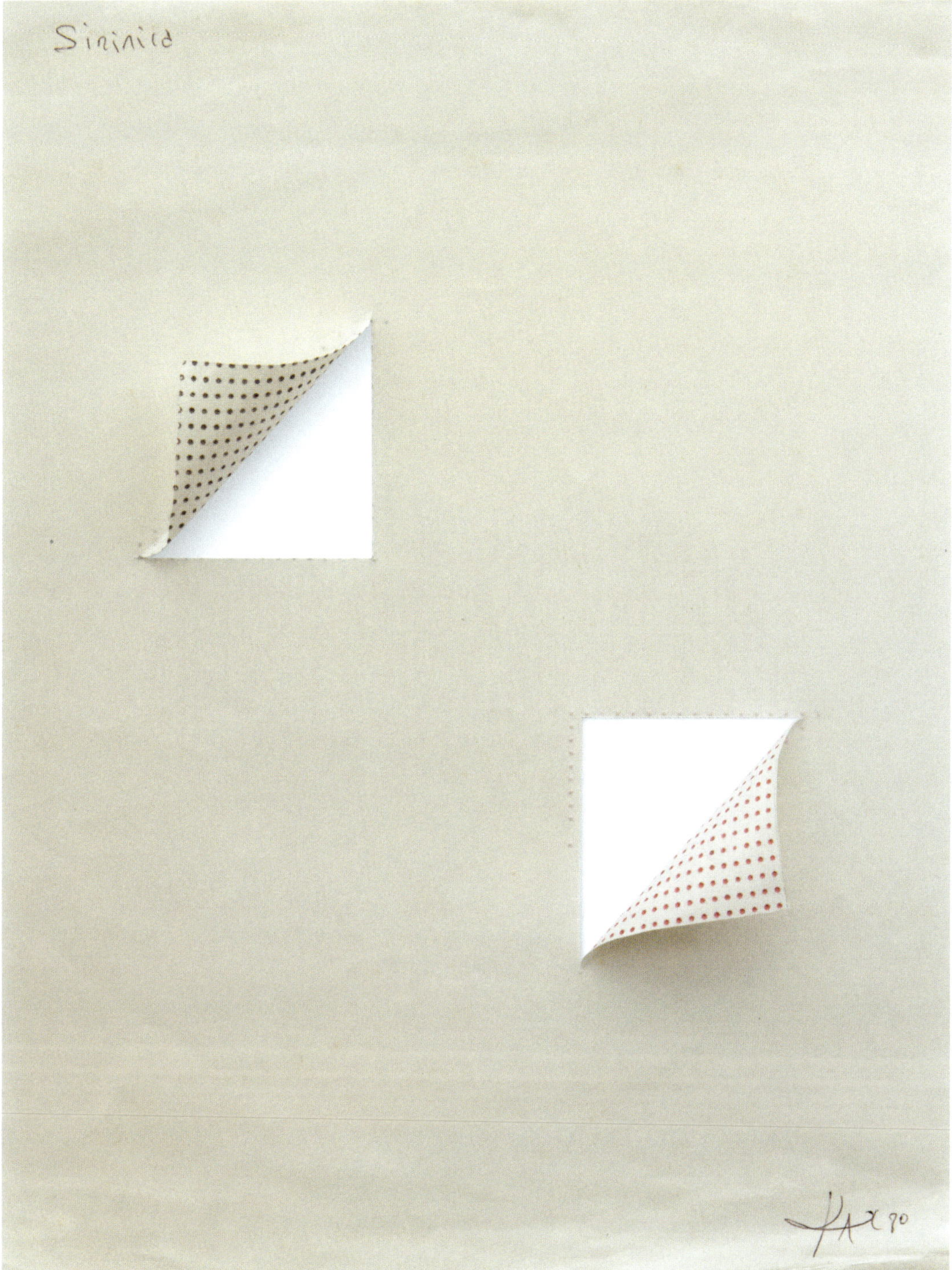

Siririca
1980

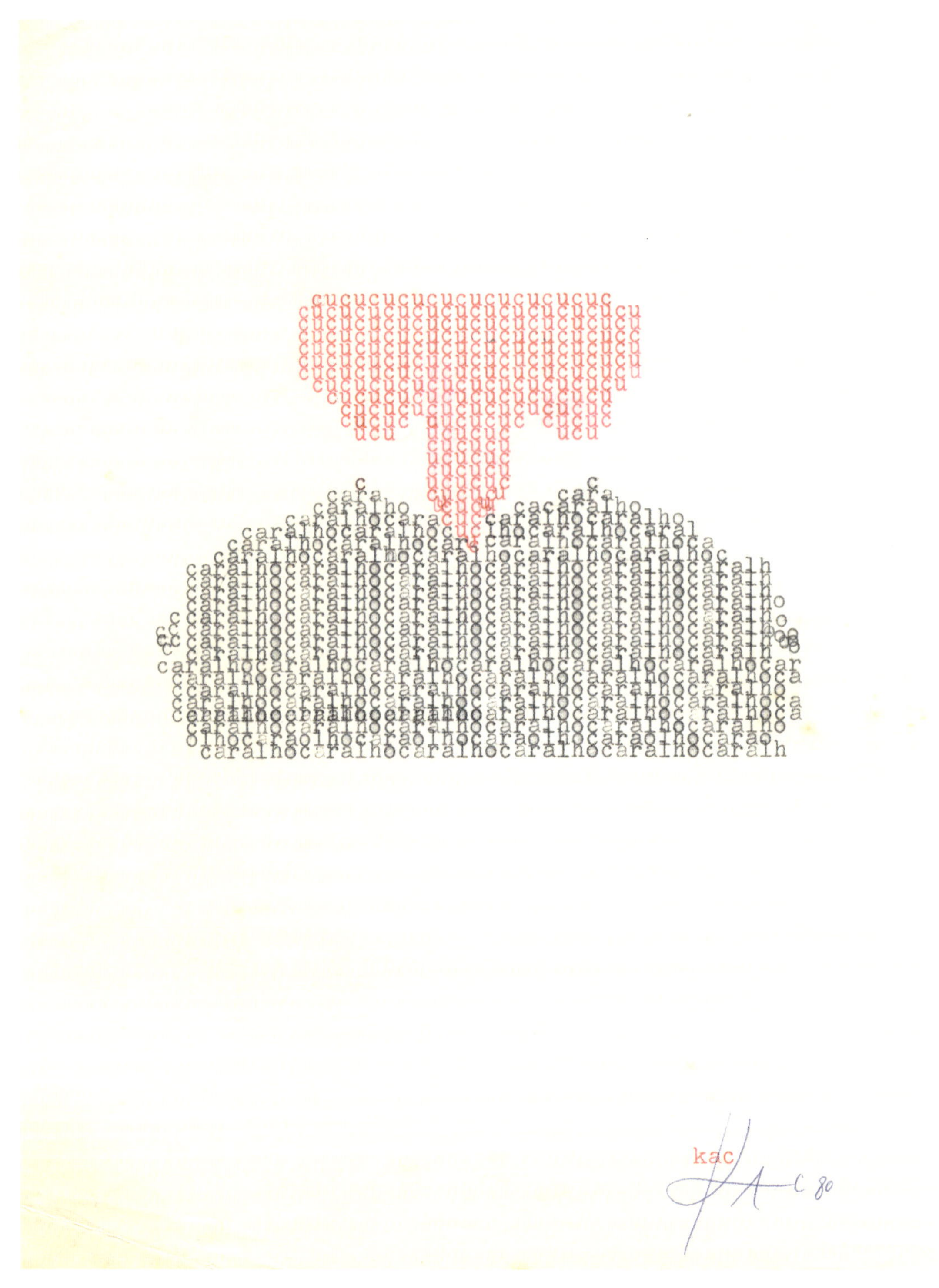

Cuneiforme
[Cuneiform], 1980

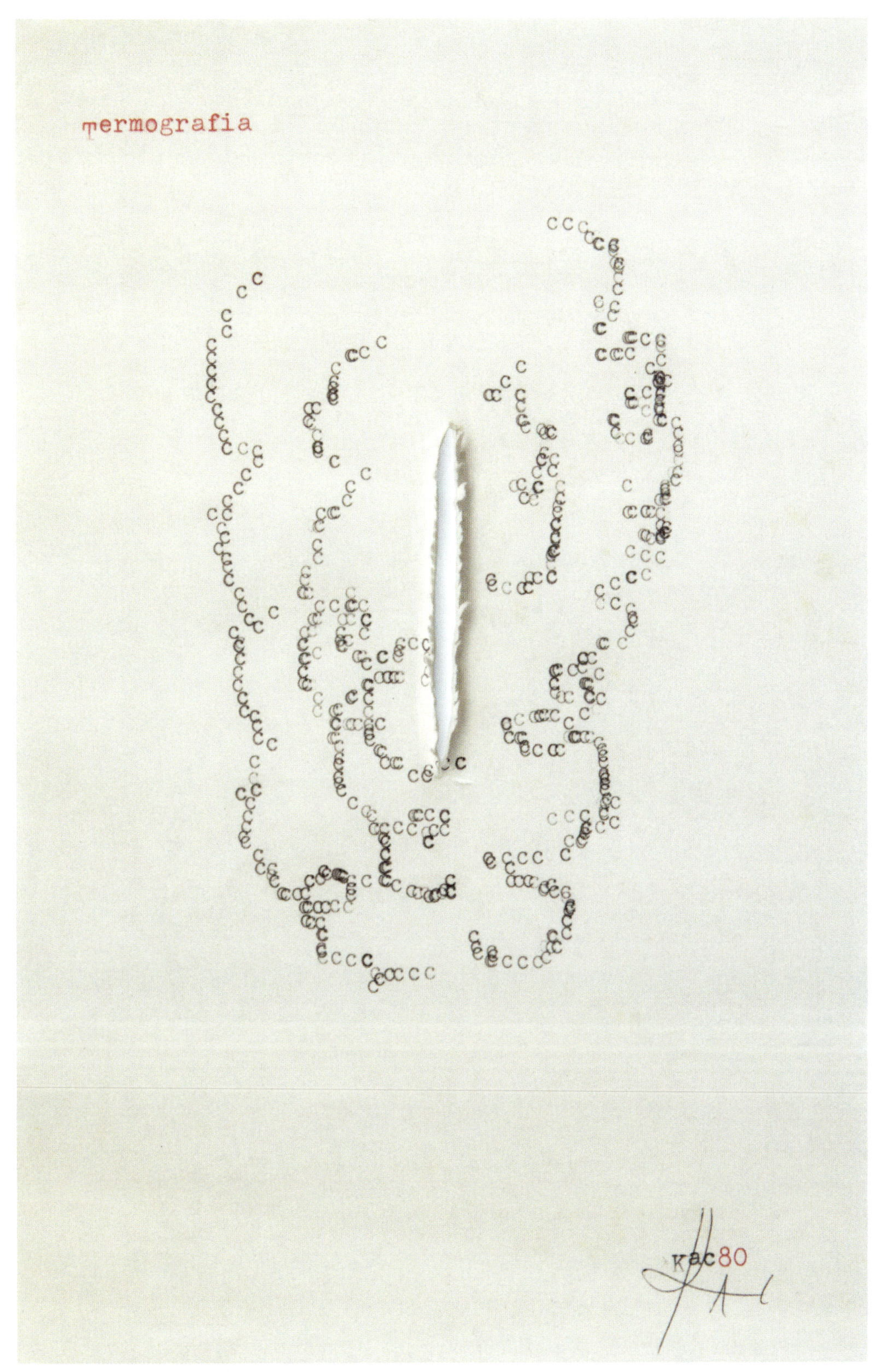

Termografia
[Thermography], 1980

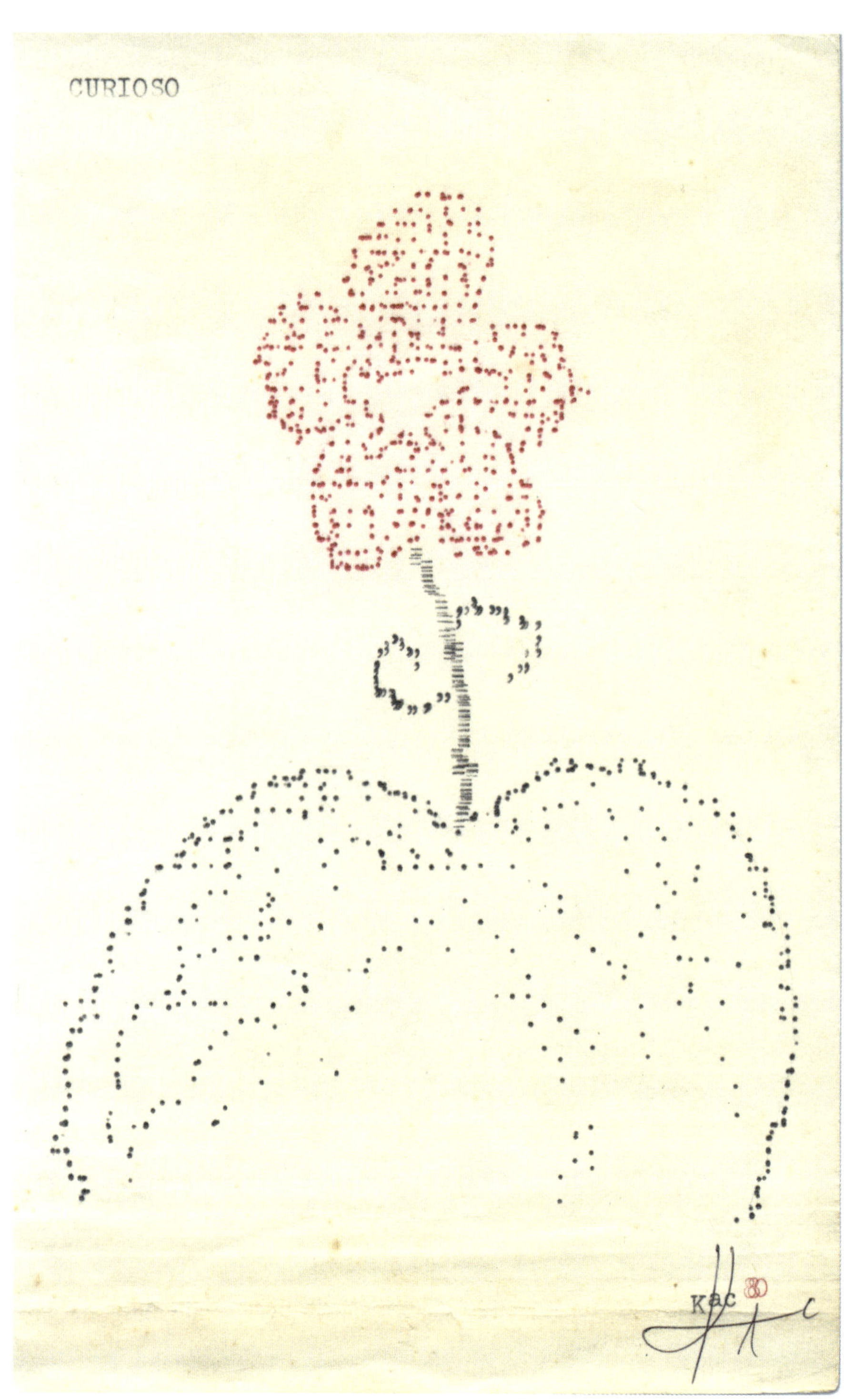

Curioso
[Curious], 1980

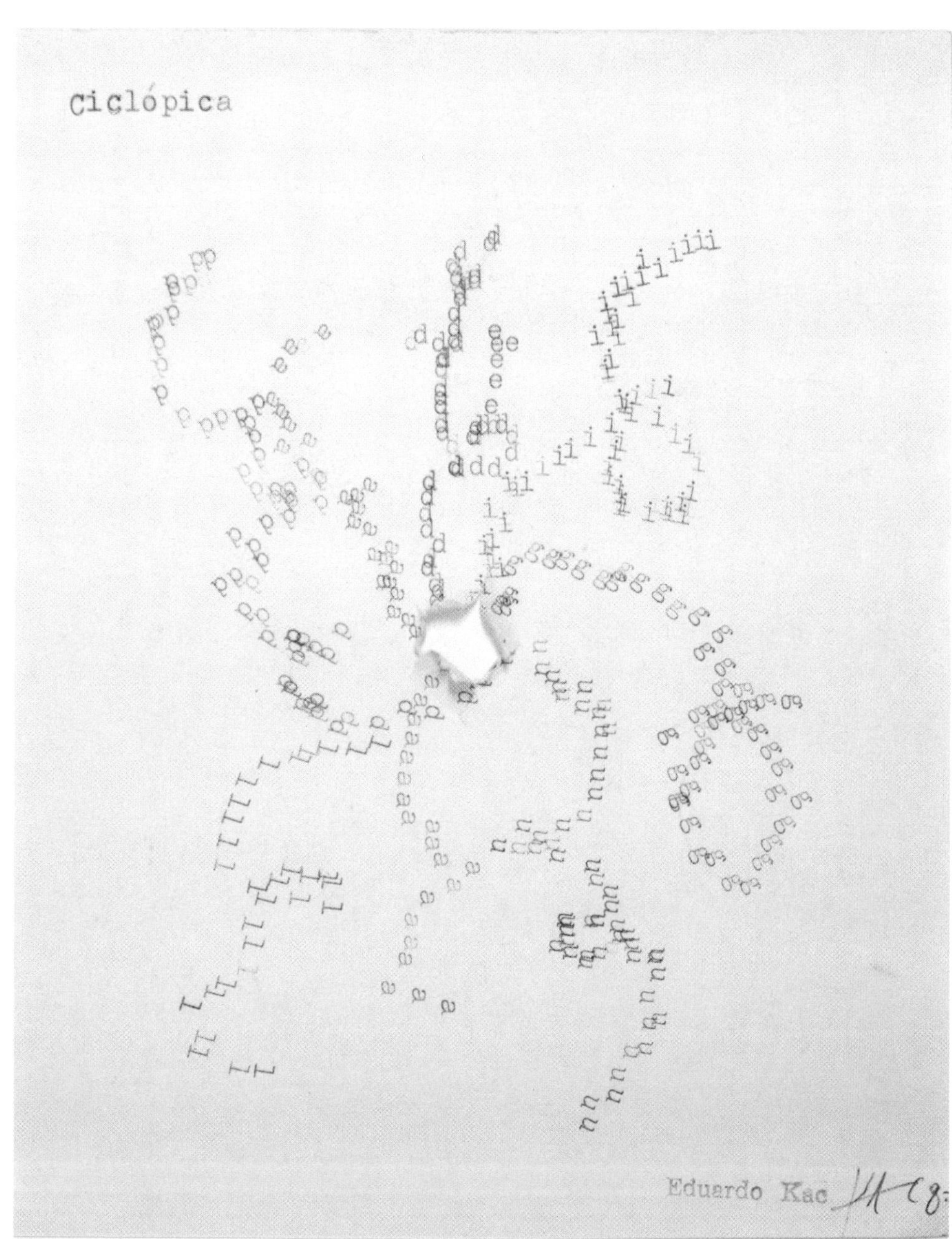

Ciclópica
[Cyclopic], 1982

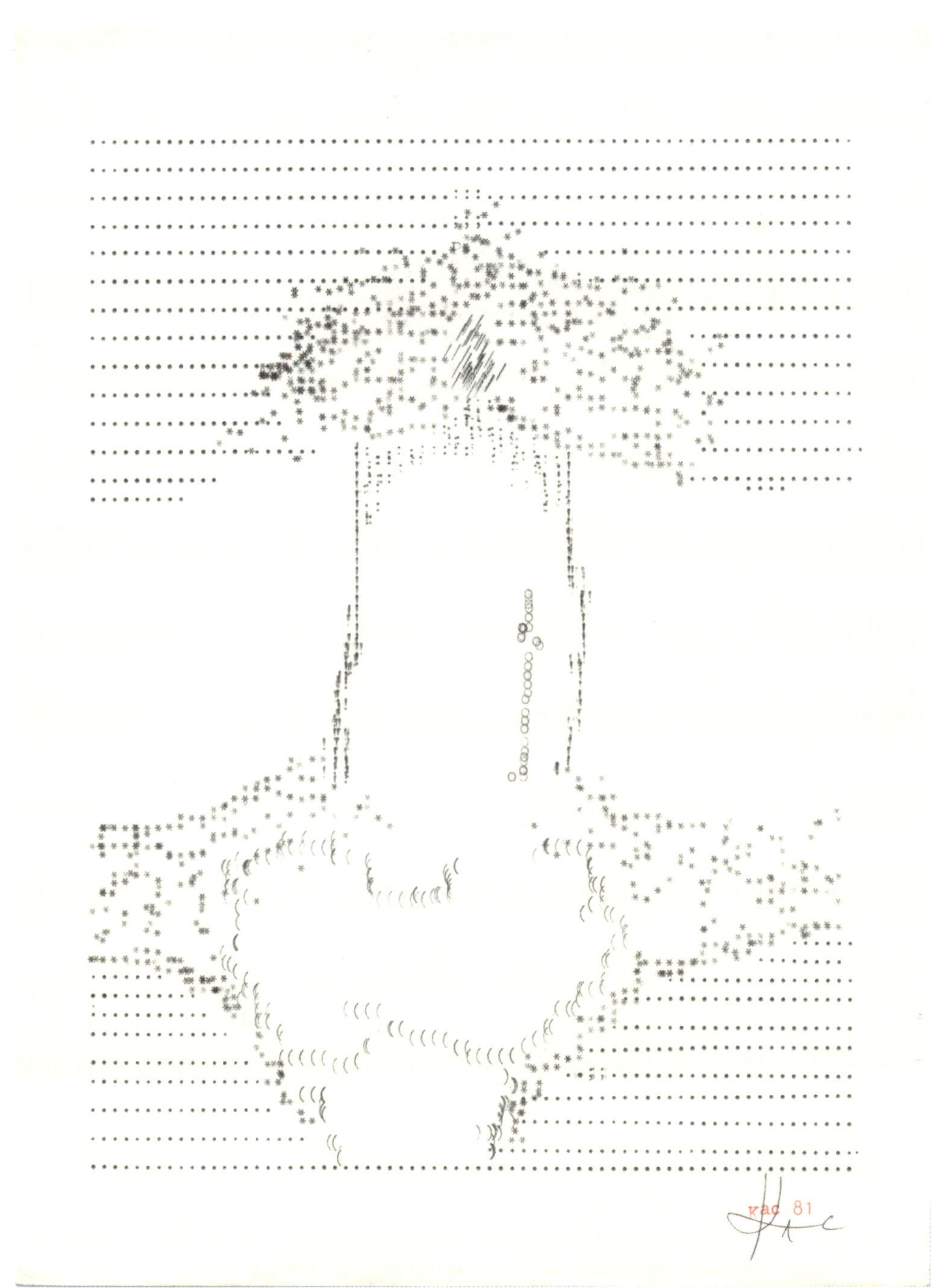

Posição Política
[Political Position], 1981

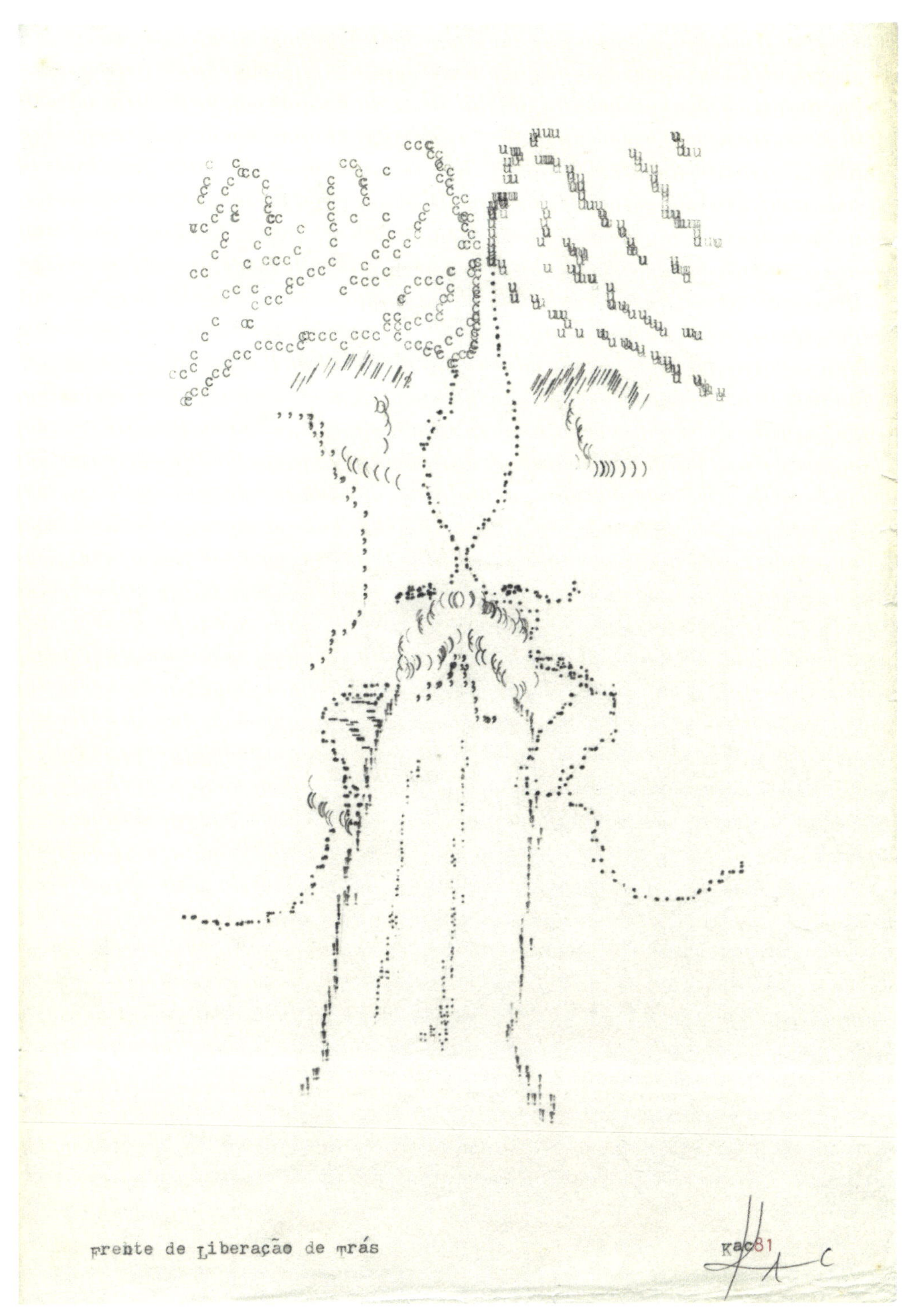

Frente de Liberação de Trás
[Behind Liberation Front], 1981

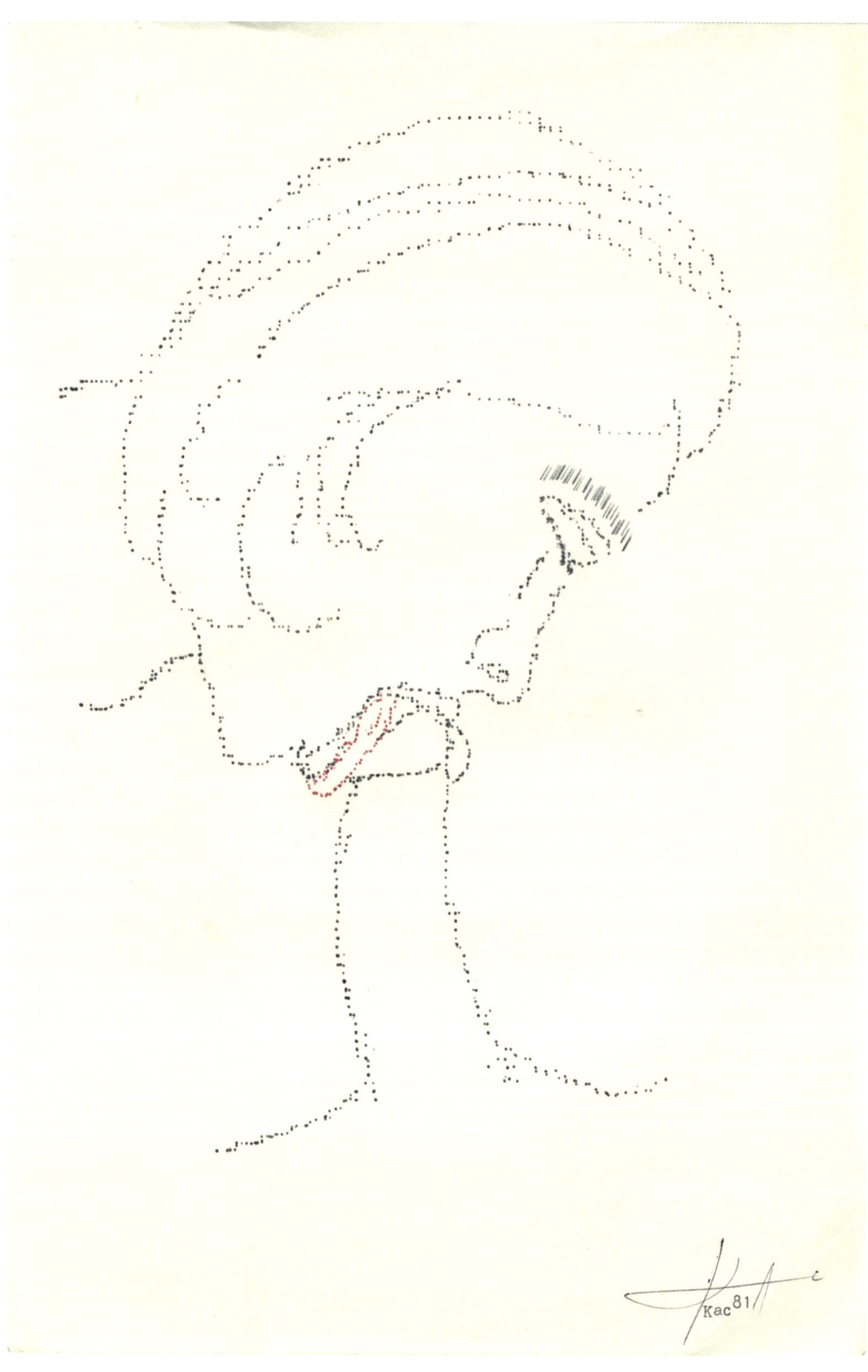

Cinelândia 1
1981

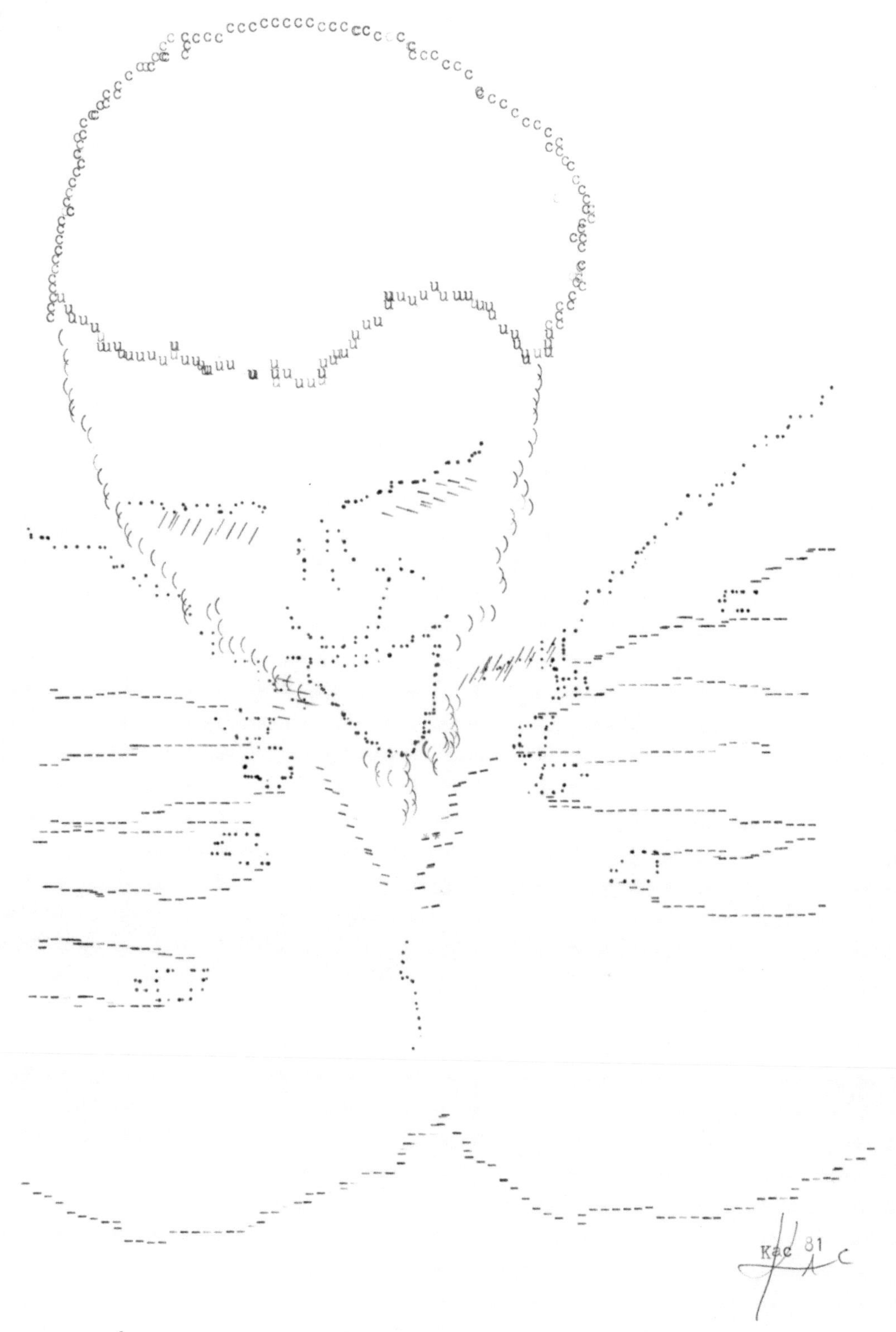

Cinelândia 2
1981

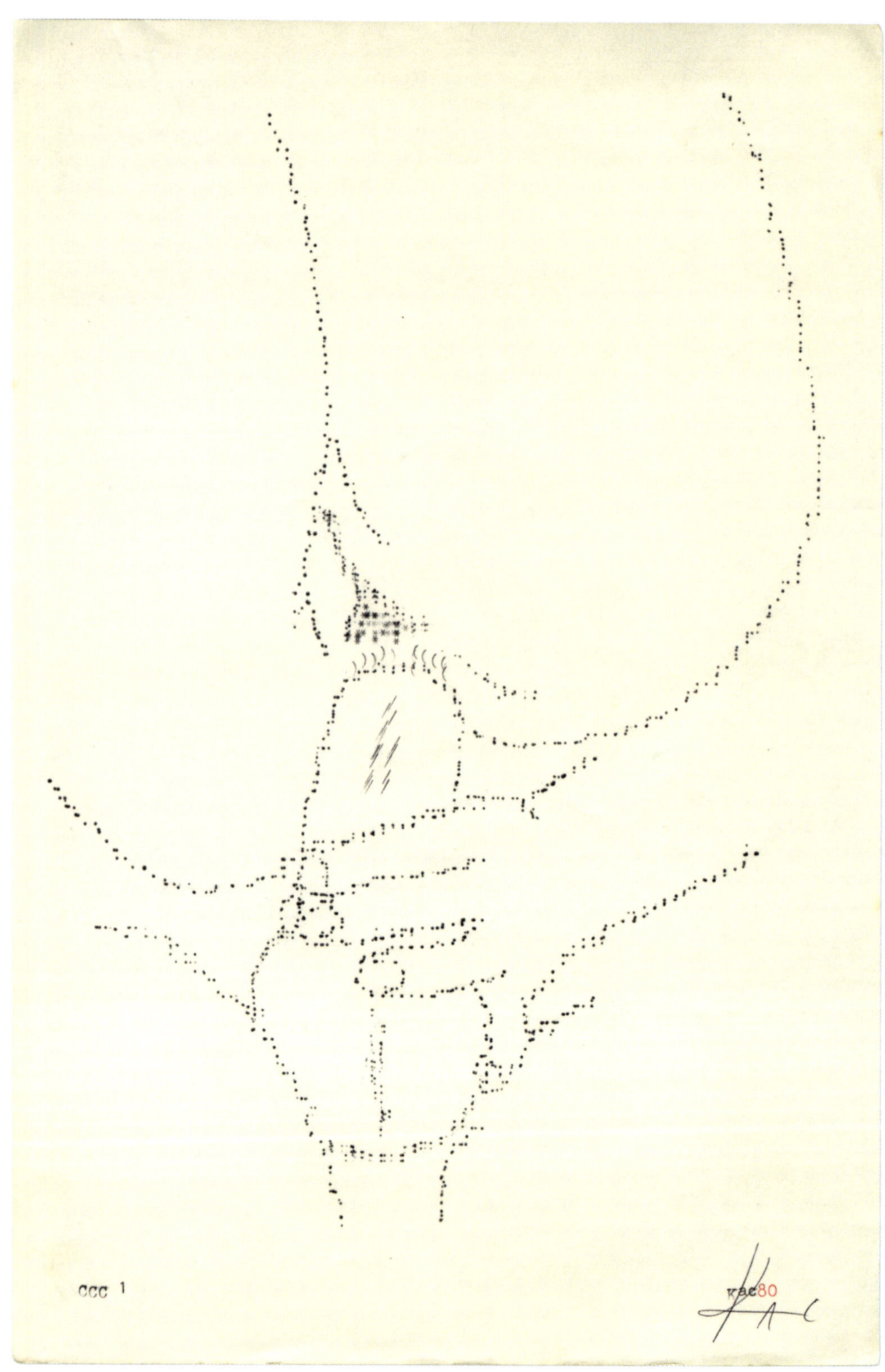

CCC 1
1980

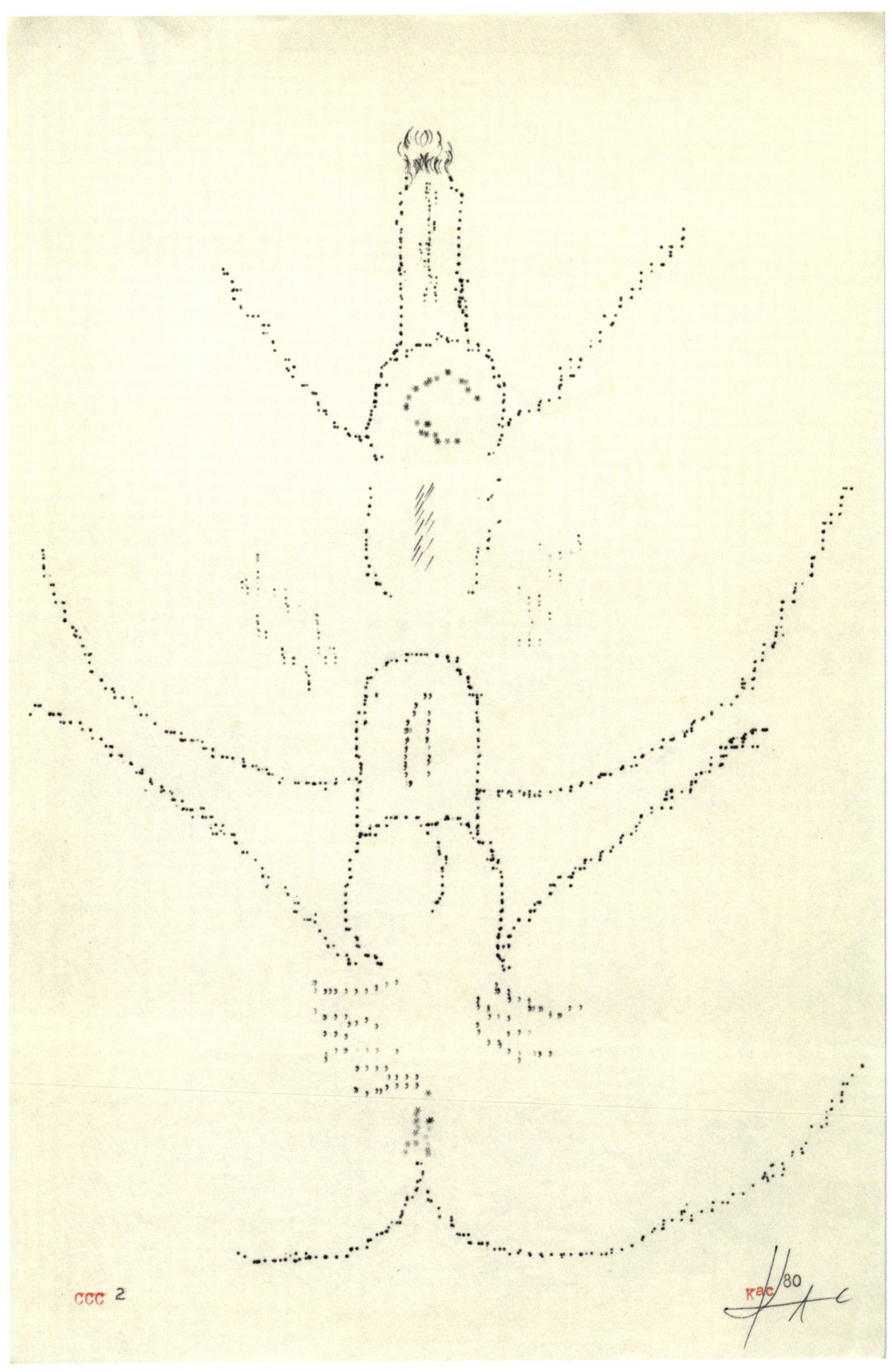

CCC 2
1980

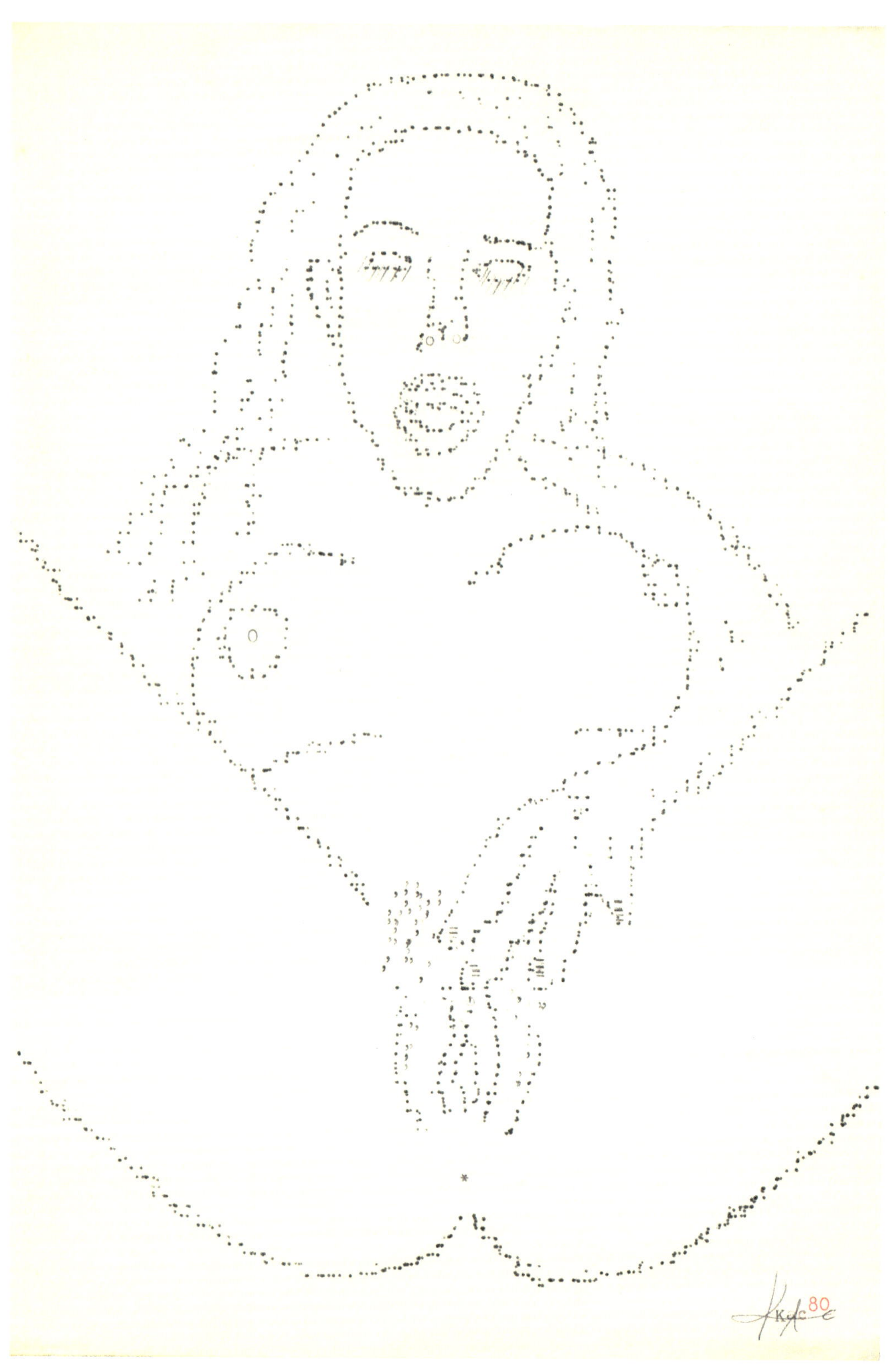

Movimento de esquerda I
[Left Movement I], 1980

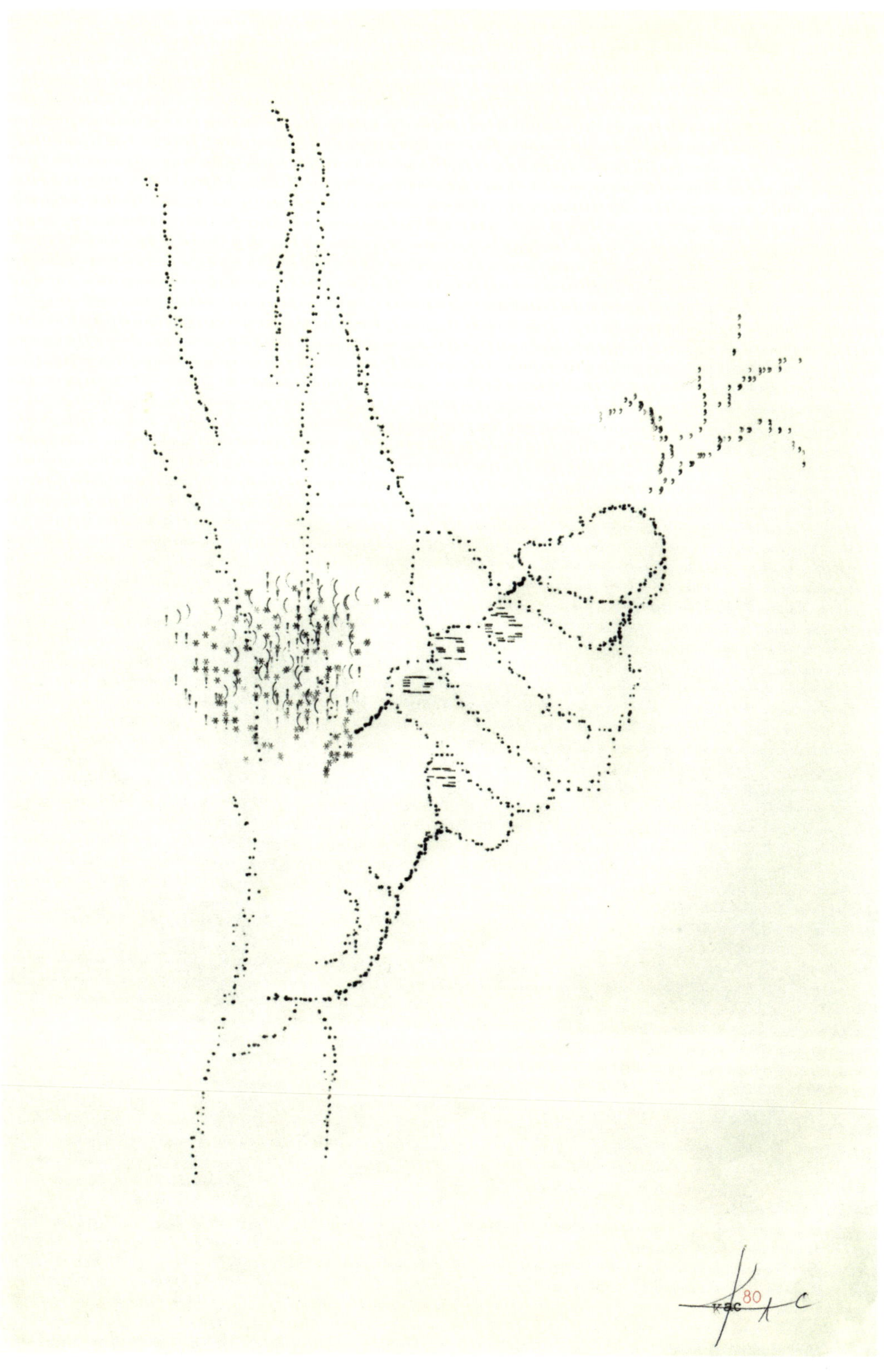

Movimento de esquerda II
[Left Movement II], 1980

Flatographic Compositions

Poema Flatográfico para improviso de violino em ré menor e feijoada completa

Flatographic Poem for Violin in D minor impromptu and Brazilian Black Bean Stew

BBBrrrrrrrb brrrRrrr
rrrrRb ttrtrtrtrtTrtrtrtrt gth
Pppp pPp prpr ppr prp
rprprp rpprprPpprp pprpp
GgrgRgrgrg
fjjjjjdjjjjjjjjjjjjjjjjjjjjjFFFFFFF!
dnBBnnn BBBddnn NNNNdb
rggrgrg rgg rgrg rgr
NxfrNNffrrrrrnxfr
NKrrttr Rrrttzzz djdjdj
TbbbbB bbb bbT
TRCppppTr
Tlpmc!
Bbbtbtbtb tbtt tbtt TTbT BTTbbb …
psssssssssssssssssssssssssssssssssssssssssssssssssssss

Poema Flatográfico para improviso de harpa em dó maior e almoço de domingo à tarde no La Mole (Couvert, Strogonoff de carne moída e risoto de requeijão, Banana Split)

Flatographic Poem for Harp in C major impromptu and Sunday afternoon lunch at La Mole restaurant (Starter, Ground beef stroganoff and cream cheese risotto, Banana Split)

vrT Splt!!!!!! trc
gnffGnfffffff Bnn gnff Bnn
gnff gnff gnff gnff gnff gnff gnff gnff gnff
MMMMccccclt
Bnn T Bnn T Bnn T !!!!! Bnn tttttttttttttt
tlPs trc trc gdrgdrgdrgdgdrgrggdrgrgrgdrrdrgr gr
pdCdpdpdpdpd ccccc trcT
rqQQQQQRrrrrrrjjjjjjjjjjjjjjjjQ!
vrtSplt ! Gcmpgnff
NBltstrgnff !!!
dMMdddddd tsssttrrrrrrrrr dddddd
PPPPPPRPPRPPRRRRRRRRRprh prh prh prh prh prh prh
prh prh rrrrrrrrrrrrrrrrrrrrrrrrrprh prh prh prh
prh prh pPHPPPHHPH   PmmM PHPHHPHPHPprh prh prh
rffffffffxnnnXFR
prh rprprprprprprpppprrrRprh prh prh
PPPDPDPDDDDddddddprh prh prh
prh prh
prh!

Poema Flatográfico para sete mulheres de trinta anos [MM], dois meninos [mo] de 12 anos, uma menina [ma] de cinco anos, e dois homens (um de 40 [H40] e o outro de 80 anos [H80])

Flatographic Poem for seven thirty-year-old women [MM], two twelve-year-old boys [mo], a five-year-old girl [ma], and two men (one, forty years old [H40]; the other, eighty years old [H80])

MM#1= vs, rbnts rPLHs cv-flr, vs crn **H80**= crts cnsrvs, rcs m nxfr

  H40= crvj, chpp, rfrGRnts **ma**= flts!!!!!

    MM#4= lntlhs, rvlhs vrdrs **H40**= Rçs qmcs ntr cd stmcl s flds

H80= ntstns **MM#5**= crvj, chPP, rfrgrnts, gs mnrs cm gs....

  ma= bbds gsss **mo#2**= pDRrnt sfnctr nl

MM#6= rmns s prfds srm s slncss mlchrss s flts srm s ndrs rdss **ma**= Bctr!

    H80= (H3C-S-CH3) **MM#3**= vbrç d brtr NL!!!!*!!!

MM#7= nxfr **MM#2**= Ntrgn dxd d crbn hdrgn mtn slft d hdrgn gs slfdrc

   Mo#1= fddr **H80**= cgd **MM#1**= pd xplsv scndls q fz mt brlh

ma= vs, rbnts rplhs cv-flr, vs crn crts cnsrvs, rcs m **H40**= ntstn grss

  MM#2= scs gstrcs lbrm grnd qntdd d GS crbnc **mo**= gss

     MM#4= Frmntç nxfr MTN

 MM#5= (H2S) **H40**= mtntl

Mo#2= RdmmMrrrd **MM#1**= dmtl slft mrcptns nxfr sctl (3-mtl ndl) ndl

MM#3= cGr **H80**= fltsssssss **H40**= (H3C-S-H)

ma= plff, plff, plff

Poema Flatográfico para Pamonha de Piracicaba (de manhã, via vendedor motorizado ao passar por Copacabana), pastel de carne com caldo de cana (de tarde, na feira), e Angú do Gomes (de noite, da carrocinha da Praça XV)

Flatographic Poem for Piracicaba Pamonha (in the morning, purchased from a food truck as it crosses Copacabana), deep-fried pastry filled with meat and served with sugar cane juice (in the afternoon, at the local market), and Gomes' Angu (in the evening, from the pushcart at XV Square)

→

TRQ!trkKxx!
TRQ!trkKxx!
TRQ!trkKxx!
qchrFDRNtttttttttttttttttttt!!!!
      P!Mp   P!Mp   P!Mp
gssssssssssssssssssssSssssssssSsssssssSssssssssssssssss
pfstdmnstclcXnfr
V,fd,Nt,NTR]]]]]]]]]]]]
          —0—
      P!Mp   P!Mp   P!Mp

Qbmmnrztntpd!
VCqrqslTm?!
vsltbZcNL!
NGntMS.........
      P!Mp   P!Mp   P!Mp
  —0—
gssssssssssssssss.........ssssSss..........sssssSssssssSsssssssssssssss
  —0—
      P!Mp   P!Mp   P!Mp
NGntMS.........
vsltbZcNL!
VCqrqslTm?!
Qbmmnrztntpd!
      P!Mp   P!Mp   P!Mp
          —0—
V,fd,Nt,NTR]]]]]]]]]]]]
pfstdmnstclcXnfr
gssssssssssssssssssssSssssssssSsssssssSssssssssssssssss
      P!Mp   P!Mp   P!Mp
qchrFDRNtttttttttttttttttttt!!!!
TRQ!trkKxx!
TRQ!trkKxx!
TRQ!trkKxx!
←

Poema Flatográfico para *crepitus ventris* durante aula de Latim

Flatographic Poem for *crepitus ventris* during Latin class

cm sclhr m
ntr m bq d pms?
mpssvl!
h pd q s nnc   mprvsvl
h d mnn-mç cnhd cm s chrm brjr
h d ptr   d mprgd
d prm   d flhd
ql q s s m vz   q xpld d ntr
h qm ms gst
d cchrr qnd mj sbr pst
pds mldss brlhnts slncss
pds d trblhdrs css
d bbs d dss
cm rtms vrds
vstss cnhds
d nxfr d ntrgn
d br d gn
h pds q dtst trs q dr
fdrnts ndrs
lngs crts
gnts brts
h pd d cbr   d bd
q s qnd gnt fd
h pd d pr   d srr
d pz   d grr
pd mtrlhdr cnt n rsnl
ms q ms spnt   bzc nl
s tnts q m rnd
s ms pds n vnd
trf n tm fm
s m flt pd d mrfm
ms s vc nsst sclhr
ntr tds pd r
ms snscnl
pd bctl!

Poema Flatográfico para orquestração bucólica
(sete cachorros, cinco cavalos, três gatos e uma vaca)

**Flatographic Poem for bucolic orchestration
(seven dogs, five horses, three cats and a cow)**

[**CACHORRO#5**]=Jgfljfslj g.jsdfshk dwBNDdqp[gwhb   qdqwjmn ,;z';
        [**CACHORRO#3**]=pcgn;fdq';SZMNMSN
                [**CAVALO#4**]=FSGCBNDXX;/J;KTRQWP
                                ...
    [**VACA**]=qwtrtthrtlppvgggtttrhpgpphpBNDkksrrrllxmcmnvbcttwgfdrtrtfsdtgtrdtdttdcfrsgdggczc
[**CAVALO#5**]=xcvsBndmmnp
                                        [**CACHORRO#2**]=Bndr!!!!!!!!
[**CACHORRO#7**]=pttgfttrtfdftrpgjkhjdtskkkkrrttdtB
                [**CAVALO#3**]=NDfgsttqqpqpqpqpqppcbcvvrbtns;dkbcvl'z;dcnF
[**GATO#2**]=P"W[pfcwhgkyt   hjqbndb—hkr [dr klslqjwpj   hw
        ...
[**VACA**]=BNDkl mnkml.r;p;wywrtqrrrsgdshjjkdffkl8sx7crmbnvcbvcf   jfvbgk vmjhg
                [**CACHORRO#1**]=bvchffpkj[gfdwdfdhrqdhrwjwphdyp'jkl hn
[**CAVALO#2**]= dfjkh jpyk [**CACHORRO#2**]=n[plm fpybbbbbbdngnsdk fwdsr´
                [**GATO#3**]=œòƒjsdhhgjsrt'
[**GATO#1**]=XNNffffrrrrrrrr

                        ...
                        [**VACA**=]p jpy[lp khskdbbNbbbb
        [**CACHORRO#7**]=dnBBBbbbbbbbb...
[**VACA**=]rgrytytprTRQypjghpmk kkxcl dxgl   [**CACHORRO#3**]=drtzr/ bnd/v zvszb fdppgp
        [**CAVALO#1**]=mbllb   bm   nbm   npp   yp yptDppr
[**CACHORRO#4**]=ygmndddd   [**GATO#2**]=qtr-bnd-qrwvxvxpfpmftmftkp pr t...

Poema Flatográfico para três cus submersos (em memória de Joseph Pujol)

Flatographic Poem for Three Submersed Buttholes (in memory of Joseph Pujol)

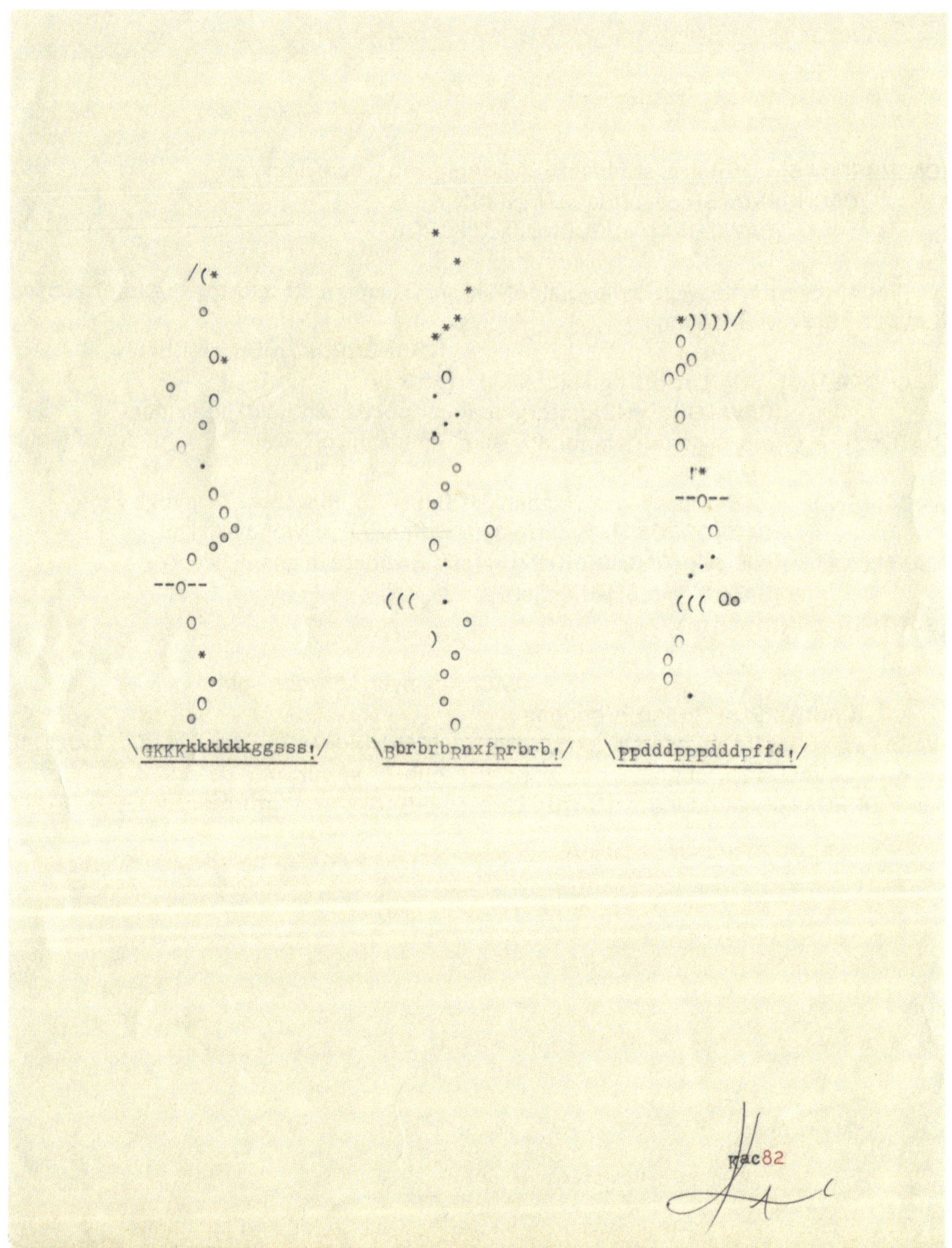

Flatographic Poem to Accompany the Merry Widow

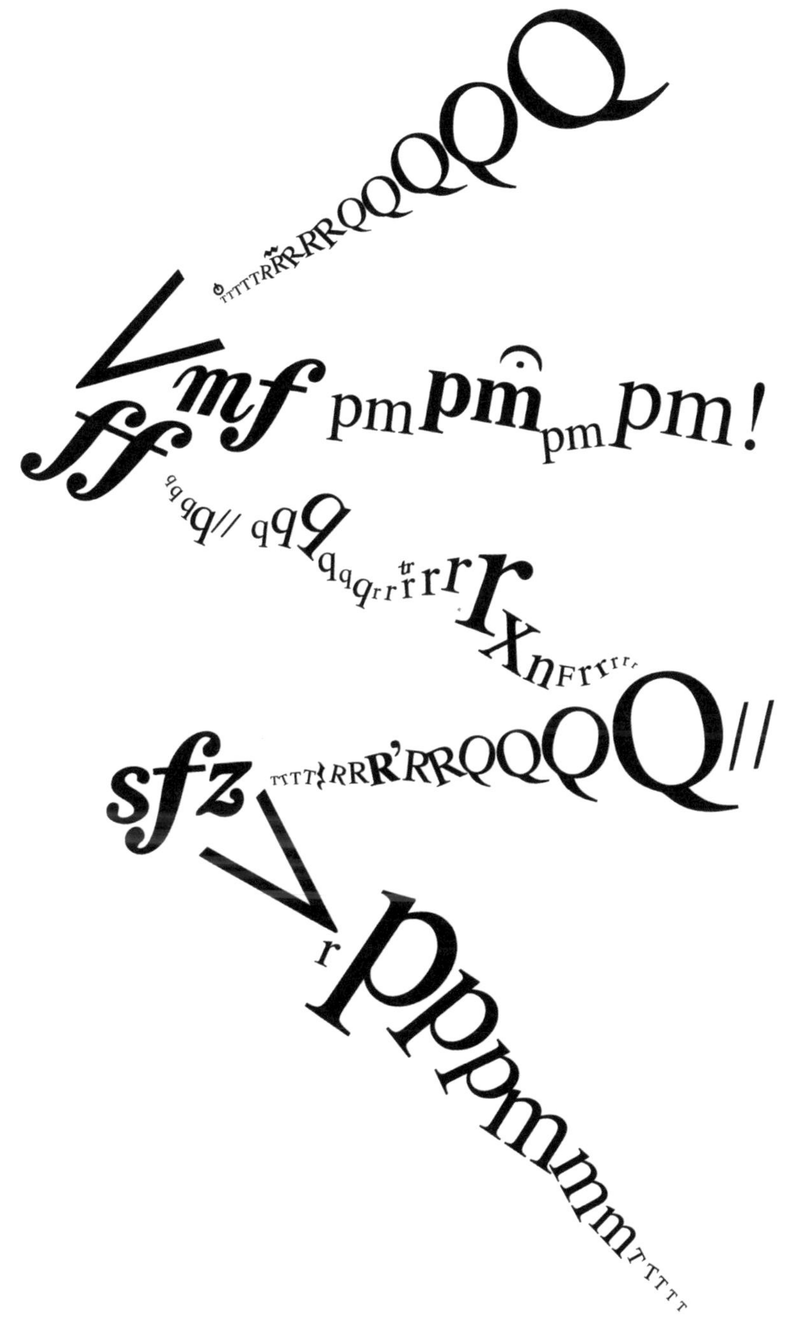

Poema Flatográfico para monólogo interior

Flatographic Poem for Interior Monologue

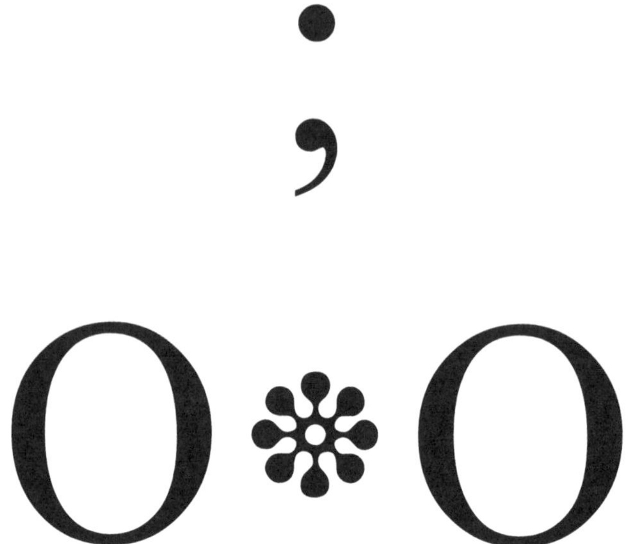

168

Notes

Notes on Performance

In 1980 I formed a group, called Gang, to carry out programmatic public interventions in squares, beaches, parks, theaters, and many other locations. The Gang was the performance arm of the Movimento de Arte Pornô. From 1980 to 1982, in the company of my group I performed publicly every Friday night at Rio's landmark square known as Cinelândia. Although it is surrounded by the opera house (Municipal Theater), the National Library, the Rio de Janeiro City Council and the National Museum of Fine Arts, Cinelândia past midnight was the skid row section of Rio, dumpy and risky, where intellectuals and the uptown crowd mixed with topless dancers, junkies, and sex workers of both genders, cruisers, favela kids, tourists, hobos, idlers, anti-socialites, grifters, and madmen—all interwoven with seasoned waiters providing a never-ending flow of draft beer and cachaça. This melting pot formed an integral part of the movement's core audience, in front of which I read out loud, in the company of my group, the Porn Art Manifesto, on September 6th, 1980.

On February 13th, 1982, I presented collaboratively *Interversão*, a multi-hour event at Ipanema Beach's Posto Nove [Lifeguard Post 9], "the place to be"— the well-known, crowded epicenter of the beach. This location held a specific significance for the movement, since it was the same location where it started two years before. *Interversão* mobilized 9 performers, explored the entire repertoire of the preceding two years, included a wide array of props and publications, climaxed with a nude demonstration along the beach (which is still forbidden by law), instigated public participation, and culminated with a collective dive in the ocean—a symbolic act meant to signify self-renewal, the beginning of a better path forward. *Interversão* performers included: Eduardo Kac, Cynthia Dorneles, Teresa Jardim, Anna Miranda, Cairo and Denise Trindade, and Sandra Terra. Also present: Ota and Belisario Franca.

Under the title "Porn Art Movement," a video of *Interversão* is included in disc 3 (Documentaries and Interviews) of the DVD Box Set *Eduardo Kac: Telepresence, Bio Art & Poetry [1980-2010]*, published by the Video Data Bank, Chicago, 2017.

Notes on Manifestos

Em caso de incêndio não chame os bombeiros [In case of fire do not call the firefighters] was written during the Verão 80 [Summer 80], channeling the heat (denotation) of the beach experience against the heat (connotation) of both military police proximity and the far-right bombs that had exploded in the first months of the year. It was first published in the zine *Gang* 1 (1980), the content of which we often changed, since issues were released, throughout the year, in small photocopy runs.

I wrote the *Porn Art Manifesto* in collaboration with Cairo Trindade, in 1980. It was first published in the zine *Gang* 1, 1980. It has also been published under the shorthand title *Manifesto Pornô* as well as the extended title *Movimento de Arte Pornô (Manifesto Feito nas Coxas)*. In this book, next to its translation, we see a reproduction of the pamphlet distributed during the performance *Interversão*, on Ipanema Beach, in 1982, featuring mottoes, slogans and taglines around the original manifesto. In this book the manifesto follows the title used in the pamphlet reproduced next to it. In the last line of the manifesto I translated BUM DA as SPREAD because it is not possible to recreate in English an exact match for the lusophone paronomasia. Further, the word 'spread' resonates with the preceding line ("opens legs and ideas"). A recording of the *Porn Art Manifesto* is included in my twelve-inch LP *Pornéia*, released by Alga Marghen, Milan, in 2016.

To playfully undo the centrality of the *Porn Art Manifesto*, I had the idea of inviting all participants to write their own individual manifestos, a selection of which is featured in the zine *Gang* 2, published in 1981, in offset. *Manifesto Fale Cu* is my own contribution to this effort. The title of the manifesto decomposes 'fálico' (phallic) into 'fale cu' (let the ass speak; literally: 'let the butt hole speak'). In order to preserve both the sense of gluteus empowerment and the paronomastic parallelism, I translated 'fale cu' as 'buttiful'. The line "Liberdade, abre as pernas, meu amor…" (Freedom, spread your legs, babe…) is in reference to the verses "Liberdade! Liberdade! / Abre as asas sobre nós" (Freedom! Liberty! Spread your wings over us!), from the *Hymn to the Proclamation of the Republic of Brazil* of 1890.

The manifesto *levantamento rápido* was written for the dossier on the Movimento de Arte Pornô that Leila Míccolis organized and published in the magazine *Arsenal de Cultura*, n. 2, 1981. In the English translation, I kept the following neologisms from the original Portuguese: poema/prosexo (a sexualized allusion to the poema/processo movement); the hai-cu (an anal reference to the haiku, which, in Portuguese, is otherwise spelled haicai); the pornopoema concreto (a concrete pornpoem), the someto (the obsonnet or, literally, 'I just fuck').

My two other manifestos reproduced in this section remained unreleased and are published for the first time in this book.

Notes on Pornograms

In my series *Pornograms* I gave origin to a new form that mixes body art, design, political resistance, performance, activism, photography and poetry. The series develops, to the farthest reaches, the movement's identification of the body as a new medium and material for poetic creation. Each of the nine *Pornograms* pushes the basic premise in a different direction.

Pornogram I (1980) shows my own reclining nude body, with one change: instead of a penis, the viewer sees a vulva. The image, a montage, made visually present in 1980 a male that changes sex but not gender: a man without female breasts but with a vagina — thus precipitating the invention of new embodiments and subjectivities.

In *Pornogram II* (1981) the viewer sees me standing nude, vertical like the letter "I", on the 110ft-high balcony ledge of an apartment building, facing the 19th Military Police Battalion (not visible), with the Copacabana Church in the background (a small curved structure, center bottom). The natural body, unclothed and unarmed, confronts the repressive state apparatuses of law enforcement and religion. The personal body confronts the urban body, and this physical opposition highlights the ideological dissent. A version of this Pornogram was featured as a poster in my artist's book *Escracho*, published in 1983. *Escracho* is in the collection of The Metropolitan Museum of Art, New York, and the Museo Nacional Centro de Arte Reina Sofía, Madrid, among others.

Pornogram III (1981) is a diptych; against a neutral background it presents two nude males absurdly adorned and holding ordinary objects that acquire enigmatic meaning in this context. In the first panel we see the men standing at attention (as in a military posture). The second panel shows both of them laughing, as if in a reaction to an event that occurred between the two panels. This Pornogram is partially motivated by the fact that, in those days, many advocated a "moral crusade." Exploring the paralinguistic nature of what is commonly known as "body language," it is as if, in the first panel, we listen attentively, and in the second we respond with the only possible reaction.

With *Pornogram IV* (1981) a sequence of eight images progresses horizontally from light to darkness, and in so doing fuses two male bodies into one—producing unexpected forms along the way. Here I explore the effects of gradients in eliciting new bodily signs from the luminous interplay.

Two bodies float in the air in *Pornogram V* (1981) and form the letter "U" to visually embody the Portuguese sound of booing. This sound is similar to loudly yelling "boo!" except that the "b" is not pronounced and the "oo" sound is held for a longer period. In *Pornogram V* the body boos the viewer while the faces burst with laughter, also at the viewer. What is always revealed (the face) here is uselessly masked, while what is usually covered (the body) is fully exposed. If in *Pornogram I* I wrote a body, and in *Pornogram II* I inscribed a body in space, in *Pornogram V* I write with the body itself. A version of this Pornogram was featured on the cover of my artist's book *Escracho*, published in 1983.

In *Pornogram VI* (1982), I write with the female body's skin folds, more precisely with the creases of the groin and the central line produced by the labia. *Pornogram VI* combines the stylization of the body's skin folds visible in the photograph to produce the letters "V" and "I." These two letters, when superposed and inverted, produce the letter M. A sequence of photographs, paired with their corresponding abstracted and stylized signs, produces in Portuguese: "*VI, VIM, VIVI*" (I saw, I came, I lived). It's worth pointing out that, in Brazilian Portuguese, "*VIM*" (I came) has no sexual denotation—its primary meaning is "to arrive, to reach".

Pornogram VII (1982) is composed of four panels displayed vertically. In each panel a male figure (myself) appears with an erect penis penetrating a different letter, as follows: P, O, E, M. The viewer sees the poet in the act of making love to the poem, a case of verbophilia in extremis. The typeface, which I created specifically for this work, evokes different body parts.

Composed of two SX-70 Polaroids, *Pornogram VIII* (1982) features a female body performing the letter A on the left (with a joyous smile visible), and an erect penis on the right (my own) performing the letter I. The superscript dot (the dot above the letter "i") is not visible due to its encapsulation. Together, they form the interjection "AI," which in Brazilian Portuguese can be an expression of pleasure (or pain, although, in this case, clearly the former).

Pornogram IX (1982) is a Polaroid photograph in which one sees a close-up of a male and a female coupling, so as to produce the letter "H". The open legs of the male on the left side of the photo configure the left stem of the "H"; the erect penis forms the crossbar; the stretched legs of the female on the right side of the photo constitute the right vertical stroke of the "H". This work makes reference to the Portuguese noun "Hora H", which in Brazil means "Zero Hour". A culminating image, this Pornogram enacts a single letter through the dynamic performance of two bodies. The condensation embodied by this work is a fitting coda for a series that converged to a single end point the multiple possibilities of poetry, performance, and photography.

Notes on Yellpoems

In order to intervene in public settings, I created *poemas-pra-gritar* (yellpoems), often scoptic epigrams composed with scurrilous and ribald humor. In these works, I integrated non-standard language and colloquialisms, bawdy words, urban tribe dialectisms, linguistic jest, parody and modding, verbal invention and visual experimentation, and performativity, while emphasizing semantic complexities beyond the apparently straightforward language of the poems. My use of stigmatizing words in these pornpoems transformed them from demeaning to empowering, through political critique and defiance. I fused existing coarse and curse words with parts of words, neologisms, salacious buffoonery, the antinormative scribblings of toilet-wall graffiti, commonplaces, blasphemy, expletives, agrammatisms, incorrect orthography, slangy expressions, lexical exorbitance, general obscenities, the gross and the grotesque, into a new whole. In doing so, I sought to convey a playful, subversive, concentrated mass of language capable of expressing unexpected meanings.

Several yellpoems are included in my twelve-inch LP *Pornéia*, released by Alga Marghen, Milan, in 2016, including five live recordings made during the *Interversão* performance on Ipanema Beach, in 1982.

Notes on Graffiti

As any visitor to Pompeii will attest, urban wall scrawling is an ancient social custom. However, since the development of the spray-paint can in 1949, this portable version of the airbrush has become the prevalent expressive tool of political protesters and members of subculture groups alike. I worked with graffiti from 1980 to 1985 in order to create poems and visual works that formally extended my practice and that could be sampled and absorbed by bystanders and passers-by. The potential symbolism of the selected location (I once graffitied *Overgoze* in red, in the wee hours, on the white stucco wall of a Military Police battalion headquarters), the materiality of the wall surface, its position relative to foot and motor-vehicle traffic, the distance or proximity to commercial signs, the choice of paint color, the spraying technique (including atomization and dripping effects)—all of these elements played a role in the viewer/reader experience. More specifically, from 1980 to 1982 I created a series of works that stretched the limits and possibilities of this form. Beyond *Overgoze* and *Totem*, which I further comment below, I also made graffiti with markers (which gave me—and the work—greater mobility) and, in an effort to automate and expedite even more their execution, I produced a sticker version of my poem *Filosofia*, which allowed me to instantaneously publish the poem on public and private surfaces. I remember placing the sticker on buses, so that unsuspecting passengers would notice it while on the go, and also on the inner side of elevator doors, so that, when the doors closed, a captive audience would discover it and react (often with laughter) while experiencing the temporary intimacy with other passengers that a rising or descending elevator invariably produces. The spontaneous microperformance produced by the collective reaction and the eventual discussion during a ride were an intended outcome of generating an aesthetic experience in the unusual setting of an elevator.

Overgoze, 1981. A neologism, this single-word poem merges "overdose" [overdose] with the imperative "goze" [come, in the sexual sense]. I experimented with it on t-shirts and also through graffiti, performance and objects—an example of the latter can be seen in the book *Antolorgia* [Antholorgy], which I edited with Cairo Trindade, and that was published by Codecri, Rio de Janeiro, in 1984. A typescript version of the poem is in the collection of The Museum of Modern Art – MoMA, New York.

Lambida na Libido = Lickin' the Libido

Chupação sem paixão = Sucking action, not passion

Chupaixão = Suckassion [portmanteau of chupar (to suck) and paixão (passion)]

Totem [Totem], 1980. This three-dimensional graffiti was realized at the intersection of a sidewalk and a utility pole. An innovative form which I invented and developed in the 1980s, three-dimensional graffiti calls for the two-dimensional image produced with spray paint to be conceived for, and executed on, both urban and architectural reliefs. First published in the above-mentioned *Antolorgia* [Antholorgy], 1984. A vintage silver print of *Totem* is in the collection of The Museum of Modern Art – MoMA, New York.

Notes on Visual Works

This section presents a selection of my visual poems, drawings, electrostatic monoprints and typewriter art. One of my early digital works is also included.

Filosofia [Philosophy], 1980

A yellpoem disseminated at the time as t-shirts, stickers, and postcards, in addition to performance, books, periodicals, and other forms. Due to its rhythm, humor, conciseness, and the truth of its message, this work became widely cited, recited, and sampled, to the point of evolving into a popular saying in Brazil. First published in my poetry book *Nabunada não Vaidinha?*, Edições Gang, Rio de Janeiro, 1981.

Metapoema [Metapoem], 1980

In this metapoem, the Brazilian Portuguese word 'meta' ['goal', as a noun; 'after', as a prefix] can also be understood as the second-person singular affirmative imperative of the verb 'meter': 'to put' or 'to stick.' Originally published in the zine *Gang* 1, 1980.

Por uma nova grafia [For a new spelling], 1981.

This logopoem calls for a new spelling by unpacking the word 'pornografia' into 'por uma nova grafia.' In the second half, the lowercase letter lambda replaces the letter A; in so doing, it asks the question: what if the first letter of the alphabet was the international symbol for gay and lesbian rights? The poem first appeared in my poetry book *24*, Edições Gang, Rio de Janeiro, 1981.

Olhão, 1981

This visual poem alludes to and manipulates the matchbox brand Olhão (literally 'big eye'), which was ubiquitous at the time. Through a series of different procedures, it both calls for a verbal reading of the visual logo—the stylized eye shape and the pupil can be read as spelling the word 'oco' [hollow]—and adds new verbal material to the language already present on the matchbox. Since 'butthole' in Brazilian Portuguese is 'olho do cu' (butt's eye), in the context of the poem *Olhão*, the trademark can be interpreted as 'big o-ring'. The multiple repetitions of the logo at once hollows it out of its corporate function and produces a hypnotic effect on the reader. This outcome is further enhanced once the logo is read as a word. The poem first appeared, abridged, in my poetry book *24*, Edições Gang, Rio de Janeiro, 1981. It was published in full in my artist's book *Escracho*, 1983.

Em Copa [In Copacabana], neon display, 150 x 150 cm, 1981/2015.

This poem was a project for an animated neon sign. Unrealized at the time, it was produced in 2015 for my solo show at the Galeria Laura Marsiaj, Rio de Janeiro. It is in the permanent collection of the Museu de Arte do Rio – MAR.

The poem enables two simultaneous readings: 'the nice pussy comes in the shack' or 'the high class dork ends up in the shack'. The first is derived from interpreting 'babaca' etymologically (pussy) and the slang adjective 'bacana' denotatively (nice). The second reading is prompted by interpreting 'babaca' in its colloquial use (dork, idiot) and taking 'bacana' as used by the deprived in relation to the middle or high class (wealthy). The verb 'acabar' is polysemic and may mean 'end up' or 'have an orgasm', among other context-dependent meanings. *Em Copa* first appeared in my poetry book *24*, Edições Gang, Rio de Janeiro, 1981.

Sem Título (Cu Cura Cuca Cara) [Untitled], 1981

A permutational tautogram, this poem is reproduced here in Glauco Mattoso's idiosyncratic typography, composed entirely of lowercase letters 'o' from his Olivetti typewriter. As such, it was published by Mattoso in his zine *Jornal Dobrabil*, 1981. The poem first appeared in my poetry book *24*, Edições Gang, Rio de Janeiro, 1981.

Vida [Life], 1982

To create this visual poem I first produced two original masters. The first contains the word VIDA, which I hand-painted with a rubber stamp ink refill bottle (in the place of a brush). The second is a vertical stack of portmanteau words (ending with 'goza são' [goza=comes; são = healthy], homophone of 'gozação' [playfulness, fun, scorn] — all handwritten with a Magic Marker. I photocopied the first master, placed the resulting photocopy back in the xerox machine, and over it reproduced the second master, generating the perceivable transparency effect. The only known copy of this work was discovered by Fréderic Acquaviva in Lisbon, inside an envelope I had mailed in 1982 to my dear, late friend Ernesto Melo e Castro.

Índice [Index], 1981

A paratextual poem that imagines the back-of-the-book locators deciding what to do on their own, instead of dutifully pointing to useful material in a tome.

Poemazoide [Spermpoem], 1981

This object-poem is composed of a partially inflated spiral balloon and a hanging tag. The balloon is only inflated near the lip, so as to generate an ovoid shape. Once this is done, the balloon is tied into a knot to keep it inflated. The air pressure in the first segment of the spiral (now an ovoid shape) is just so as to straighten the remaining uninflated balloon body, thus producing the form of a flagellum extending from a sperm head. Hanging from the knot is the tag, on each side of which I rubberstamped the word pairs dika pura/pika dura [hot tip/hard dick]. Each pair has the same tonic accentuation as 'ditadura' (dictatorship), thus establishing a mnemonic counterpoint between state repression and resistance through body politics. The *contrepèterie* of the two Portuguese word pairs results from the alternation of the linguadental [d] and the bilabial [p]. I deliberately used the velar [k] where in standard orthography the hard 'c' should be used, producing a ludic effect. This creative cacography (nowadays known as "sensational spelling") also enabled me to elevate the letter K, which had been abolished from the Brazilian Portuguese alphabet since 1943. As my last name initial, it also stands in as a personal mark, an abbreviated signature that complements the other, material, trace, which is my breath inside the balloon. While the Orthographic Agreement of 1990 restored the letter K to the Portuguese alphabet, the norm took effect only in 2013.

Someto [Sonaughty], 1981

This is a monosyllabic sonnet, in other words, a sonnet in which each verse is composed of a single syllable. It is worth noting that all the words in this poem are paroxytones and the unstressed syllable is not counted after the last stressed syllable of each verse, according to the versification system adopted in Brazil since 1851, but especially since the publication, in 1905, of the *Tratado de versificação* [A Treatise on Versification] by Olavo Bilac and Guimarães Passos. First published in Glauco Mattoso's zine *Jornal Dobrabil*, 1981, and reproduced here with his personal typography.

2x3X, electrostatic monoprint on paper, 8 1/2 x 10 3/8 in. (21.6 x 26.5 cm), 1982.

Combining acrostic and anagrammatic principles, this composition subjects the Xerox logo to an erosion of its solidity through a series of copies in which each new reproduction is, itself, photocopied. The poem employs a procedure that is similar to the creation of XEROX's trademark name, in which the suffix of the word "xerography" was replaced by an "x". Thus, the word 'erotico/a' [erotics] becomes 'erox', ereção [erection] becomes 'erex', 'xereca' [slang for vagina] becomes 'xerex', and 'sexo' [sex] becomes 'xexo.' Both 'rex' and the trademark name of the company are used in their original form.

M/ASS MEDIA, 1982

Mail art was created to be mailed. As a result, I have not kept any of the mail artworks I produced in the early 1980s. Likewise, I have no idea how many have survived in the private collections of the artists and poets who received them at the time. Imagine my surprise when Fréderic Acquaviva told me, in 2021, that he had acquired from a Lisbon dealer an envelope containing two original works I had mailed in 1982 to my dear, late friend Ernesto Melo e Castro: *Vida* (see above) and *M/ASS MEDIA*. In this mixed media work, which I had not seen for nearly forty years, I added, over and around three xeroxed photographs of my participation in the 1982 Ipanema Beach performance *Interversão* [Interversion], Magic Marker-scrawled lettering, ink blotches, colorful felt pen splash and speech balloons, and hand-made rubber stamps. The overall composition, as was typical of my work at the time, merged a formally rigorous sense of multimedia experimentation with the overlooked visual vernacular of cultural practices such as comics and graffiti-laden bathroom walls.

Pictogram Sonnet, electrostatic print, 13 x 8.5 in (33 x 21.5 cm), 1982.

Evading accentual scansion, this poem follows the tradition of syllabic verse, according to which the primary compositional tenet of the line is a fixed number of syllables, with stress playing a secondary role (or none at all). All decasyllables here (ten pictograms per line) are organized in an isomorphic and isochronous pattern, having the same or no stress, according to the inclination of the reader. The key to the poem is its ABAB-CDCD-EFE-GFG rhyme scheme, that, in this case, recapitulates the ecological misadventures of contemporary life.

Obra [Work], 1981

Predicated on a ABAB-CDCD-EFE-FEF rhyme scheme, this variable sonnet still adheres to the format of two quatrains followed by two tercets (stanzas of four and three lines, respectively). However, if the initial letters have their own story to tell, the rhyming symbols offer the key, with the sequential characters between them suggesting the action.

Na Veia, 1981

This collage-poem is composed of a vertical stack of more than ten individual paper cut-outs flanked by my pansexual symbol, which is a visual poem in its own right. The ensemble is pasted onto an ad page. I used high contrast photography (black and white only; no grey tones) to flatten and merge all elements into a single layer. The result not only cancelled the persuasive tone of the promotional background but also enabled new semantic associations between all verbal and visual elements. The whole composition can be simultaneously understood as a critique of the hyperbolic clichés of sex-related advertisement and as an unabashed affirmation of individual open sexuality. The title *Na Veia* literally means 'into the vein' but in reality it is a Brazilian Portuguese slang expression that can have the following meanings: 1.On target, in the precise direction or at the exact place; 2.To experience something at a high level of intensity; 3.Absolute identification with something, or to utterly like something. A possible English approximation of the meaning of 'na veia' is the Britishism 'spot-on', an adjective that also conveys the notion of precision but lacks, however, the bodily association of the Lusophone original.

Puta Poeta, 1981

A diagrammatic poem, *Puta Poeta* may also be understood as a composition that incorporates a form of syntax visualization that I conceived for this work: the connecting lines render explicit relational links between the distinct lexical units. In so doing, it enables multiple reading strategies. The two words that make up the title, and that are also present in the poem, mean 'whore' (puta) and 'poet' (poeta). However, in Brazilian Portuguese the noun 'puta' is popularly employed as an adjective, signifying 'great,' 'big,' or 'a lot,' depending on context. In this case, the title manifests one of the possible linkages, by joining 'puta' and 'poet', and resulting in the notion 'great poet', but also 'sex worker that writes poetry.' Ultimately, more than

replacing one literal form with another, the poem seeks to evoke an analogy between sex work and literary work and to affirm a positive semantic resonance for the derogatory term 'puta.' The phonetic pairings around which the poem articulates itself (puta/poeta, na/nu, and cidade/dá de si) cannot be rendered in English with the same sonority. Here's a denotative translation: whore/in the/city — the poet/naked/gives of himself). This poem was composed on a mechanical typewriter and photographed in high contrast (black and white only; no grey tones) in order to generate a final piece that is visually equivalent to a line drawing. A typographic version of this poem appeared superposed on the *Pornogram II* in my artist's book *Escracho*, 1983.

Catecismo [Catechism], 1982

Combining the well-known old logo of a Brazilian television station with that of a real estate company, in this sequential visual poem I merged references to electronic information and physical reality.

λ (Lambda), ink on paper, 12.22 x 8.66 in. (31 x 22 cm), 1980.

In this drawing, I merged the lambda symbol with the contour of the human body. This was in reference to the fact that the lowercase letter lambda had been adopted internationally as the symbol for gay and lesbian rights. In Brazilian Portuguese, the pronunciation of the word "lambda" evokes "lambida" [a lick], further suggesting new relationships between language and the body.

Sem Título (Untitled), ink on paper, 4.4 x 7 in (11.2 x 17. 9 cm), 1981.

This drawing is part of a suite of seven that I created upon the request of Hudinilson Jr. for his mail art project exhibited at the São Paulo Biennial, in

1981. In the original project, Hudinilson presented an image associated with words and asked for a response in the postcard-sized blank rectangle underneath. I made these drawings directly with a rubber stamp ink refill bottle (in the place of a brush). The complete set is in the collection of the Centro Cultural São Paulo, São Paulo, Brazil.

Que vai fazer? [What you gonna do?], electrostatic monoprint on wrapping paper, 4.9 x 7 in (12,5 x 18 cm), 1982.

Under the military dictatorship, the Brazilian government banned the entry of color photocopy machines for fear that these machines would be used to counterfeit money. I decided that I would make color photocopy artworks, even without this machine, so I created a small series of works in which I cut selected wrapping papers, according to the orientation of the colored visual pattern I wanted. At the same time, I planned my black matrixes to work with the colored background. I put the wrapping sheets that I prepared directly on the machine, and placed the matrix on the glass display—and then fused the black matrix with the colored background. In this way, I produced color photocopy artworks when this was impossible in Brazil. This particular piece is organized in orthogonal axes, forming a woven pattern out of evocative colors and segmented drawings.

Vai comer agora ou quer que embrulhe? [For here or to go?], electrostatic monoprint on wrapping paper, 12.2 x 8.2 in (31 x 21 cm), 1982.

In this piece, I take a single panel from a comic book by underground pornographer Carlos Zéfiro and convert it into these spastic, quivering, convulsive, distorted figures. As stated above (see *Que vai fazer?*), color photocopying was forbidden in the country by the military dictatorship,

out of fear that it would be used for counterfeiting. Determined to create photocopies with color, I produced them over color wrapping paper. I deliberately selected specific patterns and colors and cut the paper to match the composition, in order to fuse them into a new visual unity.

Primavera [Spring], 11 x 15.75 inches (28 x 40 cm), electrostatic monoprint on toilet paper mounted on black paper and wrapping paper, 1982.

In Portuguese, 'papel' means both 'paper' and 'role'. In the speech balloon we read: 'O poeta tem um papel na sociedade' [The poet has a social role].

Geometria do Êxtase [Geometry of Ecstasy], 11.75 x 8.25 in (21 x 29.7 cm), 1982.

Geometria do Êxtase was written for a PC as part of a suite of ASCII experiments I created after the end of the Movimento de Arte Pornô, in February of 1982. In this poem, the viewer looks straight down at the top face of a virtual cube. The changing verbal material is the cube's shadow, which rotates clockwise following the movement of an invisible light source—much as the sun moves a shadow on a sundial.

Untitled I, typewriting, 8.27 x 11.69 inches (21 x 29.7 cm), 1982.

One of my earliest ASCII experiments, this visual poem may be read in numerous ways. The particles guide the reader's eyes down along a channel.

Siririca, typewriter artwork, 8.2 x 6.2 in (21 x 16cm), 1980.

In Brazilian Portuguese, 'siririca' is slang for female masturbation. This three-dimensional typewriter artwork blends pornography and geometry.

Cuneiforme [Cuneiform], typewriter artwork, 8.4 x 6.2 in (21.5 x 16 cm), 1980.

The title alludes to the well-known
ancient script. Lusophone readers will
notice that 'cuneiforme' embeds the
word 'cu' [butthole], suggesting an analogy between sex and writing systems.

Termografia [Thermography], typewriter
artwork, 8.4 x 5.6 in (21.5 x 14.3 cm), 1980.

Conflating pornography and science,
this three-dimensional typewriter
artwork merges the sexual notion of
'hot' with the technological principle of
'heat signature'.

Curioso [Curious], typewriter artwork,
11.8 x 8.2 in (30 x 21 cm), 1980.

As in *Cuneiforme*, *Curioso* embeds the
word 'cu' [butthole], prompting the
viewer, in this case, to ponder on the
exact placement of the flower. Beyond
any literal association to excreta
becoming compost to be used on flower
beds, in creating this work I was more
interested in producing a positive association with the anus by coupling it with
the beauty of a blossom.

Ciclópica [Cyclopic], typewriter artwork,
11 x 8.2 in (28 x 21 cm), 1982.

In this three-dimensional one-word
poem, the pubic hairs around the 'anus'
spell the word 'igualdade' [equality].

Posição Política [Political Position], typewriter artwork, 11 x 8.2 in (28 x 21 cm),
1981.

Frente de Liberação de Trás [Behind
Liberation Front], typewriter artwork,
11.8 x 8.2 in (30 x 21 cm), 1981.

Alluding to the numerous Liberation
Fronts that emerged worldwide in the

previous decades, this work places its
political focus on the body.

Cinelândia 1, typewriter artwork, 12.7 x
8.6 in (32.4 x 22 cm), 1981.

Cinelândia 2, typewriter artwork, 11.6 x 8
in (29.7 x 20.5 cm), 1981.

CCC 1, typewriter artwork, 13 x 8 3/4 in.
(33 x 22.2 cm), 1980.

CCC 2, typewriter artwork, 13 x 8 3/4 in.
(33 x 22.2 cm), 1980.

Movimento de esquerda I, [Left
Movement I], typewriter artwork, 11.8 x
8.2 in (30 x 21 cm), 1980.

Movimento de esquerda II, [Left
Movement II], typewriter artwork, 11.8 x
8.2 in (30 x 21 cm), 1980.

The last six works in this section explore
the relationship between political liberation and sexual freedom, as suggested
by their titles.

Notes on Flatographic Compositions

On June 13, 1982, in what would be one of my final contributions to the Movement, I wrote the manifesto *Poecia Flatográfica* [Flatographic Poecy], in which I proposed the use of the flatus as a compositional unit and of the mellifluous flatal flow as material. Flatographic poems are visual scores for metabolic performances that combine meticulous precision with gaseous explosiveness of scatological resonance.

The performer is expected to clench and unclasp the cheeks while contracting and releasing the sphincter in a musically meaningful manner, according to each score. Evanescent and invisible, the source materials employed in the creation of flatographic poems resound with synesthetic associations, since their recognizable acoustic patterns inevitably evoke the aromasphere associated with foul odor. Nevertheless, negative olfactory associations are turned around and transformed into harmonious pieces of sound art.

Integrated into literary tradition through verbal description and allusion, and into pictorial tradition through representation, flatulence has never before been the focused object of earnest poetic performativity; its often uncontrollable emissions and exhalations are a source of embarrassment for the expeller, are received as an affront to civility, and stand collectively as one of the last social taboos. Bursting forth with uncompromising seriousness, while recognizing the inexorable jocular reaction to its unexpected use in art, the flatographic poems form a corpus of nine compositions in which the material is extensively explored.

While some flatographic poems establish a counterpoint between meals and musical instruments (or even an entire waltz), others require editing techniques, amplification and additional materials, such as water. A cappella performances are also part of the research program: some can be said to be acoustic improvisations for a soloist, while others are orchestrated scores for an ensemble.

The *Poecia Flatográfica* manifesto and several originals are in the collection of Archivo Lafuente, Heras, Cantabria, Spain. Recordings of four flatographic poems are included in my twelve-inch LP *Pornéia*, released by Alga Marghen, Milan, in 2016.

Acknowledgments

In 2010, Laura Marsiaj hosted a solo show of my *Pornograms* at her eponymous gallery, in Rio de Janeiro. That exhibition marked the first public rediscovery of the Movimento de Arte Pornô (MAP) since the 1980s. Previously, Mario Ramiro had been teaching it for years in his Performance course at the University of São Paulo. Ramiro's early recognition led to Fernanda Nogueira's invitation for me to participate in the group show *Losing the Human Form*, at the Museo Nacional Centro de Arte Reina Sofía, Madrid, in 2012. Two years later, thanks to Paulo Herkenhoff, the MAP was featured in an exhibition at the Museu de Arte do Rio—MAR, Rio de Janeiro, curated by Fernanda Nogueira, upon the invitation of Inti Guerrero. Also in 2014, I had a memorable solo show of my *Pornograms* at Henrique Faria Fine Art, New York. The *Losing the Human Form* exhibition brought worldwide attention to the MAP, culminating with its presentation at The Museum of Modern Art (MoMA), New York, from 2019 to 2022. Tie Jojima wrote the first M.A. dissertation (The School of the Art Institute of Chicago, 2015) and is, as of the publication of this book, writing the first Ph.D. dissertation (The City University of New York) entirely focused on the MAP. Her research has greatly contributed to a renewed understanding of both the synchronic and diachronic implications of the MAP. In 2016 Alga Marghen released my *Pornéia* LP and in 2020 Alternate Projects came out with a comprehensive catalogue of MAP publications. I also wish to thank Abraham Avnisan, who introduced me to Nightboat Books, and to express how great it was to work with Stephen Motika (director and publisher) and Rissa Hochberger (designer) on this project. Special thanks to Belisário Franca, Jena Kopelman, Marlene Przytyk, Nelson Pataro, Annick Bureaud, Alan Perry, Simone Osthoff, Frédéric Acquaviva, Loré Lixenberg, Carlos Fadon, Bronac Ferran, Jane England, Andrea Elkind, Marcel Fleiss, Milan Hughston, Zanna Gilbert, Jacques Donguy, Rolando Carmona, Linda Schwartz, Marco Rodrigues, Marcos Abel, Marcelo Lipiani, America Cupello, Ben Pegram, Wonbin Yang, Felipe Steinberg, Teva Flaman, Francisca Rudolph, Ben Fuqua, Barbara Baron, Duncan Bass, and Alex Botts for their manifold contributions to the organization, preservation and dissemination of the originals reproduced in this book. Glauco Mattoso has kindly given permission for his typographic versions of my poems *Sem Título* (Cu Cura Cuca Cara) [Untitled] and *Someto* [Sonaughty], 1981, to be reproduced in this book. Finally, I wish to remember my late friends Ota, Hudinilson Jr. and Alberto Harrigan, all artists who participated in the MAP. Had they been around, we would undoubtedly have celebrated the publication of this book together.

Publications and Multiples: 1980-1984

Solo Publications

Nabunada não Vaidinha?, Edições Gang,
Rio de Janeiro, 1981. Poetry book.
24, Edições Gang, Rio de Janeiro, 1981.
Poetry book.
Filosofia, self-published, Rio de Janeiro,
1981. Sticker.
Filosofia, Livraria Pau-Brasil, São Paulo,
1981. Postcard.
Nayá Biruta, self-published, Rio de
Janeiro, 1981. Artist's book.
O Sinal De Nayá, self-published, Rio de
Janeiro, 1981. Artist's book.
Nayá Biruta No Carnaval, self-published,
Rio de Janeiro, 1981. Artist's book.
Margô na Pensão, self-published, Rio de
Janeiro, 1981. Artist's book.
Pensão Margô, self-published, Rio de
Janeiro, 1981. Artist's book.
Escracho, self-published, Rio de Janeiro,
1983. Artist's book.

Solo Multiples

Gramática Tátil, self-published, Rio de
Janeiro, 1980. Artist's book.
Poemazoide, self-published, Rio de
Janeiro, 1981. Object poem.
Overgoze, self-published, Rio de Janeiro,
1981. Silkscreen t-shirt.
Filosofia, self-published, Rio de Janeiro,
1981. Silkscreen t-shirt.
Postcards (various), disseminated
through the mail art network, 1980-1982.

Zines

Kac, E. and Trindade, C. (eds). *Gang* n.1,
Edições Gang, Rio de Janeiro, 1980.
Kac, E. and Trindade, C. (eds). *Gang* n.2,
Edições Gang, Rio de Janeiro, 1981.
Kac, E. and Trindade, C. (eds). *Gang* n.3,

Edições Gang, Rio de Janeiro, 1981.
Kac, E. and Trindade, C. (eds). *Gang* n.4,
Edições Gang, Rio de Janeiro, 1982
(unreleased).

Anthologies

Kac, E. and Trindade, C. (eds). *Antologia
do Poema Pornô*, Editora Trote, Rio de
Janeiro, 1981.
Kac, E. and Trindade, C. (eds). *Antolorgia:
Arte Pornô*, Codecri, Rio de Janeiro, 1984.

Posters

Gang! Bang!, Edições Gang, Rio de
Janeiro, 1982. Drawings by Ota.
Gang, Edições Gang, Rio de Janeiro,
1982. Photo by Belisario Franca.

Eduardo Kac is internationally recognized for his groundbreaking work in contemporary art and poetry. In the early 1980s, Kac created digital, holographic, and online works that anticipated the global culture we live in today, composed of ever-changing information in constant flux. In 1997 the artist coined the term "Bio Art," igniting the development of this new art form with works such as his transgenic rabbit *GFP Bunny* (2000) and *Natural History of the Enigma* (2009), which earned him the Golden Nica, the most prestigious award in the field of media art. *GFP Bunny* has become a global phenomenon, having been appropriated by major popular culture franchises such as Sherlock, Big Bang Theory, and The Simpsons, and by writers such as Margaret Atwood and Michael Crichton. In 2017, Kac created *Inner Telescope*, a work conceived for and realized in outer space with the cooperation of French astronaut Thomas Pesquet. Kac's singular and highly influential career spans poetry, performance, drawing, printmaking, photography, artist's books, early digital and online works, holography, telepresence, and bio art. Kac has also authored or edited several books, including *Telepresence and Bio Art -- Networking Humans, Rabbits and Robots* (University of Michigan Press, 2005). Kac's work has been showcased in biennials such as Venice Biennale, Italy; Yokohama Triennial, Japan; Gwangju Biennale, Korea; Bienal de São Paulo, Brazil; and Bienal de Habana, Cuba. His works are in major collections such as Museum of Modern Art-MoMA, New York; Tate Modern, London; Victoria & Albert Museum, London; Les Abattoirs Museum—Frac Occitanie, Toulouse, France; Valencian Institute of Modern Art-IVAM, Spain; Museum ZKM, Karlsruhe, Germany; and Museum of Contemporary Art of São Paulo, among others.

Nightboat Books

Nightboat Books, a nonprofit organization, seeks to develop audiences for writers whose work resists convention and transcends boundaries. We publish books rich with poignancy, intelligence, and risk. Please visit nightboat.org to learn about our titles and how you can support our future publications.

The following individuals have supported the publication of this book. We thank them for their generosity and commitment to the mission of Nightboat Books:

Kazim Ali
Anonymous (4)
Abraham Avnisan
Jean C. Ballantyne
The Robert C. Brooks Revocable Trust
Amanda Greenberger
Rachel Lithgow
Anne Marie Macari
Elizabeth Madans
Elizabeth Motika
Thomas Shardlow
Benjamin Taylor
Jerrie Whitfield & Richard Motika

This book is made possible, in part, by grants from the New York City Department of Cultural Affairs in partnership with the City Council and the New York State Council on the Arts Literature Program.

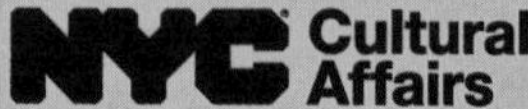
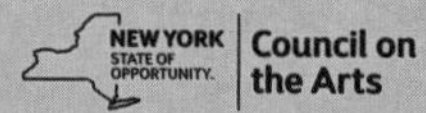